LATIN AMERICA, THE COLD WAR, AND THE WORLD POWERS, 1945-1973

Volume 9, Sage Library of Social Research

SAGE LIBRARY OF SOCIAL RESEARCH

Also in this series:

Latin America, The Cold War, & The World Powers 1945-1973

A Study in Diplomatic History

F. Parkinson

Volume 9
SAGE LIBRARY OF
SOCIAL RESEARCH

 SAGE PUBLICATIONS   Beverly Hills   London

For information address:

SAGE PUBLICATIONS, INC.
275 South Beverly Drive
Beverly Hills, California 90212

SAGE PUBLICATIONS LTD
St George's House / 44 Hatton Garden
London EC1N 8ER

Printed in the United States of America

International Standard Book Number 0-8039-0412-6(P)
0-8039-0413-4(C)
Library of Congress Catalog Card No. 74-77289

FIRST PRINTING

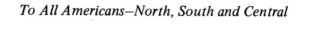

To All Americans—North, South and Central

TABLE OF CONTENTS

PREFACE

Research for this book has been conducted from sources available in Great Britain, as well as during a field trip in 1971 lasting nearly six months and covering six Latin American countries which was financed jointly by the Social Science Research Council and the Royal Institute of International Affairs. While I wish to express my deep gratitude to both of these institutions, I feel I owe a special debt to the staff of Chatham House. My special thanks must go to Mr. Andrew Shonfield, then director of studies at that institution, for having responded so readily to the idea of a book on this subject, and to his successor, Mr. J. E. S. Fawcett, for having encouraged me to persist in my task.

This book has been constructed from materials gathered in Great Britain among the following institutions: the British Museum; the Royal Institute of International Affairs; Canning House; the Foreign Office Research Library; the Bank of London and South America; the Institute of Latin American Studies in the University of London; Latin American embassies in London; the University of London Library in Senate House; the London School of Economics and Political Science; and University College London. My thanks are due to the staff of all of these libraries and archives for the patience with which they have dealt with my frequent enquiries.

As for sources tapped during my stay in Latin America, my gratitude to statesmen, diplomats, academics, journalists, staff of institutions and newspaper archives, businessmen, and Latin Americans from all walks of life, all of whom have given me generous advice and treated me with the customary hospitality with which one associates Latin America, is enormous. It would be impossible to name them all here, and invidious to single out a few for special mention.

F.P.
London

ABOUT THE AUTHOR

DR. F. PARKINSON is Senior Lecturer at University College London, where he has been teaching since 1952. He is a graduate of the University of London, and a World War II veteran of the British army. He was Assistant Director of the London Institute of World Affairs from 1967 to 1970, and from 1957-1970 Assistant and Managing Editor of the Institute's *Year Book of World Affairs* of which he currently is serving as chairman of the panel of advisers to the editorial board. Dr. Parkinson has traveled throughout the world and has contributed numerous articles to scholarly journals.

Chapter I

LATIN AMERICA AS A PAWN OF THE

WORLD POWERS (1945-1950)

After the end of the Second World War, most Latin American countries turned their attention to their relationship with the United States in an effort to commit the latter to continued inter-American cooperation.[1] With this aim in view it was agreed in principle at the Chapúltepec conference of American States (excluding Canada) in March 1945 to conclude an inter-American defense treaty which would form part of wider inter-American organization. After a great deal of delay an Inter-American Treaty of Reciprocal Assistance (the Rio Treaty) was eventually signed on September 2, 1947, providing for the adoption of collective measures, including the use of force, in the event of a direct or indirect threat to any of the contracting parties.[2]

The idea that the United States could be so bound was, however, valid only on the assumption that (a) the Americas could be effectively insulated from extra-hemispheric influences; and (b) that Latin American and United States interests vis-à-vis the outside world would continue to be broadly identical. Within two years these optimistic assumptions stood invalidated by the advent of the Cold War, and the United States began to use the inter-American system as a means of ensuring the diplomatic conformity of the governments of Latin America. In the light of these unforeseen developments, the proposed Inter-American Treaty of Reciprocal Assistance assumed new and altogether ambiguous characteristics.

Though all the governments had signed the treaty, scepticism was rife in many quarters. In the Chilean Congress, Radomiro Tomic, a prominent member of the Chamber of Deputies, voiced strong misgivings,[3] while Argentina's Radical Party opposed it.[4] The important National Party of Uruguay, which claims to have a tradition of neutrality going back to the early nineteenth century, refused to take part in the Rio conference, as it saw vassalage to the United States as its inevitable consequence.[5] The Mexican government, keen on obtaining such a treaty in 1945, was no longer so in 1947.[6] On the other hand, President G. González Videla of Chile accepted the treaty without reservations and welcomed United States proposals for inter-American military coordination, including the creation of a joint military staff.[7]

While the main field of tensions in the Cold War was situated in Central Europe, the United States and the Soviet Union tended to regard the states of Latin America as pawns. The Soviet leaders hardly bothered to distinguish between the United States and its allies on the one hand, and the countries of Asia and Latin America on the other.[8] After the conclusion of the Rio Treaty in September 1947 they could even claim with a measure of plausibility that, unlike most Asian states, the countries of Latin America had become vassal states of the United States.

For its part, Latin America was slow in establishing diplomatic contact with the Soviet Union. Mexico and Uruguay had found little profit in their diplomatic relations with the new Russia before the Second World War. Mexico, still resentful over the scant respect of her sovereignty shown by the Soviet rulers when Trotsky was murdered by their agents on Mexican territory in August 1940, relented only in 1942 when K. Oumansky, former Soviet ambassador to the United States, was accredited head of the Soviet mission in Mexico City. Diplomatic relations were never broken off after that.

Argentina agreed to Soviet representation only after the war, and only after E. Stettinius, Secretary of State of the United States, had acted as the encouraging intermediary. Ambassador M. Sergeyev presented his credentials on May 2, 1947. Brazil similarly consented to diplomatic relations only when it was apparent that the Soviet Union would play a major part in the United Nations, and J. Suritz, a veteran Soviet diplomat, presented his credentials on December 30, 1945, after Brazil had officially announced the resumption of relations on April 2 of that year.[9] Chile had backed Soviet representation not even in the days of the *frente popular* (1938-1940). It was under the impression that the Soviet Union would continue to cooperate closely with the Western powers in peacetime that President A. Ríos consented to the establishment of diplomatic relations on January 9, 1945, and allowed Ambassador G. Zhukov to be appointed on August 31 of that year.[10]

However, both Brazil and Chile broke off relations with the Soviet Union in 1947. A series of offensive articles in Soviet newspapers provided the cause for the breach in the case of Brazil,[11] while President González Videla of Chile severed relations in November, 1947, accusing the Soviet Union of trying to sabotage the Chilean economy.

In Latin America, as in Europe, the year 1947 marked the end of the post-war period of stalling in world affairs,[12] and Latin America's Communists turned themselves into determined partisans in the Cold War. Chile and Brazil provided cases in point.

In 1946, President G. González Videla of the Chilean Radical party had accepted Communist electoral support[13] in an attempt to revive the frente popular of old, only to find the political rationale of such a combination invalidated by a shift in the foreign policy of the Soviet Union, to whom the Chilean Communists looked for guidance. But González Videla's good faith vis-à-vis the three Communists he appointed to his government may fairly be questioned. According to a confidential dispatch from Santiago by the ambassador of the United States, Claude Bowers, on November 18, 1946, the Chilean president had informed him that he had had to offer the Communists some seats in the cabinet, but that he had "no doubt that these Communists will not linger long in the government"; he did not "wish to force them out immediately after taking office."[14] The Communists were compelled to leave the government in 1947. In Brazil, where the Communists had made a fine showing at the polls in 1946 and looked like establishing themselves as the acknowledged representatives of the working class, they were outlawed in 1947.[15] In both countries the barely concealed contempt in which Latin America was held in Soviet foreign policy was a major factor in facilitating the repression of the Communists.[16]

Soviet foreign policy also made it easy for the United States to take Latin American acquiescence, if not always wholehearted support in the Cold War, for granted, and to fit the region relentlessly into its own scheme of priorities, where it ranked near the bottom. The severe shortage of dollars had spread from Western Europe to Latin America in 1947, and from 1947 on the idea developed that if only Latin American governments showed sufficient anti-Communist zeal at home and enough anti-Soviet enthusiasm abroad, a sound psychological basis would exist for substantial United States economic aid to the region. Most Latin American statesmen were slow in grasping the fact that the global scheme of priorities of the United States in the Cold War was determined by hard considerations of diplomatic and military strategy. The Latin American region seemed immune to Soviet "penetration" and strategically remote from Soviet military power, and George Marshall, Secretary of State of the United States, was able to declare categorically at the Rio conference of August 1947 that there would be no Marshall Plan for Latin America, since what capital was available for foreign aid would have to be directed towards Western Europe, which was in real danger of economic and moral collapse.[17] Consequently, the Latin American share of United States aid between 1946 and 1960 never exceeded 4.8 percent.[18]

Because of the exigencies of the Cold War, most governments were disheartened and demoralized, and they sought salvation in an uncertain cooperation with the United States.

An exception to Latin America's apparent helplessness in this period was the foreign policy of Argentina under President Juan Domingo Perón. Argentina's great initial strength under him lay in the large reserves of foreign exchange amassed during the war.[19] The economic crisis which had hit Britain during the summer of 1947 and rendered her sterling balances abroad inconvertible into "hard" currencies made it impossible for Perón to promote massive industrialization by imports of United States capital and he squandered his sterling balances in purchasing the British-owned Argentine railways.[20] Believing in the imminence of a third world war, Perón bought far larger quantities of arms and industrial equipment of all sorts than could reasonably be justified on grounds of military prudence.[21]

The explanation of this lay in his expectations of the future. He was under the spell of the geopolitical school of Professor Karl Haushofer far more than any of the fascist doctrines of Hitler or Mussolini,[22] and it was his exaggerated belief in the tenets of German geopolitics that led him to overestimate the military and political value of land-power, to underrate that of sea-power, and to expect an Axis victory as late as 1944. When this did not materialize, he predicted a rapid disintegration of Allied unity which would lead to another world conflict.[23] Merely confirmed in this belief by what happened after 1945, he began to base his foreign and economic policies on a grandiose long-term strategy designed to meet these expectations. His capital mistake in this respect was to expect a "hot" war instead of a "cold" one.

He envisaged the creation of a Latin America under Argentine or, at the most, joint Argentine-United States hegemony able to pull its own weight in international conflict, and in association, on a basis of equality, with the United States and the British Empire.[24] When his expectations failed to materialize, he had to alternate frequently between offers of cooperation with the United States and efforts to oppose her by brandishing the concept of a "third force." That concept formed part of his wider and more ambitious doctrine of *justicialismo,* defined as being halfway between "capitalism" and "collectivism" in both the economic and social field, and equidistant between the Soviet Union and the United States in world affairs.[25] He was the first Latin American statesman to practise a policy of deliberate neutralism but was also the first to appreciate its numerous ambiguities.[26]

In spite of the extraordinarily tactless behavior of Spruille Braden, United States ambassador in Buenos Aires, in his attempt to prevent Perón's election in 1946, he sent General von der Becke to Washington in search of modern weapons for his armed forces; but the talks foundered on the insistence of the United States on Argentine compliance with obligations laid down at the Chapúltepec conference of March 1945.

On August 1, 1946, for the first time, Perón declared his loyalties in the Cold War openly by announcing that in the event of a world conflict Argentina would range herself on the side of the United States, which seemed gratified. Spruille Braden was compelled to resign[27] and on June 3, 1947, the White House announced officially a change of policy. No further ostacles remained to full Argentine participation at the forthcoming Rio conference on hemisphere security, where in August 1947 the Argentine representatives acknowledged the courtesy of the United States by raising no objections to the proposed inter-American pact of reciprocal assistance,[28] although, characteristically, Perón postponed ratification until the outbreak of the Korean War in 1950. In February 1948, hard on the heels of the Communist coup in Czechoslovakia and in a moment of anti-Communist panic, Perón even declared that "a clash between capitalist and Communist imperialism is coming" in which Argentina would side with the United States.[29] It seemed as if he had cast his lot irrevocably with the latter.

Soon, however, neutralist elements began to creep into Argentine foreign policy. J. A. Bramuglia, the foreign minister, criticized a blatantly anti-Communist resolution which the United States had placed before the Ninth Inter-American Conference at Bogotá in March 1948 on the ground that "communism is not stopped by passing resolutions, but by improving the living conditions of our peoples who have been exploited by the privileged classes." He insisted that "before fighting consequences, it is preferable to overcome the causes," and went on to denounce both "imperialistic capitalism" and "materialistic communism" while making a subtle appeal to his fellow Latin Americans to follow the "middle road of social justice represented by the Perón government."[30] In the United Nations he persistently pursued a line opposite to that taken by the United States.[31]

In June 1946, at the same time as he was making overtures to the United States, Perón resumed diplomatic relations with the Soviet Union. In April 1947 a Soviet commercial mission was installed in Buenos Aires in the hope of negotiating a trade agreement with Argentina. However, Perón's failure to object to the conclusion of the Rio treaty disappointed Moscow, and thereafter relations between the two countries began to cool.[32] Nonetheless, all suggestions made by Brazil and Chile that Perón should follow their example and break off diplomatic relations with the Soviet Union were steadfastly ignored by him, a sure sign that he wished to keep his options open.[33]

His policy bore some fruit when, after December 1948, Bramuglia, foreign minister and president of the Security Council of the United Nations, enhanced Argentina's international prestige by playing the "honest broker" in skilful mediation between the United States and the Soviet Union over the Berlin crisis, the most serious instance of diplomatic conflict so far.[34]

NOTES

1. Olga Pellicer de Brody, *México y la Revolución Cubana* (Mexico City, 1971), maintains that a group of highly placed Mexican officials in the Ministry of Foreign Affairs regarded inter-Americanism as the belated fulfilment of the ideas of Bolivar.

2. For a close legal analysis of the treaty, see A. van Wynen Thomas and A. J.

Thomas, *The Organization of American States* (Dallas: Southern Methodist University Press, 1963).

3. Tomic put his objections thus in August 1947: "There is only one extracontinental menace of aggression conceivable in the next twenty years: Russia. And if war comes, it will not be a war started between Chile and Russia, Bolivia and Russia, Argentina and Russia. . . . It will be war between the United States and Russia. In such an event the (proposed) military pact makes it obligatory for Latin America to tie the fortunes of its arms and its national destiny to the arms . . . of the North. It is a decision of tremendous historical magnitude. . . . It is a poor way of beginning to united America." Quoted in A. Magnet, *Nuestros vecinos justicialistas* (Santiago: Pacífico, 1955), p. 155.

4. Arturo Frondizi, their principal spokesman, attacked the whole procedure in the following terms: "Immediate necessities of maintaining an economic stability, which (the government) did not know how to defend with a policy of effective undertakings, will today carry the nation into the Rio Pact and perhaps tomorrow to the delivery of the petroleum and the control of our economy." See Conil Paz and G. Ferrari, *Argentina's Foreign Policy, 1930-1962* (South Bend, Ind.: University of Notre Dame Press, 1966).

5. See C. Lacalle (ed.) Directorio del Partido Nacional, *El Partido Nacional y la Política Exterior del Uruguay* (Monteverde, 1947), pp. 3-17, 22, and 729-730 respectively.

6. See J. Torres Bodet, *Memorias* (Vol. 2) *La victoria sin alas* (Mexico City: Porrúa, 1969), pp. 129-163. At the Bogota conference of 1948 Mexico successfully prevented the creation of a permanent inter-American general staff. See ibid., pp. 244-245.

7. See *New York Times*, July 8, 1947. The removal of the Communists from the Chilean government by President González Videla coincided with the Rio conference, where it caused a sensation. See *El Mercurio*, August 27, 1947.

8. See Molotov's contemputous reference to the Latin American states as satellites of the United States at the San Francisco conference in April 1945, in L. Mecham, *The United States and Inter-American Security, 1889-1960* (Austin: University of Texas Press, 1961), p. 427. In one committee meeting, the Soviet foreign minister derided Mexico's foreign minister, E. Padilla, as a puppet of the United States. See ibid., p. 269.

9. *The Times*, April 3, 1945. P. Leão Velloso, Brazilian minister of finance in 1945, talking to a journalist from the United States about Brazil's diplomatic relations with the Soviet Union, remarked that "It was only your insistence which caused us to take the Soviet serpent to our bosom officially." See E. Tomlinson, *Look Southward, Uncle* (New York: Devin-Adair, 1959), p. 120.

10. See J. A. Ríos, *Mensaje de S.E. en la apertura de las sesiones ordinarias del Congreso Nacional; 21 de Mayo 1945* (Santiago, 1945), p. 39, about the opening of diplomatic relations.

11. Controversy still surrounds this important subject. According to President Dutra, relations were severed with the Soviet Union because of a "violent press campaign" in which "unjustifiable attacks" were made. On instructions from Rio de Janeiro, Mario de Pimentel Brandão, Brazilian ambassador in Moscow, protested, but his note was returned by the Soviet government. At this point the Brazilian govern-

ment decided to break off diplomatic relations. (See E. G. Dutra, *Mensagem apresentada ao Congresso Nacional* [Rio de Janeiro, 1948], pp. 40-41.)

Oswaldo Aranha, leading Brazilian statesman, was to write later of this episode: "The break in our relations with the Soviet Union in 1947 did not result from any popular pressure or action on the part of the political parties." See O. Aranha, "Relações diplomáticas com a União Soviética," 1 *Revista Brasileira de Política Internacional* (1958), pp. 18-26, at p. 19. See also a significant debate in the Brazilian Chamber of Deputies on whether Pimentel Brandão had advised to break off relations in *Anais da Câmara dos diputados,* Vol. 2, 1952, pp. 207-218; and *Ministério das Relacões Exteriores, Documentos, Ruptura de Relacões Diplomáticas entre o Brasil e a URSS* (Rio de Janeiro, 1947). Also *Jornal de Commercio,* April 23, 1952, for a letter by M. de Pimentel Brandão, then secretary-general of the Itamarati, addressed to Raul Fernandes, concerning this controversy.

12. See C. Contreras Labarca, *La Lucha del pueblo por la reorganización de Chile* (Santiago, 1948), p. 10, who affirms that the Chilean Communists began to support Soviet hard-line policies after the failure of the London conference of foreign ministers in March and April 1947. See also G. González Videla, *Programa del Gobierno de los partidos de la izquierda aprobada por unanimidad en la Convención Democrática Popular y suscrito par el candidato del pueblo* (Santiago, 1946).

13. See J. Guzman Hernández, *Gabriel González Videla. Biografía y análisis crítica de su programa* (Santiago: Universo, 1946). Acknowledging the electoral support he had obtained from the Communists, González Videla appointed three Communists to relatively unimportant government posts in 1946. See S. Cole Blasier, "Chile: a Communist Battleground," 65 *Political Science Quarterly,* September 1950, pp. 353-375, especially pp. 368-374, which deal with the government's rupture with the Communists.

14. See United States Department of State, *Foreign Relations of the United States,* Vol. IX (Washington, D.C., 1946), at p. 612: Ambassador Bowers to Assistant Secretary of State Braden.

15. During the presidential elections of December 2, 1945, Yeddo Fiúza, the Communist candidate, polled 10 percent of all votes cast. In Congress the Communists were able to secure 9 percent of all seats in the Lower House and one Senator. The Communist position was severely compromised by a statement made by Carlos Luíz Prestes, the Party leader, in March 1946, according to which he would side with the Soviet Union in the event of war. The Communist party was made illegal by a court decision in 1947 and all Communist congressmen were expelled in January 1948. See T. E. Skidmore, *Politics in Brazil 1930-1964* (New York: Oxford University Press, 1967), pp. 63-64.

Already on May 13, 1945, only five days after the formal end of the war in Europe, J. N. da Fontoura, Brazil's foreign minister, asked for an immediate settlement of the Argentine problem, explaining that Russia was the new danger. See *New York Herald Tribune,* May 14, 1945.

16. In Cuba the Communists joined a coalition government in December 1945, but they would no longer follow the weak "Browder line" of 1944. See Francisco Calderió (Blas Roca), "The United States, Teheran and Latin America," 3 *Political Affairs,* March 1945, p. 269. On September 4, 1946, *Hoy,* their organ, launched an attack on the United States and Britain for their policies towards Greece. For the

first time in ten years the Communists were isolated at the elections in 1948. On the
latter point, see H. Thomas, *Cuba* (New York: Harper & Row, 1971), p. 757.
17. *New York Times,* August 21, 1947. It is interesting to see that Sumner
Welles, experienced statesman and one of the principal authors of the policy of the
Good Neighbor, urged at that time that there should be a Marshall Plan for Latin
America. See *New York Herald Tribune,* October 19 and 23, 1948. See also Rómulo
Betancourt's speech in this sense at the Ninth Inter-American Conference on April 6,
1948, reprinted in R. Betancourt, *Hacia una América Latina democrática e integrada*
(Caracas: Sendero, 1967), pp. 161-163.
18. See J. F. Rippy, "United States Post-War Aid to Latin America," 14 *Inter-
American Economic Affairs* (1961), pp. 57-65, at p. 59.
19. In 1945 the country could draw on credits of $1.76 billion in the United
Kingdom and the United States, and held the equivalent of 62 percent of foreign
exchange and gold reserves of the whole of Latin America. It is true that Brazil,
Cuba, and Mexico, among others, had similarly accumulated large reserves of foreign
currency; but sixteen million Argentines had amassed as much foreign exchange as
had 72.5 million Brazilians, Cubans, and Mexicans. See A. Magnet, op. cit., p. 110.
20. On this point, Conil Paz and G. Ferrari, op, cit., p. 155 et. seq.
21. A. Magnet, op. cit., p. 115.
22. For further details, see Liisa North, *Civil-Military Relations in Argentina,
Chile and Peru* (Berkeley, Calif.: Institute of International Studies, 1966), and L. M.
de Pablo Pardo, "La posición geográfica de la Argentina como factor de su política
exterior," 4 *Revista de la Facultad de Derecho y Ciencias Sociales* (1949), pp. 205-
515.
23. For details, see O. Holmes, "Argentina and the Dream of Southern Union,"
in University of Texas Institute of Latin American Studies, *Political, Economic and
Social Problems of the Latin-American Nations of Southern South America* (Austin:
University of Texas Press, 1949), pp. 43-57.
24. Alejandro Magnet, distinguished Chilean diplomat, in his book, *Nuestros
vecinos justicialistas* (Santiago: Pacífico, 1955), reprints the full text of the manifesto of the rebel officers *(Grupo de oficiales unidos)* which was drafted in April
1943 and circulated in May of that year. See op. cit., pp. 136-137. Magnet makes the
point that these officers never worked for Germany, and acted merely to create the
international conditions which, they hoped, would favor the fruition of their designs.
E. Díaz Araújo, *La Conspiración de '43. El GOU: una experiencia militarista en la
Argentina* (Mendoza: Universidad Nacional de Cuyo, 1969), however, questions the
existence of the GOU manifesto.
25. See R. J. Alexander, *Prophets of the Revolution* (New York: Macmillan,
1962), pp. 246-266. See also R. Picirilli, "Política internacional argentina: El justicialismo," 3 *Revista de derecho internacional y ciencias diplomáticas* (1953),
pp. 7-152; and O. G. Usinger, "Fundamentos de la política international Argentina,"
in ibid (1950), pp. 151-244.
26. See *Mensaje del Presidente de la Nación Argentina General Juan Perón, 84ta
Sesión del Honorable Congreso, Primer Mayo, 1950* (Buenos Aires, 1950), pp. 26-27.
27. *New York Times,* June 5, 1947.
28. See S. Bagú, *Argentina en el mundo* (Mexico City: Forido de Cultura
Economica, 1961), pp. 105-106.

29. *La Prensa*, February 15, 1948.

30. Conil Paz and G. Ferrari, op. cit., p. 168.

31. Thus he refused to support Indonesia in her struggle for independence from the Netherlands; and voted against all attempts to coerce South Africa in her dispute over South-West Africa. See *La Prensa*, April 5, 1948.

For an excellent general survey of Argentina's neutral tradition, see R. E. Modern, "La neutralidad de la República Argentina en las dos guerras mundiales," 2 *Revista Jurídica de Buenos Aires* (May-August, 1966), pp. 139-218.

32. *Neue Zürcher Zeitung*, September 20, 1947.

33. *New York Times*, October 20, 1947.

34. *La Prensa*, December 4, 1948. An agreement to set up a United States Military Mission in Buenos Aires was signed in Washington on October 6, 1948. See 19 *Department of State Bulletin*, October 17, 1948, p. 494.

Chapter II

THE IMPACT OF THE KOREAN WAR (1950-1953)

Before the outbreak of the Korean War on June 25, 1950, the Latin American countries had the worst of all worlds. Despised by the Soviet Union and taken for granted by the United States, their room for diplomatic maneuver was extremely narrow. The Korean War held out the prospect of swift release from all or most of these disabilities, and for the first time in the history of the Cold War, Latin America's governments had a chance of adopting policies of their own and of participating in some significant decision-making. It was not, as will be shown, a part for which they were properly prepared.

Under a so-called gentlemen's agreement of 1946, two Latin American states would always be elected as nonpermanent members on the Security Council, and in June 1950 these happened to be Cuba and Ecuador. It fell to their representatives to support the resolutions of June 25 and 27, 1950, which called for collective military measures by the United Nations in defense of South Korea.[1] Since Yugoslavia was opposing the second and stronger resolution of June 27, 1950, while India and Egypt abstained, the two Latin American votes were essential in producing the two-thirds majority required to pass the resolution.

Once the decision had been taken in the Security Council, Trygve Lie, Secretary-General of the United Nations, sent a call for material support in favor of the United Nations forces to all member countries so that the governments of Latin America were compelled to reveal their attitudes in this conflict in their replies. But few Latin American governments were eager or, for that matter, able to assume major commitments, and in some of the largest countries opposition was provoked to any active measures of support, particularly to the dispatch of troops to Korea. The general response to the United Nations therefore turned out to be a varied one, and only one country—Colombia—sent troops.

Another difficulty posed itself when the United States, strongly championing the course of South Korea, began to apply political pressures on Latin America with a view to a tightening of measures of military and economic defense in close cooperation with her. Here, too, the responses of the Latin American governments varied.

As regards Argentina, the US State Department had let it be known in January 1950 that it wished Argentina to ratify the Rio Treaty.[2] On May 17, 1950, the Export-Import Bank announced the extension of a credit of $125 million to a group of Argentine banks, and on May 29, 1950, the *State Department Bulletin* carried an article suggesting that economic relations with Argentina would "contribute to the furtherance of inter-American solidarity." Perón, however, was still holding back. At the beginning of June 1950 he informed the United States in highly ambiguous language that "in the event of war, you will defend your part of the hemisphere, and we will defend ours."[3]

The outbreak of the Korean War precipitated a rapprochement with the United States, and though Bolivia, Ecuador, Guatemala, and Peru had not ratified the Rio Treaty either, Perón now speedily did so.[4] Beyond that, Hipólito Paz, the new foreign minister, informed the United Nations of Argentina's intention to fulfil her obligations under the Charter and to provide aid to the best of her ability in support of the United Nations resolutions on sanctions,[5] thereby suggesting that Argentine troops might be sent to the Korean battlefront. That such a contingency was not remote was attested by the exchange of telegrams between the Secretary-General of the United Nations and the foreign ministry in Buenos Aires, in which the latter agreed that "the United Nations Command may enter into direct consultation with the Argentine government."[6]

Though the Radicals were opposed to any close cooperation with the United States, most of the opposition to active measures came from the Left, including the left wing of the Peronista movement itself. Serious street demonstrations were organized, allegedly by Peronists, in Rosario, and it has even been claimed that certain trade unions authorized political strikes.[7] Harping at length on the general perplexities of the situation and drawing attention to the slowness of the British, French, Italian, and Brazilian governments to take similar action, spokesmen of the Left intimated that the first obligation in Korea rested on the countries receiving Marshall Aid, and not on Argentina, pictured as a victim of the policy which underlay Marshall Aid.[8]

In view of unexpectedly strong opposition at home, Perón considered it wise to inform a meeting of workers on July 17, 1950, that he would "assume the attitude desired by the Argentine people and no other," adding that "Argentina knows what she wants to do today and tomorrow, and she will do it in her own good time and for her own sake, and not for the sake of anyone else."[9] Allowing for some hyperbole, this was the first step in the process of retraction and an indication that some public decision, either through Congress or by way of a referendum, would be necessary. Finding himself with insufficient support to carry the policy he had initiated, Perón tried to hide behind public opinion, and soon behind an ingenious legalism also.

As the prospects of a quick United Nations victory in Korea faded, Perón retreated further from his original position by publicly hinting at the desirability of adopting a full-blooded neutralism, going so far as to suggest that the ABC-powers[10] should be reassembled to protect Latin America from the imperialist powers.[11] As deadlock ensued in Korea, Perón—determined not to send troops, come what may—seized on any pretext for going back on his earlier promises to the United Nations,[12] and ultimately Argentina's only tangible contribution to the war effort of the United Nations in Korea amounted to no more than a shipment of frozen meat.[13]

Brazil reacted far more cautiously than Argentina and therefore avoided the need for backsliding, but her caution may have been due as much to fear of the strength of the Communist movement in the country—as revealed at the polls in 1946—as to uncertainty within the armed forces and elsewhere within the country regarding Brazil's role in the Cold War.

In spite of the fact that only vaguely cooperative assurances had been given by the government to the United Nations, popular disquiet was created by rumors that Brazilian troops would be sent to fight in Korea, which had to be denied publicly by Canrobert da Costa, minister of war, [14] while similar assurances were provided by Raul Fernandes, President Dutra's foreign minister.[15] On the other hand, the foreign minister informed *Tribuna da Imprensa* in December 1950 that Brazil could not remain neutral, and that the only point at issue was the extent of the commitment.[16] During the same month President-elect Getúlio Vargas announced that, on taking power, he would support the United Nations and give the United States the same amount of cooperation as during the World War.[17]

Yet, it has been established that Vargas was subjected to considerable United States pressure to participate actively in the Korean War, which he greatly resented. On one occasion he informed his cabinet that he would sooner do without a projected United States loan of $500 million than give in to that pressure.[18] Neves da Fontoura, his minister of foreign affairs, has since revealed that "Vargas was really allergic to United States policy."[19]

Vargas called to order those officials in the *Itamarati* (the Brazilian Ministry of Foreign Affairs) responsible for furnishing an optimistic draft of instructions for General Gois Monteiro on his forthcoming mission to Washington on the grounds that it might have misled the United States regarding the political intentions of Brazil.[20] Brazilians, he wrote on that occasion, must not hand themselves over "like sheep to be sacrificed." The true intentions of Brazil were outlined by the president in a number of letters to his chief of Civil Cabinet, as follows: (a) the defense of Brazil; and (b) military cooperation, on a treaty basis, with the United States, or, possibly, with the United Nations, involving the willingness of Brazil to make available scarce raw materials.[21]

Vargas' position was not an easy one, since in addition to pressures from the United States he also had to take into consideration the Communist party—which, though illegal, was still a force to be reckoned with—and the armed forces. The military, always a potential force in Brazilian politics, were not, however, united on all issues, and they reacted to the outbreak of the Korean War by exhibiting some neutralist currents which had hitherto lain dormant. Thus, General Cesar Obino, chief of the Joint General Staff, proved anxious to keep the country out of the war, whilst General Gois Montero, the army's chief-of-staff, gave warning in May 1951 that, in the event of war, the nation would have to think of its own security first before participating in collective military measures. [22] On January 5, 1952, General Estillac Leal, a staunch opponent of Communism, stressed the national character and mission of the armed forces, expressing his belief that "the country had passed the stage in which the national destiny lay in a choice between Communism and Fascism."[23]

Communist influence on some extreme nationalist officers existed also, leading to a major political crisis in December 1950. During that month an article appeared in the *Revista do Clube Militar,* the official organ of the influential Military Club in Rio de Janeiro—of which at that time an ardently nationalist major was president—which suggested that the United States was responsible for starting the war in Korea and recommended that Brazil should preserve the strictest neutrality in the contest. In the ensuing storm of indignation 600 officers issued a manifesto denouncing the "Russophil" views expressed in the article, and in mid-December the directorate of the club announced the suspension of the *Revista* in order to ensure that the officer corps would have "the climate of unity which it must have."[24]

Divisions over foreign policy also emerged in the Ministry of Foreign Affairs, where J. A. Lins de Barros, head of the Ministry's Economic Department, remarked that it was "poor business . . . not to maintain relations with Russia," and in February 1952, two "unofficial" government delegations attended the World Economic Conference in Moscow. Other officials, however, maintained that the issue of an economic rapprochement was separate from that of a resumption of diplomatic relations with the Soviet Union.[25] The position of Brazil's strategic raw materials, particularly minerals, was temporarily solved only when all export controls were placed in the hands of a national committee under the chairmanship of Foreign Minister da Fontoura.[26] In the end, Brazil contented herself with a financial contribution to the United Nations.

Mexico, under the leadership of President M. Alemán, came out in favor of the United Nations action in Korea. M. Tello, under-secretary of foreign relations, replied to Trygve Lie's telegram by affirming that "Mexico . . . will faithfully fulfil the obligations incumbent on her as a member of the United Nations" and hoping that the latter would succeed in restoring peace.[27] In his State of the Union Message of September 1, 1950, Alemán announced that Mexico would, as a matter of principle, support the democratic powers in any war, and would not remain idle in the face of a possible "collapse of civilization." He informed the country that his administration had sent food and medicine to send arms and war materials to Communist countries.[28] Considerable apprehension was felt regarding the length of Mexico's coastline, and the government's anxiety in this respect was alleviated only by the speedy transfer of two light cruisers, four destroyers, and four coast guard vessels from the United States Navy to that of Mexico.[29]

Even before the question of a military pact with the United States arose, public opinion had, however, become agitated about possible military involvements under existing commitments. In reply to a series of questions from the left-wing *Partido Obrero-Campesino Mexicano*, the foreign ministry was compelled to issue a statement on the subject in 1951, insisting that Mexico had no obligation to defend the territory of the United States or to supply "armed contingents to the United States when its government considers that country attacked." Mexico, the ministry went on to explain, would limit herself to defending her own territory in case of aggression.[30]

The outbreak of the Korean War happened to occur at a time when the country's commercial relations with the United States were undergoing a period of strain after the cancellation of the current trade agreement between the two countries.[31] Consequently, while the initial battles were in progress in Korea, Mexico found it politic to proclaim her desire to trade with the entire world by buying and selling where it was most profitable—an implied rebuff of the United States.[32]

Uruguay was ill-equipped to face the coming trials of the Cold War. In the constitutional sphere she had failed to evolve machinery for effective decision-making, while in the economic field she was excessively dependent on export earnings.

The typical form of government in Uruguay was the *colegiado* system, in which all parties are allowed proportional representation on the National Executive Council, Uruguay's cabinet. In 1933 the system was abolished and replaced by a presidential one, only to be reintroduced in 1951. Adequate for dealing with problems of foreign policy in normal times, the system tended to break down once subjected to major strains, largely because it tended to magnify the role of personalities on the National Executive Council, few of whom could claim any following in the country. Moreover, divisions of outlook in matters of foreign policy cut across both the main parties, the *colorados* and *blancos,* the representatives respectively of chiefly urban and rural interests.

A major split in the field of foreign policy had occurred within the blanco party in the 1930s, when the Independent Nationalists broke away from Dr. Luis Alberto de Herrera's Nationalists. The Herreristas remained neutral during the Second World War, in sharp contrast with the marked friendliness displayed by the government towards the Allies. The efficient conduct of Uruguay's foreign policy was gravely compromised by this division, and it was only the military victory of the Allies which caused the Herreristas to be temporarily eclipsed in the field of foreign affairs after the war.[33] The Cold War gave the Herreristas a new lease on political life. Traditionally suspicious of the Western powers, they adopted a sceptical attitude towards the West over Korea which was tempered only by an intense ideological dislike of the Soviet Union, and in doing so attracted support from many who wanted to be subject to "neither Stalin nor Truman."[34]

The presidential system, still functioning at the outbreak of the Korean War though on the way out, allowed the government to align itself firmly with the United States, while pledging all aid possible to the United Nations concerning Uruguay's resources and geographical position.[35] In March 1950 Communists and Herreristas had combined to oppose the proposed Treaty of Commerce, Friendship, and Economic Development with the United States,[36] but the ratification by the United States Senate of the treaty greatly facilitated the government's decision on August 26, 1950, to offer military assistance to the United Nations in Korea.[37] But Martin Trueba, elected president in November 1950, gave an assurance that Uruguay would enter the war only in the event of it spreading beyond Korea.[38] By way of material support, Uruguay formally pledged $2 million in September 1950 to be used at the discretion of the United Nations and made a donation of 73,000 blankets to the forces fighting on the United Nations side in Korea.[39] In October 1951 the government announced that it had put two training ships of the destroyer class and an unspecified number of foot soldiers at the disposal of the United Nations to serve, according to the Ministry of Foreign Affairs, either in the defense of the American Continent or in any other place in accord with the Charter of the United Nations.[40] No troops were sent to Korea.

In Cuba the administration of President Prío Socarrás ranged itself solidly behind the United Nations and the United States but confined its cooperation to the economic sphere. In December 1950 the president gave a pledge that Cuba would use its mineral wealth to support the defense program of the United States and the Western powers.[41] Internally the government experienced some difficulties over (a) the projected rupture of diplomatic relations with the Soviet Union; (b) the suppression of the Cuban Communists; and (c) the despatch of troops to Korea.

In November 1951, Prío Socarrás, a fierce anti-Communist, petitioned the government to break off diplomatic relations with the Soviet Union and other Communist countries, and to outlaw the Communist Party.[42] However, it fell to Fulgencio Batista to take active steps in this direction. Having seized power in a coup in March 1952 in an effort to prevent his defeat in a regular presidential election, Batista was quick to assure the United States that Cuba's place in the Cold War was at the side of the United States; that Cuban troops would be available for service in Korea if required; and that his government would fight side by side with the United States in a "hot" war. After these assurances, recognition of his régime by the United States was swift,[43] and the new Cuban administration promptly severed diplomatic relations with the Soviet Union on April 2, 1952.[44]

A number of internal measures had to be taken against the Communists, some of dubious constitutionality. Ex-President R. Grau San Martín and Ramón Vasconcelos, minister without portfolio in the Varona cabinet, protested against these, and the latter also resigned from the government. The prime minister countered by presenting what he termed proof that Cuban Communism was at the center of Soviet espionage in the Americas by displaying a number of envelopes bearing the letterhead *Prensa continental* which had been addressed to Communist agents in all countries of the Western Hemisphere; but the actual contents of these letters was never revealed.[45] Talks between Batista and the Communists before the projected elections in 1952 came to nothing because of disagreement on matters of foreign policy: Blas Roca, on behalf of the Communists, stated that in a world war he would back the Soviet Union; whereas Batista indicated that he would support the United States.[46] It was only under Batista that energetic action was taken against the Communists when *Hoy*, the Communist daily, was suppressed in July 1953,[47] and the Communist Party itself outlawed on October 31, 1953.[48]

In 1951 Prío Socarrás sent a request to Congress to dispatch a thousand Cuban troops to Korea.[49] It is noteworthy that opposition to this step—which seems never to have been contemplated seriously—came not only from the well-organized Communists, but also from left-of-center forces. Dr. Roberto Agramonte, who was later to be Dr. Castro's first foreign minister—and was at that time a presidential candidate and a loyal supporter of cooperation in the defense of the Western Hemisphere, both through the United Nations and the OAS—was prominent among these.[50]

In Ecuador the occurrence of the Korean War might well have caused a sharpening of the existing antagonism between the followers of the nationalist Jóse Maria Velasco Ibarra and those of the cosmopolitan Galo Plaza Lasso, had it not been for the smouldering border dispute with Peru which threatened to break out once more during 1950. Galo Plaza Lasso, who had taken over as president on September 1, 1948, was inclined to back the United Nations to the hilt. During a visit to the United States in June 1951 he announced that Ecuador would fight beside the United States to keep Communist tyranny out of the Western Hemisphere[51] and also called for the information of a standardized Latin American legion to be held in readiness for action on behalf of the United Nations.[52] But the frontier dispute, which erupted in October 1950, August 1951, and again in October 1952 prevented Ecuador from doing anything tangible.

Colombia, though driven by bitter and sanguine civil war, dispatched a battalion of troops to fight in Korea, and consequently became the only Latin American country to sign the armistice agreement and the security pact which were concluded simultaneously in July 1953.[53]

The Korean War encouraged the United States Administration— empowered by the National Security Act passed by Congress in 1951—to conclude bilateral military assistance pacts with its allies the world over, and to buttress multilateral security arrangements, such as NATO and the Rio Treaty, which seemed too loose to take swift and effective measures in an emergency. The Mutual Security Act of 1951 provided for $38,150,000 of direct military assistance to Latin America, to be used in those countries whose participation was judged by the president as indispensable.[54] In furtherance of this objective, a Meeting of Consultation of Foreign Ministers of the OAS was called at the behest of the United States in March 1951, and resolved that "the strengthening of their defenses" was the most urgent task of all American states.[55]

Argentina[56] and Bolivia did not enter into negotiations for a Mutual Assistance Agreement with the United States; Mexico's negotiations collapsed; while the pacts which were concluded had a difficult passage in the legislatures of Brazil, Chile, and Uruguay.

TABLE 1

MILITARY ASSISTANCE AGREEMENTS ENTERED BY LATIN AMERICAN COUNTRIES WITH THE UNITED STATES

Brazil	March 7, 1952
Chile	April 9, 1952
Colombia	April 17, 1952
Cuba	March 15, 1952
Dominican Republic	March 6, 1953
Ecuador	February 20, 1952
Guatemala[57]	June 18, 1955
Haiti	January 28, 1955
Honduras	May 20, 1954
Nicaragua	April 23, 1954
Peru	February 22, 1952
Uruguay	June 30, 1952

When the United States invited the Mexican government to enter into negotiations for a military pact, President Alemán was ready to oblige. Negotiations were begun in February 1952, collapsed almost immediately because of determined opposition, and compelled the president to explain lamely that "in all international problems we always place our country first."[58] The Mexican Communists had largely succeeded in mobilizing the generally prevailing antipathy to the proposed pact and were able to induce the ruling *Partido Revolucionario Institucional* (PRI) to suspend negotiations *sine die*.[59]

In July 1953 Francis White, ambassador of the United States, intimated that the pact was still open to negotiations; but under Ruiz Cortines, the new president, the practical possibilities of doing so had shrunk to vanishing point.[60]

Preparations for the Mutual Assistance Agreement with Brazil were completed in January 1952. By its terms Brazil bound herself to contribute war material and troops for the defense of the Western Hemisphere, while the United States undertook to provide $50 million from the $7.3 billion available for military aid.[61]

Opposition to ratification developed almost immediately,[62] producing a wave of nationalist feeling during which Vargas was able to pass the controversial legislation for the establishment of Petrobrás, the state monopoly for the extraction of oil.[63] The bill to ratify the Mutual Assistance Agreement was held up in the economic committee of Congress, where the fear was expressed that, under its implied terms, Brazilian troops might have to be sent to Korea, and that the government would be under an obligation to sell raw materials to the United States at prices dictated by the latter.[64] President Vargas himself had to intervene in order to push the bill through that delicate committee stage.[65] When the act eventually passed the House in February 1953, the price of ratification was simultaneous legislation restricting the government's right to send troops abroad. It may have been a coincidence that the Export-Import Bank of Washington released a loan of $300 million at the same time, the largest one Brazil had had.[66] Even so, the Senate was able to complete ratification of the Mutual Assistance Agreement only one day before it would have lapsed automatically under Brazilian constitutional law.[67]

In Chile, President González Videla committed the government to a Mutual Assistance Agreement without hesitation, and in spite of considerable opposition to it. The pact was signed on April 9, 1952, and rapidly moved through the appropriate channels for ratification.[68] However,

Carlos Ibáñez, candidate at the forthcoming presidential elections, who had accepted the electoral support of the *Partido Socialista Popular* in June 1952, opposed ratification[69] and attacked the proposed agreement during his election campaign.[70] He also agitated for the legalization of the Communist Party, advocated a resumption of diplomatic relations with the Soviet Union, and called for the diversification of Chile's foreign trade.[71]

Upon election, Ibáñez attempted to break the strategic embargo on the sale of copper to Communist countries which the Mutual Assistance Agreement had imposed.[72] But, in spite of Soviet willingness to buy, he changed his mind[73] and also dropped his objections to ratification, explaining that he was "with the West" and would "fight for the West."[74] The Left in Chile had been roundly deceived, and Chile continued to pursue the policies initiated by González Videla.

In Uruguay the ratification of the pact after signature took about twelve months. The reason for the delay was the clash between the Batllistas—a faction of the ruling Colorado Party—and the Herreristas. On November 4, 1952, the Herreristas proposed a national plebiscite on the question of ratification, but their motion was rejected in the Senate as unconstitutional, and on November 18, 1952, the pact was ratified.[75] There was, however, a strong suspicion that elements both in Congress and in the Council acquiesced because they considered the agreement of practical value primarily against the dreaded Perón régime in neighboring Argentina.[76]

The efforts of the United States to align the states of Latin America solidly behind it after the outbreak of the Korean conflict met with a mixed response. Though, in the flush of the first excitement, Argentina and Mexico showed a definite desire to fall in with the United States in supporting the United Nations in Korea to the extent of direct military participation, these desires were quickly extinguished. Attempts on the part of the United States to apply pressure on Latin America to enter into mutual assistance agreements with her merely aroused opposition, so that finally, with the exception of Colombia, it was made vitually impossible for any government in the region to mobilize its material resources to any significant extent in support of United Nations action in Korea.

Though all Latin American governments were represented on the Inter-American Defense Board which, acting on the basis of the resolution passed at the Fourth Meeting of OAS Foreign Ministers at Washington in March 1951, had produced its "General Plan" for the defense of the Western Hamisphere in November 1951,[77] it was becoming more and more evident that it was the relatively strong countries of Latin America that were the least inclined to commit themselves to Cold War alignments and to be tied down in specific military pacts with the United States outside the existing security system of the Rio Treaty.

The net effect of the Korean War on Latin America was, on the contrary, to alert its politically articulate sections to the full implications of the Cold War for their region and to take up positions accordingly.

NOTES

1. On June 28, 1950, the OAS Council merely sanctioned these decisions of the Security Council.

2. *New York Times,* January 23, 1950.

3. *Christian Science Monitor,* June 20, 1950.

4. *La Prensa,* June 29, 1950, and Paz and Ferrari, op. cit., p. 169.

5. *La Prensa,* June 30, 1950, and July 1, 1950. Also Paz and Ferrari, op. cit., p. 169.

6. Paz and Ferrari, op. cit., p. 170.

7. Paz and Ferrari, op. cit., p. 171.

8. *Hispanic-American Report* 3 (August 1950), pp. 29-30. Henceforeward referred to as H.A.R., this Report is published by the Institute of Hispanic-American and Brazilian Studies, Stanford, Calif.

9. P. Lux-Wurm, *Le Péronisme* (Paris: Librairie générale de droit et de jurisprudence, 1965), p. 209.

10. The reference here is to President Yrigoyen's attempt to create a bloc of neutral states composed of Argentina, Brazil, and Chile during the First World War.

11. H.A.R., August 1950, p. 31. On August 22, 1950, Perón met at the Casa rosada with Hipólito Paz, his foreign minister, and J. Remorino, his ambassador in Washington, in a high-level conference on foreign policy. Remorino returned almost at once to the United States with a message for the Department of Defense there. See G. Blanksten, *Perón's Argentina* (Chicago: University of Chicago Press, 1953), p. 257.

12. In April 1951, for instance, he explained that Argentina could not send troops abroad because the United States and her allies were not supporting Argentina's claims to the Falkland Islands. See H.A.R., May 1951, p. 31, quoting an article by Perón in *Democracia* of May 1951.

13. *La Prensa,* September 15, 1950.

14. 3 H.A.R., August 1950, p. 35. That these rumors were not altogether far-fetched was borne out nine months later when Vargas' foreign minister, João Neves da Fontoura, brought back from a visit to Washington President Truman's reply to a letter sent by the Brazilian president in which Brazil was assured of United States support, but which also contained clear hints regarding the need of having Brazilians fighting in Korea. See 4 H.A.R., May 1951, pp. 35-36.

15. Jornal do Commercio, *A Política Exterior do Brasil na gestão do Chanceler Raul Fernandes* (Rio de Janeiro, 1951), p. 62.

16. H.A.R., December 1950, p. 36. His views were not shared universally by leading Brazilians. Oswaldo Aranha, for instance, prominent *getulista*, veteran statesman and diplomat, and recently president of the Security Council of the United Nations, took the view that the government should consider carefully what path to follow in the event of war.

17. 4 H.A.R., January 1951, p. 36.

18. See L. Fontes and G. Carneiro, *A Face Final de Vargas. Os bilhetes de Getúlio* (Rio de Janeiro: O. Cruzeiro, 1966); especially the section on "Pressures on Brazil to fight in Korea," pp. 75-77.

19. See J. Neves da Fontoura, *Depoimentos de um ex-Ministro* (Rio de Janeiro: Simões, 1957), p. 128.

20. L. Fontes and G. Carneiro, op. cit., p. 75.

21. Ibid., pp. 75-77.

22. L. Continho, *O General Góes Depõe* (Rio de Janeiro, 1956), at p. 517.

23. See *Anais da Câmara dos Diputados*, vol. 1 (1952), p. 76.

24. T. E. Skidmore, *Politics in Brazil, 1930-1964* (New York: Oxford University Press, 1967), p. 105. For a full account of this episode by a left-wing military historian, see N. Werneck Sodré, *Historia Militar do Brasil* (Rio de Janeiro: Civilização Brasileira, 1965).

25. 5 H.A.R., February 1952, pp. 37-38.

26. Ibid.

27. *El Excelsior*, June 30, 1950.

28. 4 H.A.R., September 1951, p. 10. It is believed that it was General R. R. Limón, Alemán's minister of war, who energetically vetoed any idea of a dispatch of Mexican troops to Korea. On July 20, 1950, Alemán was still able to assure the Governor of Texas that Mexico would fulfil her international commitments. On the latter point, see *El Excelsior*, July 21, 1950.

29. 3 H.A.R., August 1950, p. 9.

30. Ibid., vol. 4, March 1951, p. 17.

31. Ibid., vol. 3, August 1950, p. 9.

32. Ibid. A study published by the United Nations Economic Commission for Latin America (ECLA) six years later made the point that Mexico had profited considerably from the economic boom generated by the Korean War, so that it was to take her two years after the termination of hostilities to reattain the high levels of economic activity achieved in 1951. See United Nations Economic Commission for Latin America, *El desequilibrio en el desarrollo económico latino-americano: el caso de México*, vol. 1 (Santiago, 1957), p. 60.

33. On this point, see A. E. Solari, *El Tercerismo en el Uruguay* (Montevideo: Colección Carabella, 1965). The leading Uruguayan commentator and academic, E. Rodríguez Fabregat, writing in *Marcha*, May 28, 1971, claims that Herrera told an emissary of the United States government that the war in Korea was not "a civil war but one of United States intervention."

34. Ibid., pp. 17 and 22.

35. See República Oriental del Uruguay, *Mensaje del Poder Ejecutivo a la Asamblea General al inaugurarse el Ier período de la XXXVI Legislatura* (1951), pp. 3-5.

36. 3 H.A.R., March 1950, p. 27.

37. Ibid., August 1950, p. 34.

38. 3 H.A.R., March 1951, p. 31.

39. See República Oriental del Uruguay, *Mensaje del Poder Ejecutivo a la Asamblea General al inaugurarse el Ier período de la XXXVI Legislatura* (1951), pp. II/5.

40. 3 H.A.R., October 1951, p. 34.

41. For this purpose a subcommittee of the Senate Armed Forces Committee urged the administration to reopen the Nícar nickel mine in Oriente province in which the United States had invested $32 million during the Second World War. See 4 H.A.R., December 1950, p. 21.

42. 4 H.A.R., November 1951, p. 17.

43. *New York Times,* March 14, 1952; and March 28, 1952.

44. Ibid., April 4, 1952.

45. 3 H.A.R., August 1950.

46. See H. Thomas, *Cuba* (New York: Harper & Row, 1971), p. 773.

47. *New York Times,* July 27, 1953.

48. Ibid., November 1, 1953.

49. See H. Thomas, op. cit., p. 768.

50. 5 H.A.R., February 1952, p. 17.

51. *New York Herald Tribune,* June 22, 1951.

52. Ibid., June 27, 1951.

53. See Colonel J. Polanía Puyo, "Colombia's Participation in the Korean Campaign," in *Inter-American Defense Board Yearbook* (Washington, D.C., 1953), p. 5.

54. Mecham, *The United States and Inter-American Security, 1889-1960* (Austin: Texas University Press, 1961), p. 335.

55. Connell-Smith, *The Inter-American System* (London: Oxford University Press, 1966), pp. 158-159.

56. A Mutual Assistance Agreement was signed only on May 10, 1964.

57. The signature was obtained only after the overthrow of the Arbenz Administration in June 1954.

58. *New York Times,* February 24, 1952.

59. 5 H.A.R., February 1952, p. 8. Mexico's left-wing intellectuals played a prominent part in the campaign against negotiations. David Alfaro Sequeiros, the celebrated mural painter, revolutionary, former friend of Trotsky but now ardent supporter of the Soviet government, painted a picture of President Truman waving a sheaf of dollar bills over a manacled *peon;* Emilio Fernández, well-known film director, Enrique González Martínez, famous poet, and numerous other intellectuals were also found among the active opponents of the proposed pact.

60. Ibid., vol. 6, August 1953, p. 10.

61. *The Economist,* April 26, 1952.

62. 5 H.A.R., January 1952, p. 38. General Góes Monteiro, chief-of-staff of the army, advised Vargas to reject the proffered Mutual Assistance Agreement. See L. Coutinho, *O General Góes Depõe* (Rio de Janeiro, 1956), p. 517.

63. General Góes Monteiro, chief-of-staff, advised the rejection of the agreement. See L. Coutinho, op. cit., p. 517.

64. See also N. Werneck Sodré, *Historia Militar do Brasil* (Rio de Janeiro, 1965), p. 311.

65. For the Congressional debate on ratification, see *Anais da Câmara dos diputados,* Vol. 5 (1953), pp. 88-118, 179-188, 331-346, and 543-583.

66. 6 H.A.R., March 1953, p. 33.

67. Ibid.

68. According to the United States ambassador in Santiago, the Radical party was split. On May 6, 1952, he was informed by González Videla that the pact would be ratified. Irrarázaval, the foreign minister, made the vote in Congress one of confidence. See C. G. Bowers, *Misión en Chile* (Santiago, 1957), p. 335. On June 2, 1952, the Foreign Relations Committee of the Chamber of Deputies approved ratification by seven votes in favor and three against, with one abstention, whilst the voting pattern on the floor of the Chamber was 78 in favor and 21 against. See 5 H.A.R., June 1952, p. 30. The Senate also gave its approval. See *El Mercurio,* July 4, 1952.

69. 5 H.A.R., June 1952, p. 30. At a meeting in Santiago's Teatro Caupolicán to discuss the projected agreement with the United States both Ibañistas and left-wing Socialist supporters of Allende showed themselves against it. See *El Mercurio,* June 16, 1952.

70. In the Senate he referred to the projected agreement as "dangerous to our sovereignty and degrading for the armed forces." See E. Würth-Rojas, *Ibáñez. Caudillo enigmático* (Santiago: Pacifico, 1958), pp. 222-223. The main points of opposition as set out by the Political Council of the *Movimiento Nacional y Popular* which promoted Ibáñez' candidacy were (a) that such a weighty decision should not be taken a few months before a presidential election; (b) that the agreement would infringe the principle of multilaterality established at Rio (1947) and Bogotá (1948); and (c) that it would disturb the good relationship among Latin American peoples. See *El Mercurio,* April 8, 1952.

71. *New York Times,* September 10, 1952. See also Bowers, op. cit., pp. 337-338.

72. Ibid., August 22, 1953. *La Nación* (Santiago) indignantly denied rumors according to which Baltasar Castro, Socialist president of the Chamber of Deputies, had gone to Moscow to arrange a sale of copper. See 6 H.A.R., December 1953, pp. 31-32; but an unsuccessful attempt to sell copper to Poland was made in the course of that year. (Evidence kindly supplied in a personal interview to the writer in Santiago on July 12, 1971, by Oscar Waiss, who in 1959 had been under-secretary of state in the Ministry of Mines and Labor.)

73. *New York Times,* November 4, 1953.

74. *Time Magazine,* December 14, 1953.

75. 5 H.A.R., November 1952, p. 35. For a voice of approval of the pact, see A. L. Ciasullo, *El Uruguay y la solidaridad interamericana (El Tratado de Asistencia Militar con Estados Unidos)* (Montevideo: Revista de derecho publico y privado, 1952).

76. *Marcha,* the left-of-center periodical of Montevideo, whilst in general defending a neutralism in the Korean War (see its editions of April 20, 1951, May 11, 1951, and June 8, 1951), carried an article on July 11, 1952, by a proponent of the agreement, entitled significantly *"El Tratado militar con Norteamérica y el imperialismo argentino,"* which would confirm that suspicion.

77. Mecham, op. cit., p. 333.

Chapter III

THE GUATEMALAN CRISIS (1953-1954)

The two classical episodes of direct confrontation in the Cold War—Berlin and Korea—had both proved inconclusive but had taught the two principals to act with greater circumspection in the future. Caution at this stage was also advisable because, by the time of the conclusion of the armistice in Korea on July 27, 1953, both superpowers were in possession of the hydrogen bomb and busy devising means whereby its swift delivery could be assured.

Though little or nothing had been achieved towards solving the issues underlying the Cold War, the new military technology called for profound modifications in its scenario. Henceforth direct confrontation would have to be avoided and the main field of contention shifted to an intermediate zone of underdeveloped countries comprising an area in Asia south of the Far East, the Near East, Latin America, and—later still—Africa. This vast geopolitical space was to serve at once as buffer and battlefield. The system of indirect confrontation was about to supplant the system of direct confrontation in the Cold War.

The new scenario suited the principals because in a basically unstable world they alone commanded strength, stability and confidence, and possessed the capacity to intervene swiftly almost at any point in the rest of the world. Yet, some price had to be paid. While the new areas could perform the function of buffers, they were capable of providing fresh grist for the mills of the Cold War in a manner not entirely welcome to the world powers; for though the absolute military strength of the principals was now unrivalled, their tactical scope was restricted.

Theoretically it was open to the world powers by all manner of maneuvers to "penetrate" the underdeveloped world in attempting to gain a foothold there and to undermine the adversary's position in it; but in practice the scope for such strategies proved to be surprisingly narrow. Whereas under the system of direct confrontation they had it firmly within their power to initiate a crisis, the time and place of crisis under the new system were no longer of their own choosing. All they could do now was to react to crises which had their origins within the intermediate zone of underdeveloped countries. In those circumstances the advantage belonged not to the principal that could initiate more cleverly, but to the world power that could react faster and adapt its tactics and general approach to the conditions prevailing within those areas. There was to be little or no room for deliberate contrivance.

With the principals in deadlock, a denouement could only be the result of developments within the underdeveloped areas. Henceforth, conflict in the underdeveloped world was to be primarily endogenous. It would arise from within the area and develop autonomously. Such conflict might reach a stage where it got out of control, and theoretically this was the proper point for intervention by the principals. The practical difficulty with such intervention lay in the impossibility of gauging the precise moment of action if debâcles were to be avoided. Ultimately it was for the principals to decide whether a conflict in the underdeveloped world had passed the local stage and had, in the context of the Cold War, become global.

This imposed new burdens on the diplomatic and military skills and resources of the world powers. In deciding on the criteria to guide them in their decision to intervene, the principals had ultimately to judge what ultimate effect endogenous conflict would have on the world balance of power. Ideological considerations would usually provide the pretext rather than the basic cause for intervention; they would also supply the code in which political communication among the parties was conducted. Latin America was a case in point.

The Guatemalan crisis was the first of the predominantly endogenous type of crises of the Cold War in Latin America. Its roots were strictly local and its subsequent development autonomous. There was nothing to suggest that it had been deliberately fomented from abroad, yet, it threatened to envelop both principals in the Cold War.[1]

Juan José Arévalo, a left-wing intellectual of "Populist" sympathies,[2] elected in 1945 to give practical expression to the longing for reforms, produced a program of social and economic reconstruction which brought him into sharp conflict with the United Fruit Company, owner of extensive holdings of plantations in the country, and also with the United States ambassador, who gave that company his firm support.[3]

It would be quite wrong to assume, however, that enmity from these two sources affected the principles of Arévalo's foreign policy. On the contrary, González Arévalo, his foreign minister, had condemned aggression in Korea and given a firm assurance that "the people of Guatemala will never accept the totalitarian form of government represented by Communists and practised by them."[4] Arévalo himself had defended the Rio Treaty against criticism in the National Assembly in August 1950,[5] and ordered positive steps to be taken against the country's Communists in October of that year.[6]

A crisis emerged under Arévalo's successor, Lt. Col. Jácobo Arbenz, who won the elections of November 10-12, 1950, by a wide margin.[7] In March 1951 Arbenz declared the aim of his government to be the promotion of capitalism, and in view of the perennial tensions between the landowning and business classes of Guatemala this would seem a credible enough intention.[8] In the same month, Manuel Galich, the foreign minister, denied that there had been any Communist infiltration of the government.[9]

In February 1952 the left-wing parties formed a National Democratic Front which included the Communists and constituted a clear majority in Congress.[10] At this stage developments in Guatemala began to show certain affinities with those preceding the civil war in Spain in 1936. In March 1952, Estrada de la Hoz, a Communist, was elected president of Congress.[11] In December 1952, Dr. Raúl Osegueda, the new foreign minister, announced that he was opposed to any outside influence, whether from the Left or the Right, and affirmed that the central concern of the government must be the defense of the national interest. He emphasized that he was not a member of the Communist Party.[12] It looked as if Guatemala was firmly set on a foreign policy of principled neutralism.

The Communists undeniably—and largely because of the marked lack of political sophistication prevailing in the country[13] —succeeded in occupying important posts[14] in the State, particularly in the police, in the Department of Agrarian Reform, and in the trade union movement. In addition to speeding reforms already initiated by his predecessor, Arbenz, from February 1953 onwards, took the critical step of expropriating land owned by United States companies, particularly the United Fruit Company.[15] The administration of President Eisenhower interpreted these measures as forming an integral part of the Cold War and as directed specifically against the United States. Thus, Arbenz was naively accused by the State Department of treating the Guatemalan Communists "as an authentic domestic political party and not as part of the world-wide Soviet Communist conspiracy."[16] It is interesting to note that the State Department expressly denied being concerned with developments in Guatemala because private United States interests were affected, insisting that it was interested only in opposing the Soviet Union.[17] This protestation had the ring of genuineness and would confirm the theory of the intrinsic primacy of strategic over all other considerations in the motivation of United States diplomacy towards Latin America, as expressed in the Monroe Doctrine.

On January 29, 1954, the Guatemalan government claimed the existence of a plot to invade the country with the support of President L. Somoza of Nicaragua and the United States Administration. Col. G. Castillo Armas and Gen. M. Ydígoras Fuentes, two Guatemalan emigrés living in Nicaragua, were expressly named, but the United States immediately rebutted these charges.[18]

In March 1954 the issue of the threat of "international communism" to the Western Hemisphere was raised at the Tenth Inter-American Conference meeting in Caracas, where the United States was intent on having the Guatemalan government condemned or at least discredited in Latin American eyes.[19] The attempt was only partially successful, as the conference refused to endorse positive action, contenting itself instead with generalities.[20]

Tensions were rising rapidly, as military measures were taken on both sides. The Guatemalan government had tried in vain to obtain arms from the United States first, then from other Western governments, and Arbenz ultimately turned to Eastern Europe. In February 1954 Major A. Martínez travelled to Switzerland to arrange payment for arms to be shipped to Guatemala from the Polish port of Szczecin in the chartered freighter Alfhem.[21] This consignment of arms arrived in Guatemala in mid-May

1954, and according to one source amounted to 2,000 tons of small arms in the main,[22] enough perhaps to turn the balance of power in Central America decisively in Guatemala's favor. The arrival of those arms was the subject of public exchanges between Guatemala and the United States. Guatemala asserted that the United States government had obstructed the purchase of arms in other countries, while Dulles maintained that Guatemala had a military establishment "three or four times" the size of its neighbors Nicaragua, Honduras, and El Salvador, and that the shipment of arms from Szczecin had been both devious and secret.[23] The breach between the United States and Guatemala was now irreparable, but formal diplomatic relations continued. On May 19, 1954, Nicaragua severed relations with Guatemala, and five days later the United States announced an emergency airlift of arms to both Nicaragua and Honduras.[24] A spokesman of the United States administration announced disingenuously that no arms were being sent to Guatemala because of "obvious uncertainty about their use."[25] It has been admitted that the Central Intelligence Agency and the United States Administration were directly involved in the invasion of Guatemala by a force of anti-Communist Guatamalan exiles under the command of Col. Castillo Armas.[26]

The Arbenz régime was unable to defend itself. In the first place, it had failed to follow up its initial steps of acquiring arms from Eastern Europe by substantive assurances of aid in the event of intervention. It had therefore merely its own store of arms to pit against what could easily have developed into a series of aerial deliveries of arms from the United States on the scale of the Berlin airlift of 1948-1949. Secondly, the régime and particularly the Communists in it, had never succeeded in securing the full allegiance of the armed forces.[27] It was only on June 25, 1954, one week after the invasion of Guatemala had begun from neighboring Honduras, that Arbenz ordered arms to be distributed to left-wing paramilitary organizations. The army leaders refused to comply, and on June 27, 1954, demanded Arbenz' resignation.

On the diplomatic plane, Guatemala suffered from the legal ambiguities which had been introduced into the overlapping security systems of the United Nations and the Rio Treaty, which made it impossible to establish whether the organs of either institution were competent to deal with this case. On June 18, 1954, Guatemala formally complained to the Security Council, invoking Articles 34, 35, and 39 of the UN Charter. During the session of the Security Council on June 20, 1954, Guatemala requested that Honduras and Nicaragua be ordered to apprehend the invaders, and that an observation commission be constituted to verify the accusations that these two governments had connived at the intervention. Brazil and Colombia, as Latin American members of the Security Council, presented a draft resolution which, if it had not been vetoed by the Soviet member, would have referred the complaint to the OAS. After the defeat of the resolution, the Security Council voted unanimously for a termination of all hostilities. On June 22, 1954, Guatemala renewed its complaint to the Security Council on the ground that its resolution was not being complied with and the aggression was continuing. By a narrow vote the Security Council decided not to hear that complaint.

Meanwhile, in the OAS, ten member governments, including the United States, had called for the convening of an OAS meeting of foreign ministers to investigate the "intervention of the international Communist movement" in Guatemala, and on June 23, 1954, the Inter-American Peace Committee of the OAS voted unanimously to create a Commission of Enquiry to proceed to Guatemala, Honduras, and Nicaragua, but at this point Guatemala decided not to cooperate with the OAS, possibly because she had recognized the Security Council, on which she had the Soviet Union to support her, as the more promising organ in which to fight her case.

This raised an important matter of principle, as in the course of the debate within the Security Council no conclusion could be reached as to whether the matter before it qualified as an "act of aggression," as Guatemala maintained at first, or a "dispute," as Guatemala later intimated it might be. In the case of the former the Security Council would have had primary jurisdiction, whereas in the latter jurisdiction would have fallen to the OAS.[28]

However, though on the surface the Security Council may have been the preferable institution as far as Guatemala's case was concerned, it would still have been perfectly lawful under the UN Charter for the case to be transferred to the OAS under the ultimate jurisdiction of the Security Council. The Arbenz government would, therefore, after all, have been well advised to concentrate on and cooperate fully with the OAS in an effort to achieve the speedy dispatch of its Commission of Enquiry to the scene to establish the undoubted complicity of the governments of Honduras and Nicaragua and bring world opinion to its side. The commission had just reached Mexico City from Washington when the Guatemalan government fell, as valuable time had been lost in the Security Council.[29]

The indirect intervention of the United States raises the problem of the peculiar ideological superstructure which the statesmen in the United States had erected on top of the building of the Monroe Doctrine. John Foster Dulles, Secretary of State of the United States, tried to use the machinery of the inter-American system for inducing the Latin American States to enter the lists of the Cold War on the side of the United States, and though not the first Secretary of State to do so, he was the first to use the ideological issue of "international communism" in conjunction with the issue of the security of the Western Hemisphere. At the Tenth Inter-American Conference held at Caracas in March 1954 he introduced a resolution condemning the machinations of "international communism" in such a way as to allow enforcement action to be taken in any issue under that heading under the terms of the Rio Treaty. Specifically, the resolution proposed that the OAS declare "that the domination and control of the political institutions of any American State by the international Communist movement . . . would constitute a threat to the sovereignty and political independence of the American States . . . and would call for appropriate action in accordance with existing treaties."[30] The confusion created between the ideological issue and that of security was to persist in inter-American relations.

It may, however, be questioned whether United States policy towards Latin America, as manifested by the Eisenhower Administration during and after the Guatemalan crisis, was as strongly motivated by fear of "international communism" as would appear at first sight. It would seem that ideological considerations take second place to strategic-diplomatic ones. The prime test in this instance was the Bolivian revolution in 1952, a major social and economic upheaval, during which the tin mines were nationalized and the large estates, particularly prominent in Bolivia, divided among the peasants. The entire class of wealthy landowners who had formed the political backbone of the *ancien régime* was crushed in the process. The government of the United States not only recognized the revolutionary government, but subsequently granted it economic aid on an ascending scale.[31]

The outcome of the Guatemalan crisis produced a sense of profound shock in Latin America, where it was realized that the region was not immune to Cold War crises. Even a major clash of arms in Latin America was no longer to be regarded as far-fetched.

In Latin America, the Guatemalan crisis had revealed a peculiar pattern of support for the United States, with Batista's Cuba, Trujillo's Dominican Republic, and Odría's Peru giving Dulles their "vigorous support."[32]

Further support for the position of the United States came from Nicaragua, El Salvador, and Venezuela, "all under dictatorships."[33] Guatemala apart, the only noticeable attempts at opposing United States endeavors to isolate the Arbenz government came from Argentina and Mexico and were half-hearted.

At the Washington conference of March 1951, Manuel Galich, Guatemala's foreign minister, had attacked the notion that the concepts of ideology and security ought to be fused in the Cold War, maintaining that a clear distinction had to be made between "elements of opposition" which, by implication, may be Communist, and "subversive agents of an extra-continental power."[34] At Caracas in 1954, Guillermo Toriello, former Guatemalan ambassador in Washington and newly appointed foreign minister, accused the United States and its associates of showing the "negative flag" of anti-Communism to prevent progress. According to one anonymous Latin American delegate to the conference, he "said many things some of the rest of us would have liked to say if we dared."[35]

Argentina and Mexico had opposed a resolution of the Washington meeting of OAS foreign ministers in March 1951 urging all members of that organization to earmark armed forces and resources for the joint defense of the Western Hemisphere,[36] and abstained from voting for the anti-Communist resolution at Caracas in March 1954 on the ground that it infringed the cardinal principle of non-intervention.[37]

While Perón—determined not to rush to the support of the United States and suffering the penalty, as happened at the outbreak of the Korean War in 1950—disapproved of United States policy towards Guatemala, he was unwilling to follow Guatemala in seeking support in Eastern Europe. Together with Uruguay, a very reluctant consenter at Caracas, Argentina led a group of Latin American governments in the Council of the OAS which favored the consideration of the Guatemalan crisis in its most acute stage under the innocuous procedural heading of "the general situation," rather than the potent "intervention of the international Communist movement" in Guatemala. This group argued explicitly but unsuccessfully that all interventions, and not just "Communist" ones, "may interfere with the political, economic or military sovereignty of any State."

In Mexico, the pro-United States attitude conspicuous under President Alemán (1946-1952) was giving way to more circumspect policies, as was evidenced by President A. Ruiz Cortines' appointment of Narciso Bassols, generally felt to be left-inclined, as presidential adviser in February

1954.[38] The Guatemalan crisis released a number of political pressures hitherto contained, as public opinion began to get agitated. On May 29, 1954, former President Cárdenas (1934-1940) sent a message to Cortines and addressed a meeting of newspaper publishers on June 7, 1954, expressing grave concern at developments in the Guatemalan crisis, in which he saw a danger to the Western Hemisphere.[39] However, after the conclusion of the crisis, Cortines removed Bassols from his post by sending him safely out of the way on a mission to Europe.[40]

These vacillations revealed a lack of consensus regarding Mexico's policy over issues of the Cold War and led to the appearance of rifts within the ruling *Partido Revolucionario Institucional* (PRI). Three "presidential" factions sprang up. One rallied round ex-President Alemán and favored a policy of close cooperation with the United States; one supported ex-President Cárdenas, a determined opponent of the United States; and the third centered on the incumbent President, Ruiz Cortines, who tried to steer a middle course.[41] Mexican policy in the Cold War would henceforth depend upon the interplay of these three factions, each of which was capable of upsetting the delicately maintained internal balance essential for the working of the Mexican political system.

Uruguay's conduct during the Guatemalan crisis mirrored a political dichotomy within the National Executive Council. At the Caracas conference the Uruguayan delegation was among those who had cheered the Guatemalan foreign minister yet approved the resolution on "international communism" that Toriello had so eloquently opposed, and Dr. E. Jiménez de Aréchaga, international lawyer of world renown and head of the Uruguayan delegation, issued a curiously phrased apologia for this action by explaining that the Uruguayan delegation had contributed to its approval "without enthusiasm, without optimism, without joy, and without feeling that we were contributing to the adoption of a constructive measure."[42] Uruguay also took the unusual step of appending a statement to the final act of the Caracas conference which explained that her delegation could not have adhered to the resolution on "international communism" without also adhering to the final act, with its reiteration of the principle of non-intervention.[43] This tortuous diplomacy was the result of the need for reconciling the conflicting opinions on foreign policy held by members of the National Executive Council.[44]

In Chile, the administration of President Ibáñez, which had set out to criticize the United States and began to seek a merger of the political and economic interests of all underdeveloped countries,[45] soon began to feel frustrated "by the imperialism of the Soviet Union" and by "Marxist" agitation in the country.[46] Consequently, Chile went along with the policy of the United States throughout the Guatemalan crisis.

It is worthwhile to point out, however, that the *Partido Socialista Popular* (which excluded the Allende faction of the Socialists) left the Ibáñez government in 1953, and that the Christian Democrats (still called *falange nacional*) were critical of the government's policy in the Guatemalan crisis, though they considered it essential to back the United States once the crisis was over.[47]

Ecuador, under President Velasco Ibarra, showed some hesitation. In 1953 the president had hailed the United States as an "efficient dam against Soviet totalitarianism" and proclaimed his loyalty to "Pan-Americanism."[48] At Caracas no opposition was offered by Ecuador on the issue of "international communism," but on June 21, 1954, the foreign minister stated that he was "worried" about the Guatemalan situation,[49] and in August 1954 Velasco Ibarra, addressing Congress at Quito, decried "American intervention" in that country, emphasizing that every country has the right to have the kind of government it wants. He warned that intervention was something "contagious."[50]

The main lesson learnt by the governments of Latin America from the Guatemalan crisis was that in the face of a major international crisis they were inexperienced and without articulate policies. It had also begun to be realized that coordination of policies among at least the major Latin American powers was essential if the course of events was to be affected in any way.

NOTES

1. R. N. Adams, writing in 1960, correctly predicted that "what is happening in Guatemala may provide us with a better grasp of what is happening today in Cuba and what may happen tomorrow in the Dominican Republic or elsewhere." See his essay on "Social Change in Guatemala and U.S. Policy," at p. 231 of Adams et al., *Social Change in Latin America Today* (New York: Harper & Row, 1960).

2. For a classification of Populist parties in Latin America, see T. Di Tella, "Populism and Reform in Latin America," in C. Veliz (ed.) *Obstacles to Change in Latin America* (London, 1965), pp. 47-74.

3. See J. Slater, *The OAS and United States Foreign Policy* (Columbus: Ohio State University Press, 1967), p. 116. On the nature of the United Fruit Company, see S. May and Galo Plaza Lasso, *The United Fruit Company in Latin America* (Washington, D.C.: National Planning Association, 1958).

4. 3 H.A.R., August 1950, p. 16.
5. Ibid., p. 8.
6. Ibid., October 1950, p. 15.
7. R. M. Schneider, *Communism in Guatemala, 1944-1954* (New York: Praeger, 1959) gives the election results as follows: Arbenz, 267,000 votes; Ydígoras Fuentes, 74,000; García Granados, 29,000.
8. 4 H.A.R., March 1951, p. 10.
9. Ibid., May 1951, p. 11.
10. Ibid., p. 12.
11. 5 H.A.R., February 1952, p. 11; also Schneider, op. cit., pp. 86-87.
12. 5 H.A.R., March 1952, p. 11.
13. Ibid., December 1952, p. 10.
14. Schneider, op. cit., p. 197, expresses the view that "Arbenz favored the Communists more for their abilities and virtues than from any belief in Communism."
15. See R. N. Adams, "Social Change in Guatemala and U.S. Policy," in R. N. Adams et al., op. cit., pp. 267-270. See also Schneider, op. cit., pp. 185-217.
16. United States, Department of State, *Intervention of International Communism in Guatemala* (Washington, D.C., 1954), p. 69. See also ibid., "Expropriation of United Fruit Company Property by Government of Guatemala," 29 *Department of State Bulletin,* September 14, 1953, pp. 357-360.
17. D. M. Dozer, *Are We Good Neighbors?* (Gainesville: University of Florida Press, 1959), p. 342.
18. 7 H.A.R., February 1954, pp. 11-12.
19. On this point, see Slater, op. cit., pp. 117-121.
20. See Connell-Smith, op. cit., pp. 161-163.
21. Schneider, op. cit., pp. 309-310.
22. Slater, op. cit., p. 21.
23. J. E. S. Fawcett, "Intervention in International Law," in Academie de Droit International, 103 *Recueil des Cours,* Vol. 1 (1961), pp. 372-383.
24. 7 H.A.R., June 1954, pp. 14-15.
25. Ibid., pp. 10-11.
26. On this point, see the account rendered by J. Slater, op. cit., in footnote 32 on p. 131 of his work.
27. See Schneider, op. cit., pp. 311-316.
28. On all these points, see Fawcett, op. cit.
29. For further details, see Mecham, op. cit., p. 447; and Clissold, op. cit., pp. 229-230. Arbenz admitted later that his firm belief in the United Nations had been a mistake. See Schneider, op. cit., p. 312.
30. Pan American Union, Tenth Inter-American Conference, *Chronological Collection of Documents,* 3 vols. (Washington, D.C., 1954), Dec. 10, "United States Declaration on Solidarity for the Preservation of the Political Integrity of the American States against International Communism."
On December 3, 1953, J. M. Cabot, assistant secretary of state of the United States, gave assurances that his government adhered to a policy of non-intervention, but expressly excepted from the meaning of his remarks "international communism" which was "another matter." See 6 H.A.R., January 1954, p. 11.

31. One of the best brief accounts of this aspect of the United States policy towards the Bolivian Revolution is to be found in R. W. Patch, "Bolivia; United States Assistance in a Revolutionary Setting," in R. N. Adams, op. cit., pp. 108-176. For United States efforts to aid Bolivia, see an account of the Mann-Andrade talks in 6 H.A.R., August 1953, p. 31. In April 1956 the Bolivian ambassador in Washington conferred the National Order of the Condor of the Andes on Dr. Milton Eisenhower for his recommendations to aid Bolivia. See ibid., vol. 9, May 1956, p. 111.

Juan Lechín, prominent Bolivian labor leader, referred to the nationalization of tin as "this brilliant step in the fight against imperialism." See ibid., vol. 5, October 1952, p. 26. Victor Andrade, Bolivian ambassador in Washington, took pains to explain that this did not represent a social trend. See ibid., October 1952, pp. 26-27.

On the general problem, see further R. F. Smith, "The United States and Latin American Revolution," 4 *Journal of Inter-American Studies,* January 1962, pp. 89-104.

32. The phrase is Mecham's, in op. cit., p. 442.

33. Ibid., p. 443. Mecham adds that Panama and Uruguay tried unsuccessfully to add to the proposed resolution of Caracas a condemnation of racial discrimination, respect for human rights, and support for higher standards of living.

34. See Guatemala, Ministerio de Relaciones Exteriores, *Guatemala ante América* (Guatemala City, 1951), pp. 56-58.

35. Mecham, op. cit., p. 442.

36. *Washington Post,* April 6, 1951.

37. See Isídro Fabela, "La conferencia de Caracas y la actitud anticomunista de México," 45 *Cuadernos Americanos,* (May/June 1954), pp. 1-44. Also Luis Padilla Nervo—foreign minister of Mexico at the time—in ibid., pp. 45-56, which contains the full text of his speech.

38. 7 H.A.R., March 1954, p. 9. Bassols' views on foreign policy may be gauged from the contents of an article he wrote after the Washington conference of OAS foreign ministers in 1951. See N. Bassols, "Veinte ratones y un gato, o la conferencia de Washington," 2 *Revista guatemalteca,* July/September 1951, pp. 5-18.

39. See A. K. Smith, *Mexico and the Cuban Revolution. Foreign Policy Making in Mexico Under President López Mateos, 1958-1964* (Ithaca, N.Y.: Cornell University Press, 1970), p. 7.

40. 7 H.A.R., July 1954, pp. 7-80.

41. Ibid.

42. *New York Times,* March 16, 1954.

43. Connell-Smith, op. cit., p. 163.

44. On the freer platforms of the floor of the General Assembly of the United Nations the Uruguayan delegate expressed his dissatisfaction with the restricted facility of access which Latin American governments had to the organs of the United Nations, a complaint which, taken in the present context, provides evidence of real concern on the part of Uruguay at the turn of international events in Latin America. See 7 H.A.R., November 1954, p. 11.

45. Speech by A. Olavarría Bravo, the foreign minister, reported in *El Mercurio,* December 25, 1952.

46. 7 H.A.R., May 1954, p. 32.

47. See the speech made by Eduardo Frei, their leader, in the Senate on April 27, 1954, in E. Frei, *Pensamiento y acción* (Santiago: Pacífico, 1956), pp. 222-224; and E. Frei, *Las relaciones con Estados Unidos el caso de Guatemala* (Santiago: Pacífico, 1954), p. 7.

48. *New York Times,* August 12, 1953.

49. *Christian Science Monitor,* June 22, 1954.

50. 7 H.A.R., August 1954, p. 27.

Chapter IV

PRELUDE TO THE CUBAN REVOLUTION (1959-1960)

Once the shock of the Guatemalan affair had spent itself, the expectations of Latin American governments began to run high again. Believing that the Cold War would not settle over Latin America after all, they felt free to concentrate on economic development.

Their expectations seemed to be confirmed by the new direction the Cold War was taking. In the autumn of 1955 arms shipments from Czechoslovakia—whence similar shipments had been made to Guatemala in the spring of 1954—arrived in Egypt, upsetting the carefully devised balance of power in the Middle East and opening a new field for Cold War diplomacy in the process. A new and strategically close focus had been provided for the attention of the principals; one, it could plausibly be surmised, that would hold the attention of all involved for a long time to come. Compared with the Middle East, Latin America appeared an unprofitable field for Cold War activities.

These expectations were based on false assumptions. In spite of the Guatemalan experience, the exogenous element of Cold War crisis in the area was overrated. It is with hindsight only that the period preceding the Cuban Revolution assumes a new importance in the history of the Cold

War in Latin America, showing that a multitude of subsequent diplomatic events were largely a function of internal change that occurred between 1954 and 1959.

By 1954 the economic boom generated by the Korean War had spent itself and the Republican Administration in Washington was beginning to feel the pressures brought to bear on it by internal economic interests, to which it was specially prone, and which resulted in protectionist economic policies harmful to traditional Latin America exports to the United States.

The consequence was growing frustration in Latin America in face of the failure of the United States Administration in underwriting the stability of Latin America's economies as part and parcel of a comprehensive policy of Cold War, and a tendency to cast round for autonomous strategies of economic development.

In the political sphere, the inherent conservatism of the Eisenhower Administration made for a diplomacy of the anxious preservation of the status quo in Latin America, viewing any political innovation as potentially dangerous to the general stability of the area. This, too, was bound to produce a reaction in Latin America in the long run.

Symptomatic of these trends was the fall of Perón in Argentina in September 1955. Perón had tried to find a political stance which would enable him to reconcile change at home with a stable policy in world affairs, but in this he was unsuccessful.[1]

One of his main economic worries was to stop the dollar hemorrhage from which Argentina was suffering by developing the country's oil wells in preference to a policy of spectacular industrialization. The capital for this would normally have come from the United States, but as large sections of Argentines were resolutely opposed in principle to such a course Perón shrank from taking such a step at first, trying to maintain a nervous neutralism between the United States and the Soviet Union. His earlier refusal to be stampeded into breaking with the Soviet Union enabled him to conclude in 1952 the first major trade agreement with the Soviet Union in Latin America,[2] and later to negotiate with the Soviet government for the dispatch of oil-drilling experts, while at the same time carrying on parallel negotiations with the United States for aid in the development of Argentina's oil fields.[3] It was during this period that Leopoldo Bravo, Argentine ambassador in Moscow, was accorded the highly unusual privilege of a personal, and, as it turned out, cordial interview with Stalin in February 1953;[4] that the two governments signed a trade agreement for $150 million on August 5, 1953;[5] and that Bravo was still able to send optimistic dispatches to Buenos Aires as late as October 1953.[6]

It was because of the advent of the Eisenhower Administration that a gradual but nevertheless fundamental change came over Argentine policy. Dr. Milton Eisenhower, the President's brother, visited Buenos Aires on July 30, 1953;[7] and though the oil contracts Perón signed in the course of 1954 with the Atlas Corporation and, during the following year, with Standard Oil, foundered on the rocks of internal opposition, in September 1954 Perón was still reported as willing to go along with Washington in anti-Communist moves provided only they were "more than just passing anti-Communist resolutions."[8]

From there onwards developments were swift. In December 1954 H. F. Holland, assistant undersecretary of state of the United States in charge of Latin American affairs, conferred with Perón in Buenos Aires whilst United States financial experts were on their way there.[9] In April 1955 Perón finally made up his mind that private foreign capital was essential for the development of Argentine oil resources.[10] In July 1955 A. F. Nufer, ambassador of the United States in Buenos Aires, noted happily that private United States investments in Argentina were greater than those of any other country, adding for good measure that "the voting records of our two countries in all recent international conferences show a gratifying pattern of agreement on important issues."[11]

In the measure in which Perón's relations with the United States improved, Moscow's distrust increased, introducing an ambivalent element into Soviet-Argentine relations which reflected itself in the wavering attitude of the Argentine Communists. For a while both Vitoria Codovilla and Rodolfo Ghioldi, their two veteran leaders, advocated opposition to Perón, while Rudolfo Puiggros, another Communist leader, favored supporting him. The latter had his way at the end of 1952, but, because of the President's attitude of friendly expectancy towards the new administration in Washington, Soviet support for Perón was gradually withdrawn.

Perón's fall ushered in a period of confusion as the scope of Argentina's political life was circumscribed by the military, who were doggedly anti-Communist in outlook without insisting on a break of diplomatic relations with the Soviet Union.[12] A major clarification of the confused post-Perón imbroglio seemed to offer itself with the election of Arturo Frondizi, leader of the *Unión Cívica Radical Intransigente*,[13] as President in 1958. A lawyer by training and a veteran of Argentine politics, Frondizi was known to hold views on foreign policy and economic development which had a recognizably neutralist and Marxist flavor,[14] but the repercussions of the Cuban Revolution would show that Frondizi's policy, though reflecting some of his basic tenets, was to be less simple.

In Brazil, President Juscelino Kubitschek (1956-1961) embarked on an ambitious program of industrialization which saddled the country with the dual legacy of escalating inflation and a chronic deficit. To sustain the explosive rate of economic development of about seven percent, Kubitschek turned hopefully to the United States in an effort to persuade her to underwrite Brazil's uninterrupted progress in return for a Brazilian diplomatic commitment to the West.

Both the Brazilian Communists and the Soviet Union, who had placed high hopes in him,[15] were disappointed by the President's foreign policy and shocked by his suppression of the quasi-Communist League of National Emancipation in June 1955,[16] while Carlos Lacerda, brilliant journalist and fierce political opponent of Kubitschek, attacked Kubitschek's diplomacy in a series of critical articles in *Tribuna da Imprensa* of Rio de Janeiro in July and November 1956, written from Portugal. Greatly impressed by President Nasser's successful defiance of the Western powers over the nationalization of the Suez Canal Company, Lacerda called for the adoption of a clear "neutralist" position in foreign affairs.[17]

Attacks like these could, on their own, do little to induce the President to alter course. On the contrary, taking advantage of the hostile reception given to Vice-President R. N. Nixon during a tour of Latin America in mid-1958, Kubitschek proposed to President Eisenhower the launching of economic aid on a large scale to Latin America under the slogan "Operação Panamericana,"[18] which was presented as a device to strengthen the ability of Latin America "in the struggle for a balance of power." "Operation Pan America must be understood as a corollary of the general strategy of the West," was the way in which Kubitschek expressed this in terms of Cold War strategy; and "within the framework of Operation Pan America, the struggle becomes identified with the struggle against stagnation and underdevelopment."[19] Brazil's foreign policy was to follow in the wake of that of the United States,[20] and there was to be no resumption of diplomatic relations with the Soviet Union.[21]

The response of the United States to Kubitschek's proposals was, however, lukewarm,[22] and as a result, balance of payments difficulties continued to plague Brazil, compelling Kubitschek in increasing measure to move in directions not originally envisaged, and eventually to reexamine the basis of his entire foreign policy.

Kubitschek's difficulties presented unexpected opportunities to Soviet diplomacy. In an article in *Visión*, an all-Latin American illustrated magazine with a wide circulation published in Mexico City, which appeared at the beginning of 1956, the Soviet prime minister, N. A. Bulganin, had extended an invitation to all Latin American governments to develop their economies with the aid of the Soviet Union.[23] At first Brazil was not interested in suggestions of this kind, but prominent voices were raised in favor of a revision of Brazil's attitudes in this matter.[24] When in December 1957 Rio's Communist daily reported Khrushchev's definite interest in renewing trade relations with Brazil,[25] Oswaldo Aranha,[26] head of Brazil's delegation to the United Nations, informed France-Presse in New York that Brazil should, in his opinion, renew commercial and diplomatic relations with the Communist countries. At the end of the year José Alkmin, minister of finance and generally considered the leader of the so-called young wing of the *Partido Social Democrático* (Kubitschek's own party), concurred.[27] In January congressional deputy and business leader B. Machado Neto expressed the view that trade between Brazil and the Soviet Union was desirable, and for the first time Kubitschek felt compelled to admit that Soviet trade offers "deserve to be studied."[28]

Brazil's developing dispute with the International Monetary Fund, which happened to coincide with fresh commercial offers on the part of the Soviet government,[29] made matters worse for the government. On the one hand, it was confronted with a rigid IMF insistence on balancing its budget before being allowed to make further drawings (and to the development-minded Kubitschek this was anathema); but on the other hand, the Soviet Union was doing its utmost to assure Brazil of its commercial goodwill.[30]

Gradually the administration began to yield. At the inter-American conference in Washington in November 1958, called to discuss Operation Panamerica, Brazil's chief delegates announced that Brazil would henceforth look for trade openings in both the Soviet bloc and Communist China.[31]

The IMF was now beginning to be regarded as an obstacle to Brazil's economic progress, and conformity with its wishes the symbol of Brazilian subservience to foreign capital. Roberto Campos, advocate of internal adjustments to meet the objections of the IMF—though not as fast as the latter would have wished—became a target of attacks.[32] In June 1959 Kubitschek instructed his representatives at the IMF in Washington to break off negotiations with the Fund, and in August 1959 Roberto

Campos was shifted from his post,[33] though he continued to act as adviser to the government. On August 4, 1959, H. Láfer was appointed foreign minister in place of Negrão da Lima.[34]

In retrospect, it is difficult to avoid the impression that in breaking with the IMF Kubitschek had crossed a Rubicon. For although the change produced no immediate dramatic results, it can now be seen to have set Brazil on a new course in her foreign policy. A note of bitterness crept into presidential announcements. The blame for Brazil's economic failings were placed at the door of international finance, as Kubitschek complained.[35] On July 27, 1959, the president announced angrily that "Brazil has come of age. We are no longer poor relations forced to stay in the kitchen," and that the country could manage without aid.[36]

It was after the break with the IMF that signs appeared attesting to Kubitschek's serious desire to balance his hitherto one-sided economic attachment to the United States by a rapprochement with the Soviet Union.[37] In spite of a warning by United States Ambassador John Cabot Moors in October 1959 that the adoption of a new Brazilian attitude towards the Soviet Union in political and economic matters could be achieved only at the cost of endangering Brazil's security, as well as that of the United States,[38] Kubitschek sent a seven-man trade mission to Moscow, where, on December 9, 1959, a document was signed to regulate Soviet-Brazilian trade, a document which also envisaged vaguely but significantly "the possibility of refining in Brazilian plants the import of Soviet crude oil."[39] In December 1959 President Eisenhower, worried about the break between Brazil and the IMF, requested Kubitschek to repair his relations with that financial organization. Kubitschek would not agree, but W. Moreira Sales, Brazil's ambassador in Washington, was approached by representatives of the IMF, which subsequently modified its former stiff attitude towards Brazil.[40]

In April 1960 a Soviet commercial mission arrived in Brazil,[41] and during 1960 also Brazil signed new trade agreements with Poland and Czechoslovakia and expanded trade relations with East Germany.[42]

Kubitschek's term was drawing to a close and he was anxious to show some results. In July 1960 he addressed another unavailing letter, couched in desperate language, to President Eisenhower,[43] and in his New Year broadcast which ushered in the year 1961, Kubitschek complained bitterly about the world's international financial institutions, referring to their philosophy as "an outmoded orthodoxy" and to their policies as an "archaic conservatism."[44] Sorrowfully he had to admit that "in spite of

strenuous efforts" made by Brazil, the great powers of the West continued
to attribute secondary importance to the problems of Latin America.

At the end of Kubitschek's term of office—when the shadows of the
Cuban Revolution were beginning to be cast over Latin America—Brazil
was in a receptive mood for proposals for an alternative foreign policy.[45]
The gradual change of Kubitschek's foreign policy was not due to the
worsening economic situation only, for opposition to his foreign policy
had also begun to develop in the highly sensitive field of strategic raw
materials.[46] The first nuclear agreement with the United States was
concluded in 1940, and was followed by the so-called Second Atomic
Agreement signed in February 1952. On March 15 of the same year, Brazil
signed a Military Assistance Agreement with the United States containing a
special clause concerned with the furnishing of equipment, services, and
particularly basic and strategically important materials for the purpose of
common defense.[47]

These agreements contained conditions considered harmful to the
national interest by the general staff of the Brazilian armed forces, as they
affected research in this field and its application to industrial ends.[48]
When on November 16, 1955, the provisional government of Nereu Ramos
signed the Fourth Atomic Agreement with the United States lively opposition developed,[49] and in February 1956 the newly installed President
Kubitschek was compelled to appoint a Parliamentary Commission of
Enquiry into all aspects of these agreements liable to be considered
prejudicial to the interests of Brazil. In May 1956 Prof. J. da Costa
Ribeiro, chairman of the Brazilian Atomic Energy Commission, urged
closer cooperation with the United States in this sphere,[50] but during the
same month Gen. A. Teixeira dos Santos, chief-of-staff of the armed forces,
opposed any easy accommodation of the United States.[51] In June 1956
Congressional Deputy Renato Archer displayed documents "proving
United States interference in Brazil,"[52] and claiming the existence of a
secret clause binding Brazil to supply the United States unconditionally.[53]
In July 1956 Kubitschek was compelled to abrogate the one-year-old
agreement on the export of fissionable material to the United States,[54]
and on August 30, 1956, the Brazilian government approved new guidelines for a National Policy of Nuclear Energy which restricted the scope of
future agreements of this kind concluded with foreign powers.[55]

The crisis in Brazil's foreign policy may also be illustrated by the
government's difficulties in persuading Congress and the National Security
Council to consent to an agreement with the United States involving the

lease of the island of Fernando de Noronha to sixty radar technicians from the United States for the purpose of tracking missiles. Negotiations had been proceeding in secret for a year before news of it reached the public late in 1956. In December of that year the foreign ministry published details of the projected agreement, stressing Brazil's obligations under the treaties of 1947 and 1952.[56] It was only because of the great influence exerted by the president personally in the Brazilian Congress; by his assurance that the station would be operated jointly;[57] and by Washington's announcement on January 8, 1957, that it was making available in three annual instalments $117 million of the $138 million resulting from the sale to Brazil of surplus agricultural products[58] that opposition to the scheme eventually crumbled.[59] It is significant, however, that the process of reassuring the public in this matter was not achieved until after the revolt had taken place within the president's own party, the Social Democrats, and was quelled only with some difficulty by the efforts of Adm. E. do Amaral Peixoto, party leader and son-in-law of the late President Vargas.[60] The National Security Council was not won over by Kubitschek until January 21, 1957.[61]

Mexico, too, began to concentrate more than ever on the task of economic development.[62] After her experience in the Guatemalan crisis a degree of revulsion was felt for the OAS and a preference for the United Nations.[63] Thus, in 1956 J. Castañeda, a prominent Mexican statesman-writer, counselled Mexican disengagement from the Rio Treaty,[64] and in March 1958 Luis Quintanilla, Mexico's ambassador to the OAS, expressed himself opposed to the idea of Latin American disarmament on the grounds that this would leave the defense of the Western Hemisphere at the mercy of the United States.[65] The only remaining Mexican statesman with a liking for multilateral diplomacy was Padilla Nervo.[66] How careful Mexico had become not to be involved in the Cold War was shown in July 1956 when there were fears that by participating in the projected meeting of the presidents of the Western Hemisphere in Panama, she might be confronted with a demand to sign some anti-Soviet statement. The final declaration of that meeting was therefore modified to meet these Mexican wishes.[67]

A new era in Mexico's foreign relations began in 1958 with the election to the presidency of A. López Mateos, who described the political stance of his administration as "on the extreme Left within the Constitution." He was determined to reactivate Mexico's foreign policy. If, however, the new president was expecting a smooth passage for his plans, he was to be disappointed. Mexico's difficulties in foreign policy were to mount during his period of office, as a result of the Cuban Revolution, and face him with an unexpectedly close involvement in the Cold War.

Owing to its internal cleavages, the Chilean Left was unable to affect the course of the country's foreign policy during the Guatemalan crisis; but two years later, in 1956, it produced an impressive rally by uniting the various Socialist splinter groups in a new and vigorous Socialist Party of Chile,[68] and this success was followed by the formation of the *Frente de Acción Popular* (FRAP), a regalvanized and far more left-wing form of the defunct *frente popular,* in which the Socialists and Communists would be able to call the tune. But whilst the Communists slavishly followed every minute turn in Soviet foreign policy, the Socialists were attracted by the diplomacy of Perón and, after 1955, of Tito.

As the general election approached in 1958, and as left-wing optimism soared,[69] visions of a radical bloc of left-of-center governments in South America provided further cause for optimism: with Salvador Allende Heading a FRAP government in Chile, Arturo Frondizi directing a radical administration in Argentina, Paz Estenssoro in control in Bolivia, and a friendly *colorado*-dominated coalition holding sway in Uruguay, reactionary Paraguay would find herself encircled, and Brazil would be isolated. There would be a widespread upsurge of left-wing sentiment everywhere in Latin America from which unity—which Perón had unsuccessfully sought to obtain by economic means—would spring from political action. Expectations such as these received further incentives from the successful revolt against Pérez Jiménez in Venezuela in January 1958.

Impressed by the unexpected revival of the Left, President Ibáñez began to revise his tactics as the presidential elections of 1958 were approaching. A new receptiveness was shown to the Communists and trade was sought with the Soviet bloc, and on March 20, 1958, it was announced that Chile had agreed to sell to the Soviet Union 10,500 tons of copper wire of a nonstrategic type.[70]

The great hopes entertained by the Chilean Left were not fulfilled. Allende, leader of FRAP, lost the elections by an extremely narrow margin;[71] and the *colorados* of Uruguay suffered electoral defeat in 1958. The good showing of the Chilean Left at the polls was nonetheless not to be without lasting effects on the subsequent foreign policy, as Jorge Alessandri, the new president, had to tread warily abroad for fear of inviting serious difficulties at home.

In the years before the Cuban Revolution, Uruguay continued to be beset by difficulties inherent in her economy and constitution. Unusually dependent on foreign markets for her staple exports and finding the United States market restricted, Uruguay was forced to seek new markets in Eastern Europe.[72] Consequently, during the season 1957-1958 the Soviet Union, which had not bought any wool from Uruguay between 1956 and 1957, became the leading buyer of raw wool,[73] and a further boost to the diversification of her foreign markets was given by the victory of the *blanco* party at the polls in November 1958 when Benito Nardone, known to favor trade with all countries irrespective of ideological considerations, emerged as the most important personality in the Uruguayan government.[74]

Diplomatic relations with the Soviet Union could hardly be left unaffected by these developments, and—after an interruption of eight years— were reestablished in September 1955.[75] A setback in Soviet-Uruguayan relations was suffered as a result of a revulsion of feeling aroused by the events in Hungary in 1956, which prompted F. Gamarra, the foreign minister, to instruct the Uruguayan delegation at the United Nations to oppose the claims of the Kadar regime.[76] It is, however, significant of the confused attitudes in the Cold War that it should have been Sen. Eduardo Haedo, a Herrerista, who insisted that Britain and France were equally culpable in respect of their seizure of Port Said.[77]

It may readily be seen that in embarking on a period of intensive economic development, Latin America was experiencing a crisis of change of major psychological and political proportions, leading on to an epoch of upheaval bound to cause complications with the United States, whose policy it was to preserve the political status quo as far as possible. The Cuban Revolution acted as a powerful catalyst in this process.

NOTES

1. See A. P. Whitaker, *Argentine Upheaval* (London: Atlantic Press, 1955).
2. Clissold, op. cit., pp. 180-181, for details.
3. *Neue Zürcher Zeitung*, January 24, 1954.
4. See "Stalin's Interview with Argentina's Ambassador," 9 *The World Today*, March 1953, pp. 97-99.
5. Clissold, op. cit., pp. 180-182.
6. 6 H.A.R., October 1953, p. 37.
7. H. L. Matthews, veteran correspondent, quoted Vice-President A. Tesaire of Argentina as saying it had been this visit which turned the tide in the diplomatic

relations between Argentina and the United States. See *New York Times*, August 13, 1953. However, it is worth noting that in 1954 the Soviet Union was for the first time among Argentina's leading buyers, and in December of that year became Argentina's fourth-best customer. See *Neue Zürcher Zeitung*, August 8, 1954; and *New York Times*, December 19, 1954.

8. *New York Herald Tribune*, September 19, 1954.

9. *New York Times*, December 7, 1954.

10. Ibid., April 3, 1955.

11. 8 H.A.R., July 1955,.p. 333.

12. See B. Lieuwen, *Generals versus Presidents* (London, 1965).

13. The Radical Party had split in 1957 into the *Unión Cívica Radical del Pueblo* under Ricardo Balbín, and the *Unión Cívica Radical Intransigente* under Arturo Frondizi.

14. See Frondizi's *Petróleo y Política* (Buenos Aires: Transición, 1954).

15. *Izvestia* of October 4, 1955, had described his election as a victory of democratic and progressive forces.

16. 9 H.A.R., July 1956, p. 310.

17. In November Lacerda referred to the State Department of the United States as the tool of United States trusts, advocate of "phoney" non-intervention, cowardly betrayer of democratic forces, guilty of incompetence and superficiality in Latin America. See ibid., November 1956, p. 551.

18. See "Proposal 'Operation Panamerica' put forward by the Government of Brazil, August 9, 1958," in Royal Institute of International Affairs, *Documents on International Affairs 1958* (London, 1962), pp. 428-429. See also J. Kubitschek, *Mensagem ao Congresso Nacional* (Rio de Janeiro: Congresso Nacional, 1959), p. 45.

19. Ibid., p. 430. In a note of August 9, 1958, addressed to all Latin American missions accredited to his government, Kubitschek maintained that "Operação Panamericana" was meant "to place Latin America . . . in a condition to take part more effectively in the defense of the continent." See J. Kubitschek, *A Marcha do Amanhecer* (São Paulo, 1962), p. 176.

20. However, R. Rubottom, emissary of the United States, tried hard to introduce an element of anti-Communist ideology in his talks with Kubitschek. Interview with ex-President Kubitschek kindly granted in Rio de Janeiro on April 24, 1971.

21. 11 H.A.R., April 1958, p. 229.

22. See Connell-Smith, op. cit., p. 271. Dulles, the Secretary of State of the United States, who visited Brazil in July 1958, and who on that occasion declared himself opposed to a loan to *Petrobrás*, the state-owned and -operated oil concern, could not be persuaded by Kubitschek to agree to a meeting of American presidents to consider the plan. See 11 H.A.R., August 1958, p. 464. Even a telegram sent by the Brazilian chief executive to President Eisenhower urging Latin American participation at a summit meeting was to no avail. See ibid., July 1958, p. 402.

23. For the general background to the offer, see the present writer's "Soviet Aid to Underdeveloped Countries," 11 *Year Book of World Affairs* (London: London Institute of World Affairs, 1957), pp. 184-205. At the Moscow Economic Conference of 1952, Soviet representatives had offered the unofficial Brazilian delegation a million tons of badly needed wheat in return for traditional Brazilian exports. See 5 H.A.R., April 1952, p. 48.

24. *New York Herald Tribune,* October 8, 1956. As Kubitschek was to remark later, Soviet aid "puts the West in a position of competition of the country to be aided, provided the countries of the Soviet bloc act as buyers of primary products for which there are insufficient markets." See J. Kubitschek, *A Marcha do Amanhecer* (São Paulo, 1962), p. 179.

25. *Imprensa Popular,* December 3, 1957.

26. See O. Aranha, "Relações Diplomáticas com a União Soviética," 1 *Revista Brasileira de Política Internacional* (1958), pp. 20-26.

27. 10 H.A.R., December 1957, p. 690.

28. Ibid., January 1958, pp. 50 and 52 respectively.

29. Ibid., October 1958, p. 581.

30. The International Monetary Fund wanted the rate of inflation in Brazil reduced to 6 percent; Kubitschek, on the other hand, regarded a rate of 20 percent as reasonable in the conditions ruling in Brazil at the time. Statement made by ex-President Kubitschek in a personal interview kindly granted on April 21, 1971.

31. *New York Times,* November 26 and 27, 1958.

32. In early 1959 the Brazilian Communist Party had launched an attack on Campos as a stooge of Wall Street. See Skidmore, op. cit., p. 384.

33. Ibid., p. 181. See also C. de Paiva Leite, "Brazilian Development: One Problem and Two Banks," 14 *Inter-American Economic Affairs* (1960), pp. 3-24; and E. Chaves Neto, "O Presidente Kubitschek e o Fondo Monetário Internacional," 5 *Revista Brasiliense,* July/August 1959, pp. 1-8.

34. See Ministerio das Relações Exteriores, *Gestão do Ministro Láfer na pasta das Relações Exteriores. De 4 de agosto de 1959 a 31 de janeiro de 1961* (Rio de Janeiro, 1961).

35. "We have not yet obtained from the international financial authorities the cooperation which we might expect, given our importance in the contemporary world, and which would have greatly facilitated the internal task of monetary stabilization as well as contributing to an acceleration of our own development." See *Mensagem ao Congresso Nacional* (Rio de Janeiro, 1960), p. 76.

36. 12 H.A.R., July 1959, p. 406.

37. Castilho Cabral, author of *Tempos de Jânio e outros tempos* (Rio de Janeiro, 1962), informed Quadros in a letter dated August 19, 1959, that he had learned that Horacio Láfer, Brazil's foreign minister, had advised Secretary of State Christian Herter of the United States during the Santiago conference of hemisphere foreign ministers of Brazil's intention to resume diplomatic relations with the Soviet Union. See ibid., p. 274.

38. 12 H.A.R., October 1959, p. 575.

39. *Resenha do Govêrno do Presidente Kubitschek* (1956-1961), Vol. V: Year 1960, Part I (1962). For the text of the Soviet-Brazilian agreement, see 30 *Vneshnaya Torgovlya,* July 1960; and Royal Institute of International Affairs, *Documents on International Affairs 1959* (1963), pp. 403-406.

40. Statement made by ex-President Kubitschek in a personal interview kindly granted in Rio de Janeiro on April 21, 1971.

41. *Resenha do Govêrno do Presidente Kubitschek* (1956-1961), Vol. V: Year 1960, Part I (1962), pp. 245-247. See also S. F. Chenchikovsky, "Torgovye otnosheniya mezhdu SSSR i Braziliei uspeshno razvivayutsa" ("Trade Relations between

the USSR and Brazil develop successfully"), 30 *Vneshnaya Torgovlya*, July 1960), pp. 14-15. A note on the Chenchikovsky mission may also be found in 3 *Revista Brasileira de Política Internacional*, September 1960, pp. 174-175; and O. Onody, "Relações Comerciais do Brasil com o blóco soviético," ibid., pp. 38-72.
Already on December 17, 1958, the Brazilian Foreign Ministry had confirmed that negotiations towards the establishment of trade relations with the Soviet Union were in progress and that the subject had been topical for a year. See *O Estado de S. Paulo*, December 19, 1958.

42. United States, Department of State, *Communist Economic Policy in the Less Developed Areas* (Washington, D.C., 1960), pp. 35-37.

43. In this letter he wrote *inter alia:* "This is not an appeal for generosity, but to reason ... a necessity to battle in the only efficient way against the Cold War which creeps into our continent and is about to engulf it." And again, "Reasons of a purely strategic order are not always good reasons, and many times calculations based on them have to be revised, and tactical criteria modified." *Resenha*, op. cit. above in note 5, pp. 214-216.

44. J. Kubitschek, *Discursos preferidos no quinto ano de mandato presidencial, 1960* (Rio de Janeiro, 1961), p. 476.

45. Hélio Jaguaribe, a leading Brazilian writer and industrialist, produced an important book in Rio de Janeiro in 1958 entitled *O nacionalismo na atualidade brasileira* in which he demanded "a position of greater autonomy with regard to the United States and the great European Powers, inclining, at the same time, toward a neutralist line in regard to the United States-Soviet conflict," (p. 187).

46. For details, see General A. de Souza, Jr., *O Brasil e a Terceira Guerra Mundial* (Rio de Janeiro: Biblioteca do Exercito, 1959), pp. 287-301; and J. Neves da Fontoura, *Depoimentos de um ex-Ministro* (Rio de Janeiro: Simoes, 1957), on the position under the Vargas Administration in 1951. Da Fontoura expressly denies that there was any pressure on the part of the United States on Vargas to provide a monopoly of strategic materials in Brazil to them as an alternative to the dispatch of Brazilian troops to Korea.

47. Because of technical obsolescence, a new Third Atomic Agreement had to be signed on August 20, 1954. This was supplemented by these conventions on August 3, 1955: the Cooperation for the Civil Use of Atomic Energy; the Joint Program of Cooperation for the Civil Use of Atomic Energy; and the Joint Program of Cooperation for the Prospecting of Uranium Resources in Brazil. See United States, "Atomic Energy," Agreement of August 3, 1955, 6 *Treaties and Other International Agreements* (1955), Part 2, pp. 2583-2594.

48. De Souza, op. cit., pp. 290-291. In a personal interview held in Rio de Janeiro on April 17, 1971, ex-President Kubitschek confirmed that there was considerable opposition on the part of the military and of Congress.

49. See R. Sanders, "The Bogey of Yanqui Atomic Imperialism," 13 *Inter-American Economic Affairs* (1959), pp. 43-46.

50. 9 H.A.R., June 1956, pp. 262-263.

51. Ibid.

52. Ibid., p. 361. For a comprehensive exposition of the nationalist view, see O. Guilherme, *O Brasil e a Era Atómica* (Rio de Janeiro, 1957).

53. R. Sanders, op. cit., p. 42.

54. R. Sanders, ibid., p. 45.

55. The full text of this document is to be found in de Souza, op. cit., pp. 292-295.

56. 9 H.A.R., December 1956, pp. 605-606.

The Ministry of Foreign Affairs sought to link the agreement between Brazil and the United States over Fernando de Noronha with both the Rio Treaty of 1947 and the Mutual Assistance Agreement of 1952. See *Relatório do Ministério das Relações Exteriores* (1957), pp. 38-40.

57. *New York Times,* January 22, 1957.

58. 10 H.A.R., January 1957, p. 42.

59. In an interview kindly granted to the writer on April 17, 1971, ex-President Kubitschek explained that Brazilian officers had been eager on that occasion to be informed of the technical secrets involved, only to be reassured by President Eisenhower that only very few officers in the United States forces knew them. Kubitschek favored the scheme on purely utilitarian grounds. Brazil was not in a position to shoulder the financial burden of such a scheme.

60. *New York Times,* January 22, 1957. An opinion sample taken from Brazilian legislators in 1961 showed that 45 percent were against, and only 26 percent in favor of the establishment of a long-range missile base in Brazil. See L. A. Free, *Some International Implications of the Political Psychology of Brazilians* (Princeton, N.J.: Institute for International Social Science, 1961).

61. 10 H.A.R., January 1957, p. 42. For the text of the five-year agreement, see United States, Part I, "Defense: Establishment of Guided Missile Station on Island of Fernando de Noronha," January 21, 1957, 8 *United States Treaties and other International Agreements* (1957), pp. 87-90.

62. Between 1955 and 1958 heavy direct investment of foreign capital in Mexico reached $100 million per year. See R. Vernon, *The Dilemma of Mexico's Development* (Cambridge, Mass.: Harvard University Press, 1963).

63. See Olga Pellicer de Brody, "México en la OEA," 6 *Foro Internacional,* October/December 1965, January/March 1966, pp. 288-302, at pp. 288-291.

64. J. Castañeda, *México y el orden internacional* (Mexico City, 1956), p. 45.

65. 11 H.A.R., March 1958, p. 141.

66. Pellicer de Brody, op. cit., p. 299.

67. 9 H.A.R., July 1956, p. 326.

68. See E. Halperin, *Nationalism and Communism in Chile* (Cambridge, Mass.: MIT Press, 1965); especially ch. 4, pp. 121-135.

69. See C. Véliz, "A Latin American Union?" *New Statesman and Nation* (London) July 19, 1958.

FRAP was committed in the field of foreign policy on four points, as follows: (a) renunciation of the Military Assistance Agreement with the United States; (b) renunciation of all inter-American commitments, especially those within the OAS; (c) opposition to the establishment of foreign military bases on Chilean territory; and (d) the development of a policy which would unite and tie Chile and Latin America to the bloc of Afro-Asian countries, with the object of developing a common strategy to help dependent countries. See FRAP, *Un camino nuevo para Chile: el programa del gobierno popular* (Santiago, 1958), pp. 16-17.

70. 11 H.A.R., March 1958, p. 159.

71. The figures were as follows: Alessandri, 386,192 votes; Allende, 354,300

votes; Frei, 254,323 votes; Bossay, 189,182 votes; Zamorano, 41,224 votes. Figures from *The Times,* September 5, 1958.

72. 8 H.A.R., January 1955, p. 140.

73. 11 H.A.R., August 1958, p. 461. For the relevant documents regarding economic agreements with the Soviet Union, see Consejo Nacional de Gobierno, *Mensaje del Poder Ejecutivo a la Asamblea General al inaugurarse el 3 er periodo de la XXXVII Legislatura* (1957), pp. II/113-123.

74. 11 H.A.R., November 1958, p. 631. In 1958 also Uruguay's foreign minister, C. Secca Ellauri, criticized Pan-Americanism as "suffering from lack of content." See E. Yrrazaval Concha, *América Latina en la guerra fría* (Santiago: Nascimiento, 1959), p. 184.

75. H.A.R., September 1955, p. 435.

76. 9 H.A.R., December 1956, p. 603. The Uruguayan Institute of Public Opinion found at that time that only 6 percent of those interviewed thought that the Soviet Union was not a genuine danger to the non-Soviet world. See M. Alisky, *Uruguay. A Contemporary Survey* (New York: Praeger, 1969), p. 155.

77. 9 H.A.R., November 1956, p. 549.

Chapter V

THE CUBAN REVOLUTION (1959-1960)

The Cuban Revolution, like the Guatemalan one, was endogenous in character and autonomous in its subsequent development.[1] There is little empirical evidence of any hard and fast views on foreign policy held among Castro's July 26 movement in the mountains, and any account of the development of Castroite conceptions of foreign policy has, in the main, to rely on a psychological explanation. Two main groups of revolutionaries may be distinguished from this angle: the *serranos,* operating in the mountainside: and the *llaneros,* operating in the plain (including the cities).[2] Because of the harshness of the conditions under which they had to labor, the former acquired a radical political outlook, while the llaneros retained a sense of political moderation.

The serranos contained a relatively moderate element within their ranks, as witness the subsequent records of men like Felipe Pazos, who was to be for a short time Castro's president of the Bank of Cuba; Raúl Chibás, leader of the *ortódoxos,* to whom Castro himself used to belong; and the two partisan commanders Manolo Ray and Huber Matos. All of these were to desert Castro eventually. As personalities they were easily overshadowed by the two charismatic radicals, Ernesto Guevara and Raúl

Castro (Fidel Castro's brother). Guevara regarded the revolution as all-continental in character from the start, and not confined to Cuba.[3] Castro himself was undecided but showed a temperamental tendency to side with the radicals.

The crucial factor in the ultimate triumph of the radical serranos was their acute sense of power, expressing itself in their great concern with military and economic considerations. Guevara's economic conception of the revolution was rooted in the belief in the need for the development of the Cuban economy through extensive diversification of both industry and agriculture.[4] This implied (a) a system of central planning at home; and (b) the coordination of Cuba's foreign trade with that of other centrally planned economies, necessitating the close association of the Cuban economy with the economies of Eastern Europe, and the replacing of the unreliable United States market for Cuba's sugar by that of the Soviet Union, which—correctly, as it turned out—was considered to be stable.

The Communists had no hand in the formation of this policy. Carlos Rafael Rodríguez, leading member of the *Partido Socialista Popular* (PSP), was so much in the dark that he feared a Puerto Rican type of industrialization dependent on the United States, and he reacted to Castro's rejection of this with much relief.[5] Blas Roca, leader of the PSP, suggested tentatively that the Soviet Union might take Cuba's sugar surplus, citing the example of Egyptian cotton by way of illustration.[6] Those who emphasized the need to retain military power in the hands of the serranos, above all Raúl Castro, favored the preservation and strengthening of the rebel army, their living symbol of power and political preponderance.

The role of the PSP was never decisive.[7] In aligning Cuba diplomatically with the Soviet Union it acted as a catalyst, not as a motor, and it joined the serranos too late to color their basic convictions substantially. However, the Communists did prove to be a subsidiary force of alertness and resource, two qualities which they applied in exercising judicious pressure on the revolutionary government and on the Soviet Union.

Two distinct but mutually exclusive Cuban Communist conceptions of policy emerged. One was associated with Aníbal Escalante, long time influential editor of *Hoy*, the Communist daily; and the other one with Blas Roca, secretary-general of the Party. According to Aníbal Escalante, the foremost tactical need of the Communists was to detach and eventually annex the radical element in the serrano group to the PSP, much in the same way as had been done in China by Mao Tse-tung vis-á-vis the left wing of the Kuomintang.[8] Blas Roca, on the other hand, proved to be the pure pragmatist, unimpressed by the glitter of historical parallels and able to pick out the unique features of the Cuban Revolution. Though keeping his options open for a long time, his own thesis was developed at a surprisingly early stage. In essence this was much closer to that of the radical serranos than to that of his fellow Communists.[9] In particular, Blas Roca was able to recognize the crucial role of the rebel army; the importance of preserving the legality of the PSP; and the incipient tendencies in Cuba's foreign policy to veer away from the United States and towards the Soviet Union, as exemplified in what he called the end of "Plattism" and "geographical fatalism."[10]

The first revolutionary government in Havana was based on a united front of anti-Batista revolutionaries and found political expression in a left-of-center stance both at home and abroad. Roberto Agramonte, *llanero* and *auténtico,* was the first foreign minister. Castro pronounced the official revolutionary ideology to be "humanism," which he defined as "government by the people, without dictatorship and without oligarchy; liberty with bread and without terror."[11]

Though the foreign policy pursued by the revolutionary government accorded with these principles, there were early signs in the Revolution of a Cold War situation in the making. On January 9, 1959, Guevara remarked that the Communists had earned the right to be a party.[12] More significantly, on January 13, 1959, Castro was reported as saying that the Platt Amendment—by which Cuba had bound itself in 1901 to consult the United States before taking any major decision in the field of foreign policy—was finished,[13] adding that Cuba would adopt an equidistance between the United States and the Soviet Union. The following day, he announced that if United States marines invaded Cuba, 200,000 *gringos* would die.[14] On April 1, 1959, he gave warning that Cuba would not be another Guatemala.[15]

The radical tendency in Cuban foreign policy was first made the subject of public debate during the visit to Havana of José Figueres, former president of Costa Rica, in March 1959. Figueres had long been an advocate of a left-of-center solution for Latin America's ills, implying friendly but not uncritical cooperation with the United States in foreign affairs.[16] He now advised Castro to be anti-Communist at home and abroad on the ground that the United States would not tolerate anything else.[17] Castro, who spoke after Figueres at the same mass rally of workers, merely reaffirmed his own neutrality in the Cold War.[18]

Though Castro's reaction was nonchalant at first, there was an immediate reaction from the Communists, as well as certain indignation outside Communist ranks.[19] It may have been in response to those ractions that Castro, on March 22, 1959, expressly repudiated Figueres' suggestion of a pro-United States foreign policy based on geographical and economic realism. He also took the opportunity of declaring Cuba's neutrality "in the event of a world war" and accused the United States of being Cuba's real enemy.[20]

Cuba's foreign policy nevertheless proceeded placidly for the time being, conforming for all intents and purposes to the canons of *figuerismo*. Thus, during a visit to Venezuela, Castro told Congress in Caracas that he was in favor of the formation of a "democratic bloc" within the OAS.[21] An alignment between Cuba and Venezuela seemed not only natural, but the continuation of existing Caribbean traditions of diplomacy.

In January 1959 Castro announced that the basic pattern of the Cuban struggle was suitable for application against Somoza in Nicaragua, adding that Latin America as a whole would require similar revolutions.[22] However, Castro stressed his adherence to the principle of non-intervention— which had never in practice been observed by any *figueristas* in the Caribbean area—and made a distinction between revolutionary struggle (with its concomitant, the spirit of solidarity), and diplomatic correctness. Thus, in mid-February he was reported as opposed to a diplomatic rupture with Trujillo on grounds of the ineffectiveness of such a move. Assistance to revolutionaries in the Dominican Republic was, however, a different matter, and a revolutionary government in that country would be immediately recognized by Cuba.[23] Further evidence of his figuerista leanings in foreign policy was supplied when Castro attended the inter-American economic conference in Buenos Aires where he asked for economic aid from the United States for Latin America to the extent of $30 billion over ten years, a figure which in retrospect must be regarded as realistic.[24]

During his visit to Washington in April 1959, Castro reiterated his concept of equidistance between the United States and the Soviet Union; refused to commit himself on the question of taking sides in a hypothetical war between the United States and the Soviet Union;[25] reaffirmed the Rio Treaty; and avowed that in the context of the global Cold War his heart was "with the West."[26]

These ambiguities were not to last much longer, and soon those of his followers in the llanero camp most committed to figuerismo would be eliminated. Prominent among these were President M. Urrutia and R. Agramonte, the foreign minister.[27] At the beginning of March Urrutia caused a stir by a speech delivered on the occasion of the presentation of the credentials of the new ambassador of the United States, Philip Bonsal, in which he called specifically for a rapprochement with the United States. The Communists immediately launched an attack, accusing Urrutia of trading a pro-United States and anti-Soviet foreign policy in exchange for United States condemnation of the institution of dictatorship in Latin America generally.[28] On June 12, 1959, Agramonte resigned along with four other ministers and was replaced as foreign minister by Raúl Roa,[29] a populist llanero, who ushered in a radical, as distinct from a moderate, form of figuerismo in foreign policy. On July 18, 1959, Agramonte's resignation was followed by that of Urrutia,[30] and Osvaldo Dorticós assumed the office of president.

Both the presidency and the foreign ministry were now safely in the hands of reliable, radical llaneros and the revolution was rapidly acquiring radical overtones at home and abroad. Agrarian reform involving a certain amount of expropriation of foreign property was carried out, and Roa was able to reject a protest from the United States regarding the manner in which land reform was being executed.[31] On June 26, 1959, notwithstanding earlier pronouncements on principle to the contrary, Castro broke off diplomatic relations with Trujillo.[32]

So far Cuba's radicalism had shown itself in relation to the "oligarchies" of Latin America only. There was as yet nothing to indicate a desire to intervene in the Cold War. Roa was still using clearly recognizable figuerista imagery in describing Cuban foreign policy to the Fifth Meeting of OAS Foreign Ministers held at Santiago, Chile, in August 1959, where he described the position of his government as of "neither the third, nor the fourth, nor the fifth position";[33] or when he informed the General Assembly of the United Nations in September 1959 that Cuba's revolution was "an autonomous one . . . not red, but olive green."[34]

There is little doubt that in September 1959 a new phase started in the evolution of diplomatic conceptions in the Cuban leadership,[35] a development which would lead to a progressive worsening of relations with the United States, closer relations with the Soviet Union, and—as a logical sequel—to a steadily increasing involvement in the Cold War. But whether diplomatic tensions with the United States were the cause or the effect of changing political conceptions in the Cuban leadership is not by any means clear as yet.

Castro's gradual conversion to doctrinaire anti-imperialism, as distinct from mere anti-Plattism—which was regarded only as a corrective, though a long overdue one—appears to have resulted from his growing conviction that the United States was obstructing the course of revolutionary developments in Cuba. The two key figures among the radical serranos, E. Guevara and Raúl Castro, took possession of the levers of power and began to give Cuban foreign policy a new shape. In June 1959 President Nasser of Egypt had invited Castro to visit Cairo.[36] Guevara went in his place, combining the visit with a three-month tour of Europe, Africa, and Asia. On June 30, 1959, it was reported from Cairo that Guevara had met Soviet representatives and subsequently stated that trade relations with the Soviet Union might provide a basis for the eventual resumption of diplomatic relations between Havana and Moscow. It was as a result of Guevara's soundings at Cairo that a trade agreement was concluded by R. Botí, the Cuban minister of economy, during the International Sugar Conference then in session in London.[37] Large-scale imports of Cuban sugar into the Soviet Union were nothing new, however. During the Batista régime, Cuba ranked third in hemispheric imports from the Soviet Union and fourth in exports to the Soviet Union[38] after 1955, and, as yet, the Soviet-Cuban deal does not seem to have caused undue alarm in Washington, where a quota of 3,110,655 tons was assigned to Cuba for 1960 out of a total of 9,400,000 tons.[39]

The idea of barter agreements with socialist countries was first suggested by Guevara on his return home,[40] and it was precisely at this juncture that Castro announced his new economic policy of ambitious industrialization, based on the principle of priority of industry over agriculture,[41] which would suggest a causal connection between these two events. Guevara himself was placed in charge of the National Bank, with full powers to carry out the new economic policy. On October 16, 1959, the old Ministry of Defense was abolished and Raúl Castro appointed minister of the Revolutionary Armed Forces, with full control over the police.

From late November 1959 onwards it became increasingly evident that Cuba's foreign policy was being activated in two directions: (a) the old policy of neutralism acquired a new, active and radical edge, greatly reinforcing a tendency which had been apparent since the advent of Roa at the foreign ministry;[43] and (b) relations with the Soviet Union were being actively fostered on the Cuban side. The first tendency showed itself in the attempt to organize a conference of underdeveloped countries in Havana, whilst the second manifested itself in negotiations for a high-level Soviet person to visit Cuba.

In December 1959 President O. Dorticós announced that Raúl Roa would visit the Mediterranean region in order to canvas support for the idea of a conference. Roa's visit was a disappointment, as only Yugoslavia and Egypt showed any interest.[44] Equally disappointing was the response from Latin America: Argentina, Brazil, Chile, and Uruguay declined the invitation on the pragmatic grounds that they would be attending the inter-American conference at Quito (which was never held) where the identical subject would be discussed.[45] Only Panama accepted without reservations.[46] Roa was compelled to cancel the conference in August 1960.

Thus rebuffed, Cuba was rapidly drifting into isolation, and on January 20, 1960, Castro admitted in a telecast that Cuba had become "a solitary nation."[47] Relations with the United States were now more important and critical than ever before. On January 26, 1960, President Eisenhower expressed the hope that Cuba would not fall victim to Soviet intrigues.[48] At this point Castro appears to have been wavering, or so it appeared to Argentina's ambassador, J. A. Amoedo, on January 27, 1960, as to whether to accept an offer from Washington.[49] In any event, a non-committal reply was delivered by Dorticós. Amoedo asserts, however, that this was not the end of the matter, and that his own attempts at mediation continued to show promise "until the arrival of Mikoyan."[50]

At the end of November 1959 at the latest, Cuba was anxious to establish closer relations with the Soviet Union, and at the beginning of November 1959 hints were dropped that the visit to Mexico by Mikoyan, Soviet Deputy Prime Minister, might present a suitable opportunity for making direct contact, if only on a preliminary basis, with the Soviet Union.[51] Cuba's secret moves in this direction must have been successful, for Mikoyan arrived in Havana on February 4, 1960.

On the following day Eisenhower set forth several points which he thought would "furnish reasonable bases of a workable and satisfactory relationship" between Cuba and the United States. He maintained that the United States adhered strictly to a policy of non-intervention in the domestic affairs of other countries; reiterated that his government had consistently endeavored to prevent illegal acts in territory under its jurisdiction directed against other governments; and viewed with increasing concern the tendency of spokesmen of the Cuban government to create the illusion of aggressive acts and conspiratorial activities aimed at the Cuban government and attributed to United States officials and agents.[52]

Mikoyan stayed until February 13, 1960, ostensibly to open a Soviet exhibition in Havana. On that day he signed a trade agreement with Cuba committing the Soviet Union to buy 425,000 tons of sugar in 1960 and a million tons per year during the subsequent four years. The agreement also provided for a Soviet credit of $100 million.[53] On May 7, 1960, the two countries exchanged ambassadors.[54]

The radical serranos, who ultimately emerged victorious, were men given to action, and not—like the llanero Communists—to endless theorizing. Political extroverts par excellence, it is unlikely that they ever had a clear vision of the diplomatic future of Cuba. Javier Pazos maintains that until the middle of 1960 Fidel Castro considered himself as a Nasser-like leader of a neutralist movement in Latin America, who thought that the United States would ultimately come to terms with him.[55] What probably weighed heavily with the radical serranos was the problem of the supply of arms. The United States had been reluctant to supply these to the revolution, and the only substantial source during 1959 had been Belgium. That the serranos, for years dependent on their personal weapons for their physical survival, should have developed an instinct for seeking effective armament need not cause any surprise. Nor, in the circumstances, could it be thought unnatural that among the first governmental acts performed by Castro should have been the closing of the United States military mission in Havana. In June 1959, long before relations between Cuba and the United States had shown any signs of serious deterioration, Castro considered the purchase of $9 million worth of arms from the United States. It was the United States which refused to supply them, compelling Castro eventually to turn to the Soviet Union for an alternative source.[56] In October 1959 the Cuban government was further alarmed on learning that the United States was trying to prevent the sale of British jet planes to Cuba on the ground that this might aggravate tensions in the Caribbean.[57]

A month later, on November 13, 1959, the Cuban government's note *In Defense of National Sovereignty* contained an ominous passage making reference to the government's intention to obtain weapons "from whoever may be willing to supply them" because of orders blocked by the United States. It was estimated that Cuban expenditure on arms during 1959 amounted to $120 million, leaving a mere $67 million in reserves.[58] In February 1960 President Eisenhower placed an embarge on shipments to Cuba of arms, munitions of war, and other articles "intended to be or being exported from the United States, together with the means used or intended to be used in effectuating the illegal transportation."[59] At the same time Cuba competed with Chile for the vacancy of a non-permanent seat on the Security Council,[60] thus delivering an indirect challenge to the principle of solidarity of the Latin American states under the terms of the so-called gentlemen's agreement of 1946.

Further fuel seems to have been added to the flames of indignation of the Cuban leadership when the French vessel *La Coubre,* carrying a cargo of Belgian arms, exploded in Havana harbor on March 4, 1960. It was this event that probably provoked Castro, who suspected sabotage, into denouncing the Rio Treaty on the following day, March 5, 1960; though it may also have been a reaction to President Eisenhower's statements about Cuba in Rio in February, when he said "We would consider it intervention in the internal affairs of an American State if any power, whether by invasion, coercion or subversion, succeeded in denying freedom of choice to the people of any of our sister republics."[61] Castro justified the action by maintaining that the United States was making attempts to "incite the Latin American countries against us with this Pact of Rio de Janeiro, by which we do not feel bound because the Revolution never signed it."[62] On March 17, 1960, the CIA was promptly authorized by the United States government to equip a force of Cuban exiles with a view to invade Cuba, although no particular urgency appears to have been attached to the project.[63]

On June 9, 1960, Raúl Roa, Cuba's foreign minister, was still able to proclaim with some pride that "we shall not have to choose between the East and the West";[64] but during the last week of that month Raúl Castro, minister of the Revolutionary Armed Forces, visited Czechoslovakia,[65] and on July 8, 1960, finally, Fidel Castro was able to announce the imminent arrival of arms, without specifying the source of the supply. It is, however, known from a statement made later by Guevara, that the first consignment of arms for Cuba from Eastern Europe originated in Czechoslovakia.[66] It is at this stage that the Soviet Union first became involved in Cuba's dispute with the United States, and that a Cold War dimension was added to this dispute. On January 6, 1961, diplomatic relations between the two countries were finally broken off.[67]

But economic factors were also involved from the start. The stake of United States business in the Cuban economy was enormous. On a per capita basis, the book value of United States enterprises in Cuba was over three times the value for the rest of Latin America as a whole.[68] More than $1 billion was invested in public utilities, sugar mills, cane and tobacco plantations, ranches, commercial establishments, and industries. The United States was the traditional supplier of between 70 and 80 percent of Cuba's imports and had taken 60-70 percent of Cuba's exports.[69] In April 1960 the Cuban government agreed to pay the United Fruit Company $6,118,407 over twenty years in bonds at 4½ percent. The company valued its property in Cuba at approximately $32 million.[70] This set in motion attempts in the United States Congress to reduce the Cuban sugar quota by way of retaliation. On April 19, 1960, Soviet oil began to arrive in Cuba,[71] but the United States oil refining companies, which monopolized this activity in Cuba, refused to refine that oil. According to one source, a high-level person travelled to Moscow after that to assure a regular flow of refined Soviet oil to Cuba, enabling Castro to expropriate the United States oil companies on June 29, 1960.[72] On July 6, 1960, Eisenhower reduced the Cuban sugar quota by 700,000 tons, and again the Soviet Union stepped into the breach by offering to take the differential amount.[73] Both Soviet moves had been shrewd ones, showing up United States diplomacy as crude, impetuous, and fumbling. The United States secretary of state, Christian Herter, persisted in this course, pleading before the House Committee on Agriculture for the approval of the amendment of the Sugar Act,[74] and on July 16, 1960, the United States protested against the Cuban law of nationalization as "discriminatory, arbitrary and confiscatory."

Cuba now charged the United States with economic aggression before the Security Council,[75] but the charge was rebutted by the United States representative, Henry Cabot Lodge.[76] The Security Council decided to adjourn, and neither the Soviet Union nor Poland opposed the move.

Having obtained Soviet assurances regarding the purchase of Cuban sugar and continued deliveries of Soviet refined oil, the Cuban government was encouraged to look forward to a direct Soviet commitment regarding its territorial integrity and political sovereignty. What had given them more ground than anything else for optimism was the spontaneous statement by Khrushchev on July 9, 1960, which implied Soviet willingness to use missiles in order to defend Cuba.[77] And although Khrushchev subsequently modified his statement in the sense that it was "really symbolic,"[78] the psychological impetus which the statement had imparted to Cuban diplomacy could hardly be overestimated.

Now that Cuba was armed, the last encumbering vestiges of figuerismo could be discarded, and the Revolution spring into diplomatic action at the San José meeting of foreign ministers in August 1960, where the diplomatic entente with Venezuela, now considered embarrassing, was jettisoned. At the same time Castro solemnly and categorically denounced the Military Assistance Agreement which Batista had concluded with the United States in 1952. After September 1960, Cuba's foreign policy moved rapidly into line with that of the Soviet Union, and between September 1960 and January 1961 an impressive number of fundamental steps was taken by Cuba to ensure the finality of the new course. In the economic field, another tour of Eastern Europe and China by Guevara ensured closer coordination with the Socialist countries,[79] and Cuba left the International Monetary Fund and the World Bank. On the political level, a joint Cuban-Chinese communiqué proclaimed complete agreement on "the current international situation"; [80] on December 11, 1960, Guevara was able to express his wholehearted support for the Moscow Declaration of 81 Communist parties of December 6, 1960; and on December 19, 1960, Cuba and the Soviet Union issued a joint communiqué expressing solidarity with the Socialist camp.[81] At home, the merger between the 26th July Movement and PSP was agreed in principle.

Cuba's own autonomously evolved policy towards the underdeveloped countries was similarly adjusted to conform with that of the Soviet Union. Before the annual General Assembly of the United Nations met, Roa announced Cuba's support of the Algerian revolution and her approval of the admission of Communist China into the United Nations.[82] During the session, Castro denounced the United Nations action in the Congo; came out in favor of the reform of the Security Council and the Economic and Social Council of the United Nations;[83] and called for a nuclear-free zone in Africa:[84] All demands in strict accord with Soviet initiatives. Whilst in New York he also cultivated neutralist statesmen like Nasser, Nehru, Tito, and Nkrumah.[85]

Within less than four months Cuba had completed her alignment with the Soviet Union, broken with the United States, and turned herself into a determined partisan in the Cold War. It may have been a coincidence that this was done while there was a change of administration in Washington where John Kennedy, the new president, inherited from the outgoing Eisenhower Administration a critical situation on its doorstep which showed every sign of rapid deterioration.

The Cuban Revolution: Latin America's Response

Provided only the character of the Cuban Revolution would conform to the model of moderate social reconstruction, there was little or no reason to suppose that the advent of Dr. Castro to power in Havana should arouse undue fears among the Latin American countries whose class structures had undergone some degree of modification. It was only in the Central American-Caribbean region,[86] in the Andean region, and in Paraguay, where social structures were still of the traditional kind, that the revolution was regarded with a cold indifference not unmixed with some apprehension. When Dr. Castro's policies turned from reforming pragmatism to revolutionary socialism, even the relatively reformed countries of Latin America began to be gripped with the fear of serious social repercussions. It is, however, doubtful whether the strength of these apprehensions would have sufficed to spark off crises without the element of Cold War to give the former a sharp edge.

To the governments of Latin America, the diplomatic issue was posed in the form of a dilemma. Were they to allow the United States to assume the mantle of protector of the Western Hemisphere against the Soviet Union and its de facto ally Cuba, and risk direct or indirect intervention by the United States in their internal affairs? Conversely, were they to regard the Soviet Union as a suitable counterweight to the excessive influence of the United States?

Latin America's answer to these questions varied roughly according to the social ethos and diplomatic traditions prevailing in the country concerned. The immediate reactions of the governments to the emergence of revolutionary Cuba were in accord with their social perception of the new régime there. Fears of political and even military intervention ran highest in Guatemala and the Dominican Republic. Colombia, Venezuela, and Costa Rica, not, at first, without considerable sympathies for the Cuban Revolution, were to modify their attitudes considerably in due course.

The countries whose societies had experienced a fair measure of modernization—Mexico, Bolivia, Uruguay, Chile, Argentina, and Brazil—tended to feel protective about the new Cuba and adopted a neutral stance. This group received the somewhat erratic support of Ecuador, not by any means a country with a reformed social structure. Implicit in the diplomatic attitudes of these governments was the belief that, left to its own devices, the Cuban Revolution would readily settle down to a quiet coexistence with the rest of the Americas.

The Fifth Meeting of Consultation at Santiago (August 12-18, 1959)

The restless Caribbean, now further disturbed by the advent of a revolutionary government in Havana, provided sufficient cause for diplomatic worry to call for a meeting of consultation of foreign ministers of the OAS. At Santiago[87] the representatives of what were later to be the two chief antagonists of the Cold War in the Western Hemisphere were still speaking essentially the same political language. Thus, Raúl Roa, Cuban foreign minister, was able to condemn roundly "an interpretation of non-intervention which shielded dictatorships from international action to safeguard human rights"[88] and to attack hostile wireless transmissions from the Dominican Republic as an act of true intervention;[89] while the representative of the United States—ironically, in the light of later developments—came out strongly in favor "of the principle of non-intervention and against attempts to overthrow governments by force in the hope of establishing democracy."[90] Equal scepticism regarding the prospect of collective intervention was expressed on that occasion by other Latin American statesmen also.[91]

But tensions between Cuba and the United States increased steadily, and on July 9, 1960, Khrushchev hinted at the possibility of Soviet missiles going into action in defense of Cuba. This caused alarm in the Americas and a conference of OAS ministers was convened at San José in August 1960 to review the new situation. The conference consisted of two meetings, the sixth and seventh, held consecutively to discuss the situation in the Dominican Republic and Cuba respectively.

The Sixth Meeting of Consultation at San José (August 16-21, 1960)

At San José the United States was determined to keep the Soviet Union out of the Western Hemisphere by isolating Cuba, a potential Soviet ally.

On June 6, 1960, the Inter-American Peace Committee had published a report which contained an "uncompromising indictment of the Trujillo régime."[92] Instinctively the Cuban government attacked the substance of the report, fearing it might provide a precedent for subsequent action against the revolutionary government in Havana,[93] but by so doing found itself in the company of the Trujillo government, not an enviable position. But it was not only the Cuban government which had begun to shift its ground.

On June 24, 1960, Venezuela brought charges of aggression against the government of the Dominican Republic which formed the substance of discussion at the sixth meeting.[94] The majority of delegates now requested the imposition of sanctions against the Dominican Republic under the terms of the Rio Treaty. But though, if proved true, the actions of the latter constituted a flagrant violation of the principle of non-intervention, the United States chose to reverse its previous attitudes on this issue by shifting the emphasis from the principle of non-intervention to that of democracy. What was demanded now was the holding of duly supervised elections in the Dominican Republic, rather than any action capable of bringing down the Trujillo régime and thus facilitating the advent of a pro-Castro government in the Dominican Republic. A proposal in this direction by the United States encountered strong opposition from Mexico and others[95] and had to be abandoned, as both Trujillo and Castro were now attacking the United States, and "on occasion the former hinted at accommodation with the Soviet Union."[96]

Thus, within the space of a year both Cuba and the United States had neatly reversed their tactical positions for reasons connected not with the subject matter at hand, but because of considerations of Cold War.

The Seventh Meeting of Consultation at San José (August 22-29, 1960)

If the sixth meeting had its portents of crisis, the seventh—which immediately followed the sixth at San José—saw the reincarnation of the ghost of "international Communism" of the Caracas conference of 1954, with Christian Herter, secretary of state of the United States, trying to establish the thesis that "the installation of a Communist régime in any American Republic would automatically involve the loss of a country's independence."[97]

Turbay Ayala, Colombia's foreign minister, followed suit by stressing the ideological rather than the strategic aspect of the issue, insisting that the point under discussion was not the conflict between Cuba and the United States—in which case there would be much reason for popular support of the Cuban revolutionaries—but the conflict between the Soviet Union and the United States, between "democracy" and "Communism"; in such a basic struggle no American state had the right to remain neutral.[98]

Raúl Roa, Cuba's foreign minister, expressed Cuba's willingness to settle her differences with the United States bilaterally. Already on July 18, 1960, Cuba had gone to the Security Council of the United Nations complaining that: "the drastic reduction of the sugar quota (of the United States) constitutes an international crime of economic aggression."[99] In doing so, and bypassing the OAS in the process, the Cuban revolutionary government served notice that, where the United States was concerned, it did not consider the OAS a suitable place for obtaining a fair hearing.

The attempt of the United States to get Cuba condemned through the indirect device of "international Communism" met considerable opposition, causing keen embarrassment for at least two delegations, whose foreign ministers preferred to resign rather than append their signatures to the Declaration of San José[100] because, though Cuba was not mentioned by name, they considered it as being directed against the Cuban revolutionary government. The Peruvian foreign minister, Raul Porras Barrenechea, offered his resignation to President Prado, and J. B. de Lavalle, Peru's ambassador to the OAS, had to sign the document.[101] Similarly, Ignacio Luis Arcaya, Venezuela's foreign minister, refused to sign the final act of the seventh meeting. He was recalled and resigned subsequently. M. Falcón-Briceño, ambassador in Washington at the time, was appointed to sign.[102] The period of tacit cooperation between Cuba and Venezuela against the Trujillo régime was at an end, and soon the two would have daggers drawn, the bitterest opponents in the Cold War in Latin America.

While most Caribbean and Central American governments, with the exception of Cuba and Haiti, stressed the internal dangers of Communism, H. Láfer, Brazil's foreign minister, neatly traced a direct causal relationship between underdevelopment and the advent of Communism,[103] while Argentina's foreign minister, D. Taboada, insisted that Latin America's underdevelopment "facilitates in increasing measure the intervention of Communism in many of our countries."[104] Turbay Ayala, Colombia's foreign minister, who was extremely careful not to cast any approbrium on the internal character of the Cuban Revolution, put all the blame on the sinister designs of Soviet diplomacy, to the extent of excusing Cuba of any diplomatic responsibility.[105] He was fascinated by the fear of the unity of the hemisphere being undermined and replaced "by an alliance of underdeveloped countries of all geographical latitudes . . . which could give the relations between peoples the dimension of the class struggle."[106]

Of the remainder, Cuba refused steadfastly to repudiate the friendship of the Soviet Union and China, in spite of having been expressly asked to do so by Argentina and Ecuador,[107] and immediately after the meeting threw down the gauntlet by proclaiming the challenging Declaration of Havana.[108]

Until the San José conference, Cuba and Venezuela seemed natural allies. Their internal and external developments showed marked parallels until divergences were appearing in 1960 serious enough to lead first to a break in relations and ultimately to bitter hostility.

The key figure in Venezuela was Rómulo Betancourt, whose freely elected government rested on a coalition between his own party, *Acción Democrática*,[109] and the Christian Democratic *Comité Organizador por elecciónes independientes* (COPEI); and while the former was the majority party, it lacked an absolute majority in Congress, necessitating the formation of a broad coalition which included the *Unión Republicana Democrática*, a centralist party which, in matters of foreign policy, was to diverge from AD and COPEI. AD's marked sense of ideology and geopolitical self-consciousness is well demonstrated in its first policy pronouncement after the fall of Pérez Jiménez in 1958, as follows: "*Acción Democrática* considers that Venezuela, and Latin America in general, has an economic and geopolitical community of interest with the country of greatest power in the hemisphere: the United States ... because if we deny that Venezuela can be a satellite of the United States, we equally reject the idea that a Venezuelan political party could become an ideological satellite of the Soviet Union and that it could function as a chessboard pawn in the international strategy of the so-called Eastern bloc."[110]

Relations with the Soviet Union subsequently suffered on both political and economic grounds. As early as December 1958 Betancourt announced that a decision on the resumption of diplomatic relations with the Soviet Union would be reached by a "cold factual and objective analysis," [111] but though in July 1959 a congressional committee recommended this step, as well as the recognition of Communist China, Rafael Caldera, leader of COPEI, vetoed this.[112] In May 1960 an indirect contact with the Soviet Union was made at long last, but the deterioration of Venezuela's relations with Cuba prevented a follow-up.

One of the principal oil exporting countries in the world, Venezuela became enmeshed in the Cold War in the economic as well as the political field, since—as a traditional supplier of crude oil to Cuba—she was directly affected by the oil-refining crisis developing between Cuba and the United States in 1959. Still ostensibly neutral in that dispute, Venezuela retaliated quietly by switching her purchases of sugar from Cuba to Brazil.[113] But in the early 1960s the Soviet Union became a major exporter of oil to Western Europe, arousing the Venezuelan government's fears that these sales, made on favorable terms, might undermine the position of Venezuelan oil in those markets.[114] In June 1960, finally, the Venezuelan minister of mines and coal, J. P. Pérez Alfonso, announced that his country would stay neutral in relation to Cuba's decision to refine crude oil from the Soviet Union, and that it would be Venezuela's policy not to extend her participation in oil operations beyond her own frontiers.[115] In July 1960 relations with Cuba had deteriorated to a point at which Venezuela saw herself compelled to send an official protest to Havana. The occasion was a statement by Guevara that the Venezuelan president was a "prisoner of an allegedly democratic régime controlled by lackeys of Pérez Jiménez" which "long since should have used firing squads to eliminate its enemies."[116] This was strong language by any standards, and Venezuelan moderate opinion was antagonized by it, especially as just before Guevara's outburst the Chamber of Deputies in Caracas had agreed to a motion giving support to the Castro régime by reaffirming its right to determine its own destiny.[117] It was in such a psychological climate that things came to a head between the two countries, as well as within the government coalition, as a result of developments at the OAS conference at San José in August 1960. Represented by J. L. Arcaya, her foreign minister—a member of URD—Venezuela pursued a robust neutralist line during the seventh meeting. Maintaining firmly that within the conception outlined by him there was room for the establishment of relations with all countries of the world, including the Socialist countries, Arcaya refused to sign the Declaration of San José.

His action made it impossible for the government to defer an outright diplomatic choice between the United States and Cuba. Opposition to Betancourt had been mounting on the Left, and a new, pronouncedly Castroite party—ultimately to take the name of *Movimiento de la Izquierda Revolucionaria*—had broken away from AD. Jóvito Villalba, leader of URD, denounced the San José declaration in indignant terms also, thus endangering the continuation of the coalition.

In those circumstances, Betancourt could either endorse Arcaya's pro-Cuban line and risk estrangement with the United States and its supporters in the OAS for the sake of retaining the increasingly problematic diplomatic friendship of Cuba; or, sensing a brewing conflict between itself and Cuba, throw in its lot with the United States and the majority members of the OAS and risk the fierce hostility of the Castro régime.

At first Betancourt tried to dissuade Arcaya from persisting in the course of action he had elected to take at San José, but having failed to do so, he recalled Arcaya and replaced him as Venezuela's official delegate to the San José conference with M. Falcón Briceño, Venezuelan ambassador to the United States, leaving no doubt whatever as to where Venezuela stood. Betancourt even went to the length of requesting the conference to strike off Arcaya's remarks from the official record.[118] In order not to take matters to extremes and to avoid a final breach with Cuba, the three coalition parties agreed to issue a statement in support of the Cuban Revolution, while at the same time impartially condemning both pro-Castro and anti-Castro groups active in Venezuela.[119] A month later Arcaya resigned, but was again backed by the URD. But this could not be the end of the matter, for the Cold War was casting an ever-lengthening shadow over Venezuela and, both within the government and the country, was leading to a state of ominous polarization between Left and Right. On November 18, 1960, the internal rift was complete when the URD retired from the ruling coalition.[120]

Betancourt may have calculated that, since a choice had to be made, it was better to sacrifice Cuba for the sake of United States support over the Trujillo issue and to secure United States backing in any future difficulties with Cuba. He may also have felt confident to handle any opposition at home emanating from the URD or from Castroite elements. Subsequent events would show that, acting from his own premises, the risks he took abroad were justified, but that he gravely underestimated the costs incurred at home in terms of political unrest and years of armed insurrection. In the end, however, his régime survived a period of severe trials at home and abroad, and—first of all Venezuelan presidents—he and his successors were able to complete their full legal term in office.

The Mexican delegation found itself in a quandary at the seventh meeting which is reflected in the reservation made to the final act in the sense that the condemnation of extra-hemispheric intervention in America was in no way to be construed as a threat against Cuba.[121] Mexico was unwilling to introduce ideological restrictions in inter-American diplomacy, and M. Tello, the foreign minister, averred that it was the aim of his government "to make Cuba feel that her destiny is in America."[122]

A high degree of sensitivity as regards the principle of non-intervention was also to be found in the case of Bolivia, where—as in Mexico—it was historically rooted. This emerged in E. Arze Quiroga's address, which showed surprisingly little concern with Khrushchev's "rocket" threat and contained a high degree of identification with the Cuban Revolution.[123]

Argentina reacted to the issues raised at the seventh meeting with some nervousness. That the Frondizi administration was worried about the way in which the Cuban Revolution was developing was evident. On July 13, 1960, already the foreign ministry in Buenos Aires had sent a cable to the

Argentine ambassador in Havana instructing him to implore the Cuban government not to approve of "manifestations that signify meddling of extra-hemispheric Powers in American affairs" and "to express its disapproval of any statement which may be construed as interference by an extra-continental Power in American hemisphere affairs."[124]

Argentine diplomacy was thrown off its stride by a serious defect in communications. On August 22, 1960, the Argentine delegation at the San José conference presented a project envisaging the convocation of a special conference within ninety days for the purpose of preparing a treaty on (a) the rights and obligations of states taking part in the struggle against Communism; and (b) the most suitable method and institutional form of the struggle.

But it was one thing to be anti-Communist and suspicious of the Cuban government's foreign policies, but quite another to approve the issue of blank cheques for indiscriminate anti-Communist action within the inter-American system. The foreign minister's cable containing the report of the project elicited an immediate rebuke from the president, who claimed that newspaper reports were the first he had seen of it and asked Dr. Taboada to stick to agreed instructions in future. Taboada replied that his action had been in accord with instructions received.

It is not necessary to impute bad faith to either of these men. On the contrary, their misunderstanding highlights the uncertain reactions of some Latin American governments when faced with Cold War crisis in which the entire region was now gripped.

NOTES

1. Some of the technical preparations for Dr. Castro's campaign against the Batista régime were made in the United States and Mexico—though without the connivance of their governments—but this fact can hardly detract from the general thesis presented here.

2. See an article in *Revolución,* July 31, 1963, under the title "Frank País fue el jefe en el llano."

3. Suárez, op. cit., p. 40 et seq. It was significant that on February 16, 1959, the day Fidel Castro was appointed prime minister, *Revolución,* principal organ of the serranos now in office, carried an editorial announcing boldly that "The revolution will be the permanent revolution which the theorists have been clamoring for." See ibid., pp. 45-46.

4. J. O'Connor, "On Cuban Political Economy," 79 *Political Science Quarterly,* June 1954, pp. 233-247, felt that economic considerations predetermined the subsequent character of the revolution.

5. *Hoy,* March 8, 1959.

6. Ibid., April 2, 1959.

7. On the relationship between Castroites, Communists, and the Soviet government, see E. Gonzalez, "Castro's Revolution, Cuban Communist Appeal, and the Soviet Response," 21 *World Politics,* October 1968, pp. 39-68. H. Thomas, *Cuba* (New York: Harper & Row, 1971), p. 923, claims that some younger Communists in 1957 had become impatient with the party's non-violent approach towards the Batista régime.

8. *Hoy,* January 28, 1959. Castro may have held this against him subsequently, though what was to happen in actual fact was the reverse: the radical element of the serranos annexed the Communists, though the latter were able to supply a coherent political philosophy. The radical serranos, moreover, never let go of their overall control.

9. H. Thomas, op. cit., develops the reverse thesis, attributing this role to Carlos Rafael Rodríguez, while picturing Blas Roca as a typical *apparatchik.* In my opinion it was Blas Roca who initiated policies of his own, while Rodríguez merely waited for clues from Moscow.

10. See *Hoy,* January 11, 1959.

11. Speaking in New York on April 24, 1959. See *New York Times,* April 25, 1959.

12. United States Senate, *Events in United States-Cuban Relations* (Washington, D.C., 1963), p. 3.

13. *Revolución,* January 14, 1959. The Platt Amendment was abolished by President F. D. Roosevelt in 1934.

14. See Manuela Samidei, *Les Etats-Unis et la Révolution Cubaine* (Paris, 1968), p. 50.

15. *Revolución,* April 2, 1959.

16. At the time of the Guatemalan crisis, for instance, Figueres had counselled moderation in the matter of reform for fear of provoking the United States. Semidei, op. cit., p. 51. It was notable that the Costa Rican government under President Figueres had adopted much gentler methods in dealing with the United Fruit Company than the Arbenz Administration in Guatemala. See 6 H.A.R., December 1953, pp. 14-15.

17. *New York Times,* March 23, 1959. See also J. Figueres, "No se puede escupir a una política exterior," 4 *Revista de ciencias políticas y sociales,* July/ September 1958, pp. 461-470.

18. H.A.R., as in note 5.

19. *Hoy,* March 11, 1959.

20. *New York Times,* March 23, 1959.

21. 12 H.A.R., January 1959, p. 26.

22. *Revolución,* January 23, 1959.

23. *Revolución,* February 20, 1959.

24. *New York Times,* May 3, 1959.

25. *New York Times,* April 18, 1959.

26. 12 H.A.R., April 1959, p. 205.

27. In July 1957 Agramonte, an ortódoxo, had written to the editors of the *Hispanic American Report* attacking Batista and pledging his support of Castro.

28. *Hoy*, March 3, 1959.

29. It is interesting to recall that Roa had signed a letter of protest against the Soviet invasion of Hungary in 1956. See *New York Times,* November 27, 1956.

30. On July 13, 1959, Urrutia had attacked the Communists in a television interview. For the former president's version of events, see M. Urrutia, *Fidel Castro & Co., Inc.* (New York: Praeger, 1964), especially pp. 49-53.

31. The Cuban government could have claimed with justification that it was acting lawfully on the basis of the Constitution of 1940, Art. 90 of which expressly laid down that "The law shall restrictively limit acquisition and possession of land by foreign persons and companies, and shall adapt measures tending to return the land to Cuban ownership."

32. Suárez, op. cit., p. 68.

33. OAS, Pan American Union. *Quinta Reunión de Consulta de Ministros de Relaciones Exteriores. 12-18 de agosto de 1959* (Washington, D.C., 1961), p. 109.

34. *New York Times,* September 25, 1959. Castro had used the same language on May 21, 1959. See T. Draper, *Castro's Revolution. Myths and Realities* (London: Thames & Hudson, 1962), p. 83.

35. To underline Cuba's neutrality in the Cold War, the Cuban delegation at the United Nations abstained on the vote over the admission of Communist delegates to the seat reserved for China. See E. B. Glick, "Cuba and the 15th United Nations General Assembly. A Case Study in Regional Disassociation," 6 *Journal of Inter-American Studies,* April 1964, pp. 235-248.

36. 12 H.A.R., June 1959, pp. 321-322.

37. In June the United States had rejected a request from Castro for an increase in the Cuban sugar quota. See Semidei, op. cit., p. 59.

38. See R. L. Allen, *Soviet Influence in Latin America. The Role of Economic Relations* (Washington: Public Affairs Press, 1959), p. 9. During the war Cuba had supplied some rum, sugar, and tobacco to the Soviet Union. In 1946 the Soviets exported small quantities of books, musical instruments, and liquor to Cuba. By 1948 there was hardly any trade at all. See Cuba, Dirección General Estadística, *Comercio Exterior 1948* (Havana, 1950), p. 31. It was reported that Soviet purchases of Cuban sugar in 1955 exceeded 500,000 tons. See *New York Journal of Commerce,* May 10, 1955.

39. 12 H.A.R., December 1959, p. 665.

40. *Revolución,* September 15, 1959.

41. Fidel Castro, *Informe Económico sobre Cuba* (Havana, 1959), pp. 39-40.

42. Goldenberg, op. cit., pp. 188-189; Draper, op. cit., pp. 65-66.

43. On his return from his three-month trip, Guevara had praised Egypt and Yugoslavia, the two most radical neutralist states. See 12 H.A.R., September 1959, p. 488.

44. 13 H.A.R., January 1960, p. 26; and *Revolución,* January 20, 1960.

45. 13 H.A.R., January 1960, p. 26.

46. Ibid., April 1960, p. 241.

47. *New York Times,* January 22, 1960.

48. Ibid., January 27, 1960.

49. J. A. Amoedo, "Negotiating with Fidel Castro," *New Leader* (New York), April 27, 1964.

50. Ibid.

51. *Revolución,* November 3, 1959, as cited in Suárez, op. cit., p. 81.

52. United States Department of State, *Foreign Policy Briefs,* February 5, 1960.

53. Suárez, op. cit., p. 84.

54. *Pravda,* February 22, 1960.

55. J. Pazos, "Cuba—Was a Deal Possible in 1959?" 148 *New Republic,* January 12, 1963, pp. 10-11. H. Thomas, op. cit., would go no further than stating that Pazos, Boti, and Fidel Castro had discussed the conditions for Cuba's neutrality in the abstract only (p. 1205).

56. Suárez, op. cit., pp. 71-72.

57. *New York Times,* October 17, 1959. Britain actually gave in to the United States on that point. On the question of the supply of arms from Britain to Cuba, see Royal Institute of International Affairs, *Documents on International Affairs 1959* (London, 1963), pp. 389-391.

58. *El Excelsior* (Mexico City), March 5, 1960.

59. United States Executive Order No. 10863 of February 18, 1960, as printed in 44 *Department of State Bulletin,* March 1960, at p. 362.

60. 13 H.A.R., February 1960, p. 99.

61. Ibid., March 1960, p. 175.

62. *New York Times,* March 6, 1960.

63. Suárez, op. cit., p. 88.

64. See *El Sol,* an Uruguayan Socialist paper of Montevideo, June 10, 1960.

65. Suárez, op. cit., p. 93.

66. United States Congress (Senate), *Events in United States-Cuban Relations, a Chronology 1957-1963* (Washington, D.C., 1963), p. 18.

67. 13 H.A.R., June 1960, p. iv. On the inevitability of the escalation of both perceptions and expectations on both sides, see M. Zeitlin and R. Scheer, *Cuba: Tragedy in Our Hemisphere* (New York: Grove, 1964). There is some evidence to support the view that the White House took a hard line from the start, whereas the State Department tried to be conciliatory. See D. D. Eisenhower, *Waging Peace. The White House Years,* Vol. 2 (New York: Doubleday, 1965). R. N. Nixon, *Six Crises* (New York: Doubleday, 1962), claims to have recommended the creation of a Cuban exiles legion as early as April 1959. His account imputes a waiting intention even to Edgar Hoover, head of the FBI, and to A. Gardner and E. F. Smith, two former ambassadors to Cuba (pp. 351-352). For the El Salvador conference of twelve United States ambassadors to the Caribbean region, see *Hoy,* April 14, 1959. See also J. Hickey, "The Role of Congress in the Cuban Disaster," 14 *Inter-American Economic Affairs* (1961), pp. 67-89.

68. L. L. Johnson, "United States Business Interests in Cuba and the Rise of Castro," 17 *World Politics* (1965), pp. 440-459.

69. D. Horowitz, *The Free World Colossus* (New York: Hill & Wang, 1965), p. 201, supplies the following information regarding United States interests in Cuba before 1960: 80 percent of utilities; 90 percent of cattle ranches; 100 percent of oil refining; 50 percent of public railways; 40 percent of the sugar industry; and 25 percent of all bank deposits.

70. *New York Times,* April 6, 1960.

71. Suárez, op. cit., p. 92.

72. Ibid., p. 93. In ordering the United States oil companies to refine Soviet crude oil, Castro was able to rely on the Mineral Fuel Law of 1938, which allowed the compulsion of foreign-owned oil refining companies to deal with Cuban crude oil.

73. Suárez, op. cit., p. 93. On December 16, 1960, Eisenhower fixed the Cuban sugar quota at zero for the first quarter of 1961.

74. 43 *Department of State Bulletin,* July 11, 1960, pp. 58-59.

75. "Economic aggression contrary to the basic terms of the relevant international treaties and agreements and to the fundamental principles of the United Nations." Roa's letter to the president of the Security Council, July 11, 1960, UN Doc. S/4378. Art. 15 of the Charter of the OAS lists "coercive measures of an economic or political character" as illegal.

For Roa's accusations before the Security Council, see United Nations Security Council, O.R., 874th meeting, July 18, 1960, pp. 1-27.

76. United Nations Security Council, O.R., 875th meeting, July 18, 1960, p. 761.

77. Clissold, op. cit., pp. 256-257.

78. 13 H.A.R., October 1960, p. 694.

79. 13 H.A.R., October 1960, p. 695, suspected that Guevara had tried to persuade the Soviet Union to turn over its sugar fields to other crops and take Cuban sugar instead. The same publication reported Guevara in November 1960, p. 789, as negotiating an interest-free loan of $60 million and the exchange of one million tons of sugar for rice and other commodities in Peking. Finally, in December, 1960, H.A.R., p. 876, reported the signing of an agreement between Guevara and Mikoyan which formalized a series of previous agreements. See also "Cuba's Economic Gamble," *The Economist,* January 14, 1961.

80. United States Department of States, *Events in United States-Cuban Relations, a Chronology 1957-1963* (Washington, D.C., 1963), pp. 19-20.

81. Ibid.

82. *New York Times,* September 14, 1960.

83. E. B. Glick, "Cuba and the 15th United Nations General Assembly. A Case Study in Regional Disassociation," 6 *Journal of Inter-American Studies,* April 1964, pp. 235-248.

84. E. B. Glick, "Castro and the Neutrals," 73 *The Commonweal,* October 1960, pp. 87-89.

85. See *New York Times,* September 22-24, 26, and 28, 1960.

86. On the case of Panama, see E. Castillero Pimentel, *Política Exterior de Panama* (Panama, 1961).

87. For a systematic discussion of this problem, see M. M. Ball, "Issue for the Americas: non-intervention versus human rights," 15 *International Organization* (1961), pp. 21-37.

88. See Connell-Smith, op. cit., p. 242. Senator Salvador Allende, leader of the Chilean left-wing coalition FRAP, an ardent supporter of Cuba, called for an OAS blockade of all dictatorships in Latin America. See *Hoy* (Havana), July 26, 1959.

89. OAS, Pan American Union, *Quinta Reunión de Consulta de Ministros de Relaciones Exteriores, 12-18 de agosto de 1959* (Washington, D.C., 1961), pp. 113-114. The full speech takes up pp. 108-116.

90. Connell-Smith, op. cit., p. 242.

91. OAS, *Quinta Reunión*, p. 69.

92. Mecham, op. cit., p. 419.

93. Ibid. In a letter addressed to President Betancourt of Venezuela by President Dorticós of Cuba dated August 23, 1960, the latter requested an undertaking that Arcaya's denial of any intention on the part of Betancourt to raise the general problem of the exclusion of governments which have not resulted from elections from the OAS were genuine and not in any way directed against Cuba. Betancourt refused to give such undertaking. See R. Betancourt, *Hacia América Latina democrática y integrada*, 2nd ed. (Caracas: Sendero, 1967), p. 51.

94. H. Thomas, op. cit., maintains that Texaco, Royal Dutch, and Esso refused to refine Soviet crude oil in Cuba out of a sense of solidarity with Venezuela (p. 1288).

95. President López Mateos stated in his annual Message to Congress on September 1, 1960, that Mexico had "opposed other measures which would have been construed as interference by the OAS in the internal affairs of the Dominican Republic." See H. F. Cline, op. cit., p. 315.

96. Mecham, op. cit., p. 421.

97. 43 *Department of State Bulletin*, September 12, 1960, pp. 395-407.

98. Cline, op. cit., p. 317.

99. Security Council, O.R., 15th year; Supplement for July, August, and September 1960, pp. 9-10; Roa's letter to the president of the Security Council of July 11, 1960 (Doc. S/4378).

100. The Declaration of San José (a) condemned intervention by an extracontinental power in the affairs of the American republics and declared that the acceptance by any American state of such intervention jeopardized American solidarity and security; (b) rejected attempts of the Sino-Soviet powers to exploit the political, economic and social situation in any American state as threatening to hemisphere unity and security; (c) declared that no American state may intervene for the purpose of imposing on another American state its ideologies or political, economic, or social principles; and (d) proclaimed that all members of the OAS are under an obligation to conduct themselves in accordance with the principles stated in the Declaration of Santiago and to comply with the provisions of the Charter of the OAS. See Mecham, op. cit., pp. 460-461.

101. 13 H.A.R., November 1960, pp. 631-632.

102. Ibid., October 1960, p. 537.

103. Ministério das Relações Exteriores, *Gestão de Ministro Láfer na pasta das Relações Exteriores* (Rio de Janeiro, 1961), p. 20.

104. A. A. Conil Paz and G. E. Ferrari, *Argentina's Foreign Policy, 1930-1962* (South Bend, Ind.: University of Notre Dame Press, 1966), pp. 187-188.

105. "It is possible that, without wishing it, the Cuban government has fallen into the implacable claws of Soviet strategy." Ibid., p. 60.

106. Ibid., p. 62.

107. *Guardian*, August 25, 1960. For Argentina's request, made on July 13, 1960, see Paz and Ferrari, op. cit., pp. 187-188; for Ecuador's, made in the Security Council of the United Nations, see United Nations Security Council, O.R., 15th year, 876th meeting, July 18, 1960, p. 27.

Frondizi's former junior foreign minister criticized the Argentine note to Cuba because it was based on the Monrovian conception and maintained that Argentina should have adopted the role of arbiter between the factions at San José. See C. A. Florit, *Política Exterior Nacional* (Buenos Aires: Arayu, 1961), pp. 53-54.

108. Clissold, op. cit., pp. 258-259.

109. For its background, see S. J. Serxner, *Acción Democrática. Its Origin and Development* (GainesvilleJ University of Florida Press, 1959); and J. D. Martz, *Acción Democrática. Evolution of a Modern Political Party in Venezuela* (Princeton, N.J.: Princeton University Press, 1966).

110. Acción Democrática, Secretaría Nacional de prensa y propaganda, *Ratificación de principios teóricos y de orientación programática normativos de Acción Democrática* (Caracas: Secretaria Nacional de Prensa y Propaganda, 1958), p. 20.

111. 11 H.A.R., December 1958, p. 678.

112. Ibid., vol. 12, July 1959, p. 387.

113. 13 H.A.R., July 1960, p. 463.

114. See R. J. Alexander, *The Venezuelan Democratic Revolution* (New Brunswick, N.J.: Rutgers University Press, 1964), p. 142.

115. 13 H.A.R., June 1960, p. 394.

116. Betancourt went out of his way to explain that the plotters would not have to face a *paredon* (firing squad) "as is done in some countries," an oblique reference to Cuban practice. *Revolución* of Havana criticized this statement, and Raúl Roa, the Cuban foreign minister, explained condescendingly that this did not reflect popular opinion in Venezuela. See ibid., p. 321.

117. 13 H.A.R., July 1960, p. 462.

118. 13 H.A.R., August 1960, p. 538.

119. Ibid.

120. *Le Monde,* November 19, 1960.

121. OAS, *Septima Reunión,* p. 417.

122. Ibid., p. 80.

123. Ibid., pp. 118-125.

124. Conil Paz and Ferrari, op. cit., pp. 187-188.

Chapter VI

THE CRISIS OF THE BAY OF PIGS (1961-1962)

The constant deterioration in the relations between Cuba and the United States produced a complete diplomatic break on January 3, 1961. This, however, was not a starting point of a new phase, but rather one development amongst many in the intensification of the Cold War in Latin America. President Kennedy allowed preparations for an invasion of Cuba by the Cuban exiles to continue on the assumption that the venture would be as successful as had been that against Guatemala in 1954. The invasion, which was carried out by Cuban émigrés stationed in Florida in April 1961, lacked proper logistical support—particularly air cover—by the United States, and was repulsed by Castro.

To Latin America's statesmen the situation in April 1961 must have been alarming from whichever angle it was viewed. No longer could it be hoped—or pretended—that the Cold War would be nipped in the bud in Latin America.[1] Not only was Castro able to defend himself against the type of invasion launched against him in April 1961, but he also regarded his revolution as a phenomenon that would sweep far and wide across Latin America.

The Cold War was complicating ordinary diplomatic conduct and casting doubt on some fundamental assumptions regarding the principles which had hitherto governed inter-American relations. Governments chiefly affected by these doubts were anxious not to involve Latin America further in its closing diplomatic web and to undo as many as possible of its hamstringing threads. Some of them began to grope around in search of a new system of diplomatic consultation. They were motivated not only by fear of the United States and a recognition of the dynamic nature of the Cold War, but also by the prospects of political repercussions at home. Already one country's domestic politics—Venezuela's—had been thrown out of gear.

Thus, a group of Latin American states emerged after the San José conference whose broad responses towards the Cold War were roughly identical and whose members were to develop their foreign policies on approximately parallel lines. Neutralism in Latin America, unlike its counterpart in Afro-Asia, was never raised to the plane of diplomatic principle.[2] Roberto de Oliveira Campos, the distinguished Brazilian statesman and economist, put it thus:

> Observers are likely to find a growing urge in the Latin American countries for an *independent foreign policy,* reflecting both the need of those countries to assert their national personalities and their different interpretations of Cold War issues. It is altogether too simple, however, to dismiss the policy of independence . . . as just another manner of *neutralism,* or an exhibition of pro-Castro feelings. For, in fact, the independent policy of Latin America countries differs substantially from Afro-Asian neutralism. Firstly, they are not systematically non-aligned, since they remain faithful to the inter-American system. Secondly, they do not show interest in the formation of a third power bloc, symmetrically distant from the two big centers of power. Thirdly, they have chosen Western institutions of representative democracy and capitalism, even though practising these imperfectly, while the typical neutral country has not yet crystallized its choice between democracy and private enterprise on the one hand, and authoritarian socialism on the other.[3]

He went on to list three reasons for a tendency on the part of certain Latin American governments to choose "independent" foreign policies: (a) *traditional:* because of a historical attachment to the principle of non-intervention; (b) *legal:* because of the imprecision of the instruments provided by the OAS; and (c) *pragmatic:* due to fear of aggravating domestic tensions, and scepticism regarding the effectiveness of the imposition of sanctions under the Rio Treaty.[4]

The precise motivations of Latin American governments tending towards cautious independence in the Cold War within the region varied from case to case, and a brief survey would therefore be in order.

Brazil's efforts under President Jânio Quadros, and to a lesser extent under his successor, Joâo Goulart, to combine the search for a world role[5] with a determined neutralism in the Latin American Cold War had relatively few causal connections with domestic politics, being primarily determined by diplomatic considerations. It must, however, be borne in mind that Quadros inherited a trend in this direction from his predecessor Kubitschek, who had been motivated by economic considerations primarily.

President López Mateos of Mexico would no doubt have relished a world role if internal political conditions had permitted it. Mexico's moderate neutralism proved to be a function largely of her internal politics, which at once provided the drive and set the limits to Mexico's policies in the Cold War.

Argentina's tendencies in this direction under the guidance of President Frondizi were shaped mainly by her desire to play a leading part in the economic modernization of Latin America, which imparted a great deal of energy to Argentine foreign policy; but much of this was nullified by the work of countervailing forces at home.

Chile's cautious independent policies were both generated and restricted by a precarious domestic constellation of political forces, while Uruguayan tendencies in this direction suffered perennially from the weak mechanism of decision-making with which she was encumbered. Bolivia's attitude in the Cold War had strong overtones of isolationism dictated by the need of her ruling elites to be identified with nationalist self-expression.

Ecuador alone among this group of countries developed a strategy which was strictly rooted in a local problem entirely unconnected with the Cold War—namely her dispute with Peru—which prompted some Ecuadorean statesmen from time to time to attempt to make local gains by pursuing a tactical neutralism in the Cold War.

The initiator of fresh Latin American initiatives was Argentina under President Frondizi, whose singleminded policies tended to be given far less publicity than the flamboyantly neutralist but less persistent tactics of President Quadros of Brazil, whose psychological impact on Latin American diplomacy in the Cold War far outstripped his own positive achievements. Undisturbed by internal opposition, Frondizi and Quadros might in the long run have established new and exciting patterns of Latin American policies, and glimpses of the promised land could be obtained at their meeting in Uruguaiana in April 1961, where they resolved on the future coordination of their policies.

The historical roots of the agreement of Uruguaiana reach back beyond the advent of Fidel Castro to power in Havana. According to Frondizi[6] the central purpose of the policy initiated by him was the traditional Argentine one of creating in the *cono sur* of South America a strong multilateral combination composed of Argentina, Brazil, Chile, Uruguay, and Peru. The first of these agreements was concluded with Uruguay in 1958,[7] and was to serve as prototype for the next and most important step: an identical agreement with Brazil.

Frondizi's optimistic assumptions were well expressed by one of his junior foreign ministers, Florit, who maintained that it was "indispensable that our countries, those of the south of the hemisphere, gather the political and economic resources necessary for achieving the required balance within the system, neutralizing the predominance of the Caribbean region, in order to align and integrate Latin American policy."[8]

The first moves were made when President Kubitschek was invited to visit Buenos Aires, an invitation which was not, on technical grounds, acceptable to him. Similar technical grounds were also pleaded at first by President Quadros, Kubitschek's successor in 1961. It was because of the growing currents of the Cold War, which were now affecting the whole of Latin America, that Quadros finally agreed to meet Frondizi at the bordertown of Uruguaiana at the beginning of April 1961.[9]

Frondizi's basic idea was to create a Latin American combination capable of mutual self-help in the economic sphere and able to face the world powers politically. He relied on President Kennedy to underwrite this policy.[10] Kennedy seemed to approve Frondizi's conception in principle, but there would seem to be some doubt as to the extent to which he was prepared to carry it into practice, since the whole experiment was regarded in Washington with extreme mistrust and in the political perspective of the Cold War. After all, Kennedy was at that time going ahead with plans for the invasion of Cuba which, when they were first communicated to Frondizi by President Eisenhower who had initiated the operation, had met with Frondizi's determined disapproval.[11] What the United States probably feared more than anything else was that a compact with Quadros might set off a wave of neutralism which would swamp in its entirety Frondizi's original conception,[12] and assimilate it to a strategy forcefully recommended by a leading Brazilian writer before.[13]

Here was the making of a substantial diplomatic axis in Latin America capable of cutting across the confines of the inter-American system and bringing an element of freshness into the diplomatic relations of the Americas. However, the new diplomacy was never allowed to run its full course. Checked by military coups in Argentina (1962) and Ecuador (1963), and later in Brazil and Bolivia (both in 1964), what little diplomatic solidarity had been achieved among members of the group crumbled, leaving only Mexico to hold the ring.

In the rest of Latin America a group of "hard-liners" emerged gradually as the determined Cold War opponents of Cuba and, in some cases, as pacemakers of the United States.

Cuba's principle of policy in relation to these was clarified in a note addressed to the Argentine government in March 1961, in which she insisted on negotiations through bilateral channels on a plane of equality.[14] For its part, the United States made it clear that this was a problem for the OAS to solve, and not one that allowed of a bilateral solution.

There were many indications that Cuban foreign policy at this period was taking a turn towards greater militancy. For the first time, Yugoslavia became the butt of Cuban criticism.[15] In Latin America itself even governments with left-wing participation were not immune from Cuban attack. The new government resulting from a populist-military coup in El Salvador in February 1961, which included such figures as Castillo, a man of eminently pro-Castro sympathies, was a case in point.[16] It was only for a brief period, and, it would seem, as a direct consequence of the attempt to invade Cuba at the Bay of Pigs in April 1961 that Cuban foreign policy mellowed,[17] as the Cuban press displayed a marked friendliness towards the governments of Brazil, Ecuador, and Mexico, which had been outspoken in their condemnation of the Bay of Pigs venture.[18] However, the fall of Quadros in Brazil on August 25, 1961, ushered in a new era of Cuban militancy. Brazilians were exhorted by Dr. Castro to copy the example of Cuba,[19] and at the Cairo preparatory conference for the forthcoming Belgrade conference of non-aligned countries on July 5, 1961, Cuba advocated the admission of Bolivia and Ecuador but opposed that of Argentina and Chile. She also opposed the admission of a Brazilian observer at the Belgrade conference,[20] and proved exceedingly difficult in sponsoring invitations of genuinely non-aligned states, such as Cyprus and Tanganyika.[21]

At the Belgrade conference, Cuban radicalism caused some political embarrassment to the two principal sponsoring governments, Yugoslavia and India, who saw their influence fade in the face of the new radical governments of Cuba and Africa.[22] President Dorticós chose this occasion for making a militant speech[23] in which he expounded diplomatic principles which differed in no way from those currently espoused by the Soviet Union.[24]

A new element was injected into the diplomatic patterns of Latin America by the advent of President Quadros of Brazil. Students of international relations must be grateful to L.A. Free for having undertaken an opinion survey of Brazilian political opinion[25] at the time of Quadros' tenure of office, from which it would appear that his policy enjoyed widespread support.

Jânio Quadros had won his political spurs as governor of the state of São Paulo, one of the three key states in the federation (the other two being Minas Gerais and Rio Grande do Sul), where he established a reputation for efficient government. But he brought to his new office of president a mercurial temperament coupled with a belief that the United States of Brazil could be run on the same lines as the state of São Paulo, a belief which was to prove to be his undoing.

It is possible that he had a political formula whereby measures of internal retrenchment, bound to arouse misgivings after the palmy days of unrestrained economic expansion under his predecessor Kubitschek, could be combined with a spectacular diversification in the sphere of foreign policy which, he believed, would offset the unpopular measures he was taking at home. Thus, Quadros launched a drastic program to curb inflation involving a considerable lowering of the subsidy on essential imports, such as wheat and oil. Though this resulted in price rises of bread and an increase in bus fares, he got into the good books of the IMF, which announced the granting of a package of foreign credits of $2 billion in May and June 1961.[26] International financial circles were also pleased by his currency reform,[27] and in April the United States Administration took the decision to back the Quadros Administration financially.[28] Indeed, during his election campaign Quadros had given the impression of an ultra-conventional Latin American statesman eager to seek foreign investment, an attitude which cost him the support of the Communists, which went to his rival, Marshal H. Texeira Lott, a nationalist.[29]

Most of these acts were confined to the strictly domestic problem of combating inflation. In foreign policy the new president acted in quite a different and totally unconventional way. Thus, he was quick to modify his earlier stand against *Petrobrás,* the Brazilian oil-producing monopoly, and even began to oppose the principle of participation of foreign firms in Brazilian oil production.[30]

Six months before his election Quadros carried out a reconnaissance which included visits to India, Egypt, Yugoslavia, and Cuba; the leading exponents of "neutralism" in the underdeveloped world. Only two developed countries, Japan and the Soviet Union, figured on his itinerary. The United States was a notable absentee. On his return Quadros remarked significantly that Brazil also needed a Nasser.[31] A later post-election but pre-inauguration tour included France, Great Britain, Yugoslavia, Italy, Spain, and Portugal. He turned down an invitation to visit President Eisenhower and hedged over one extended to him by President-elect Kennedy. The nature of his attitude towards the United States is well illustrated by his willingness to see Kennedy in Brazil but not in the United States.[32]

João Goulart, on the other hand, elected vice-president, a member of the left-of-center *Partido Trabalhista Brasileiro* (PTB), travelled to China and the Soviet Union after his election, possibly in an attempt to compel the new administration in Brasilia to resume diplomatic relations with the latter and recognize the government of the former.[33] In July 1961, when the contours of Brazil's new foreign policy were already plain, the PTB, at its convention in Brasilia, endorsed Quadros' policy. In this he was helped by Lionel Brizola, Goulart's brother-in-law, one of the radicals within the movement. Goulart was consequently elected to head a mission to China.[34]

What marked Quadros' new foreign policy was his series of attempts to play an active part not only in inter-American relations, but as far as possible on a world scale also. Although his overall conception of foreign policy shows some surprising similarities with that elaborated by Hélio Jaguaribe in his work *O nacionalismo na atualidade brasileira,* published in 1958, there can be no doubt that Quadros had arrived at his conclusions independently, without any recourse to academic theories.

To achieve his objective Quadros tried to break out of the Western Hemisphere in all directions:[35] (a) by developing relations with Afro-Asia;[36] (b) by redeveloping ties with the Communist countries; and (c) by taking great care to divide his diplomatic favors between the United States and the Soviet Union and her allies.

A few days after his inauguration Quadros was reported eager to meet the "leaders of countries which he regards as holding an international position similar to that which Brazil ought to adopt," a desire which earned his policy the name *neutralismo interessado*.[37] As he himself put it a little later: "Solidarity with the Afro-Asian peoples in their struggle for emancipation is an absolute necessity."[38]

A special relationship with Africa is a theme which had intrigued many Brazilians from the 1950s onwards.[39] One Brazilian author argued in 1956 that Brazil would have to play the role of a mediator in the Afro-Asian world,[40] and in a television interview of March 1962 in which he tried to justify his actions while in office, Quadros actually confirmed that he had wanted to see Brazil cast in the role of both promoter and moderator among the Afro-Asian States.[41] He certainly regarded Brazil as "the link, the bridge, between Africa and the West."[42]

On May 17, 1961, a dialogue took place within the Commission of Foreign Relations in the Chamber of Deputies on the exact meaning of the terms "neutralist" and "independent" between Sra. Ivete Vargas and A. de Melo Franco, Quadros' foreign minister. The latter maintained that the principle of solidarity with member states of the OAS was by no means incompatible with that of independence in Brazil's foreign policy. He cited the case of President Nasser's foreign policy, which similarly combined a free hand in foreign affairs with definite obligations towards the Arab League.[43]

In an outspoken article in a periodical in the United States, Quadros explained that "Brazil, either through misinterpretation or distortion of its better judgment, spent many years without regular contacts with the countries of the Communist bloc, even to the point of having only roundabout and insufficient trade relations with them."[44] After two days in office, he instructed his foreign minister, A. de Melo Franco, to resume relations with Hungary, Bulgaria, and Rumania—relations with Czechoslovakia and Poland had never been interrupted—and gave an indication of his desire to resume diplomatic relations with the Soviet Union also.[45] Staking Brazil's claim to diplomatic independence in an unprecedentedly clear-cut manner, he also hinted that he might want to recognize the government of Communist China.[46] This desire was all the more surprising, not to say sensational, as only one country in the Western Hemisphere—Cuba—had so far done so, and that only in September 1960. A fortnight later, Quadros instructed Brazil's delegation at the United Nations to support the inclusion of an item on the agenda of the General Assembly regarding the question of Chinese representation.[47]

It is difficult to avoid the impression that in his anxiety to demonstrate his independence from the United States, Quadros saw fit to be consistently cool, and on occasion downright rude, to the United States and some of its representatives.[48] Seven months after his resignation in 1961, the former Brazilian president justified his actions by referring to a series of provocative acts by two United States diplomats, whom he named as A. A. Berle, then coordinator of Latin American Affairs in the Department of State, and John Moors Cabot, United States ambassador in Brasilia.[49] In one of his first decrees he put an abrupt end to the training of Brazilian military personnel abroad; and since it was the United States to which the vast majority of Brazilian officers and men had gone for training in the past, this must be regarded as a deliberate affront.[50] Typical also was his treatment of A. A. Berle in February 1961.[51] Quadros, who happened to be in Rio de Janeiro at the time of Berle's arrival, pointedly omitted inviting Kennedy's representative to share the presidential plane to Brasilia, where Quadros wanted to meet him. During the interview itself, Quadros showed himself reserved, even though his friendliness to a representative to *Prensa Latina,* the Cuban news agency, whom he received on the same day and who brought a personal gift from Guevara, was exuberant.[52] In February 1961 the president went to the length of withdrawing recognition from the governments of the Baltic States.[53] At the end of May 1961 he let it be known that he would welcome any head of state who would care to visit Brazil.[54] When an official invitation to visit Washington was made[55] it was accepted gracefully enough but followed barely a fortnight later by the acceptance of an invitation to see Khruschev in Moscow.[56]

The height of tactlessness was the Brazilian president's decoration of E. Guevara on August 21, 1961. The Cuban minister was awarded the order of the *Cruzeiro do Sul,* an honor which is normally bestowed on any visiting statesman of some importance,[57] and would have caused little comment. In the circumstances, however, it was considered of special diplomatic significance.[58]

Before the polls opened for the presidential elections in November 1960, Quadros had accepted an official invitation from Havana to visit Cuba to show the Brazilian public that he was bold enough to do so, while his rival, Marshal H. Texeira Lott—who enjoyed Communist electoral support—was not.[59] Lott had even accused Quadros of "neutralism" and asserted that Brazil's best interests lay in support of the West against the Soviet bloc.[60] Thus the paradoxical situation arose that Quadros was "internationalist" at home and "nationalist" abroad, whilst Lott was "nationalist" at home and "internationalist" abroad. At a news conference on April 14, 1961, he called for "comprehension and tolerance" towards the Castro régime[61] and in his ex post factum address on television in March 1962 he maintained that he had sympathized with the desire of Cuba for "economic and social emancipation."[62] His policy towards Cuba was, however, perfectly in accord with the principle of non-intervention which has provided a cornerstone in the program on foreign policy of the *Movimento Popular Jânio Quadros.*[63]

The problem of Cuba had meanwhile assumed much wider proportions, and the new president showed considerable uncertainty how to handle it in practice. To oppose the United States within the Western Hemisphere was one thing; to get involved in the Cold War in doing so was quite another.[64] The electoral program of the *Movimento Popular Jânio Quadros* had specified the United Nations as the organization in which Brazil must rest in the universal camp, and the Organization of American States as "the proper organization elected for the promotion of greater closeness and the solution of possible controversies,"[65] and Quadros had some difficulty in defining the spheres of functions between the two.

On April 14, 1961, he had proclaimed that "the government of Brazil is in favor of all or any efforts at an understanding, bilaterally or multi-laterally, in the Organization of American States or in the United Nations, that will resolve the issue between Cuba and the government of the United States,"[66] thus leaving all options of a settlement open. On May 6, 1961, de Melo Franco, Brazil's foreign minister, confirmed that the government would not be opposed to an OAS conference on Cuba, such as the United States had suggested.[67] The government's dilemma in this matter was highlighted when in reply to a question put to him in the course of a congressional hearing on foreign policy, de Melo Franco explained that Brazil was in principle opposed to the introduction of the Communist system in Latin America, but that the Castro régime could not be identified as such. Somewhat sheepishly he added on that occasion that Brazil was opposed to "international capitalism" as well as to Communism.[68]

The Bay of Pigs episode made Quadros bolder, and at the end of April Brazil found herself in the company of Chile, Ecuador, Mexico, and Venezuela in abstaining in the Inter-American Defense Board on a vote which excluded the representatives of Cuba from secret meetings of that body.[69] On April 24, 1961, the president instructed the Brazilian ambassador at the United Nations to support a Mexican proposal for a United

Nations investigation into the origins of the invasion at the Bay of Pigs,[70] and on May 10, 1961, Quadros issued a strongly worded policy statement in which, in clear allusion to the Bay of Pigs incident, he opposed any collective censure of Cuba, adding significantly that Brazil would not recognize any Cuban government established as a result of "interference by a foreign Power."[71] While he did not seem to have contemplated the possibility of individual Brazilian mediation at that stage, the idea of collective Latin American mediation must have gradually matured in his mind. It is a matter of conjecture as to what extent his subsequent policy was influenced by the exchange of views he had with President Frondizi of Argentina in Uruguaiana at the end of April 1961,[72] but it is significant that his foreign minister was able to announce in Rio de Janeiro on August 24, 1961, the eve of Quadros' resignation, with some air of certainty that "with Mexico, Chile, Argentina, Uruguay and Ecuador" everything would be done to reduce tensions between the two antagonists.[73]

At the center of opposition to Quadros' policy was Governor Carlos Lacerda of Guanabara. Now that the Cold War had invaded Latin America in strength, Lacerda's former ardor for neutralism had vanished to give way to a desire for armed intervention in Cuba.[74] The prime mover of opposition to Quadros, Lacerda made issues related to the Cold War the spearhead of his attacks, and eventually brought about the president's downfall.[75] Deciding to take an independent hand in the field of foreign policy on May 16, 1961, he declared that the presence of N. Mora, Cuban cultural attaché in Brasilia, was undesirable in the state of Guanabara[76] — an act of dubious constitutional propriety—and during a presidential banquet in honor of President Prado of Peru, Lacerda chose the occasion of the toast to the guests for attacking Brazil's policy in the Cold War: "Our present foreign policy is destructive of American unity and establishes Brazil as a diplomatic bridgehead for Russia to accomplish what the latter had initiated militarily in Cuba by way of an invasion of technicians who will prepare for all of us days of agony."[77] It was Lacerda also who protested strongly against the decoration of Guevara, Cuba's minister of the economy, by Quadros.

There can be little doubt that Quadros' Cold War postures represented the most controversial aspect of his presidential rule;[78] and though it was during the last two years of Kubitschek's tenure of presidential office that new attitudes towards the Cold War had begun to emerge in Brazil, it was under Quadros that these came fully into the open. Yet, those of his critics who believed that his resignation on August 25, 1961, would signal a return to a conventional foreign policy on the part of Brazil were to be deceived.

In earlier years President Frondizi of Argentina and his party had pronounced themselves against the adherance of Argentina to the Rio Treaty of 1947,[79] but once in office he sought a rapprochement with the United States. To establish his good faith, he visited Washington in February 1959,[80] and his foreign minister, Diogenes Taboada, announced publicly the necessity of an alliance with the United States.[81] The course of Frondizi's foreign policy in the Cold War seemed firmly set.

In the measure in which the Cuban crisis developed, a certain impatience crept into Frondizi's demands for equality of treatment with the United States. He envisaged the creation of an informal diplomatic directorate of the major American countries which had reached a minimum level of economic development. Beside the United States, these would have included not only Argentina, Brazil, and Mexico, but possibly also Venezuela and Chile. A proposal on these lines was put to Kennedy's roving ambassador, Adlai Stevenson, when he called on Frondizi in Buenos Aires in June 1961, with a demand for an immediate meeting of the presidents of the United States, Argentina, Brazil, and Mexico to discuss the problem of Cuba.[82]

Frondizi's conception of foreign policy is also reflected in a memorandum sent by Rogelio Frigerio—regarded by many as Frondizi's *éminence grise*[83]—to Stevenson, before he knew of the latter's impending trip around Latin America to canvas support for the Alliance for Progress. Frigerio put the issue bluntly: "Full inter-American meetings within the framework of the Organization of American States must be carefully prepared and *preceded by agreement among the principal countries of the system.*" (Emphasis added.)[84]

Before his advent to the presidency, Frondizi had been well-known for his economic nationalism, especially where oil was concerned.[85] On June 12, 1960, Frondizi justified the need for foreign aid[86] on the grounds that "no underdeveloped country can provide the necessary solutions under a democratic government without the decisive cooperation of the more developed countries."[87]

This explains his initial hesitation to deepen Argentina's relations with the underdeveloped countries, in stark contrast with Quadros, whose enthusiasm in this respect was unbounded. The underdeveloped world was regarded by the Argentine president primarily as a market for the country's output of semi-manufactured goods,[88] whereas Western Europe was a potential source of valuable economic aid.[89] When, at the Uruguaiana meeting at the end of April 1961, Quadros raised the question of a neutralist foreign policy, Frondizi replied resignedly that such a strategy might be theoretically desirable, but that the duty of Latin America lay in accelerating her economic development, which could only be done in conjunction with the West.[90]

Frondizi's hostility towards Soviet global policy was pronounced. Though on January 10, 1959, he had approved the acceptance of a loan of $100 million from the Soviet Union,[91] he went out of his way during his visit to Mexico barely a fortnight later—which happened to coincide with a visit by Mikoyan to that country—to declare in curiously discourteous and undiplomatic language that Mikoyan would never be a welcome visitor in Argentina.[92]

The principal object of the diplomatic flurry in which Frondizi engaged subsequently appears to have been the creation of a détente between Cuba and the United States. On February 17, 1961, he rejected an Ecuadorian proposal to launch a collective conciliatory move by the Latin American States,[93] but barely a fortnight later on March 5, 1961, this was followed by a formal offer of good offices to both Washington and Havana, indicating that he believed it both possible and desirable to encourage a bilateral solution between those two capitals.[94] According to foreign minister Taboada,[95] an opening had been detected in a twenty-two page note circulated to all Latin American governments by Raúl Roa, Cuba's foreign minister, asking urgently for help in bringing about a reconciliation with the United States. Frondizi's offer, which had been made in perfectly good faith, was, however, rejected by both sides.

Frondizi refused to give up. Spurred in his determination by the episode of the Bay of Pigs, he called a cabinet meeting on Cuba on May 20, 1961, which prompted the Argentine government to take the unusual course of announcing pointedly that Argentina supported the principle of self-determination "without exception."[96] The Argentine foreign ministry reaffirmed Argentina's basic Western orientation, but pointed to the economic underdevelopment of the region as the main cause of Cold War difficulties experienced in Latin America.[97]

At this point Frondizi undertook a diplomatic trip around South America. In Montevideo he agreed with President Haedo of Uruguay that for Latin America *fidelismo* was an internal, and not, as in the case of the United States, an external threat, requiring an approach different from that adopted by the United States. He also met President Paz Estenssoro of Bolivia.[98] The climax of this phase in Frondizi's diplomatic activity was his meeting with Quadros at the frontier town of Uruguaiana between April 20-22, 1961, arranged at Frondizi's express wish,[99] at which the two statesmen condemned outside interference and reaffirmed the principles of non-intervention.[100]

The main importance of the Uruguaiana meeting lay in its psychological impact on the governments of Latin America, many of which saw in it the beginning of a new diplomatic alignment designed to make Latin America's voice heard in the Cold War. An understanding between the two major Latin American powers could be followed by a closer diplomatic association among like-minded Latin American states and lead to hammering out of common Latin American policies in the Cold War.[101]

The invasion of the Bay of Pigs by Cuban exiles backed by the Kennedy Administration created a favorable climate for the furtherance of Frondizi's diplomatic scheme.[102] On August 18, 1961, he met Guevara, Cuban minister of the economy, who had flown in secretly from Punta del Este. Guevara wanted Frondizi to renew his attempts to ease relations between Cuba and the United States, giving an assurance that the Cuban government had no intention of entering into a military pact with the Soviet Union.[103]

But Frondizi was no longer a free agent, since he was increasingly subjected to *planteos* by the military at home.[104] The armed forces grew suspicious of Frondizi over the Guevara meeting and of Adolfo Múgica, his foreign minister, a Conservative, for having arranged the meeting. Múgica was suspected of being under the influence of Frigerio, whom the military in turn considered a crypto-Peronista.[105] On August 28, 1961, the military saw a chance to oust him. At a private party thrown by a Brazilian diplomat, Múgica had committed the indiscretion of mentioning the secret meeting between R. N. Goodwin, Kennedy's deputy assistant secretary of state for inter-American affairs, and Guevara which had taken place at Buenos Aires. The fact leaked out, Washington felt greatly embarrassed, and Múgica was compelled to resign under an ultimatum handed in by the three service chiefs.[106]

Neither Frondizi nor Múgica repented. The president assumed all responsibility, although he never explained why, beyond reasons of security, the visit had to be concealed, especially from the military cabinet. He significantly referred to the diminishing concept of the "West," intimating hopefully that he expected Argentina on account of that to be a "world power" within a decade.[107] Múgica declared his complete satisfaction with the presidential meeting with Guevara since it presaged better relations between Cuba and the United States.[108] This was the first major intervention of the Argentine military in foreign policy since the fall of Perón. Military intervention within Argentina was to increase fast during the following months and reach its climax in the arrest of Frondizi in March 1962. It was also to frustrate one of the most spectacular diplomatic developments in Latin America by preventing a movement for collective conciliation in the Cold War in Latin America.

When Adolfo López Mateos was elected President of Mexico in 1958, the Cuban revolutionaries were about to seize power in Havana. As a former chairman of the Commission of Foreign Relations, the president was eager to broaden and activate Mexican foreign policy,[109] but the totally unexpected evolution of the Castro régime in Havana frustrated this ambition.

In its early phases, the Cuban Revolution was felt in Mexico to have close affinities with the Mexican Revolution of 1910. There was the same emphasis on agrarian reform, on curbing the power of foreign enterprise, and eventually the coincidence of expropriation of United States oil companies. During his election campaign in 1958 López Mateos had stated confidently that he considered Communism to be less a danger to Mexico than to the United States,[110] and during a press conference in Caracas, Venezuela, on January 17, 1961, he was still able to announce that at the first opportunity he would visit Cuba "with much pleasure."[111] At a press conference in Rio de Janeiro three days later he declared proudly, "perhaps for countries which have not undergone a social revolution the news from Cuba is surprisingly disagreeable . . . but as Mexicans who know the sequel of a revolution with deep popular roots, we are not surprised by this news."[112]

Two developments within the Cuban Revolution served to dim Mexican enthusiasm in some quarters. There was first the rapid and radical transition from pragmatic populism to dogmatic Marxism, an experience which Mexico had never shared; and there was secondly the diplomatic alignment of Cuba with the Soviet Union, for which no equivalent existed in Mexican diplomatic experience.[113]

From the middle of 1960 onwards, developments in Cuba were causing rifts in the decision-making cadres at the top of the government structure of Mexico. The center of opposition to President López Mateos was ex-President Lázaro Cárdenas, chief executive between 1934 and 1940. In the minds of most Mexicans directly associated with a radical policy at home and abroad, Cárdenas was something of a hero in the eyes of both the Populist and Marxist Left. During the 1930s he had pursued a consistently anti-Fascist foreign policy and on September 17, 1939, had described the war as "an international conflict between ambitious, unscrupulous and imperialistic interests."[114] At first sight this record would mark him out as a fellow-traveller of Moscow, sympathetic towards the Nazi-Soviet Pact of August 23, 1939. However, after the murder of Trotsky by Stalin's agents in Mexico City in August 1940, he described the Communists as "servants of a foreign Power who are a disgrace to civilization."[115]

Cárdenas' tendency since the late 1950s had been markedly to the Left. In November 1958 he visited Eastern Europe and the Soviet Union,[116] and in October 1959 he advocated the recognition of the Communist government of China.[117] The cause of the Cuban Revolution was championed by him from the beginning. Returning from a visit to Havana in July 1959, he also began to adopt an active left-wing policy at home.[118]

Yet, it would be a mistake to regard him even at this stage as having abandoned the Mexican establishment. The challenge which the ex-president was throwing out to López Mateos was not to the latter's authority—for Cárdenas had been among the principal sponsors of the president within the PRI—but to the generally critical attitude he was beginning to adopt towards the Castro régime in Cuba and the kind of foreign policy he was promoting as a consequence.[119]

The president's changing attitude towards the revolutionary government in Havana was reflected in his message to Congress of September 1, 1960, in which he drew some sharp distinctions between the character of the Mexican and Cuban Revolutions, taking care not to name the latter.[120] Cárdenas replied by sponsoring a Latin American Conference for National Soveriegnty, Economic Emancipation and Peace which was held in Mexico City between March 3-8, 1961.[121] On March 11, 1961, he denied President Kennedy's right on his forthcoming conference with Khrushchev to speak in the name of Latin America.[122]

Cárdenas' intervention in the Cuban question was a matter of serious concern to López Mateos, as it tended to mobilize the Left against him and served to accentuate labor unrest which had broken out in 1958—before the Cuban Revolution—and with which he had to grapple throughout his term of office. This compelled him to take some repressive measures of doubtful legal propriety.[123] Mexican Congress was restless also.

Like Argentina, Mexico never contemplated a balancing act between the United States and the Soviet Union. It is true that Mikoyan was invited to Mexico City to open a Soviet exhibition there in 1959; but when Khrushchev expressed a desire to attend the festivities marking the 150th anniversary of the existence of independent Mexico in August 1960, the Mexicans declined on the curious grounds that it would not be politic to have such a high Soviet personage so soon after Mikoyan's visit, adding with unconscionable sense of humor that Khrushchev would be welcome if he ranked as ambassador.[124] Relations with the United States had been undisturbed for some years. The decade 1953-1963 was marked in Mexico by an economic recession which rendered López Mateos' internal economic policies dependent on financing by the United States.[125]

The president's apprehension of the dangers of a neutralist foreign policy may be illustrated with reference to the conference of non-aligned countries at Belgrade, whose sponsors were eager for Mexican participation. However, foreign minister Manuel Tello explained that Mexico's attendance was not feasible on constitutional grounds, as no list of participating countries had been published, and as the Mexican constitution required advance approval by Congress of any presidential trips abroad; a specious ground for refusing.[126]

In order to avoid issues of a Cold War content, Mexico tended to use the principle of non-intervention[127] to clothe its moderate neutralism in a legal garb. Thus, the legality of the economic embargo imposed by the United States on Cuba towards the end of 1960 was challenged not only on intrinsic legal grounds, but also, it is submitted, because she considered the proposed course politically hazardous. Similarly, the legality of the Inter-American Peace Committee was questioned during the San José conference in August 1960[128] basically because Mexico disapproved of the political reasons that had led to its creation in the first place.

From the middle of 1960 onwards there were growing signs of strain in Mexico's relationship with Cuba. After a number of efforts to mediate between Cuba and the United States had come to nothing in mid-1960, President López Mateos, addressing Congress on September 1, 1960, reflected somberly that he had failed in his attempts in that direction,[129] adding that "the corner-stone of Mexican foreign policy now rests on close relations with the United States."[130] This was a far cry from the exuberant mood in which the chief executive had proclaimed categorically on his return from a visit to the United States and Canada in October 1959 that there would be "no relations with Franco. No label of Communism for peoples seeking their own internal recovery."[131]

In January 1960 Castro had hinted at the possibility of holding a conference of underdeveloped countries in Havana in the autumn, but López Mateos ruled ingeniously that Mexico would send a delegation provided only that at least half of all Latin American States did likewise. This amounted to a barely concealed refusal.[132]

In January 1961 the Mexican government refused a Cuban request for oil technicians from *Petróleos Mexicanos* (PEMEX), the state monopoly organization, to help in the operation of Cuba's newly appropriated oil refineries,[133] and during the same month instituted a regular patrol of the beaches of Yucatán, the Mexican state closest to Cuba, where discontent was rife after the once-thriving sisal industry had been ruined.[134] For their part, the Cubans accused the Mexican authorities of harboring Cuban exiles and counter-revolutionaries preparing an invasion.[135] Disenchantment with Cuba in the Mexican presidency must have gone some way to reach such a pass,[136] and it is not impossible that at this point López Mateos would have been willing to go some distance towards a return to the pro-United States foreign policy of Miguel Alemán (1946-1952).[137] What prevented him from doing so was not only resistance to such a course at home, but also the attempted overthrow of the Castro regime by an invasion of Cuban exiles in April 1961.

The Bay of Pigs disaster set Mexico's foreign policy back to a course of sceptical neutrality. To the disenchantment with Cuba was added disillusionment with the United States and the Organization of American States, in which the United States predominated. There was also a sudden awareness of Cuba's new military potential.

The shock to the directors of Mexican foreign policy administered by the Bay of Pigs drama was all the more severe because, alongside several other Latin American states, Mexico had just decided to introduce a resolution at the United Nations calling on the Latin American members of that body, as well as of the Organization of American States, to assist in settling the dispute between the United States and Cuba.[138] The Bay of Pigs episode forced López Mateos' hand. Mexico withdrew from the sponsorship of the resolution in the United Nations since, worded as it stood, it could have condoned the action of the United States, and, far from drifting towards the position of the United States any longer, Mexico found herself in headlong diplomatic collision with her.

Events now moved in swift sequence. Mexico introduced a draft resolution into the General Assembly,[139] but the United States opposed it as too favorable to Cuba and because it ignored the Organization of American States. In the General Assembly the relevant points of a resolution sponsored by Argentina, Chile, Colombia, Honduras, Panama, Uruguay, and Venezuela, according to which the United States-Cuban dispute should be referred to the OAS, was defeated by a vote of 59 to 13, with 24 abstentions, leaving intact only the part calling on all members of the United Nations to "take such peaceful action as is open to them to remove existing tension." The Mexican resolution was defeated by a vote of 41 against 35, with 20 abstentions, which was short of the two-thirds majority required under the provisions of the charter. [140] What Mexico did achieve, therefore, was the blocking of a move in the General Assembly to refer the matter to the OAS.

Henceforth Mexico was to set greater store than hitherto in the political processes of the United Nations, where the enormous diplomatic weight of the United States was balanced by that of the Soviet Union and a number of extra-hemispheric states critical of the general conduct of the United States.[141]

On April 17, a day after the beginning of the landings, the Mexican Ministry of Foreign Affairs issued a strongly worded statement reiterating its firm adherence to the principles of non-intervention.[142]

The position was exacerbated by a speech by President Kennedy on April 20, 1961, in which he called in question the absolute validity in practice of "the inter-American doctrine of non-interference."[143] Ex-President Cárdenas was outraged and wished to fly to Cuba, presumably to place his services at the disposal of the revolutionary government.[144] On May 4, 1961, the Mexican Congress passed a law prohibiting service of Mexican nationals in any foreign army.[145]

After the invasion of the Bay of Pigs, the option of an *alemanista*-type of foreign policy, leaning closely on the United States was practically foreclosed. And although the Mexican authorities continued to seize quantities of propaganda material hidden in Cuban diplomatic pouches, [146] López Mateos' message to Congress of September 1, 1961, was very different in tone from that of the previous year, as he insisted on the "universal application of the principle of non-intervention."[147]

Chile's response to the first phase of the Cuban Revolution was largely conditioned by the slender majority by which President Jorge Alessandri had been elected over his rival, Salvador Allende, in 1958. The Cuban Revolution certainly heartened FRAP, the left-wing combination which was the most determined opponent of the Alessandri Administration. In the past the dominating trend in the conceptions of foreign policy among the Socialists had been a radical neutralism of the Titoist kind,[148] whereas the Communists rigidly adhered to the Soviet line. As if to atone for this rigidity, they showed themselves remarkably flexible at home, whereas the Socialists tended to regard the parliamentary system with suspicion.

This dichotomy represented a weakness in the armour of FRAP. In the defense of the Cuban Revolution both parties found not only a rallying point, but also a means of reaching common agreement in the field of foreign policy, and to that extent the political cohesion of FRAP was strengthened.[149] Allende remarked in July 1960 that the new Cuba was "showing the way for a new future for the whole of Latin America."[150]

If the Cuban Revolution raised the morale of FRAP, it certainly represented an embarrassment for the government. At the beginning of 1961 G. Vergara Donoso, Chile's foreign minister, admitted that relations with Cuba were not "cordial," but gave an assurance that, so long as there was no interference with other governments, the Cubans had the right to choose their own. The government dissociated itself publicly from all inter-American consultations regarding the imposition of diplomatic sanctions on Cuba.[151] On the occasion of the break of relations between the United States and Cuba early in January 1961, Allende sent a telegram to the Cuban ambassador in Santiago pledging FRAP's support in the event of an attack on Cuba,[152] an act not exactly calculated to relieve the Chilean government of its anxieties.

Nor did pressure on the Alessandri Administration come from FRAP only. Chilean officials also were disturbed by the pressing advances made by A. A. Berle, Kennedy's roving ambassador in Latin America, who tried in March 1961 to bring Chile's Cuban policy into line with that of the United States. Walter Muller, Chile's ambassador in Washington, had to listen to an admonition delivered by Berle in a "tone of impatience" (the phrase was Muller's) to the effect that Chile was not taking the Cuban problem seriously enough. Berle was clearly unappreciative of Chile's internal political problem, and German Vergara Donoso, Chile's foreign minister, had to inform Walter Howe, United States ambassador in Santiago, that, unlike the United States, Latin American countries had to be careful, since they had a left-wing problem at home, with the Cuban Revolution providing a banner under which the Left could gather.[153]

No official reaction came from Chile in response to President Frondizi's offer of good offices between the United States and Cuba in February 1961, and the general feeling in the administration was that the OAS was the proper place in which to pursue a détente. When the Cuban foreign minister sent a circular to all Latin American governments requesting support for Cuba's attempts to improve relations with the United States, Vergara Donoso replied evasively that Chile would give its full cooperation in any international organ in which Cuban affairs would be discussed.[154]

In April 1961 the foreign minister told demonstrators of FRAP partisans and trade unionists against the United States-sponsored invasion of Cuba at the Bay of Pigs that Chile would do everything to bring about a peaceful solution of the Cuban crisis, [155] but during the same month he left the government. Enrique Escobar Ortuzar, his successor, informed two Cuban diplomats in magisterial language that self-determination must be expressed periodically in free elections; that Chile condemned the intervention of an extra-continental power in the affairs of the continent; and that she "will not permit any country to introduce its political ideologies, its system of government or its revolution in any other."[156]

It is a moot point whether the entry of the Radical Party into the Chilean government in August 1961[157] was due to a desire on the part of Alessandri—who was suffering economic shipwreck at home—to bolster his foreign policy. Among the three ministries allocated to the Radicals was that of foreign affairs, which went to C. Martínez Sotomayor. One of the first official statements put out by him concerned Chile's intention of no longer supporting white nations in their colonialism, and expressed the surprising view that Chile "would be bound eventually to recognize Communist China as a major non-European Power."[158] In view of subsequent policies pursued by the Alessandri Administration, which amounted roughly to a continuation of the cautious, almost reluctant form of neutralism practised in the Cuban crisis hitherto, Martínez Sotomayor's statements were somewhat misleading. Alternatively, they could have been expressly designed to silence the growing volume of criticism of Chile's policy in the Cold War on the Left.[159]

In spite of her great financial dependence on the United States, the general reactions of Bolivia to the Cold War were similar to those of Chile, combining an attitude of indifference towards the Soviet Union with a policy of caution towards Cuba. Bolivia had agreed to recognize the Soviet

Union during the Second World War, but diplomatic relations between the two countries were not established before 1969. Under President Hernan Zuazo Siles (1956-1960), Víctor Andrade, ambassador in Washington, had accused the Soviet Union of trying to wreck good relations with the United States, and charged her with harming tin-producing countries by making large-scale sales of that commodity on the world market, depressing prices thereby.[160]

New policies were introduced when, on returning to office in 1960, [161] President V. Paz Estenssoro tried to hold the prospect of diplomatic relations before the Soviet Union to tempt her to aid Bolivia. Rising tensions of the Cold War seemed to favor such a move. A Soviet offer of $150 million[162] for the development of both the tin mines and oil industry of Bolivia followed on December 20, 1960, and on December 29, 1960, there came an announcement by Paz Estenssoro of his serious intention to establish diplomatic relations with the Soviet Union.[163]

Sensing a possible Soviet and Cuban opening in La Paz, the Eisenhower Administration reversed its previous policy of not aiding state-owned enterprises in Latin America; and in April 1960 *Yacimientos Petroleros Fiscales Bolivianos,* the state-owned and operated oil corporation, was allowed to apply for United States credits for purposes of re-equipment.[164] High Bolivian officials intimated that if aid were not forthcoming, a Soviet offer would be further explored, and a United States credit of $2,700 million was promptly granted in June 1960.[165]

The Soviet offer of a tin smelter served to bring Bolivian attitudes in the Cold War out into the open. Following Khrushchev's hint in New York in October 1960 that an offer might be forthcoming, the Chamber of Deputies expressed the majority view in favoring loans from the Soviet Union in preference to the United States. A vote taken in the Chamber instructed the Bolivian delegation in the United States to explore the Soviet offer, and at the same time the deputies presented a petition to the foreign minister asking him to investigate the government's intention of establishing diplomatic relations with the Soviet Union.[166]

Under continued pressure from the Left, the Paz Estenssoro Administration announced the impending departure of a mission to the Soviet Union, which did not, however, materialize. In spite of the preference of Vice-President Juan Lechín, who was also a powerful trade union leader, for the Soviet offer, the Bolivian administration went ahead with Western Germany and the United States in the "triangular" plan, which was signed on June 11, 1961.[167] Paz Estenssoro announced in August 1961 that the acceptance of a Soviet offer would complement the aid received from elsewhere; but this was no more than a gesture, probably made to stave off left-wing criticism and pressure from Lechín.[168]

On the Cuban issue Paz Estenssoro's sentiments were revealed when, in August 1960, he expressed the view that while the revolutión in Cuba was undoubtedly a "people's revolution" (*una revolución popular*), it would be a genuine mistake to allow an extra-continental power to exercise any influence in the Americas.[169] In January 1961 he announced his firm policy of not breaking off diplomatic relations with Cuba.[170] To this policy Bolivia continued to adhere strictly until relations had to be broken after a resolution passed by the OAS in July 1964. Meanwhile Bolivia's actual diplomatic relations with the Castro régime were not cordial. In June 1961 the Cuban chargé d'affaires in La Paz was accused of fomenting revolution and given his passport.

The impact of the developing Cuban crisis subjected Uruguay's delicate internal balance to severe strains, which prevented the emergence of clear-cut policies towards Cuba and the Soviet Union. Uruguay's willingness to enter into a Military Assistance Agreement with the United States in 1953 had been dictated far more by her fear of Perón's Argentina than apprehension of the Soviet Union, and, with Perón out of the way, she may have been less attached to pro-Western commitments.

These ambiguities were highlighted by the uncertainties she displayed over the Cuban crisis. The crux of the matter turned out to be the question of maintaining or breaking diplomatic relations with Cuba and the Soviet Union. Whilst Benito Nardone, leader of an important faction within the *blanco* party, favored a break with both countries, E. V. Haedo, a blanco leader who was fiercely anti-Communist at home, described Fidel Castro as "the greatest living man in the hemisphere,"[171] and in July 1961 declared himself categorically opposed to a forcible solution of the Cuban problem.[172]

Possibly because he was beginning to lose supporters to both the Communists and the Nardone faction within the blanco party, Luis Batlle, the *colorado* leader, began to assume more markedly hostile attitudes towards the United States from 1960 onwards. There was certainly growing competition from the Socialist Party, which saw in Castro an instrument of political revival.[173] In 1956, obeying the current Moscow line, the Communist Party began approaches to unity with the Socialists. By 1960 it reportedly had achieved modest success, although it would be necessary to split the Socialists' highly respected and experienced leader,

Emilio Frugoni, away from the main body in order to accomplish it.[174] It was Vivian Trias, not Frugoni, who was in the ascendancy, and it was Trias also who was in the chair—with Palacios of Argentina and Allende of Chile, both pro-Castro, as vice-chairmen—when the Fifth Conference of the Consultative Committee of the Latin American Secretariat of the Socialist International met in Montevideo between July 23-24, 1960. The resolutions passed at that meeting were in line with the Latin American policies pursued by both Cuba and the Soviet Union.[175]

The Cuban issue persisted in disturbing Uruguay's political process. On July 14, 1960, the National Executive Council had to discuss the possibility of an official complaint about the political propaganda activities of the Cuban ambassador, M. García Incháustegui; on July 28, 1960, it was told by Martínez Montero, Uruguay's foreign minister, that the pro-Western Hemisphere (that is, pro-United States) policy pursued by the government hitherto, would be maintained,[176] and a storm broke in January 1961 when Cuba's ambassador was finally declared persona non grata.[177] The decision had been taken by the Council in the absence of Haedo, who was due to take up his appointment as president on March 1, 1961, and, though having previously declared himself critical of Castro's relationship with the Soviet Union, felt that the United States was much to blame for this.[178]

The Council found itself narrowly divided on the question of a diplomatic break with Cuba: with five members voting against (but favoring some joint action against Cuba); and four (including Nardone) favoring an immediate break with both Cuba and the Soviet Union.[179] On taking office as president, Haedo intimated that he hoped a direct settlement would be achieved between Kennedy and Castro.[180]

The country's relations with the Soviet Union were complicated by the fluctuating balance of Uruguay's foreign trade, a vital factor in the general welfare of that country. In 1959 the Soviet Union was rapidly becoming the paramount factor in Uruguay's foreign trade, buying twice as much wool as the United States and taking second place only after the United States as a source of Uruguayan imports. Soviet bloc purchases from Uruguay leapt from 19 percent of Uruguay's total exports during the first half of 1958 to 34.2 percent during the same period of 1959.[181]

The question of breaking off diplomatic relations with the Soviet Union was raised on several occasions in the National Executive Council, where Nardone led the fight in favor of a break in June 1959, but the proposal was narrowly defeated. [182] In March 1960 he returned to the attack, demanding reciprocity of diplomatic representation with the Soviet Union based on equality of size in embassy staffs. [183] After the Bay of Pigs invasion, during which Uruguay showed herself mildly sympathetic towards Kennedy, the Council, angered by a note from the new Soviet ambassador, Striganov, asking for Uruguay's backing in the United Nations to end the invasion, delivered a cold reply. [184] However, relations with the Soviet Union were maintained.

The Cuban crisis had similarly adverse effects on the political system of Ecuador, where it raised in particularly acute form the unresolved problem of precedence as between the inter-American and nationalist conceptions of foreign policy. Three dramatis personae deserve to be mentioned: (a) Jóse María Velasco Ibarra, five times president (1934-1935, 1944-1947, 1952-1956, 1960-1961, and 1968-1972), brilliant demagogue and nationalist with populist leanings in the Peronista manner, his style more vigorous than his policies, but always a potent force on the Ecuadorian political scene; [185] (b) Araújo Hidalgo, an extreme nationalist and former Axis supporter turned Castroite, who tried unsuccessfully to operate within the Velasquista camp; and (c) the two moderately conservative ex-presidents, Camilo Ponce Enríquez (1956-1960), and Galo Plaza Lasso (1948-1952). Araújo Hidalgo favored the nationalist conception of foreign policy according priority to the Marañon dispute with Peru. [186] But while the latter was clearly swayed by ideological considerations in the matter of Cuba, Velasco Ibarra—who assumed the presidency on September 1, 1960—regarded the intrusion of the Cuban crisis merely as a welcome opportunity for once more pressing for the revision of the Rio Award of 1942, by which Peru had acquired the Marañon territory. Ponce Enríquez and Gala Plazo, on the other hand, were primarily inter-Americanist in outlook.

The opening shot was fired in August 1960 when Congress criticized C. Tobar Zalumbide, the foreign minister who had just resigned, for having placed hemisphere interests above national ones. [187] One day after his accession to the presidency, Velasco Ibarra announced that Ecuador no longer considered herself bound by the Rio Award, [188] and the new foreign minister, J. R. Chiriboga Villagómez, speaking from the floor of the General Assembly of the United Nations in September 1960, accused Peru of aggression. [189] In December 1960 E. Santos Campuzano, undersecretary of foreign affairs, hinted that Ecuador might take the dispute to the United Nations, and not, as would habitually have been the case, to the OAS.[190] It was in this atmosphere that Sergio Quirola, minister of education in Velasco Ibarra's new administration, travelled to Czechoslovakia in October 1960,[191] and that rumors began to circulate of an early establishment of diplomatic relations between Ecuador and the Soviet Union.[192] In mid-December the new Ecuadorian administration received a warning from the United States not to carry its differences with Peru to extremes.[193] By way of retaliation, Velasco Ibarra and Araújo Hidalgo went out of their way to praise Khrushchev's statesmanship and the wisdom contained in the latest Soviet proposals for disarmament.[194] On this occasion Araújo Hidalgo—who was minister of the interior—exclaimed ominously, "If Soviet arms are needed to defend our country, let them come!" and added, "If we need the devil, we shall seek the devil's aid and receive it."[195]

It was clear that in the government of President Velasco Ibarra there was no room for both moderate and extreme policies over Peru and Cuba. On December 17, 1960, finally, Velasco Ibarra relieved Araújo Hidalgo of his government post.[196] On December 23, 1960, he announced that Ecuador was in no danger of falling under Communist domination,[197] and in January 1961 he declared categorically that "we must defend Western liberties."[198]

However, the relentlessly developing Cuban crisis would not allow much diplomatic respite for Ecuador, and Velasco Ibarra sought refuge from it in an attitude of neutrality. In March 1961 he appointed a new ambassador to Cuba, began trade talks with Czechoslovakia, and met the Soviet ambassador in Mexico, Kosylkin,[199] thus giving new current to the belief that the establishment of diplomatic relations with the Soviet Union was imminent.

The peak of the crisis was reached in the aftermath of the Bay of Pigs episode, when Velasco Ibarra sent a telegram of encouragement to Dr. Castro, and Ecuador's ambassador to the OAS, G. Escundero, opposed a request for clemency towards the prisoners taken by the Castro government in the course of the invasion. At first Velasco Ibarra tried to maintain the diplomatic balance by refraining from open attacks on the United States,[200] but on May 9, 1961, he felt the need to condemn the invasion and proclaim Ecuador's independent line over Cuba.[201]

This, however, made matters worse. On May 12, 1961, his foreign minister, Chiriboga Villagómez, who favored sanctions against Cuba, resigned,[202] challenging the president to choose between East and West. Velasco Ibarra remained firm and accepted the resignation. On June 7, 1961, he declared in a speech, "I will not accept aggression against any Latin American country."[203] When Vice-President Carlos Arosemena returned from a visit to the Soviet Union in the summer of 1961, he was greeted by the masses with shouts of "Cuba sí! Yanqui no!"[204]

It was at this point that the president was overthrown, a victim of the Cold War in Latin America.[205] Characteristically, preparing the ground for a return in more favorable circumstances, the ex-president blamed the Communists for his downfall.[206]

In Venezuela, political tragedy followed in the wake of political drama. Unable to support the government's strongly anti-Cuban foreign policies, the URD had left the government, and a dangerous bipolarization of political forces was beginning to develop at home. In February 1961 Betancourt had to suspend certain constitutional guarantees.[207] Further confusion was added by the invasion of the Bay of Pigs in April, when Falcón Briceño supported the United States in the United Nations, antagonizing the URD even further. In the Chamber of Deputies, Villalba criticized the United States for having acted without consulting the OAS.[208] In July 1961, T. Petkov, a Communist member of parliament, was threatened with suspension of his parliamentary immunities;[209] in October 1961 COPEI was pressing for a diplomatic break with Cuba;[210] and on November 11, 1961, the formal suspension of diplomatic relations with Cuba was accomplished. Simultaneously, the first signs of armed insurrection of the Left appeared. While Betancourt, addressing the nation, promised that Venezuela would not be made a base for operations against Cuba,[211] nothing, it seemed, could now keep Venezuela away from the front line of the Cold War in Latin America.[212]

The specifically Latin American contours of Cold War were beginning to be visible. From a discussion of internal matters initially related to traditional international quarrels in the Caribbean region the crisis had unfolded until given a sharp turn by Khrushchev's "missile" threat in July 1960, which introduced entirely new strategic and psychological dimensions and gave it a pronounced character of Cold War. The San José conference in August 1960 merely served to define the issues and to set in relief the differences developing amongst the American states.

The attempted invasion of Cuba at the Bay of Pigs in April 1961 represented the first major operational move in the Cold War in Latin

America since the invasion of Guatemala in June 1954. The Cold War had invaded Latin America, and every government of the region had to come to terms with it in one way or another.

The United States followed a double-barrelled policy, trying on the one hand, ineptly, to overthrow the Castro régime in a half-hearted military adventure, while at the same time holding out the prospects of socio-economic relief in the shape of the Alliance for Progress, but the Latin American governments most inclined to subscribe to the principles of socio-economic reform were also the ones showing a growing scepticism regarding the role played by the United States in the Cold War in the Americas.

NOTES

1. As a Mexican veteran statesman put it at the time, "The Cold War has arrived in Latin America." See R. Beteta, *Entrevistas y pláticas* (Mexico City: Renovación, 1961), p. 265.

2. On this specific point, see A. Arinos de Melo Franco, *Evolução da crise brasileira* (São Paulo: Editoria Nacional, 1965), pp. 252-254.

3. See R. de Oliveira Campos, *Reflections on Latin American Development* (Austin, 1967). The chapter from which the above quotation is taken is headed "United States-Latin American Relations," and is based on a lecture delivered to a Conference on Tensions in Development in the Western Hemisphere at the University of Bahia (Brazil) in August 1963, pp. 26-27.

4. Oliveira Campos, op. cit., p. 28.

5. One of the first Brazilian statesmen to call for a world role and a turning away from diplomatic isolation was also one of Brazil's most famous statesmen. See Oswaldo Aranha, "Relações diplomáticas com a União Soviética," 1 *Revista Brasileira de Política Internacional* (1958), pp. 18-28, at p. 26.

6. Statement made in an interview kindly granted to this writer on June 22, 1971, at Buenos Aires.

7. See "Amistad argentino-uruguayo," 7 *Revista de derecho internacional y ciencias diplomáticas* (Rosario-1958), pp. 141-146.

8. See C. A. Florit, *Política Exterior Nacional* (Buenos Aires: Arayu, 1960), pp. 42-44 and p. 50.

9. This information was kindly supplied to the writer in an interview granted in Buenos Aires on June 10, 1971, by Carlos M. Mûniz, Argentine ambassador to Brazil in 1961.

10. Information kindly supplied by Oscar Camilión in an interview granted to this writer on June 16, 1971, in Buenos Aires. Camilión was, alongside Florit, junior foreign minister under Frondizi and actively engaged in giving practical shape to the latter's policies.

11. Ibid.

12. For United States duplicity towards Frondizi, see a well-substantiated article by M. Angel Scenna, "Frondizi y el caso de las cartas cubanas," 4 *Todo es Historia* (Buenos Aires), April 1971, pp. 8-37.

13. See H. Jaguaribe, *O nacionalismo na atualidade brasileira* (Rio de Janeiro, 1958). An extreme exponent of neutralism, Jaguaribe, one of Brazil's ablest political scientists, proposed a military alliance between the two countries based on nuclear armaments as a starting point of an all-Latin American neutralism.

14. See A. Conil Paz and G. Ferrari, op. cit., pp. 198-199.

15. An attack on her by *Hoy,* the Cuban Communist daily, provoked a severely critical article published in the Belgrade periodical *Kommunist,* the first time a Yugoslav paper had attacked a Cuban organ in this way. See *New York Times,* January 19, 1961.

16. See *The Times,* March 2, 1961.

17. On April 8, 1961, Castro sent a personal appeal to President Quadros of Brazil to support an Indonesian proposal to bring the dispute between Cuba and the United States before the Security Council of the United Nations. See *O Estado de S. Paulo,* April 9, 1961.

18. Carlos Olivares, Cuba's acting foreign minister, headed a mission to these three countries, but the only result of it was that President Quadros of Brazil agreed to set up a group of experts to inquire into the possibility of promoting economic relations between the two countries. See 14 H.A.R., May 1961, p. 409; and ibid., June 1961, p. 500.

19. Ibid., August 1961, p. 748.

20. *Hindu,* July 8, 1961.

21. Ibid., July 31, 1961.

22. *Observer,* August 6, 1961.

23. *New York Times,* September 3, 1961.

24. To emphasize Cuba's radicalism in foreign policy, Dorticós proceeded from Belgrade direct to Moscow. See Suárez, op. cit., p. 134. For the documents of the Conference of Non-Aligned Countries, Belgrade, September 2-6, 1961, see Royal Institute of International Affairs, *Documents on International Affairs 1961* (London, 1965), pp. 604-632.

25. L. A. Free, *Some International Implications of the Political Psychology of Brazilians* (Princeton, N.J.: Institute for International Social Research, 1961). Only one in five Brazilian congressmen mentioned the United States in answer to a question asking for the identification of the country with which Brazil should maintain specially close relations.

In answer to the question whether Brazil should follow the diplomatic path of the United States in world affairs, 28 percent of all congressmen and 19 percent of the urban public expressed themselves in the positive, while 50 percent of all congressmen and 29 percent of the urban public expressed themselves in the negative (p. 10). 63 percent of all congressmen thought Brazil should be as neutral as possible in the Cold War, as against 35 percent who thought she should not (p. 11). 30 percent of all congressmen thought that in the present world situation Brazil should take the side of the United States, against 42 percent who thought she should be neutral between

the two superpowers. No congressmen wished to take sides with the Soviet Union (p. 15). See also pp. 16-17.
Even more interesting are the findings resulting from a breakdown of the last answers according to political party (p. 17).

	P.T.B.[a]	P.S.D.[b]	U.D.N.[c]	Others
For the United States	19%	46%	50%	38%
For neutrality	46%	36%	45%	43%

a. Partido Trabalhista Brasileiro, Vice-President Goulart's party.

b. Partido Social Democrático, ex-President Kubitschek's party. (It is not in any way connected with any left-wing type of Social Democratic party anywhere.)

c. União Democrática Nacional. The general public's reaction was not very different.
30 percent of the urban, and 23 percent of the rural sample expressed a preference for the United States; 2 percent in each category for the Soviet Union, while 36 percent of the former and 16 percent of the latter wanted neutrality (p. 18).

But, according to the author, of those urban dwellers who did think Brazil should side with the United States, only one-third went so far as to feel that this siding with the United States should involve Brazil following the leadership and orientation of the United States in world affairs (p. 18).

In answer to a question whether Brazil should have close, less close, or unchanged relations with the Soviet Union, the urban sample showed 15 percent in favor of close, 18 percent in favor of less close, and 23 percent in favor of unchanged relations. The rural sample yielded 7 percent in favor of closer, 17 percent in favor of less, and 11 percent in favor of unchanged relations (p. 19).

Most surprising of all was the very high percentage of congressmen—74 percent, as against only 15 percent—who favored the establishment of regular diplomatic relations with the Communist government of China (p. 22). Almost equally surprising, by way of contrast, was the relatively high percentage of congressmen—50 percent against 12 percent—who favored a request to the United States for more loans and grants (p. 26).

26. T. E. Skidmore, *Politics in Brazil, 1930-1964* (New York: Oxford University Press, 1967), pp. 194-195.

27. *Financial Times,* March 16, 1961. See also *Relatório do Ministério das Relações Exteriores* (Brasilia, 1961), pp. 5-6.

28. 14 H.A.R., April 1961, p. 365.

29. 12 H.A.R., June 1959, p. 351.

30. Skidmore, op. cit., p. 191.

31. V. Reisky de Dubnic, "Brasiliens neue Aussenpolitik. Von der Blockfreiheit zur Solidarität mit dem Westen," 20 *Europa-Archiv,* February 10, 1965, pp. 91-100.

32. 13 H.A.R., November 1960, p. 836.

33. Ibid., p. 837.

34. 14 H.A.R., July 1961, p. 650.

35. Witness Jaguaribe's acute comment on the lack of feasibility of a neutralism confined to Latin America: "An isolated Brazilian neutralism within Latin America, without support from Europe, Japan and the Afro-Asian and Arab blocs, and

unassisted by the countries of the Socialist camp is one thing; a Brazilian neutralism enjoying the support of those forces is quite another matter." Op. cit., p. 270.

36. In his article in 40 *Foreign Affairs* on "Brazil's New Foreign Policy," published in October 1961 but written before his resignation on August 25, 1961, Quadros remarked that "colonialism . . . will from now on meet with the determined opposition of Brazil," (p. 24).

This article is largely based on Quadros' Message to Congress of March 15, 1961, excerpts of which regarding foreign policy are to be found in 4 *Revista Brasileira de Política Internacional,* June 1961, pp. 125-133. For the full message, see J. Quadros, *Mensagem ao Congresso Nacional* (Brasilia, 1961).

37. *The Times,* February 9, 1961.

38. *Le Monde,* April 14, 1961. Quadros is also reported to have remarked, "As to Africa, we may say that today it represents a new dimension in Brazilian policy." Quoted in I. L. Horowitz, *Revolution in Brazil* (New York: Dutton, 1964), pp. 79-80. Unfortunately Horowitz omits to give the date of the remark. In his Message to Congress of March 15, 1961, Quadros announced that he had instructed his foreign minister to establish a special commission for the study of Brazil's relations with Africa. See Quadros, *Mensagem ao Congresso Nacional,* p. 97.

39. For an overall treatment see M. Y. Leite Linhares, "Brazilian Foreign Policy and Africa," 18 *The World Today* (1962), pp. 532-540; and, in a somewhat partisan manner, J. Honório Rodrígues, *Brazil and Africa* (London, 1966).

It is worth noting, however, that though Brazil was the author of a proposal to create the United Nations Economic Commission for Africa, both H. Láfer and W. Moreira Sales, foreign minister and ambassador to the United States, respectively, under President Kubitschek, protested against United States grants to Africa. See D. de Carvalho, *Atlas de Relações Internacionais* (Rio de Janeiro, 1961), p. 156.

40. A. J. B. de Menezes, *O Brasil e o mundo ásio-africano* (Rio de Janeiro, 1956).

41. *Tribuna da Imprensa,* March 16, 1962. See also E. Fischlowitz, "Subsidios para a 'doutrina africana' do Brasil," 3 *Revista Brasileira de Política Internacional,* March 1960, pp. 82-95; and G. Freyre, *Uma política transnacional de cultura para o Brasil de hoje* (Belo Horizonte, 1960).

42. J. Quadros, "Brazil's New Foreign Policy," 40 *Foreign Affairs* (1961), p. 24. It must be noted, however, that Quadros was not intent on associating himself with Portuguese colonial policies, and in February 1961 he granted asylum to Captain Galvão, who had kidnapped the Portuguese ship *Santa Maria.* See *Christian Science Monitor,* February 4, 1961. He opened an embassy in Accra in March and announced that his foreign minister, Arinos de Melo Franco, would pay a visit to Senegal. See *New York Times,* March 22, 1961.

43. It is interesting to note that Jaguaribe had stated categorically in 1958 that "'a 'Sovietophil' neutralism could not survive in Latin America." See H. Jaguaribe, op. cit., p. 285.

44. Quadros, op. cit., p. 25.

45. *Daily Telegraph,* February 16, 1961, and *New York Times,* February 3, 1961, respectively. According to the journalist Carlos Castelo Branco, a close collaborator of Quadros at the time, the president gave instructions to his negotiators to show great caution in the manner in which relations with those countries were to be

reestablished. Personal interview with C. Castelo Branco kindly granted in Brasilia on May 3, 1971. Quadros finally announced his intention to resume diplomatic relations with the Soviet Union on July 25, 1961. See *Jornal do Brasil*, July 26, 1961, and also received a Soviet mission of goodwill, see *Relatório do Ministério das Relaçóes Exteriores, 1961* (Brasilia, 1962), pp. 53-54.

46. *New York Times,* February 5, 1961.

47. Ibid., February 26, 1961. J. Moors Cabot, United States ambassador to Brazil, had warned as early as October 1960 that there was a "tendency among some nations" to favor United Nations membership of Communist China. See 13 H.A.R., October 1960, p. 752.

48. Gilberto Freyre, the noted writer, remarks in his book, *New World in the Tropics: the Culture of Modern Brazil* (New York: Knopf, 1959), that "most Brazilians—even some of those who are known as sincere friends of the United States—think that their country has been, or is being, used by the United States for its narrowly national purposes without reciprocity or any special consideration for what has been Brazil's traditional policy of cooperation with the United States. Some Brazilians have even reached the conclusion that Argentina has been wiser in its policy in regard to the United States; a policy of roughness, arrogance, brutal 'realism.' They think that this policy seems to be more fruitful than the Brazilian one" (p. 321).

49. On that occasion Quadros also attacked Douglas Dillon, the United States Secretary of the Treasury, who had pressed him to adopt a pro-United States foreign policy in return for United States economic aid, and H. Dittmann, West Germany's ambassador. Telecast of March 14, 1962, reprinted in *Tribuna da Imprensa,* March 16, 1962.

50. *New York Times,* February 5, 1961.

51. *New York Times,* February 7, 1961. Ernani do Amaral Peixoto, chairman of the *getulista* Social Democratic party, defended Quadros' treatment of Berle, reminding Brazilians that the latter had been ambassador in Rio in 1945 when Vargas was overthrown. Peixoto's defense of Quadros is one more piece of evidence of the popularity which his foreign policy enjoyed in the PTB. See 14 H.A.R., March 1961, p. 262. See also J. Hickey, "The Day Mr. Berle Talked with Mr. Quadros," 15 *Inter-American Economic Affairs* (1961), pp. 58-71.

52. Jaguaribe, on the other hand, had advocated a relationship with the United States somewhat akin to that existing between members of the British Commonwealth. He wanted to see a "discreet" and "practical" neutralism which would not unnecessarily provoke the United States. See H. Jaguaribe, op. cit., pp. 285-287.

53. *New York Times,* February 5, 1961.

54. *Le Monde,* June 1, 1961.

55. *The Times,* August 11, 1961.

56. *O Estado de S. Paulo,* July 25, 1961. The invitation was tendered by M. Georgadze, head of a Soviet goodwill mission to Brazil on July 18, 1961, who brought personal greetings from Mr. Khrushchev. The true purpose of the visit appears to have been the establishment of diplomatic relations. For further details, see 14 H.A.R., July 1961, p. 652. For Khrushchev's and Brezhnev's "Messages to President J. Quadros of Brazil," see *Pravda,* August 26, 1961.

Carlos Luíz Prestes, Brazil's Communist leader, sent a letter to Quadros supporting his foreign policy. This letter was published in *A Gazeta* on August 4, 1961. See J. W. F. Dulles, *Unrest in Brazil* (Austin: University of Texas Press, 1970), p. 121. Ironically, in view of developments in Brazil after April 1964, Quadros' policy was also fully supported by the Governor of Minas Gerais, J. Magalhães Pinto. See ibid.

57. For the broad range of persons decorated in this manner, see, for instance, *Relatório do Ministério das Relações Exteriores* (Rio de Janeiro, 1949), pp. 115-123.

58. *Le Monde*, August 22, 1961. C. Mariani, Brazil's minister of finance, had backed Guevara several times during the Punta del Este Conference. See 14 H.A.R., August 1961, p. 753.

59. Castilho Cabral, op. cit., p. 183. For a full account of the visit, see pp. 183-192.

60. 13 H.A.R., August 1960, p. 563.

61. *New York Times*, April 15, 1961.

62. *Tribuna da Imprensa*, March 16, 1962. Quadros is quoted as saying (no date supplied), "In defending with intransigence the sovereignty of Cuba against interpretations of a historical fact which cannot be controlled *a posteriori*, we believe we are helping to awaken the continent to a true awareness of its responsibilities. We stand by our position on Cuba, with all its implications." Quoted in I. L. Horowitz, op. cit., pp. 179-180.

63. Cabral, op. cit., p. 291.

64. Foreign Minister Afonso Arinos de Melo Franco stated early in February 1961 that the importance of the Cuban problem in Brazil's foreign policy could be seen from the appointment of Vasco Leitão da Cunha, Brazil's ambassador in Havana, to the post of secretary-general of the Itamaratí. See *New York Times*, February 7, 1961. However, on May 6, 1961, the foreign minister intimated—somewhat rashly, as the future was to show—that in the event of Cuba turning herself into a "Popular Socialist Republic," Brazil's relations with her would undergo profound changes, as this would infringe the principles underlying the OAS. See *O Estado de S. Paulo*, May 7, 1961.

On July 6, 1961, J. Moors Cabot, the United States ambassador, stated flatly during a press conference that "the United States considers Brazil a committed nation." See ibid., July 7, 1961.

65. Cabral, op. cit., p. 291.

66. *O Estado de S. Paulo*, April 15, 1961.

67. Ibid., May 7, 1961.

68. Ibid., May 18, 1961.

69. On that occasion Brazil adopted a strictly legal position according to which it was the Council of the OAS which was the proper place for deciding this issue. See Pan American Union, *Annual Report of the Secretary General to the Council of the Organization* (Washington, D.C., 1961), p. 12.

70. *O Estado de S. Paulo*, April 25, 1961.

71. *New York Times*, May 11, 1961.

72. On the Uruguaiana meeting with Frondizi, see A. Frondizi, *La política exterior argentina* (Buenos Aires, 1963), pp. 200-202. On July 4, 1961, de Melo Franco and E. Ortúzar, Chile's foreign minister, declared their intention of coordinating their foreign policies in respect of Cuba. See 14 H.A.R., July 1961, p. 623.

73. *Le Monde*, August 25, 1961. According to Cabral, op. cit., p. 246, news was

received on the night of August 24, 1961, according to which on the following day—which was "Dia do soldado"—there was to be an announcement "on international policy."

74. Ibid., June 27, 1961.

75. That foreign policy was not the only reason for Quadros' resignation was attested by Piccioli, op. cit.; and J. W. F. Dulles, *Unrest in Brazil* (Austin, 1970), pp. 127-136.

76. *New York Times,* May 17, 1961.

77. Cabral, op. cit., p. 305.

78. I. A. C. Piccioli, *As pressões na renúncia de Jânio* (Rio de Janeiro, 1962), identifies no fewer than thirteen kinds of pressures on the president to resign. See also H. Jaguaribe, "A renúncia do Presidente Quadros e a crise política brasileira," 1 *Revista Brasileira de Ciências Sociais* (1961), pp. 272-311.

79. See Arturo Frondizi, *El Tratado de Rio de Janeiro de 1947, Recopilación de antecedentes. Posición internacional de la Unión Cívica Radical* (Buenos Aires: Unión Cívica Radical, 1950).

80. *The Times,* February 3, 1959.

81. Address to the National War School. See *Christian Science Monitor,* November 14, 1959.

82. Dardo Cúneo, *Las nuevas fronteras* (Buenos Aires: Siglo Veinte, 1964), p. 168. It was characteristic of Frondizi's way of thinking that during that meeting he should have administered a mild rebuke to President Kennedy for having gone to Vienna to meet Khrushchev without previously consulting the leading statesmen of Latin America. See Cúneo, op. cit., p. 168.

83. A. Conil Paz and G. Ferrari, op. cit., p. 195, claim such an influence for Frigerio. A developmentalist, they maintain, Frigerio's thesis in his book, *Cuba o Argentina, Dos alternativas para un problem comun: el subdesarrollo* (Buenos Aires, 1961), was that economic aid from abroad was welcome from whatever quarter it came.

84. Cúneo, op. cit., p. 168.

85. See his book, *Petróleo y política* (Buenos Aires: Transición, 1954), which carried the significant subtitle, *Contribucion al estudio de la historia económica argentina y de las relaciones entre el imperialismo y la vida política nacional.*

86. *Christian Science Monitor,* April 12, 1961. For the domestic económic background, see C. Zuvekas, "Argentine Economic Policy, 1958-1962: The Frondizi Government's Development Plan," 22 *Inter-American Economic Affairs* (1968), pp. 45-74.

87. Cúneo, op. cit., p. 213.

88. Arturo Frondizi, *Política económica nacional* (Buenos Aires: Arayu, 1963), p. 211.

89. It is curious that Quadros should not have attempted a West European orientation in his foreign policy also, especially as L. A. Free, op. cit., p. 10, provides evidence according to which 19 percent of all Brazilian congressmen would have preferred such a connection as against 22 percent who would have liked a closer connection with the United States.

90. *New York Times,* December 16, 1961. Addressing the General Assembly of the United Nations in 1959, Argentine Foreign Minister Taboada expressly dis-

claimed a policy of neutralism and reaffirmed his solidarity with "the West." See Conil Paz and Ferrari, op. cit., p. 185. In a personal interview kindly granted to this writer in Buenos Aires on June 22, 1971, ex-President Frondizi maintained that he had succeeded in persuading Quadros of the ineffectualness of the latter's conception of universal neutralism and the need for Argentina and Brazil to pull together in the task of economic development. According to Ambassador Carlos M. Muñiz, Frondizi told Quadros at Uruguaiana: "We have to be friends with our friends and when we need help we ought to get it from our friends." (Interview kindly granted in Buenos Aires on June 10, 1971).

91. This was a $100 million credit for developing the Argentinian oil industry. For details, see United States State Department, *Events in United States-Latin American Relations 1957-1963* (Washington, D.C., 1963), pp. 751, 756, 765, and 766. See also Allen, op. cit., p. 30.

92. *New York Times,* January 24, 1959.

93. *Neue Zürcher Zeitung,* March 10, 1961; and Conil Paz and Ferrari, op. cit., pp. 197-198.

94. *New York Times,* March 7, 1961. Adolph Berle, one of Kennedy's roving ambassadors in Latin America at that critical period, is quoted by this paper as saying that "it would not be feasible to think of mediation by any Hemisphere country."

95. *Christian Science Monitor,* March 14, 1961.

96. *New York Times,* May 21, 1961.

97. *Neue Zürcher Zeitung,* March 23, 1961.

98. On both these points, see 14 H.A.R., May 1961, p. 446.

99. *Neue Zürcher Zeitung,* May 2, 1961.

100. A Treaty of Friendship and Consultation was signed on April 21, 1961, in which the high contracting parties bound themselves to carry out "permanent consultations on all matters of common interest and to coordinate their activities in the continental and world-wide sphere" (Art. 1), and "for some purposes" to "maintain an exchange of information on all the questions of a relevant character in the international sphere" (Art. 2). For full details see Conil Paz and Ferrari, op. cit., p. 201 et seq. Because of Quadros' resignation in August 1961 the instrument was never ratified, but on November 24, 1961, an exchange of notes between the Argentinian and Brazilian governments expressed the intention to execute the agreement. On November 28, 1961, the form in which consultation and exchange of information was to be performed was also agreed upon. See ibid.

101. As Quadros affirmed at the opening of an Argentine art exhibition in Rio de Janeiro in the presence of Adolfo Múgica, Argentina's foreign minister, the old rivalry between the two countries was dead. See *Le Monde,* July 12, 1961. On the eve of the Punta del Este Conference, at which the proposed Alliance for Progress was under discussion, Múgica went so far as to maintain that the two countries would "act as a single country." See Conil Paz and Ferrari, op. cit., p. 206.

102. *The Unión Cívica Radical del Pueblo,* for instance, exhibited a number of neutralist reactions among its members, varying from the advocacy of an "impartial third position," condemning intervention from whatever quarter it came, to a "historical third position," regretting Cuba's trend towards communism while blaming the United States for it; to a "silent third position," isolationist and quietest in nature; to a "gentlemanly third position," which accepted Castro's victory but

requested clemency for the vanquished. See *La Nación,* cited in 14 H.A.R. (1961), p. 358.

103. *Neue Zürcher Zeitung,* August 23, 1961.

104. The Mexican newspaper *El Excelsior* explains the term *planteo* as follows: "It is a military movement in which there are no shots, but which serves the military to impose conditions on the government concerning matters of State." For an analysis of the quasi-political role of the military in Argentina, see E. Lieuwen, *Generals versus Presidents* (London, 1965), pp. 13-14.

105. *Neue Zürcher Zeitung,* August 23 and September 22, 1961.

106. *Le Monde,* August 30, 1961.

107. Conil Paz and Ferrari, op. cit., pp. 207-208. On August 21, 1961, Frondizi assumed full responsibility for the meeting with Guevara in a broadcast to the nation in which he claimed that he had given a full account of that meeting to the minister of defense, the secretaries and under-secretaries of the armed forces, the commander-in-chief and chiefs-of-staff of the three armed forces. See *La Nación,* August 22, 1961.

108. *The Times,* August 30, 1961.

109. See B. Cosío Villegas, *Change in Latin America: The Mexican and Cuban Revolutions* (Lincoln: University of Nebraska Press, 1961), which accurately reflects the views of the López Mateos wing of the PRI in this respect.

110. 11 H.A.R., January 1958, pp. 10-11. At the Bogotá conference of 1948 Mexico had supported a motion by Cuba to include the right of revolution as an attribute of popular sovereignty within the inter-American system. When put to the vote, this motion failed by one vote only. See A. K. Smith, *Mexico and the Cuban Revolution: Foreign policy-making in Mexico under President López Mateos 1958-1964* (Ithaca, N.Y.: Cornell University, 1970), pp. 6-7.

111. *Presencia Internacional de Adolfo López Mateos* (Mexico City, 1963), p. 99.

112. Ibid., p. 111.

113. During the first world war, Carranza, whose sympathies with imperial Germany were well-known, never accepted a German offer of support against the United States. The logistical opportunities for aiding Mexico were minimal. The position in the 1960s was very different in this respect.

114. Mecham, op. cit., p. 186.

115. R. García Treviño, *La ingerencia rusa en México y Sudamérica* (Mexico City, América, 1959), pp. 195-201.

116. 11 H.A.R., November 1958, p. 598.

117. Ibid., vol. 12, October 1959, p. 532.

118. See A. K. Smith, op. cit., p. 56.

119. Cárdenas received infrastructural support within the left wing of the PRI from the *Círculo de Estudios Mexicanos,* a group of left-inclined intellectuals. This was countered on the right wing of the PRI by the *Frente Cívico Mexicano de Afirmación Revolucionaria,* led by M. Alemán and A. L. Rodríguez, two former presidents. See Olga Pellicer de Brody, *México y la Revolución Cubana* (Mexico City, 1971).

120. H. F. Cline, *Mexico. From Revolution to Evolution, 1940-1960* (London, 1963), p. 328. When the Communist painter Alfaro Siqueiros, returning from a visit to Cuba in January 1960, declared that the Cuban Revolution had left the Mexican Revolution far behind, López Mateos commented typically that, while Siqueiros

represented in a certain way the pictorial desires of the Mexican people, he did not represent them ideologically. See *Tiempo,* February 1, 1960.

121. *New York Times,* March 6, 7, and 9, 1961. From this meeting there was to emerge a fully fledged, though, as the future would show, not very successful *fidelista* organization, the *Movimiento de Liberación Nacional* (MLN). However, the possibility of *guerrilla* tactics was never even discussed within that movement.

122. Cárdenas' comment was reported in the *New York Times,* March 12, 1961.

123. See Cline, op. cit., pp. 324-325.

124. 12 H.A.R., August 1960, p. 509.

125. See Olga Pellicer de Brody, op. cit.

126. *New York Times,* May 31, 1961.

127. On the history of this championship, see F. Cuevas Cancino, "The Foreign Policy of Mexico," J. E. Black and K. W. Thompson (eds.), *Foreign Policies in a World of Change* (New York, 1963), pp. 643-673.

128. See H. F. Cline, op. cit., p. 314.

129. *El Universal,* September 2, 1960. A great influence on López Mateos had been his intellectual mentor in matters of foreign policy, Isídro Fabela. The latter engaged in a polemical exchange of letters with R. C. Hill, the United States ambassador, in which he defended the Cuban Revolution. See I. Fabela, *El Caso de Cuba* (Mexico City: Cuadernos Americanos, 1960).

130. N. Rivero, *Castro's Cuba. An American Dilemma* (Washington, D.C.: Luce, 1962), p. 130.

131. Partido Revolucionario Institucional, *The Voice of Mexico in the United States and Canada. Speeches by Adolfo López Mateos.* (Mexico City, 1959), pp. 77-78.

132. 3 H.A.R., February 1960, pp. 84-85.

133. See Cline, op. cit., p. 327.

134. *New York Times,* January 22, 1961.

135. 13 H.A.R., December 1960, p. 27.

136. Castro's claim that Mexico's farmers were ready to go to the mountains and take up arms in defense of the Cuban Revolution caused some resentment. See 14 H.A.R., March 1961, p. 199. Because Cuba's embassy in Mexico City had become very active since July 1960, López Mateos assigned special officials to check on fingerprints and photos of all Cubans arriving in Mexico. See ibid., vol. 13, November 1960, p. 772.

137. In March 1961 López Mateos told a French newspaper correspondent that Mexico had "the worst impression" of Cuba's political régime. See *Le Figaro,* March 30, 1961, as cited by A. K. Smith, op. cit., p. 92.

138. *New York Times,* April 13, 1961. On the speech by L. Padilla Nervo, Mexican representative in the United Nations, asserting the competence of the United Nations "to know of a complaint or a situation between States who both belong at the same time to a regional organism," see 7 *Revista de Ciencias Políticas y Sociales,* April/June 1961, pp. 265-276. For an analysis of Mexico's policy in the OAS, see Olga Pellicer de Brody, "México en la OEA," 6 *Foro Internacional,* October/ December 1965 and January/March 1966, pp. 288-302.

139. United Nations General Assembly, O.R., 15th Session, First Committee, 1154th Meeting, April 18, 1961, Doc. A/C. 1/L275.

140. United Nations General Assembly, O.R., 15th Session, First Committee,

1149th Meeting through the 1161st Meeting, April 15-21, pp. 55-112; ibid., 995th Plenary Meeting, April 21st, 1961; Report of the First Committee (A/4744), p. 489.

141. On this point, see the learned article by J. Castañeda, "Conflictos de competencia entre las Naciones Unídas y la Organización de Estados Americanos," 6 *Foro Internacional,* October/December 1965 and January/March 1966, pp. 303-322.

142. *El Universal,* April 18, 1961.

143. *New York Times,* April 21, 1961.

144. *El Excelsior,* April 18, 1961. For Cárdenas' appeal to the world, see *Playa Giron. Derrota del imperialismo,* Vol. 3 (Havana, 1962), pp. 333-336. According to one report, confidential orders had been given to airport officials to prevent Cárdenas from taking off. See *New York Times,* April 19, 1961.

145. *El Nacional,* May 5th, 1961.

146. *New York Times,* July 23, 1961.

147. Secretaría de Gobernación, *Capitulos sobre política extranjera y Mensaje . . . del Presidente Adolfo López Mateos al Honorable Congreso de la República de México, 1 de Septiembre 1961* (Mexico City, 1961), p. 7.

148. The leading "Titoist" was the radical Socialist, Oscar Waiss. See his *Amanecer en Belgrado* (Santiago: Prensa Latinoamericana, 1956).

149. E. Halperin, *Nationalism and Communism in Chile* (Cambridge, Mass: MIT Press, 1965), pp. 70 and 136-137.

150. See S. Allende, *Cuba, un camino* (Santiago, 1960).

151. 13 H.A.R., January 1961, p. 66.

152. Ibid.

153. See a special report by Juan de Onis to the *New York Times,* March 8, 1961.

154. 14 H.A.R., April 1961, p. 352.

155. 14 H.A.R., April 1961, p. 351. The results of a poll conducted by Professor E. Hamuy on Chilean reactions to the invasion at the Bay of Pigs were as follows: 15.6 percent of all respondents approved of the invasion, whereas 61.8 percent disapproved. See L. Gross, *The Last, Best Hope. Eduardo Frei and Chilean Democracy* (New York, 1967), p. 196.

156. See *El Mercurio,* June 8, 1961.

157. *Financial Times,* August 28, 1961.

158. *Observer,* October 1, 1961.

159. The advent of a revolutionary government in Havana produced repercussions inside Chile in the sensitive field of the production and marketing of copper on which the bulk of the country's export proceeds depended. In July 1961 E. Serrano, minister of mining, announced a new plan for the expansion of the production of copper which would not only involve increased national control, but also a more intensive search for markets everywhere, including Eastern Europe. Senator F. Bulnes, a Conservative, suggested that the United States-sponsored Alliance for Progress, if adopted at the forthcoming Conference of Punta del Este, should lend Chile the money that would be required for the expropriation of the big copper companies. See *New York Times,* July 22, 1961.

The Socialist Party was emboldened to present a bill for the nationalization of the Kennecott and Anaconda copper mines, which provided for some compensation to be paid out of the profits of their operation by the state. See *Financial Times,* August

11, 1961. The government eventually decided on the transformation of the foreign copper enterprises into Chilean firms, whose sales policy was to be determined by the Chilean Department of Copper. For details, see *Neue Zürcher Zeitung*, September 20, 1961.

As if to add fuel to the flames of the internal controversy over copper, a proposal was made by the Soviet government in October, 1961, for a long-term contract for the annual purchase of 60,000 tons of Chilean copper by the Soviet Union. See *Financial Times*, October 5, 1961.

160. *New York Times*, May 6, 1958. It is ironical that the identical charge should have been preferred by President Paz Estenssoro against the United States in 1961, when President Kennedy was accused of having acted in the same irresponsible manner. For Andrade's friendly attitude towards the United States, see P. J. Alexander, *The Bolivian National Revolution* (New Brunswick, N.J.: Rutgers University Press, 1958), pp. 258-259.

161. It is noteworthy to mention that the Bolivian Communists supported both Paz Estenssoro and his predecessor, Zuazo Siles, electorally, embarrassing both by doing so. See 13 H.A.R., April 1960, p. 265.

162. Ibid., December 1960, p. 911. G. Bedregal, head of COMIBOL, the Bolivian state organization concerned with the production of the nationalized tin mines, commented bitterly during a visit to London in 1964 that, though Bolivia had sent plans, Moscow had remained silent on the offer. See *Financial Times*, June, 1964.

163. The meagre result of Paz Estenssoro's extensive trip to the Soviet Union and Eastern Europe before his election in 1960 was the opening of a legation in Prague.

164. *New York Times*, April 15, 1960.

165. Ibid., June 8, 1960.

166. 13 H.A.R., October 1960, p. 728.

167. 14 H.A.R., June 1961, p. 535-538; and ibid., July 1961, p. 636.

168. Ibid., August 1961, p. 727.

169. *Süddeutsche Zeitung*, August 7, 1960.

170. *New York Times*, January 13, 1961.

171. See P. B. Taylor, *Government and Politics in Uruguay* (New Orleans: University of Tulane Press, 1969), p. 68.

172. *Neue Zürcher Zeitung*, July 30, 1961.

173. Taylor, op. cit., p. 52.

174. Ibid., p. 50.

175. Taylor, op. cit., p. 50. For Trias' left-wing orientation, see his articles on "Imperialismo en el Uruguay," *El Sol*, January 24, 1958, and on "Marx, Lenin y la revolución latinoamericana," ibid., December 22, 1961.

176. 13 H.A.R., July 1960, p. 482.

177. República Oriental del Uruguay, *Mensaje del Poder Ejecutivo a la Asamblea General al inaugurarse el 40 período de la XXXVIII Legislativa* (1962), pp. II/4.

178. See the critical remarks made by Congressmen Michelini and Gambardella (both *batllistas*), during a debate on the subject in Congress, as reported in Cámara de Representantes, *Diario de Sesiones*, May 24, 1961, pp. 394-400.

179. *Frankfurter Allgemeine Zeitung*, February 6, 1961.

180. 14 H.A.R., March 1961, p. 258.

181. 12 H.A.R., November 1959, p. 628. For later figures, see ibid., March and

September 1963, pp. 78 and 726 respectively. It may have been in view of these developments that the Soviet Union increased its embassy staff in Montevideo considerably, thus creating a marked discrepancy in the number of employees on either side. The Soviet embassy in Montevideo employed 280; the Uruguayan embassy in Moscow only six people. See *Neue Zürcher Zeitung,* March 12, 1960.

182. Four members voted in favor, two against, with three abstentions. See 12 H.A.R., June 1959, pp. 347-348.

183. Ibid., vol. 13, March 1960, p. 207. For the details of the new régime, based on reciprocity of numbers, see República Oriental del Uruguay, *Mensaje del Poder Ejecutive a la Asamblea General al inaugurarse el 40 periodo de la XXXVIII Legislatura* (1962), pp. II/26.

184. 14 H.A.R., April 1961, p. 361.

185. For the political background to Velasco Ibarra, see C. I. Blanksten, "Ecuador. The Politics of Instability," in M. P. Needler (ed.), *Political Systems in Latin America* (London, 1964), pp. 269-288.

186. On the occasion of the nomination of Arosemena as vice-presidential candidate on May 3, 1960, for instance, Velasco Ibarra had this to say on principles of Ecuador's foreign policy: "The Ecuadorians believe in Panamericanism; we believe the United States is doing well in being part of the world balance of power . . . but it is one thing to cooperate between equals . . . but another thing to hand over one's soul." Quoted in T. Mancheno, *El Velazquismo. Una interpretación* (Quito, 1960), pp. 189-190.

187. 13 H.A.R., August 1960, p. 545.

188. *New York Times,* September 2, 1960. A meeting of the guarantors of the Rio Award, composed of the United States, Argentina, Brazil, and Chile, had rejected Ecuador's unilateral repudiation of the award.

189. See B. Wood and Minerva Morales, "Latin America and the United Nations," 19 *International Organization,* Summer 1960, p. 717.

190. 13 H.A.R., December 1960, pp. 903-905.

191. *New York Times,* October 9, 1960.

192. Originally Ecuador had announced its intention of establishing relations with the Soviet Union in April 1945. See *Daily Telegraph,* April 2, 1945. Negotiations began in December of that year but proved fruitless. See *New York Times,* December 10, 1945.

193. *New York Times,* December 14, 1960.

194. 13 H.A.R., December 1960, pp. 903-905.

195. Ibid.

196. *New York Times,* December 18, 1960.

197. Ibid., December 24, 1960.

198. 14 H.A.R., January 1961, p. 54.

199. Ibid., March 1961, p. 239.

200. Ibid., April 1961, p. 343. Ecuador's representative in the General Assembly of the United Nations explained why the problem of Cuba could not now remain within the hemisphere. See speech by B. Vinueza, as quoted verbatim in *Playa Giron, Derrota del imperialismo,* vol. 3 (Havana, 1962), pp. 154-158. This speech should be contrasted with the fairly apprehensive one made on July 19, 1960, in response to Khrushchev's rocket threat by J. Corres, Ecuador's representative on the Security

Council of the United Nations (who also happened to be president of the Security Council at that time), as reprinted in Royal Institute of International Affairs, *Documents of International Affairs 1960* (London, 1964), p. 572. The change in Ecuador's policy was remarkable.

201. *Hsinhua News Agency* (Peking), May 10, 1961.

202. *Le Monde,* May 13, 1961.

203. *Hsinhua News Agency* (Peking), June 8, 1961.

204. See Goldenberg, op. cit., p. 316.

205. Arosemena had been thrown into prison by Velasco Ibarra shortly before the latter was overthrown. For further details, see E. S. Urbanski, "Ecuador's Socioeconomic Mosaic," 46 *Current History,* January 1964, pp. 19-25.

206. *New York Times,* November 14, 1961.

207. Ibid., vol. 14, February 1961, p. 139.

208. 13 H.A.R., April 1961, p. 330. According to the official publication *Playa Giron, Derrota del imperialismo,* vol. 2 (Havana, 1962), W. Larrázabal, former provisional president of Venezuela and now ambassador in Santiago de Chile, phoned his Cuban colleague to express his solidarity (p. 80).

209. Ibid., July 1961, pp. 618-619.

210. Ibid., October 1961, p. 909.

211. Ibid., November 1961, pp. 1006-1007 and 1010-1011.

212. A full account of rising tensions inside Venezuela was provided by the president in his address to Congress in Caracas on March 12, 1962. See R. Betancourt, *Venezuela rinde cuenta* (Caracas: Imprenta Nacional, 1962), pp. 7-15.

Chapter VII

DIPLOMATIC CLIMAX:

THE CONFERENCE OF PUNTA DEL ESTE (1962)

In the autumn of 1961 Peru and Colombia, gravely disturbed by current developments in Latin America, set in motion the machinery of the OAS for convoking a meeting of OAS foreign ministers. The plan behind the Peruvian proposal of October 13, 1961, was to appoint a committee of investigation and, in the event of a positive report from it, to impose collective sanctions on Cuba under the terms of the Rio Treaty. On November 9, 1961, Colombia proposed in a similar vein that member governments of the OAS send a formal request to Havana for Cuban submission to the discipline of the inter-American system and that, in the event of its rejection, joint sanctions be imposed on the Castro régime.[1] The Colombian proposal envisaged a meeting of consultation of OAS foreign ministers on January 10, 1962, to consider "the intervention of extracontinental Powers" and, more important still, the redefinition of the principles governing the inter-American system to meet the new situation.[2]

The Peruvian proposal was proving unpopular in the rest of Latin

America, and on October 23, 1961, Argentina, Brazil, Ecuador, Mexico, and Uruguay—whose governments were showing neutralist inclinations—sponsored a proposal to delay discussions on the ground that there was a need for basic previous agreement among Latin American governments.[3] Brazil and even Venezuela disliked the idea of collective intervention, whilst Uruguay considered that the best way of countering a possible threat from Cuba was to practice the social principles laid down in the Santiago Declaration of 1959. However, the Peruvian proposal enjoyed the backing of the United States.[4]

After a heated debate in the OAS Council in Washington on December 4, 1961, the Colombian request was carried by a vote of 14 to 2, with Cuba and Mexico casting the opposing votes; but five Latin American countries—Argentina, Bolivia, Brazil, Chile, and Ecuador—abstained, as in their view the Rio Treaty was not applicable.[5]

No doubt the decision taken in the OAS Council on December 4, 1961, would have been more adverse to Colombia still, had it not been for Castro's controversial profession on December 1, 1961, of "Marxism-Leninism,"[6] which induced Uruguay to vote in favor of the Colombian proposal (instead of abstaining), and Chile to abstain (instead of opposing). It also provided the emerging group of hard liners among the Latin American governments with a much needed issue over which to fight their case. Before the OAS vote, Raúl Roa had not been altogether averse to the idea of cooperating with the Inter-American Peace Committee of the OAS in this matter,[7] but after December 4, 1961, Castro reversed this decision and barred the entry of its members into Cuba.[8]

The Punta del Este Conference

A few preliminary skirmishes at Punta del Este were followed by seven days of hectic diplomatic negotiations which finally issued on January 31, 1962, a set of provisions voted on separately as follows:[9] (a) the principles of Marxism-Leninism are incompatible with the inter-American system (Cuba opposed); (b) the principles of the Alliance for Progress are essential to the security of the hemisphere (Cuba opposed); (c) Cuba to be "excluded" from participation in the inter-American system (Cuba opposed, while Argentina, Brazil, Chile, Ecuador, and Mexico abstained); (d) Cuba to be excluded from membership of the Inter-American Defense Board (Cuba opposed); (e) all arms traffic with Cuba to be suspended and the Council of the OAS to "study" the feasibility and desirability of extending the suspension to other items (Cuba opposed, while Brazil, Chile, Ecuador, and Mexico abstained); (f) the Council of the OAS to establish a committee of five to investigate means by which help could be given to countries requesting assistance, the committee to report on May 1, 1962, (Cuba opposed, Bolivia abstained); (g) the Inter-American Commission on Human Rights to be strengthened (Cuba opposed).[10]

The attitude of the United States, after a period of initial wavering, seems to have settled down to one of solidarity with the hard liners.[11] It has been suggested that the United States might have been under strong pressure from those quarters, and the case of El Salvador, which is said to have intimated that a refusal to break with Cuba collectively could result in a military coup in San Salvador, is cited in support.[12] Some Central American governments would have liked to see the formation of a Central American-Caribbean alliance with the United States if a decision on strong collective measures against Cuba could not be obtained from the Punta del Este meeting.[13] The representative of the Dominican Republic, J. A. Bonilla Atiles, suggested slyly on January 25, 1962, that sanctions like those imposed on his country in 1960 might be adopted against Cuba,[14] whilst the president of Guatemala claims to have been instrumental in committing the United States to the camp of the hard liners.[15]

The soft liners argued that it would take at least two years to revise the charter of the OAS and would involve the cumbersome and time-consuming procedures of ratification by the Latin American legislatures.[16] On January 24, 1962, this group, composed of Argentina, Bolivia, Brazil, Chile, Ecuador, and Mexico—joined on this occasion rather uncharacteristically by Haiti—issued a memorandum which, while proclaiming the "incompatibility between the present régime in Cuba and the inter-American system," emphatically opposed the imposition of sanctions.[17] The two groups seemed hopelessly at loggerheads. On January 29, 1962, a demand for depriving Cuba of all participation in the inter-American system was made by Colombia,[18] but was adamantly opposed by Bolivia, Brazil, Ecuador, and Mexico. Argentina and Chile were working for a compromise.[19]

Although President Dorticós had attended the Belgrade Conference of Non-aligned States in August 1961, Cuba's foreign policy had come to be closely aligned with that of the Soviet Union. This may not of itself have been sufficient to cause a widening of the existing rift between Cuba and the United States had it not been for Cuban fears of another invasion expressed in October 1961 by C. Olivares, junior minister of foreign affairs, in a white paper accusing the United States of training troops for that purpose at twenty bases, both on its own territory and on that of some of the Central American States.[20]

At the eighth meeting, the Cuban attitude was defensive. Cuban representatives even entered into discussions with some Latin American diplomats for the purpose of drafting an agreement on a formula of coexistence.[21] But once excluded from the OAS, Havana reacted in two ways. In the first place, the government passed the Second Declaration of Havana on February 4, 1962, to indict those who had contrived her exclusion and to sound an ideological counterblast to the condemnation of Marxism-Leninism.[22] In the second place, it called for an advisory opinion of the International Court of Justice on the action taken against her at Punta del Este,[23] a shrewd move designed to turn the tables on those who professed to uphold the rule of law in international relations.

In spite of the shrill tone of the Second Declaration of Havana, the prospect of complete isolation in the Western Hemisphere was having some modifying effects on Cuban diplomacy. In April 1962 Carlos Rafael Rodríguez announced that Cuba would consider paying compensation for United States property nationalized by the Castro régime, provided the government of the United States bought three million tons of sugar and political differences between the two countries were settled.[24]

But on the other hand, the militant *serrano* element within the Castro régime was bidding for Soviet favor. Castro's profession of Marxism-Leninism of December 1, 1961, may be read in this context, and the Second Declaration of Havana, produced after Punta del Este and interpreted as presaging a more radical ideology condemning the "national bourgeoisie," by which Moscow was setting so much store, as incapable of discharging its historical task, the attainment of a democratic revolution.[25] The final bid for serrano supremacy was made on March 14, 1962, in an attack by Castro on Aníbal Escalante, whose early thesis of the supremacy of the PSP over the 26th June Movement has been noted. The line advocated by Blas Roca, according to which the revolution in Cuba should be allowed to run its full course under the unchallenged leadership of Castro, triumphed and was duly endorsed by Moscow in an article in *Pravda* on April 11, 1962.[26] With the radical serrano element thus riding high in Havana and with Cuba isolated in the Western Hemisphere, there was little that Moscow could do short of supporting those wielding power in Havana almost unconditionally. The PSP, and particularly Blas Roca, had no doubt been useful in persuading Moscow to back the Castro régime, but in February 1962 their immediate usefulness in Soviet-Cuban relations was at an end.

After a great deal of vacillation Uruguay turned out a moderate hard liner. This was a strange result, considering that it had been in the Uruguayan embassy in Washington that a meeting of seventeen Latin American states had taken place on October 23, 1961, on a motion proposed jointly by the governments of Argentina, Brazil, Ecuador, Mexico, and Uruguay urging that basic agreement should be reached before a meeting of foreign ministers was called.[27] When the vote was taken in the OAS Council on December 4, 1961, on the Colombian proposal for holding the conference, the conduct of Uruguay once again bore witness to the inefficiency of her general decision-making processes as, in spite of instructions received to the contrary, C. Clulow, Urugay's representative, voted in favor of the Colombian request.

This was an extraordinary action by any normal diplomatic standards.[28] Ostensibly, Uruguay's objection to the Colombian request was a purely legal one, but there were political complications. When, after Castro's profession of Marxism-Leninism of December 1, 1961, the Uruguayan ambassador to the OAS asked his government for fresh instructions, Homero Martínez Montero, the foreign minister, apparently baffled, approached President Haedo for a political ruling, and the latter decided on a tactic of abstention. There was no time to consult the National Executive Council, and consequently the ambassador found himself without instructions at the time of the vote. Using his own judgment, he voted in favor of the Colombian proposal.[29]

Eventually Haedo ruled that diplomatic sanctions only were to be called against Cuba, because (a) Marxism-Leninism was an internal affair; and (b) of the Herrerista principles of non-intervention and self-determination, but this artificial construction was too delicate to stand the hectic pace of the conference. So long as the hard liners were pressing for a break with Cuba as well as her exclusion from the OAS, Uruguay sided with the soft line group, but when the former modified their demands to exclusion only, she changed sides—though only at the very last moment[30]—to the immense embarrassment of Uruguay's spokesman at Punta del Este.[31]

Uruguay's two main political parties remained deeply divided over Cuba after the conference. C. Batlle Pacheco advocated a break with Cuba only and was joined by some *blancos,* while Nardone favored a diplomatic break with all Communist countries. A vote on the Cuban issue resulted in a majority of 5 to 4 in favor of a diplomatic break, but a reversal of the vote was brought about after the *blanco* party executive had cast its vote against a break. Diplomatic relations with Cuba were subsequently maintained, even while Batlle Pacheco and Nardone continued to agitate for a break.[32]

But even within the countries most critical of Cuba's policies, the process of policy formation proved a difficult one. In Colombia, President Lleras Camargo had pressed for the adoption of a hard line as early as July 1961, while his foreign minister, Turbay Ayala, had stated categorically that "Communism and inter-Americanism are incompatible."[33] An untoward event temporarily deflected this intransigence when Turbay Ayala was highjacked in August 1961 and taken to Havana, where he met Dr. Castro and Raúl Roa.[34] After that his attitude could never satisfy the ultra-hard liners of the Laureanista type[35] in the Colombian Senate, who ceaselessly attacked him. Eventually Turbay Ayala succumbed, and was criticized by J. J. Caicedo Castilla, his successor at the foreign ministry, for his desire to keep Cuba within the OAS. It was under Caicedo Castilla that the Colombian initiative leading to the convocation of the conference of Punta del Este was taken, and it was he who was to establish the two principal themes of the hard liners at the conference by his assertion on January 24, 1962, that "this world zone has freely and thanks to its own determination decided some time ago that it is not neutral in the Cold War,"[36] and by his claim that Cuba had disturbed the military equilibrium by its newly-found capacity to import arms and to create the strongest force in Latin America.[37]

Haiti's spectacular and probably decisive change of front in the critical closing stages of the conference has never been explained to full satisfaction, for almost up to the last minute the Haitian delegates adopted an attitude of resolute opposition to the proposed exclusion of Cuba from the OAS. On January 25, 1962, R. Chalmers, the Haitian delegate, announced defiantly that "the people of Haiti, who have maintained themselves neutral during the Caribbean imbroglio, continue to cleave to its neutrality, and will have the audacity not to renounce this vocation, and to deny support to one or the other."[38]

However, Haiti carried out a turnabout of policy.[39] According to some sources, Dean Rusk had offered Haiti substantial economic aid.[40] In Guatemala and four other Central American countries acting en bloc, there was from the beginning a determination "that a strong resolution against Cuba emanate from the . . . meeting."[41]

If the high degree if cohesion achieved by the soft line group before and during the early stages of the Punta del Este conference could have been maintained, a significant neutralist ginger group could have emerged. Such a possibility had to be taken seriously by the United States, especially as the political strictures of the group tended to be couched in terms of well-reasoned and friendly advice. Such an outcome with probably more to be feared by the United States than the open challenge by Cuba.

The Cuban Revolution opened a new and rather exciting chapter in Argentine diplomacy in 1961. On September 10, 1961, M. Angel Cárcano, a Conservative with excellent international connections, was appointed foreign minister[42] to enable the president to unfold a vigorous diplomatic activity. On January 5, 1962, Frondizi informed President Haedo of Uruguay in Montevideo that at the forthcoming meeting Argentina would adhere "to the Western and Christian philosophy proclaimed in Uruguaiana,"[43] and this ideological firmness was corroborated in a paper circulated by Argentina at the beginning of the conference, in which Cuba was condemned, *inter alia,* for suppressing representative democracy.[44]

The crucial point, however, was Argentina's stance in the matter of sanctions against Cuba. Originally opposed to the holding of the Punta del Este meeting, Frondizi was beginning to weaken during his meeting with Adlai Stevenson at Trinidad in early December 1961.[45] During the conference itself Argentina tried discreetly to prevent the imposition of sanctions against Cuba[46] by gaining time for a compromise. On the one hand, therefore, the Argentine delegation produced the concept of "incompatibility" which was to form the quasi-legal basis for the exclusion of Cuba from the OAS;[47] but on the other hand Argentina associated herself with Brazil, Mexico, Bolivia, Haiti, and Chile in calling a conference to modify the charter of the OAS so as to enable the suspension of a member state which has gone over to "the Communist camp."[48] Argentina also tried, together with the United States, to obtain a unanimous vote to consider the expulsion of the Castro government in return for the dropping of the demand for a mass rupture of relations with Cuba.[49]

The full degree to which Frondizi was forced to modify his policies in response to pressures from the military at home was only revealed after the conference.[50] Three conditions were made by the military: (a) the total revision of Argentine foreign policy in relation to Cuba; (b) the breaking of diplomatic relations with Cuba within a brief period; and (c) the resignation of M. Cárcano from the foreign ministry, as well as the removal of all members of the Argentine delegation to the Punta del Este conference.[51] To gain time, Frondizi offered to recall the Argentine ambassador from Havana as an interim solution, but this was vetoed by the chief of the Argentine air force, who insisted on a complete break of diplomatic relations.[52]

Rumors had spread, meanwhile, that the Argentine delegation at Punta del Este had been compelled to improvise a response. At this point Frondizi, now almost completely isolated, decided to reassert his authority.[53] In a speech at Parana on February 3, 1962, he emphatically denied these allegations, citing from a letter he had sent to his foreign minister for his guidance at the Punta del Este conference.[54] But military pressure intensified and diplomatic relations with Cuba had to be severed formally in February 1962. On March 30, 1962, President Frondizi himself was deposed.[55]

Under the Goulart Administration, Brazil's foreign policy was largely determined by neutralist conceptions inherited from President Quadros. However, where Quadros' neutralism had been non-ideological, Goulart's was inspired by the Populist Left, with which most of the figures in his administration were associated. Thus, F. C. San Thiago Dantas, Goulart's foreign minister during the crucial period of the Punta del Este conference, was a former *integralista* turned moderate Populist. A member of the PTB, he liked to describe himself as belonging to the "positive Left." A man of consequence and great distinction, an able politician and an outstanding academic lawyer who brought to his office a cultured intellectual style which showed itself in the clear and elegant formulation of his policies, his impact on the conduct of Brazil's diplomacy was considerable.

The guidelines of his policy were set out at a press conference on September 10, 1961. There was, he maintained, a need to "widen the circle of our relations with other countries, without ideological discrimination of any kind."[56] Consequently, as he renewed diplomatic relations with the Soviet Union in November 1961, this was justified by the need for widening Brazil's markets. He added, significantly, that in the past Brazil had been kept apart from the Soviet Union more for internal than external reasons.[57] As for the thorny issue of the recognition of Communist China, Dantas announced that this would be considered "without prejudice to the merits of the case."[58]

The crisis which led to the Punta del Este conference provided Brazil not only with a platform from which to proclaim her views, but also gave her the opportunity of taking the lead among the soft-liner group which was forming there. In November 1961 Tancredo Neves, the prime minister, defined Brazilian policy towards Cuba. Interference from the outside "by another State" in the internal affairs of Cuba, be it for internal or external reasons, was improper, and the Cuban régime should be allowed to "evolve into the fullness of democratic life."[59] On December 10, 1961, it was reported that the Itamaratí wanted the United States to issue a denial of any intention of invading Cuba in order to facilitate her reintegration within the inter-American system, and in his key speech at Punta del Este on January 24, 1962, Dantas warned that if "measures are adopted leading the country (Cuba) into an isolation without alternatives, its gratitude towards the Soviet bloc will be inevitable."[60] He urged that the door with Cuba be left open to contacts with the West, and intimated that the isolation of Cuba was not a concern of the Brazilian delegation. A legal interpretation according to which Resolution 193, adopted at the Caracas conference of 1954, had "reformed" the Rio Treaty was rejected by him as "incorrect."[61] It was inadvisable to urge Cuba to break with the Soviet bloc within a given period of time, which could only issue in the importation of "a dangerous element of radicalisation and exaltation in the internal politics of various American States."[62]

Dantas' own evolutionist philosophy was clearly implicit in his insistence that the momentary ineffectiveness of representative democracy "involves no definite incompatibility with the (inter-American) system and organism in which it expresses itself, but a deliberate and permanent acceptance of a political ideology" was incompatible.[63] He also gave clear warning against the infringement of the principle of non-intervention which had been fought for against the European powers first, and then "against the strongest nation within our own hemisphere." The implication of this bold statement could hardly be lost on the United States and the hard-line camp at Punta del Este.[64]

The full vigor of Dantas' policy is revealed by an address to the heads of missions of American states at the Itamaratí on January 12, 1962.[65] In his exposé Dantas warned that there could not at the forthcoming conference be any "interventionist or positive" solutions nor any "evasive insincere formulas." With his customary forensic skill he presented the idea of economic sanctions as both juridically objectionable and politically unwise. His basic moral proposition was contained in the assertion that Cuba had "a right to maintain this form of government and this social régime without being subjected to intervention, either unilateral or collective." Not averse to invoking pragmatic arguments in order to prove a moral proposition, Dantas cast doubt on the idea of economic sanctions on grounds of effectiveness, since, he claimed, Cuba's trade with Latin America never exceeded on average 4.5 percent of her exports and 9 percent of her imports.[66] He was careful not to mention the corresponding figures of trade between Cuba and the United States, which may not have supported his thesis.

The most controversial statement made by Dantas during the Punta del Este conference concerned his proposal for the creation of a special political and legal status for Cuba within the inter-American system. Proceeding from the assumption that a peaceful solution must be both "historically valid" and "politically effective,"[67] a proposition which he had put to the Academia Nacional de derecho in Buenos Aires on November 13, 1961, he urged upon the assembled heads of American missions at Rio on January 12, 1962, the establishment of a régime of neutralization for Cuba[68] which was to be based on a wider code of coexistence binding on all members of the inter-American system.[69] A measure of this sort he believed would be a powerful antidote to the arguments of those favoring the imposition of sanctions on Cuba.

In his speech to the conference on January 24, 1962, Dantas had proposed the creation of a special organ composed of representatives drawn from various currents of opinion to study the relations between Cuba and the rest of the Western Hemisphere, but this proposal never reached the floor of the conference.[70] He returned to this theme in his TV address on February 5, 1962—just after the end of the conference—maintaining that the incompatibility of the Cuban régime with the rest of the hemisphere would have to be resolved through a Statute of Negative Obligations, which was to be a mediating instrument.[71]

A political strategy as controversial as that pursued so singlemindedly by Dantas was bound to find its critics at home. On January 17, 1962, the conservative *O Globo* of Rio de Janeiro published a "Declaration on the Note of Ex-Ministers of Foreign Affairs" in the form of an appeal to the government to change the course of its foreign policy at this crucial juncture of the Cold War in Latin America, when so many important decisions were lying ahead. The declaration—which was signed by J. C. de Macedo Soares, J. Neves da Fontoura, V. Rao, and H. Lafer[72] —contained a virtual outline of an alternative pattern of policy for adoption by the government. Its main points can be summarized as follows: (a) neither Communist states nor states linked with Communist powers are admissible within the "continental system"; (b) exception was taken to Castro's announcement that no more elections would be held in Cuba; (c) ex-

President Quadros was taken to task for "fixing himself in a theoretical position" in the sphere of foreign policy; (d) the principle of self-determination was misapplied since "the problem created by the communization of Cuba will not resolve itself by a simple enunciation of general rules"; (e) the measures required need not comprise the use of force, but the OAS must be conceived as a "barrier to the invasion of Communism"; (f) a "position of resignation of one's arms" was unacceptable; (g) Cuba must not be allowed to invoke the principle of self-determination "under the cover of neutrality" in order to evade promises accepted by all. The declaration ended with an appeal for a return to the traditional Brazilian foreign policy of cooperation with the United States, invoking the names of Río Branco and Joaquím Nabuco in this sense.[73]

Dantas' foreign policy remained under pressure in Brazil, and it was the matter of principle, not the actual failure to put his policy across with full effect at Punta del Este, that gave rise to criticism. Vivaldo Lima, chairman of the Commission of External Affairs of Congress in Brasilia, remarked reprovingly: "Either Brazil accepts the decision adopted by the majority at Punta del Este and breaks with Cuba; or she retires from the OAS."[74] In spite of this, the Chamber of Deputies rejected a motion to vote down Dantas over the policies he pursued at Punta del Este.[75]

It is symptomatic of the nagging doubts which surrounded the subject of Dantas' foreign policy that Congress refused to approve President Goulart's nomination of Dantas as prime minister to succeed Tancredo Neves in June 1962 on two counts particularly: (a) his policy in the Cuban issue; and (b) the alleged growth of Soviet influence in Brazil.[76] The resulting departure of Dantas from the sphere of foreign policy-making did not portend the end of neutralism in Brazil's foreign policy by any means.

At the conference Chile tried at first to play the mediator between the two sides.[77] Martínez Sotomayor attacked some of the false and formal liberalism which was being expressed so freely at the conference,[78] and agreed implicitly with Dantas in refusing to regard Cuba as a menace.[79]

Mexico's position in the crisis can best be described as soft at first and hardening in face of various pressures subsequently. The Cárdenas wing in the PRI had made gains, and its views could no longer be disregarded. Thus, on October 26, 1961, President López Mateos expressed himself in forthright manner on the subject of Cuba in order to forestall possible criticism from that quarter,[80] while V. Sánchez Gavito, Mexican delegate to the OAS Council voting on the Colombian proposal on December 4, 1961, flatly told his fellow delegates that he did not believe a threat to

Latin America actually existed and tried, without success, to delay the meeting, going so far as to cast the only other adverse vote beside that of Cuba.[81] His action was backed by a special vote in the Mexican Senate.[82]

Castro's announcement on December 1, 1961, to the effect that he had always been a Marxist-Leninist, combined with Mexico's vote opposing the Colombian proposal of December 4, 1961, to hold a meeting of foreign ministers, had explosive effects at home. While President López Mateos may have gone too far to the Right in the months preceding the Bay of Pigs episode and had to move to the Left thereafter, he may have gone too far in that direction also, and to retain the political consensus on which the finely balanced political system of Mexico rests,[83] he adopted the expedient of appointing all former living presidents to form a consultative committee.[84]

The international position of Mexico was making some gesture of reassurance imperative, as her refusal to sanction the convocation of a meeting of consultation was rapidly resulting in a "slowdown of foreign investments, some flight of capital and a resultant attack on the peso."[85] At this critical point López Mateos was informed by A. Ortiz Mena, Mexico's minister of finance, and by R. Salinas Rozana, minister of industry and commerce, that—both on grounds of need for United States credit and in order to strengthen the confidence of the private investor— Mexico's stiff opposition to the strategy of the United States of isolating Cuba had to be modified.[86]

Some action was imperative to restore financial confidence. In his key speech at the conference, therefore, M. Tello, Mexico's foreign minister, on January 24, 1962, condemned Marxism-Leninism as being incompatible with membership in the inter-American system and reaffirmed Mexico's respect for "private property." His speech was promptly followed by a record volume of sales on the Mexican stock exchange.[87]

In his speech on January 24, 1962, also, M. Tello informed the meeting that when the Rio Treaty was drafted, it was not considered necessary to provide for its entry into operation in case some of the twenty republics underwent a change in its political outlook in a manner in contrast with the institutional life of the others. The principle of Cuba's exclusion from the OAS was supported by Tello,[88] who went on to make a distinction between Castro's right to exercise Marxism-Leninism at home and its impact on the functioning of an international organization.[89]

That the Mexican government was sensitive to the possible charge of hypocrisy in saying one thing before the conference and another in the course of it is shown by the statement it saw fit to append to the final act of the eighth meeting, placing it on record that "the exclusion of a Member of State was not juridically possible unless the Charter of the OAS is first amended pursuant to the procedure established in Article 111."[90] Also, the occasion of President Kennedy's visit in June 1962 was seized by the Mexican government for reaffirming the principle of non-intervention in the joint communiqué.[91] Manuel Tello, the foreign minister, expressly denied that the visit implied a change in Mexican foreign policy, whilst López Mateos insisted that any action over Cuba would have to be taken within the framework of the Charter of the OAS, since no machinery existed for isolating a member state outside.[92]

Ramón Beteta, diplomat and influential writer with a left-wing Populist bias, saw in the Mexican action in respect of the joint communiqué a striking victory for Mexico,[93] and, by implication, a stiffening of her attitude in the Cold War in Latin America; but it would be sounder to regard the actions of the Mexican government as an attempt to satisfy all factions at home in order to maintain the balance of the Mexican political system.

Though it would be idle to pretend that Ecuador's internal politics show much stability at any time, the Cuban issue, as manifested at the time of the Punta del Este conference, made a profound impact on the country. The central importance of the personality of J. M. Velasco Ibarra has been noted, but the somewhat mercurial figure of his successor, Carlos Julio Arosemena, should not be overlooked. A Velasquista who had held posts under Velasco Ibarra before, his nationalism was more pronounced than that of his leader. Arosemena was also more neutralist than Velasco Ibarra. He had visited the Soviet Union in June 1961 without cabinet permission; had, on his return, advocated the establishment of diplomatic relations with that country;[94] had praised the Soviet social experiment; and appeared on the same platform as Araújo Hidalgo.[95] This attitude strained his relations with the cautious Velasco Ibarra, and also contributed to the president's downfall.

Arosemena acceded to the presidency on November 9, 1961, and though in its composition his cabinet was moderate, he at once set out to defend Ecuador's right to trade with the Soviet bloc.[96] In December 1961 the Arosemena Administration's announcement of its unwillingness to break relations with Cuba[97] was followed on New Year's Day by a personal assurance from Arosemena to Cuba's under-secretary of foreign affairs, Sánchez Olivares, of Ecuador's support, a decision which was sanctioned by the Ecuadorean cabinet.[98]

At Punta del Este, therefore, Ecuador proved herself a consistent soft liner. On January 25, 1962, Acosta Yépez, the foreign minister, intimated by tactful implication the desirability of a regional neutralism,[99] adding for good measure that social and economic reforms were far more effective for fighting Communism in America than propaganda or political measures.[100] Acosta Yépez was disowned by his own party, the moderately conservative Social Christian Movement,[101] and a serious political crisis ensued. This made it difficult for the president to maintain the unity of his administration, and matters were hardly improved when Arosemena decorated his foreign minister for the part he had played at Punta del Este.[102] A fresh political crisis was provoked at the end of March 1962 by a highly controversial presidential interview with V. Borovsky, a *Pravda* correspondent, during which Arosemena ridiculed the idea that Cuba represented a Communist menace and expressed the hope of an early agreement between the Soviet Union and the United States.[103]

At the end of March the army garrison in Cuenca rose in revolt to demand a diplomatic break with all Communist countries; and though it failed, the army leaders took the opportunity of associating themselves with the political demands of the rebels.[104] On March 31, 1962, Arosemena was sufficiently worried to propose the holding of a plebiscite on the question of whether relations with Cuba should be broken off, but he ran into unexpected opposition from the Conservatives, who withdrew from the coalition. An ultimatum from the *Federación Democrática Nacional* demanding a diplomatic break with all countries whose governments denied the rights of man, in return for support and joining the government, was accepted by Arosemena, and relations with Cuba were duly broken off. After that the Arosemena Administration limped along on a narrow political foundation,[105] but was able to hold on until July 10, 1963, when Arosemena was unseated in a military coup.[106]

The Conference of Punta del Este represented the diplomatic climax of the Cold War within the Western Hemisphere. Yet when all political resources had been mobilized, it turned out that the main contest would express itself not so much in a headlong clash between the principals, Cuba and the United States—for these had been locked in diplomatic and political battle for some time—but in a confrontation between the loosely constituted group of hard-liners, composed of governments wishing to see harsh measures—such as far-reaching sanctions—applied to Cuba, and a group of soft-liners, held together informally and desirous of finding ways and means by which the developing conflict could be contained without engaging the undue attention of either world power. The result was an uncomfortable compromise which left the main issues open.

The lessons of Punta del Este were not to be lost on the two world powers, which would henceforth bring into play far more prominently than ever before the military element.

NOTES

1. For the note from the Colombian ambassador, see OAS, Pan American Union, *Octava Reunión de Consulta de Ministros de Relaciones Exteriores, Punta del Este, 22-31 de enero 1962* (Washington, D.C., 1962), p. 3.

2. Ibid.

3. Peru had taken the step without prior consultation with anyone.

4. 14 H.A.R., December 1961, p. 941.

5. OAS, *Acta del Consejo,* November 14, 1961, pp. 46-50.

6. Full text in *International Affairs* (Moscow), February 1962, pp. 68-69. Extracts in Royal Institute of International Affairs, *Documents on International Affairs 1961* (London, 1965), p. 34.

7. 14 H.A.R., November 1961, p. 989.

8. *New York Times,* December 19, 1961.

9. See also Connell-Smith, op. cit., pp. 177-180; also the same author, "The Future of the Organization of American States. The Significance of the Punta del Este Conference," 18 *The World Today* (1962), pp. 112-120.

10. DAS, *Final Act. Meeting of Consultation of Ministers of Foreign Affairs, Punta del Este, January 22-31, 1962* (Washington, D.C., 1962).

11. See also J. Slater, *The OAS and United States Foreign Policy* (Ohio, 1967), p. 178.

12. See D. Cater, "The Lessons of Punta del Este," *The Reporter,* March 1, 1962.

13. *New York Times,* January 23, 1962.

14. OAS, *Octava Reunión,* pp. 209-210.

15. According to his account, instructions were cabled to the Guatemalan representative to inform Rusk that it was Guatemala's intention to break up the meeting rather than to agree to a unanimous resolution of a "soft" nature. The president identified Peru, Paraguay, the Dominican Republic, and the Central American states as having supported Guatemala in this sense at Punta del Este. See M. Ydígoras Fuentes, *My War with Communism* (Englewood Cliffs, N.J.: Prentice-Hall, 1963), pp. 179-182.

16. The soft liners conducted what was virtually a parallel conference by meeting regularly at San Rafael, near Punta del Este. See "Commentarios a una

reunión de trascendencia continental: La Octava Reunión de Consulta," 11 *Revista de derecho internacional y ciencias diplomáticas* (Rosario), January/December 1962, pp. 183-192.

17. *New York Times*, January 25, 1962.

18. Ibid., January 30, 1962.

19. As for the lines of diplomatic division now made manifest at the world at large, their significance was stated by R. E. Ruiz, assistance professor of Latin American history at Smith College, United States, in a letter to the editor of the *New York Times*, as follows: "Of the Latin American countries supporting our Cuban position, ten are controlled either by dictators or traditional oligarchies; three of them represent the votes of dictators we have condemned. Of the affirmative botes, only Uruguay (and perhaps Costa Rica) can be called the voice of free nations." See *New York Times*, February 6, 1962.

20. *New York Times*, October 11, 1961.

21. 15 H.A.R., January 1962, p. 32.

22. 15 H.A.R., January 1962, p. 126. It will be recalled that the first Declaration of Havana, passed in September 1960, had served a similar purpose in relation to the seventh meeting held at San José. For a Castroite analysis of the Second Declaration, see R. Alarcón, "La Segunda Declaración de Habana," 1 *Política Internacional* (Havana, 1963), pp. 97-110. The Second Declaration of Havana asks, *inter alia*, rhetorically, "What is the history of Cuba if not the history of Latin America? What is the history of Latin America if not the history of Asia, Africa and Oceania?" See M. A. D'Estéfano Pisani, "Presencia y precisión de no-alineación," 9 *Política Internacional* (1965), pp. 73-105. The author of this article sees non-alignment as a tactical annex to the world policy of the Socialist camp.

23. See "UN Security Council Rejects Cuban Call for Opinion of World Court on OAS Action," 36 *Department of State Bulletin*, April 23, 1962. For a ratiocination of Chile's negative vote on the Security Council, see República de Chile, Ministerio de Relaciones Exteriores, 2 *Presencia internacional de Chile* (Santiago, 1962), pp. 69-72.

24. 15 H.A.R., April 1962, p. 318.

25. See R. Alarcón, op. cit., p. 104.

26. See Goldenberg, op. cit., p. 267 and Suárez, op. cit., pp. 146-153.

27. *New York Times*, October 24, 1961. It was during that meeting that Uruguay had asked that effective measures be taken within countries on the basis of the maxims established at the Santiago conference of 1959 for the defense of democracy. See 14 H.A.R., December 1961, p. 941.

28. OAS, *Acta del Consejo*, December 4, 1961. President Victor Haedo stated in Pôrto Alegre on December 6, 1961, that Clulow had voted "precipitately." See Irma Pellicer Silva, *La posición mexicana en la Octava Reunión de Consulta* (Mexico City, 1968), p. 59. See also L. S. Morrison, *Latin American Mission* (New York: Simon & Schuster, 1965), p. 157.

29. Only a detailed breakdown of voting in the National Executive Council over the main lines of policy to be pursued at the conference can convey the hopeless confusion of Uruguay's decision-making processes at this critical stage of the Cold War, as a three-way split was opening as follows: (a) in favor of diplomatic and economic sanctions against Cuba: *ruralistas:* B. Nardore, Faustino Harrison; *Her-*

reristas: J. M. Alonso; *Batllistas,* List 14: César Batlle Pacheco; (b) for an anti-sanctionist policy: *Herreristas:* E. V. Haedo, M. Echegoyen, A. Artataveytia; (c) undecided: *Batllistas,* List 15: H. A. Grauert, L. Arroyo Torres. The foreign minister, H. Martínez Montero, favored the immediate exclusion of Cuba from the OAS. See 14 H.A.R., January 1962, pp. 70-71.

30. Ibid.

31. See J. Slater, op. cit., p. 157. An official publication justifies Uruguay's policy on the ground that the most important task was to save the conference and to prevent the isolation of several Latin American states. See República Oriental del Uruguay, *Mensaje del Poder Ejecutivo a la Asamblea General al inaugurarse la XXXIX Legislatura* (1963), pp. II/4.

32. 15 H.A.R., April 1962, p. 171. See also an article, "Se pronunció contra la ruptura el herrerismo," *El Diario,* February 13, 1962.

33. Ibid., p. 623.

34. Ibid., August 1961, p. 713.

35. Laureano Gómez, an outstanding veteran right-wing statesman.

36. OAS, *Octava Reunión,* p. 79.

37. Ibid., p. 80.

38. See OAS, *Octava Reunion,* at p. 149.

39. "Haiti came to Punta del Este with the firm intention of defending the principles of non-intervention and self-determination of peoples with all they imply. Haiti remains firmly attached to these intangible principles, which guarantee an order of mutual respect in relations among peoples of different languages and cultures.

"Here Haiti has become persuaded that the fallacies of Communist propaganda cannot and should not obscure or hide the difference in philosophy which these principles represent when they are expressed by a democratic American country, and when Communist governments and their agents attempt to utilize them for their own benefit." See OAS, *Octava Reunión,* p. 302. See also L. S. Morrison, op. cit., pp. 179 and 192.

40. See R. W. Logan and M. C. Needler, *Political Systems of Latin America* (London, 1964), p. 161.

41. Ydígoras Fuentes, op. cit., pp. 171-172. There is also the former Guatemalan president's claim of the dispatch of a presidential cable from Guatemala to her ambassador in Port-au-Prince, which—allegedly by an oversight—was sent in clear, rather than in code, instructing him to leave, close the embassy, and explain that other states in Central America would follow suit. According to the same source it was in response to this action that President Duvalier of Haiti changed his mind and joined the hard-line group at Punta del Este. See ibid., pp. 181-182.

42. 14 H.A.R., September 1961, pp. 828-830.

43. Conil Paz and Ferrari, op. cit., p. 215.

44. *Daily Telegraph,* January 24, 1962.

45. *New York Times,* December 3, 1961. Frondizi suggested that Art. 39 of the Charter of the OAS be invoked to call a meeting, rather than having recourse to the controversial Rio Treaty.

46. Conil Paz and Ferrari, op. cit., p. 213.

47. This was done on the advice of Dr. J. M. Ruda, legal counsel to the Argentine delegation at the United Nations. Dr. Ruda kindly confirmed this point in

a personal interview with the writer in Buenos Aires on June 16, 1971, explaining that this was done to gain valuable time to prevent the complete failure of the conference.

48. See "Comentarios a una reunión de trascendencia continental: La Octava Reunión de Consulta," 11 *Revista de derecho internacional y ciencias diplomáticas* (Rosario), January/December 1962, pp. 183 and 187.

49. Ibid., p. 106. There is the suggestion that Argentina might have tried to persuade Uruguay to join the ranks of the anti-sanctionists. See P. S. Holbe, 44 *Current History* (1963), p. 70. An interesting analysis of the pressures exerted by the military and what the author calls "the traditional intelligentsia" is provided by Frondizi's former junior foreign minister. See C. A. Florit, *Las Fuerzas Armadas y la guerra psicológica* (Buenos Aires: Arayú, 1963).

50. See *La Prensa*, February 1, 1962.

51. Ibid.

52. *New York Times*, February 2, 1962.

53. R. Balbín, leader of the *Unión Radical del Pueblo*, condemned Frondizi's policy at Punta del Este outright, while the Left—which had looked upon the president as a defector from it on grounds of domestic policy—gave him lukewarm support only. See R. Noble, *Satelismo contra Soberania* (Buenos Aires: Arayú, 1966). Frondizi himself maintains that the military and the press were aligned against him, and that it was only the Peronists who "saw more clearly." Information kindly supplied to the author in Buenos Aires on June 22, 1971.

54. The full text is to be found in Arturo Frondizi, *La Política exterior argentina* (Buenos Aires: Transición, 1962), pp. 186-195.

55. For a complete account of the final stages of the Frondizi Administration, see 15 H.A.R., April 1962, pp. 166-167; and A. Conil Paz and G. Ferrari, op. cit., pp. 220-221. Oscar Camilión claims that R. McClintock, the United States ambassador in Buenos Aires, did his best to save Frondizi. (Interview kindly granted the writer on June 16, 1971.)

56. *New York Times*, September 11, 1961. The continuity in Brazil's foreign policy is also attested by the appointment of Afonso Arinos de Melo Franco, Quadros' foreign minister, as head of Brazil's delegation to the United Nations. The continuity of Brazil's new course was all the more remarkable on account of the large supplies of aid of all kinds that the country was receiving from the United States. Brazil received $205 million in military aid from the United States between 1948 and 1964, almost one-third of the total granted to the remaining member states of the OAS during the period. See Agency for International Development and Department of Defense of the United States, *Proposed Mutual Defense and Development Programs FY 1966: Summary Presentation to the Congress* (Washington, D.C., 1965), p. 226. It was in January 1962 that the first specific agreements under the Alliance for Progress were signed with Brazil. See 14 H.A.R., January 1962, p. 76.

57. Dantas, op. cit., pp. 6-7.

58. *New York Times*, September 11, 1961.

59. Dantas, op. cit., p. 21.

60. Dantas, op. cit., pp. 121-122.

61. Ibid., p. 123.

62. Ibid.

63. Dantas, op. cit., p. 126.

64. Ibid., p. 116.

65. Ibid., p. 106. A pragmatic justification for Brazil's abstention earlier on in the OAS, on December 4, 1961, was similarly provided by her ambassador in Washington, Roberto de Oliveira Campos, who explained Brazil's decision on the grounds that, though she disapproved of the régime in Cuba, the latter could not be toppled by external pressure. See 14 H.A.R., December 1961, p. 1139.

66. Dantas, op. cit.

67. Ibid., pp. 32-33.

68. Ibid., p. 108.

69. See "O Brasil proporá a 'institucionalização' da situação de Cuba," *O Estado de S. Paulo*, January 12, 1962.

70. Dantas, op. cit., p. 180.

71. Ibid., p. 127.

72. There was a hint that Raúl Fernandes would have been among the signatories but for his quasi-judicial status at the time as a member of a government commission.

73. For an article expressing well-reasoned criticism of Dantas' foreign policy, see "Equidistancia fingida," *O Estado de S. Paulo*, April 29, 1962, which maintains that his diplomacy was prompted by internal factors.

74. 31 *Cuadernos Americanos* (1962), p. 110.

75. *New York Times*, May 31, 1962.

76. *The Times*, June 22, 1962. For a measured appreciation of Brazil's policy at Punta del Este, see A. Amoroso Lima, a liberal professor of anti-Castro, pro-Kennedy and pro-de Gaulle views, "A Posição do Brasil em Punta del Este," 5 *Revista Brasileira de Política Internacional*, March 1962, pp. 5-16. Unlike Slater, op. cit., Amoroso Lima assumes that the United States wanted to adopt a hard line at the conference, but this was done only because Kennedy was under pressure from public opinion at home.

77. See E. Bernstein Carabantes, "Punta del Este y las erróneas interpretaciones de un tratado," 2 *Foro Internacional* (1962), pp. 518-534.

78. The full text of the foreign minister's speech is to be found in Ministerio de Relaciones Exteriores, *Presencia Internacional de Chile* (Santiago, 1962), pp. 53-63. The present reference is to p. 53.

79. OAS, *Octava Reunión*, p. 105.

80. *El Universal*, October 27, 1961.

81. OAS, *Acta del Consejo*, December 4, 1961.

82. *El Universal*, December 9, 1961.

83. See M. Ojeda Gómez, "Mexico en el ámbito internacional," 6 *Foro Internacional*, October/December 1965 and January/March 1966, pp. 247-270.

84. *New York Times*, December 10, 1961.

85. Ibid., January 21, 1962.

86. See Olga Pellicer de Brody, op. cit.

87. See "Alza notable en la Bolsa de Valores," *El Universal*, January 26, 1962. The relevant extracts from Tello's speech are to be found in L. C. Zorate, *Conferencia de cancilleres en Punta del Este* (Bogotá, 1962).

88. *El Universal*, January 25, 1962.

89. *Cuadernos Americanos*, op. cit., pp. 12-13.

90. OAS, Final Act. *Eighth Meeting of Consultation of Ministers of Foreign Affairs, Punta del Este, January 22-31, 1962* (Washington, D.C., 1962). For a general review, see J. Rondero, "Mexico en Punta del Este," 8 *Revista de Ciencias Políticas y Sociales* (1962), pp. 47-72. For a criticism by a Mexican left-wing Populist writer, see Carlos Fuentes, "Punta del Este, A Mexican Perspective," 194 *The Nation*, February 24, 1962.

91. *New York Times*, July 8, 1962.

92. Ibid.

93. Ibid.

94. *New York Times*, July 17, 1961.

95. 14 H.A.R., July 1961, p. 626.

96. 14 H.A.R., November 1961, pp. 1016-1017.

97. See Irma Pellicer Silva, *La posición mexicana en la Octava Reunión de Consulta* (Mexico City, 1969).

98. 15 H.A.R., January 1962, pp. 35-56.

99. OAS, *Octava Reunión*, p. 160.

100. Ibid., p. 164.

101. 15 H.A.R., January 1962, pp. 55-56.

102. H.A.R., March 1962, p. 248.

103. 137 *Revista internacional y diplomática*, April 5, 1962, p. 13.

104. Gesellschaft für auswärtige Politik, *Die internationale Politik 1962* (Bonn, 1968), pp. 92-93.

105. 15 H.A.R., April 1962, pp. 342-355.

106. See M. C. Needler, *Anatomy of a Coup d'Etat: Ecuador 1963* (Washington, D.C.: Institute for the Comparative Study of Political Systems, 1964).

Chapter VIII

MILITARY CLIMAX:

THE CUBAN MISSILE CRISIS (1962)

At Punta del Este, Cuba redoubled her efforts to commit the Soviet Union to her defense in the event of a direct or indirect invasion by the United States. This the Soviet Union was reluctant to do, as it would have presented a direct challenge to the Monroe Doctrine, as interpreted by the United States. Eventually, however, an arrangement was made by which the Soviet Union would refrain from giving a formal guarantee of Cuba's political and territorial integrity, but supply the means of Cuba's only effective defense: missiles and nuclear weapons. Apparently—the evidence to date is by no means conclusive—no drastic countermeasures were expected from the United States.

In the event, the arrival of Soviet arms in Cuba from mid-1960 onwards was seen as a two-fold challenge to the United States. In the first place, it laid open to question the fundamental assumptions embedded in the Monroe Doctrine, particularly the notion that changes in the status quo of the area must not come about as a result of extra-hemispheric action, whether that was done in association with an American power or not.

Second, any shipment of arms exceeding a certain volume or going beyond a certain level of sophistication could be interpreted as an attempt to tip the world strategic balance against the United States in what had become a very sensitive area.[1]

Conflicting explanations have been provided by the Cuban leadership as to the origins of the crisis. Speaking to the French journalist, Claude Julien, shortly after the crisis, Dr. Castro declared, "We have, ourselves, envisaged the possibility of asking the Soviet Union to provide us with missiles. But we had not yet come to a decision when Moscow offered them to us. We were told that by accepting them, we would add to the global strength of the socialist camp. Because we are receiving significant aid from the socialist camp, we considered that we were not in a position to refuse them. That is why we accepted them. It was not to secure our own defense, but primarily to strengthen socialism internationally."[2]

Herbert Matthews, however, the veteran correspondent of the *New York Times*, was assured by the Cuban leader that "We were the ones who put forward the idea of the missiles. . . . It was for us to do so. We showed them in an incontrovertible way that an invasion was being planned."[3]

Castro's fears gain some weight considering the increasing number of raids by Cuban exiles, particularly group "Alpha 66," and by the maneuvers of 40,000 United States marines begun on April 9, 1962, under the hardly reassuring code name "Lantphibex—62."[4] It was difficult for the Soviet government to turn a cold shoulder to the moral pressures emanating from the Cuban leadership, encouraged by Khrushchev's statement of July 9, 1960, which had held out the prospect of Soviet missile action in support of Cuba. Guevara certainly seems to have drawn far-reaching conclusions from the Soviet attitude. Two days after the Soviet premier's statement he rejoiced: "Today by force of circumstances we are practically the arbiters of peace in the world."[5] In January 1961 he wrote that "it is known that the Soviet Union and all the Socialist States are ready to go to war to defend our sovereignty and that a tacit understanding exists among our peoples."[6] On December 31, 1960, Castro made a speech in which he accused the CIA of preparing another invasion on the pretext that Cuba was allowing missile sites to be constructed on her territory,[7] and the same charge was formally repeated in a note addressed by Roa to the United Nations requesting a meeting of the Security Council in January 1961.[8] In April 1961 Khrushchev was still denying any intention of sending missiles; a denial which, in retrospect, may have been made as much for the benefit of the Cubans as that of the United States. Moral pressure was resumed by Castro on December 1, 1961, when he declared himself a Marxist-Leninist.

On February 5, 1962, hard on the heels of the Punta del Este conference, Mariano García Inchaústegui, Cuban representative at the United Nations, complained of renewed preparations by the United States to invade Cuba.[9] It is possible that, after Punta del Este, the Cuban government saw in a full Soviet commitment to defend it the only hope to deter another, and this time determined attempt by the United States to invade Cuba and overthrow the Castro régime. From February 25, 1962, onwards, therefore, Cuban efforts to involve the Soviet Union gained fresh determination. On that day *Revolución* carried an article which urged the need for full Soviet support.[10]

On March 27, 1962, came the first public indication that the Soviet Union was at last responding to Cuban appeals, as A. I. Adzhubei, Khrushchev's son-in-law and editor of *Pravda,* spelled out what Guevara had had suggested as a fact in January 1961, namely that the Soviet Union "would go to war, if necessary, to defend the Castro régime."[11] The endorsement by the Soviet government of the expulsion of Aníbal Escalante from Cuba signalled the beginning of unreserved Soviet commitment to the Cuban régime under exclusively Castroite management.[12]

Two events seem to have served to heighten Cuba's alarm and to induce the Soviet leadership to take the step of delivering the missiles to Cuba. One was a stream of indications that certain elements in the United States were growing restless with the relative inactivity of the Kennedy Administration vis-à-vis Cuba. Thus in May, 1962, J. Miró Cardona, prominent Cuban emigré leader, remarked publicly that anti-Castro action was "imperative";[13] and Spruille Braden, formerly high in the councils of the State Department and a former United States ambassador to Cuba—still influential in extreme right-wing circles in the United States—called for an all-out invasion of Cuba.[14]

The other alarming event may have been the Rapacki visit to Cuba in June 1962. During a lecture at Havana University, Adam Rapacki, Poland's foreign minister, reminded his listeners—rather tactlessly but perhaps intentionally so—that Cuba was "not a signatory of the Warsaw Pact," and referred to the "independent position of the revolutionary government of Cuba in international affairs." He also pleaded for peaceful coexistence between the United States and Cuba.[15] What the immediate Cuban reaction was must be left to surmise. However, it is known that Raúl Castro, Cuban minister of defense, was received in Moscow by Marshal M. Malinovsky, his Soviet counterpart, at the beginning of July 1962.[16]

There can be no doubt that the Moscow visit by Raúl Castro, followed by a visit by Guevara in August 1962, settled the details of the portentous missile operation. On September 12, 1962, Raúl Castro felt certain enough to proclaim with perfect self-confidence that "if they shoot, it will be the end of imperialism!"[17]

When the crisis broke on October 22, 1962, Castro put the country on a war footing, insisting on Cuba's right to possess any weapons.[18] At this point the Soviet leaders began to have second thoughts, and suggested the United Nations as a suitable forum for resolving the threatening conflict.[19] U Thant, secretary-general of the United Nations, consequently initiated mediation, and on October 26, 1962, the Soviet leadership fell in line. Cuba was left isolated.

The crisis could have been solved there and then had it not been for the determined stand taken by the Cuban government, bent on resisting the will of both the Soviet government and the United Nations. On October 27, 1962, Castro rejected the United Nations initiative of the previous day, which had asked for a suspension of the work carried out on the missile-launching sites, issuing a warning that combat planes appearing over the island would be shot down. The Soviet government, however, continued to deal with that of the United States direct, through exchange of letters between Khrushchev and Kennedy, and on October 28, 1962, Moscow announced that the missiles would be shipped back to the Soviet Union. On the same crucial day Castro set out five conditions for agreeing to the withdrawal of missiles from Cuba: (a) the United States must lift the blockade and end all economic pressures; (b) cease all subversive activities in Cuba; (c) stop all "piratical" attacks by Cuban exiles; (d) end all fights over the island; and (e) withdraw from the Guantánamo base.[20]

It was part of Khrushchev's attempted *Diktat* to ask the United Nations to comply with the wishes of the United States by sending a team of observers to Cuba to verify the dismantling, and it fell to U Thant to remind the Soviet leader that the permission of the Cuban government was essential for this.[21] Castro obliged by inviting U Thant to visit him in Havana, and on October 30, 1962, the United States air and naval blockade was lifted for two days to allow U Thant to have talks with Castro, Dorticós, Roa, and Lechuga, the Cuban ambassador in Mexico.[22]

Telecasting to the Cuban nation on November 2, 1962, Castro explained that Cuba could not prevent the withdrawal of the missiles, since they were Soviet property. Differences between the Cuban and Soviet leadership were admitted freely, but not stressed unduly, proof enough that Cuba was intent on retaining the valuable Soviet connection. Nonmissile weapons of Soviet origin, but under Cuban control, would remain.[23] Castro had no wish to be an unsuperable obstacle to a peaceful solution.

Soviet pressure was brought to bear on Castro to induce him to part with the Ilyushin-28 bombers he had received from the Soviet Union and which were under his exclusive jurisdiction. Since Kennedy insisted, Mikoyan was ultimately able to persuade Castro to acquiesce.[24] Castro was, however, left with the satisfaction of refusing to agree to any sort of inspection, and Kennedy thereupon informed a press conference on November 21, 1962, that in view of this refusal he had no option but to continue aerial reconnaissance.[25]

On November 26, 1962, Castro attacked the Khrushchev-Kennedy agreement which had been reached over his head, and gave solemn warning that "an armed conflict has been avoided, but peace has not been achieved." Castro and Dorticós laid down the principle of reciprocity which was to govern Cuba's attitude towards a settlement with the United States.[26] Thus Castro gave the world notice that for him the Cold War was not over by any means.

The Khrushchev-Kennedy Agreement

By the terms of the Khrushchev-Kennedy agreement Soviet missiles and Ilyushin-28 bombers were removed from Cuba, but Soviet troops were allowed to remain. Cuba was partially neutralized by bilateral agreement between the United States and the Soviet Union in respect of strategic weapons; in return the United States gave a pledge not to invade Cuba.[27]

The Khrushchev-Kennedy agreements also went some way towards defining the strategic boundaries of the Western Hemisphere. The Monroe Doctrine, as interpreted by the United States, was strengthened considerably, although this was the psychological implication rather than the explicit intention of the two parties. There was nothing in the agreements reflecting on the political and military status of any Latin American country other than Cuba. In his address to the Supreme Soviet on

December 12, 1962, Khrushchev on his side appeared to accept these conditions, implying that henceforth Soviet support of Cuba would be confined to the economic sphere.[28]

The Punta del Este conference of January 1962 had revealed serious disagreements among Latin American states regarding policies towards Cuba, and some of the adamant Central American and Caribbean countries canvassed the idea of forming a separate group to oppose Cuban policies in the Western Hemisphere. When the missile crisis entered into a critical stage, Dean Rusk, secretary of state of the United States, toyed with the idea of activating that group. On September 26, 1962, he met several of the ambassadors of those countries in order to launch a ten-member security organization composed entirely of the hard liners of Punta del Este.[29] Costa Rica, either on its own initiative or prompted by Dean Rusk, put forward similar proposals at the same time[30] in the hope of avoiding the frustrations experienced at Punta del Este.

The development of the crisis left no time to organize that group, and Dean Rusk had therefore to deal with all Latin American countries, relying on the element of urgency to bring them into line. A meeting of OAS foreign ministers was therefore called and assembled in New York on October 2-3, 1962, during which the secretary of state described developments in Cuba as a threat to the Western Hemisphere requiring collective countermeasures.[31]

Guatemala's president left a personal account of the way in which the crisis impinged on his country. "At four p.m. on October 16, 1962, United States Ambassador John O. Bell . . . came to my office and conferred with Foreign Minister Jesús Unda Murillo and myself." On being informed about the shipment to Cuba of Soviet missiles, "I then offered the United States the use of locations on Guatemalan soil for the installation of missile sites and military bases . . . not only to permit the country (that is, the United States) to defend itself against a possible aggression, but also to defend Central America and Guatemala from the same threat."[32]

But it was not until October 22, 1962, that the United States sent a note to the chairman of the OAS alleging Cuba had "permitted its territory to be used for the establishment of offensive weapons with nuclear capacity provided by extra continental Powers."[33] An emergency meeting of the council, acting as a Provisional Meeting of OAS Foreign Ministers, was called for the following day, October 23, 1962, and the operative sentence in Dean Rusk's speech to the council during that meeting read, "These new weapons arriving in Cuba are not only directed against the United States. Let there be no misunderstanding; there are other strategic targets in this hemisphere—in your countries—which they can devastate with their lethal loads."[34]

At the insistence of Brazil and Mexico, three separate votes were taken on the three parts of a United States resolution calling for (a) the withdrawal of all offensive weapons from Cuba; (b) individual and collective action, including the use of armed force, to halt the entry of these weapons and to prevent these from becoming an active threat; and (c) to keep the Security Council of the United Nations informed.[35] The first and third of these were passed unanimously, but the second found Bolivia, Brazil, and Mexico abstaining, even though the "recommendations" could not produce legally binding consequences.

The degree of unanimity achieved at that meeting contrasted deeply with the marked divisions which had appeared at Punta del Este in January of the same year. Latin America had given strong support to President Kennedy in his policy of direct confrontation with the Soviet Union over the missile issue in Cuba. The psychological circumstances of this decision are, however, quite unique; and to gain deeper insights into the pattern of real support obtained by the United States it is advisable to go beyond an examination of the voting pattern into a scrutiny of the type of state which responded to the call from the Pentagon of the same day (October 23, 1962) inviting the dispatch of ships to join the 50 vessels of the United States in the blockade of Cuba.[36]

The Latin American Response

The Military Reaction

With the exception of Argentina, which was under a military régime, the social-political profile of the active sanctionist states was far from reassuring. Ecuador, El Salvador, Peru, and Guatemala all conformed to the traditional type of oligarchic society which it was the avowed object of the Alliance for Progress to reform. Haiti, Nicaragua, and Honduras were under authoritarian rule, the former scandalously so. The Dominican Republic was in political turmoil. Only Colombia, Costa Rica, and Venezuela could be regarded as operating a system of representative government.

The undoubtedly representative governments of Brazil, Chile, and Uruguay refrained from complying with the call for military assistance from the Pentagon, while the semi-representative administrations of

Bolivia and Mexico also remained conspicuously inactive. Viewed in this light, it may be noticed that the political pattern of Punta del Este had survived after all in basic outline, with some modifications.

The initiative in the matter of military sanctions was taken by Argentina at the OAS Council meeting of November 5, 1962, in proposing coordinated military participation in the blockade of Cuba. In doing so, the Argentine representative had touched a raw nerve in traditional Latin American sentiment which tends to react sharply to any attempt to coordinate military forces in unison with those of the United States. Brazilian objections were overcome only when the chairman, A. Zulueta Angel, a Colombian, gave assurances of the strictly temporary character of the measures proposed, while Bolivia and Mexico abstained on several paragraphs of the resolution on the ground of constitutional incompatibility.[37]

In the event, Argentina offered two destroyers; Honduras and Peru offered troops; Colombia offered general collaboration; Costa Rica, the Dominican Republic, Guatemala, Nicaragua, and Venezuela offered the temporary use of their bases. On November 9, 1962, the United States Navy disclosed that an Inter-American Quarantine Force composed of ships drawn from the United States, Argentina, and the Dominican Republic had been formed and was to be known as Task Force 137, to operate separately from Task Force 136, which comprised United States vessels exclusively.[38] Venezuela was the only American country apart from Cuba to decree general mobilization.[39]

The Diplomatic Reaction

The near-unanimous vote cast by the Latin American states on October 23, 1962, in support of President Kennedy's quarantine measures requires further explanation. Three separate but mutually compatible explanations may be put forward. In the first place, there was the tremendous shock of the real possibility of nuclear holocaust. It matters not that this fear was not logically grounded, for the intended quarantine made the prospects of such holocaust less instead of more remote, whereas nothing pointed to immediate risk of nuclear war in the event of the undisturbed installation of the Soviet missiles in Cuba. A real emotional shock was administered to the cherished and deeply embedded notion that, in spite of the Guatemalan and Cuban crisis, there was no real prospect of Cold War issues erupting into hot war in Latin America, and still less of the epicentre of the Cold War shifting from Europe and Asia to Latin America. Secondly, there has always been in Latin America a traditional mistrust of Russia, both Tsarist and Bolshevik. Nothing in the recent history of Latin America suggested similar mistrust of the countries of Western Europe. Accounts which attempt to explain the Latin American vote of October 23, 1962, in terms of an unqualified adherence to the principles of the Monroe Doctrine are thus wide of the mark.[40] Thirdly, there was in Latin America, as elsewhere in the world, general concern about the future shape of Cuba's foreign policy, particularly when in nuclear harness. Experience had shown that well-established powers, long used to regular diplomatic practice, having acquired nuclear capability, were prepared to impose practical restraints on its use in international relations. In the case of a government run by an elite of successful revolutionaries slow in settling down to the routine business of day-to-day administration, one could not be quite so sure. The prospect of coexistence with a Cuba that was at once revolutionary in outlook and nuclear in armament was deeply disturbing to many.

It is easy to sympathize with the Latin American governments in their predicament, but this is not to admit that no other courses were open. For what was expected from those Latin American countries who had proved to be dissidents at Punta del Este only nine months before was that they should not be willing parties to the flagrant violation of the very principles they had so loudly reasserted at that meeting: (a) the political principle of non-intervention—with its corollary, self-determination—and (b) the legal principle that there can be no law without due process of legislation. There was nothing short of a failure of nerve to stop the group of dissidents of Punta del Este from voting against the critical resolutions of October 23, 1962, on the ground that they violated those principles, for this implied a degree of submissiveness to the United States in matters of principle which at least some of the dissidents of Punta del Este had not shown in the past. While the change of attitude on the part of Argentina and Ecuador can be easily accounted in terms of a decisive political shift of internal political power, no such changes had taken place in Bolivia, Brazil, Chile, and Mexico, the remaining dissidents of Punta del Este.

The government that succeeded President Frondizi in Argentina was under military orders and could be expected to favor an attitude of hostility towards the Castro régime. Typical in this respect was the announcement by E. del Carril, President G. M. Guido's foreign minister, that no "so-called neutralism" was to be tolerated in Argentina's foreign policy.[41] During the missile crisis Argentina showed herself eager to take an active part in the military operations connected with the blockade of Cuba, even though the political balance within the military had shifted from the hard, so-called red forces to the relatively moderate blue ones in September 1962.

There are strong indications that Argentina's readiness to send a naval force—which made a deep impression in Washington at the time—had been taken mainly for internal reasons, at the behest of General J. Onganía, commander-in-chief, who saw in such a move a heaven-sent opportunity to reconcile the two warring factions within the military, the reds and the blues.

Ever since the tacit alliance between Castro and Betancourt came to an end during the San José conference in 1960, [42] the Cold War has had a direct impact on Venezuela's internal affairs and external relations. At one time the administration of President Betancourt faced a near-boycott of the Left; but in June 1962 already the *Unión Republicana Democrática* (URD), led by Jóvito Villalba, dissociated itself from the Communist party, [43] and in December 1962 veered round to adopt an anti-*fidelista* line. [44] This left only the *Movimiento de la Izquierda Revolucionaria* (MIR) in opposition on the Left alongside the Communists. [45]

Venezuelan oil installations were sabotaged soon after the OAS vote of October 23, 1962, and the government ordered general mobilization on October 27. [46] Abroad, as at home, the Betancourt Administration moved with characteristic swiftness and determination. Broadcasting to the nation on New Year's Eve 1962, the president explained that Venezuela would have to be on the alert always, because it was "one of the political and military targets of the Soviet Union and of the parties which follow its ambitious plans for world domination." [47]

The quasi-neutralist tendency, which had become so marked a feature of Brazilian foreign policy under Presidents Quadros and Goulart, showed no signs of flagging. Even Dantas' failure to be elected prime minister in June 1962 had no repercussions in the sphere of foreign policy. [48] Brazil was not prepared to view with equanimity the collapse of the Uruguaiana axis with Argentina resulting from the fall of the Frondizi régime. In April 1962 President Goulart paid an official visit to Mexico to meet President López Mateos; and while the technical preparations for that occasion had clearly preceded events in Argentina, it was nevertheless apparent that Brazil welcomed the opportunity of an entente with Mexico. Neutralist overtones marked the joint communiqué issued at the end of the visit. [49]

At the emergency meeting of the Council of the OAS on October 23, 1962, Brazil had voted in favor of blockading Cuba, but with reservations—ostensibly on constitutional grounds—concerning the use of arms. [50] According to a leading article in *O Estado de S. Paulo* of October 30, 1962, the Brazilian government, dissatisfied with the development of the crisis, wished to have the draft declaration with which it was confronted at the OAS Council of October 23, 1962, revised; but as time would not permit this, had to be content with placing its basic reservation on record. Even this was done only after both the Chilean and Mexican delegates had refused to be parties to a revision of the original draft. However, and perhaps significantly—for in the meantime political pressures had been applied against the administration—the Ministry of Foreign Affairs published an official statement on the following day affirming that "the Brazilian government does not give support to the use of force that would violate the territorial integrity of an independent nation and endanger world peace." [51]

During the entire missile crisis, President Goulart was pressed hard by Brazil's military chiefs to fall in with United States policy. [52] That there must have been a considerable amount of heart-searching in governmental circles is attested by two developments. In the first place, the Brazilian delegation at the United Nations worked out a project for the denuclearization of Latin America under the auspices of an 8-member committee of the Disarmament Commission of the United Nations, intended to facilitate the acceptance by Cuba and the Soviet Union of repatriation of the missiles without loss of face and implying a quasi-neutralization of Cuba. This was officially presented to the General Assembly of the United Nations on October 29, 1962, Bolivia, Chile, and Ecuador acting as co-sponsors. [53] In the second place, President Goulart dispatched General Albino da Silva, chief of the presidential military cabinet, to Cuba on October 29, 1962, to offer mediation. [54] The gesture was no doubt intended as genuine, though the effect was largely lost by the fact that U Thant had arrived in Havana before him. [55]

Incensed by the apparent weakness displayed by the Brazilian delegation at the meeting of the OAS on October 23, 1962, Brizola demanded a public reprimand for Ilmar Pena Marinho, chief Brazilian delegate at the OAS. However, Hermes Lima accepted full responsibility, insisting that Pena Marinho had acted properly on the basis of instructions received from the government. [56] Brizola eventually relented, admitting that the

Soviet Union had "taken advantage" of Cuba's plight, and vowing that he was "never prepared to accept Cuba's transformation into a satellite of the Soviet Union"; [57] but his scorn for the United States persisted.

As for Mexico's attitude, Luis Cabrera once remarked about Mexican foreign policy that "the foes of the United States, who are always the foes of the whole of the American continent, will certainly assume to be friends of Mexico, and will try to take advantage of any sort of resentment or feeling of distrust that Mexico may have against the United States. Mexico nevertheless understands that in case of a conflict between the United States and any other nation outside of America, her attitude must be one of complete continental solidarity." [58] The weight of this tradition has proved to be considerable, and explains in part Mexico's otherwise incongruous attitude during the missile crisis.

López Mateos had set out deliberately to widen the general scope of Mexico's foreign policy, if not its general direction. [59] It is ironical that the very prosperity which encouraged the Mexican president to branch out in this manner was made possible by developments described by the Governor of the Bank of Mexico as (a) the pre-eminent place in Mexico's balance of payments occupied by foreign tourism (the overwhelming part of it from the United States), and (b) the increasing influx of long-term capital as reflected in the following comparisons: 1950: 9.9 percent of the total influx of foreign exchange; 21 percent by 1961. [60]

During the crucial weeks of the development of the crisis the president happened to be touring Asia, and on one occasion during that trip he declared it his intention "to put an end finally to the traditional policy of isolation and inertia, which disguises complexes of inferiority." [61] Addressing a meeting in India, López Mateos denied any intention of shifting the bases of Mexico's foreign policy: "In the case of Mexico the expression 'independent international policy' means neither neutralism nor the will or the aspiration to form or associate with the third bloc." [62]

In foreign policy Mexico has a tendency to "lean to the Left," and to regard left-wing dictatorships as more acceptable than right-wing ones. President López Mateos confirmed this during his Asian tour when he stated that "peaceful revolution is the best way of avoiding a bloody revolution." [63] These principles were put to the test during the missile crisis in October 1962. Early in the crisis, ex-President Cárdenas suggested that a presidential warning be given that an invasion of Cuba by the United States would have serious consequences, and M. Tello, the foreign minister, and A. Ortiz Mena, secretary of the treasury, both made it clear that

Mexico would oppose any kind of blockade of Cuba.[64] For the time being the Left rested content.

At the height of the crisis the right-wing National Action Party, led by former President Alemán, accused the López Mateos Administration of "dangerous vacillation, neutralism and sympathy for the pro-Soviet Castro régime";[65] and although these charges were hardly fair, they had to be taken seriously. The Alemanistas remained staunchly pro-United States throughout the crisis.

More serious still was the blow delivered to implicit Mexican assumptions regarding the balance of power in the Americas. To the sense of shock experienced when, by repelling the invasion at the Bay of Pigs, Cuba had shown that by Latin American standards she was capable of wielding considerable military strength, there was now added the revelation that Cuba was transforming herself into a nuclear power.

Mexico's morale was badly shaken. She even failed to associate herself, though she was asked to do so, with a Brazilian-sponsored move supported by Bolivia, Chile, and Ecuador, for the proclamation of a denuclearized zone.[66] López Mateos decided therefore to emphasize Mexico's loyalty to the Rio Treaty and to underscore the offensive nature of the weapons being installed in Cuba by announcing from Manila that if Cuba armed herself offensively," the approach of the Mexican government will also change."[67] During his flight from Manila to Hawaii, he remained under constant pressure by radio-telephone from President Kennedy to fall in with United States policy,[68] and secretly cabled President Dorticós of Cuba, on October 23, 1962, warning that Mexico could not "view with indifference a Latin American country establishing facilities for the utilization of the most destructive weapons of all times."[69] When the crucial vote was taken in the OAS on October 23, 1962, Mexico voted in favor of the blockade but abstained over the issue of the use of force.[70]

At home, Mexico confined herself to taking military measures. The navy took up defensive positions in the Yucatan Channel, but Mexico took no part in any integrated action.

However, the fine balance of Mexico's political system allows no wide deviations from the political norm. As soon as Mexico had taken up a position of cautious hostility towards Cuba, she reiterated her objections to the existence of the Special Consultative Security Committee, originally created at the Punta del Este conference, to ward off any expected encroachments on her internal sovereignty by the CIA or similar agencies acting in the name of the inter-American system. When on October 24,

1962, L. S. Morrison, United States ambassador at the OAS, called for counter-subversionary action, the Mexican representative gave an assurance that the security precautions taken by Mexico were perfectly adequate to deal with any Cuban agents.[71]

In December 1962 the Mexican Administration regained sufficient composure to take measures to counter the impression of vacillation created during the crisis. On December 11, 1962, the president granted an interview to James Reston, a United States journalist, in which one may detect a calculated effort to regain that political equilibrium at home, resting halfway between Cárdenas on the Left and Alemán on the Right, which experience since the Guatemalan crisis had shown to be essential. López Mateos repeated his approval of President Kennedy's action while blaming the United States for driving Castro into Soviet arms. As to the present, the president considered that Castro was more a problem for the United States than Mexico. Mexico had had her revolution and was not vulnerable to communism.[72]

López Mateos' interview must be regarded as an attempt to dismiss the missile crisis as a mere episode in the otherwise smooth course of Mexican foreign policy, but his ploys could scarcely hide the fact that there was little diplomatic scope for Mexico in a period of severe stress.

Bolivia had stayed away from the OAS in a protest against its refusal to take action in Bolivia's dispute with Chile over the River Lauca, but her representative returned during the Cuban missile crisis in order to voice a qualified approval of the blockade measures proposed by President Kennedy. However, the action was unpremeditated, since it was taken by the Bolivian ambassador to the OAS, E. Sarmiento Corruncho, without instructions from his government. The Bolivian government first voided this ambassador's vote before debating the situation, but eventually sanctioned it. [73] A different temper prevailed in the Bolivian Senate, controlled by Juan Lechín, which condemned the action of the United States as threatening "destruction without parallel in history."[74]

What would have been the Bolivian government's attitude if its hand had not been forced is an open question; though it may be surmised that at any rate the president, Paz Estenssoro, and most of the members of his cabinet, would not ultimately have acted differently. [75]

No instructions were received by the Uruguayan delegate attending the crucial OAS meeting of October 23, 1962, since an inconclusive debate in the National Executive Council had resulted in an inability to agree on the exact degree of force which should be authorized in connection with the blockade of Cuba. [76] A vote of abstention had therefore to be cast in the OAS. On the following day the National Executive Council reached a unanimous decision approving of the blockade in principle, with the express reservation that there was no need for Latin American forces. In Chile the shock of the missile crisis exposed the quasi-neutralism of the Alessandri Administration—which had consistently opposed the imposition of any sanctionist measures on Cuba—as purely tactical, as the government surprised everyone by the determination of its alignment with the course chosen by President Kennedy.

Only two hours after the receipt of news of the presence of Soviet missiles in Cuba, President Alessandri decided that "hemispheric action" would have to be taken in this matter. [77] The official Chilean case was presented in the Security Council of the United Nations on October 24, 1962, by D. Schweitzer, her permanent representative there, in a manner to which even hard-liners in the United States could not have taken exception. [78]

Allende, leader of FRAP, acted with great restraint, calling on Alessandri on October 30, 1962, to propose a constructive way out of the crisis. [79] The Christian Democrats took the view that, though on principle the OAS was entitled to intervene in Cuba in order to verify the presence of missiles and to remove them, the United States should not have acted without consulting the OAS. The quarantine measures taken by the United States were denounced by them as going beyond all norms of international law, but the Soviet Union also came in for their criticism for its action in introducing missiles into Cuba. [80] Only the Liberals and the Radicals supported the government unconditionally.

NOTES

1. As one historian put it: "Valid strategic considerations would be powerfully reinforced by the fundamental tradition of the United States identified with the Monroe Doctrine." L. J. Halle, *The Cold War as History* (New York: Harper & Row, 1967), p. 404.
2. *Le Monde*, March 22, 1963, as quoted in Goldenberg, op. cit., p. 275.
3. H. Matthews, *Return to Cuba* (Stanford, Calif.: Bolivar House, 1964), p. 16. For further inconsistencies, see Goldenberg, op. cit., p. 276.
4. Semidei, op. cit., p. 116.
5. *Hoy,* July 12, 1960.
6. *Obra Revolucionaria,* January 21, 1961, as cited in Semidei, op. cit., p. 115.
7. *Revolución,* January 2, 1961, as quoted by Suárez, op. cit., p. 119.

8. United Nations Security Council, O.R., 16th year, 921st meeting, January 4, 1961, pp. 10-25.

9. *New York Times,* February, 1962.

10. Suárez, op. cit., p. 147.

11. *New York Times,* March 27, 1962.

12. See Suárez, op. cit., pp. 154-155; Goldenberg, op. cit., concurs and expressly cites *Pravda,* April 11, 1962, to support this thesis.

13. 15 H.A.R., May 1962, p. 412.

14. *American Opinion,* June 1967, pp. 13-18.

15. *Revolución,* June 14, 1962, as quoted by Suárez, op. cit., p. 157.

16. Perhaps it was not altogether without significance that an article surveying the course of Soviet-Cuban relations should have appeared in Havana in June 1962 also. See J. Torras, "Dos años de relaciones fraternales entre Cuba y la Unión Soviética," 2 *Cuba Socialista* (1962), pp. 1-7.

17. Suárez, op. cit., p. 168.

18. Ibid., p. 169.

19. *Pravda,* October 24, 1962.

20. *Hoy* and *Revolución,* October 29, 1962.

21. *Revolución,* November 2, 1962.

22. 15 H.A.R., October 1962, pp. 908-909.

23. Clissold, op. cit., pp. 276-278.

24. 15 H.A.R., November 1962, p. 1004.

25. Ibid., p. 1005.

26. "The United States government demands that the United Nations verify the withdrawal of strategic weapons by inspection of our territory. Cuba demands that the United Nations verify, on the territory of the United States, Puerto Rico and other sites where aggression against Cuba is being prepared, the dismantling of the training camps of mercenaries, spies, saboteurs and terrorists, subversive centers, and bases from which piratical ships are launched against our shores. . . . If the United States and its partners do not accept inspection of their territories by the United Nations, Cuba will not accept any concept of inspection put forth by them." 15 H.A.R., November 1962, p. 1005.

27. The full correspondence between Khrushchev and Kennedy during the crisis may be found in Pachter, op. cit., pp. 217-228; Abel op. cit., *passim;* and Robert Kennedy, *Thirteen Days* (New York: Norton, 1969), pp. 163-184.

28. Pachter, op. cit., p. 249.

29. *New York Times,* September 27, 1962.

30. See J. Slater, op. cit., p. 141.

31. *New York Times,* October 4, 1962.

32. M. Ydígoras Fuentes, op. cit., pp. 221-222.

33. OAS, *Acta del Consejo,* October 23, 1962, p. 2.

34. Ibid., p. 8.

35. OAS Council, *Acts of Extraordinary Session, October 23, 1962* (Washington, D.C., 1962). See also OAS, *Inter-American Treaty of Reciprocal Assistance. Application, 1960-1964* (Washington, D.C., 1964), pt. II, p. 112.

36. *The Times,* October 24, 1962.

37. OAS, *Inter-American Treaty of Reciprocal Assistance Application, 1960-1964* (Washington, D.C., 1964), pt. II, p. 153.

38. *New York Times*, November 10, 1962; and OAS, op. cit., in footnote above, pp. 110-166, 133, and 145.

39. 15 H.A.R., October 1962, p. 910.

40. See, for instance, K. Krakau, *Die kubanische Revolution und die Monroe-Doktrin* (Frankfurt: Metzner, 1968).

41. *New York Times*, May 8, 1962.

42. Se Chapter V.

43. 15 H.A.R., June 1962, p. 528.

44. 16 H.A.R., December 1962, p. 149. The *Fuerzas Armadas de Liberación Nacional*, the military arm of the militantly pro-Castro Left, was formed on June 2, 1962. See R. Robledo Limón, "El Partido Comunista de Venezuela. Sus tácticas políticas de 1967 a 1969," 4 *Foro Internacional*, April/June, 1970, pp. 531-551 at p. 533.

45. See the critical account of a former MIR leader, G. Rodríguez, "El fracaso de la insurrección," *El Universal* (Caracas), September 3-9, 1962.

46. *New York Times*, October 30, 1962.

47. See 15 H.A.R., December 1962, pp. 1125 and 1127.

48. Ibid., vol. 15, July 1962, pp. 656-657.

49. The joint declaration affirmed "that both countries were not bound to any political or military bloc" and that there was a need "for a more equitable distribution of riches." See Ministério das Relações Exteriores, *Viagem do Presidente João Goulart aos Estados Unidos de América e ao México* (Rio de Janeiro, 1962), pp. 59-60.

50. L. S. Morrison, former United States ambassador to the OAS, asserts in his memoirs that Roberto Campos, Brazil's ambassador in Washington, was instrumental in shouldering the responsibility for Brazil's surprising assenting vote (with qualifications) on October 23, 1962. See L. S. Morrison, *Latin American Mission* (New York: Simon & Schuster, 1965), pp. 250 and 258.

51. 15 H.A.R., October 1962, p. 964. Former President Kubitschek supported the position taken by the United States in the crisis, whereas Almino Afonso, leader of the PTB in Congress, took the opposite position. Goulart's brother-in-law, Brizola, attacked both the United States and the Soviet Union for their part in promoting the crisis. See J. W. F. Dulles, *Unrest in Brazil* (Austin: University of Texas Press, 1970), p. 185.

52. Information kindly supplied to the present writer by ex-President Goulart during an interview granted in Montevideo on May 29, 1971.

53. 6 *Revista Brasileira de Política Internacional*, June 1963, pp. 309-310, contains the full details. See also *Jornal do Brasil*, October 24, 1962.

54. This was done after Hermes Lima, Brazil's foreign minister, had conferred with the chairman of the Chamber of Deputies, R. Padilha (UDN), Martins Rodrígues of the PSD, Hélio Cabral of the PSU, Plinio Salgado of the PRP, Menezes Cortes of the UDN, Bocaiura Cunha of the PTB, and Senator V. Freire—a fair cross-section of Brazil's political community. *O Estado do S. Paulo*, October 30, 1962.

55. H.A.R., Vol. 5, December 1962, p. 765. It is significant of the image in which Brazilian foreign policy was held abroad at that time that President Tito of Yugoslavia, presumably in the conviction that he was dealing with a fellow-neutralist government, sent a message to President Goulart which implied an expectation of action on the part of the latter. See ibid., p. 768. Goulart's reply referred specifically to Brazil's project for the denuclearization of Latin America. See *O Estado de S. Paulo,* October 30, 1962.

56. *Neue Zürcher Zeitung,* November 18, 1962; and *Jornal do Brasil,* October 26, 1962. According to V. T. Vasco Leitão da Cunha, Ilmar Pena Marinho was recalled to Brazil by President Goulart to account for the way the Brazilian vote was cast in the OAS Council on October 23, 1962, but was able to convince Brazil's chief executive of the soundness of that move. (Information kindly supplied to the present writer during an interview granted by Vasco Leitão da Cunha in Rio de Janeiro on April 26, 1962.)

57. 15 H.A.R., November 1962, p. 1060. See also footnote 56 above.

58. Quoted by A. Carrillo Flores, "Mexico and Latin America," 27 *Proceedings of the American Academy of Political Science,* May 1964, p. 123.

59. No important departure from the general pattern of Mexican foreign policy was evident from the president's itineraries: to the United States and Canada in October 1959; to Venezuela, Brazil, Argentina, Chile, and Peru in January and February 1960; to Asia in October 1962; and subsequently to France, Yugoslavia, Poland, the Netherlands, and Western Germany in March and April 1963.

60. O. Campos Salas, "Mexico Faces Changes in International Trade," 14 *Review of International Affairs* (Belgrade), February 20, 1963, pp. 12-14.

61. Agustín Yañez (ed.), *Proyección universal de México. Crónica del viaje realizado por el Presidente de México Lic. Adolfo López Mateos a India, Japón, Indonesia y Filipinas en año 1962* (Mexico City: Torres, 1969), p. 208.

62. Yañez, op. cit., p. 198.

63. Yañez, op. cit., p. 37.

64. 15 H.A.R., September 1962, p. 792. See also J. C. Merrill, "The United States as Seen from Mexico," 5 *Journal of Inter-American Studies,* January 1963, pp. 53-66. Narciso Bassols, prominent left-wing writer and former state official, had published a book in Mexico City in 1960 carrying the significantly critical title, *La Revolución Mexicana cuesta abajo.*

65. On this point, see Peggy Fenn, "Non-Intervention and Self-Determination as Cornerstones of Mexican Foreign Policy: Their Application to the Cuban Issue," 2 *Topic,* Autumn 1962, pp. 39-53.

66. 6 *Revista Brasileira de Política Internacional,* June 1963, pp. 309-310.

67. *El Universal,* October 23, 1962.

68. See L. S. Morrison, *Latin American Mission: An Adventure in Hemisphere Diplomacy* (New York, 1965), p. 244.

69. *El Excelsior,* October 30, 1962. The Mexican president also cabled to Kennedy and Khrushchev, setting out his position. See ibid.

70. 15 H.A.R., October 1962, p. 881.

71. *New York Times,* October 25, 1962.

72. The interview was published in the *New York Times* on December 12, 1962.

73. 15 H.A.R., October 1962, pp. 943-944.

74. Ibid. For the background of United States policy towards Bolivia, see C. W. Arnade, "The United States and the Ultimate Roots of the Bolivian Revolution," *Historia*, January 1962, published by the University of Puerto Rico, pp. 35-49; and W. S. Stokes, "The Foreign Aid Program in Bolivia," 15 *Western Political Quarterly*, September 1962, pp. 28-30.

75. In an interview kindly granted to this writer in 1971, however, ex-President Paz Estenssoro explained that he personally would not have minded seeing the installation of Soviet missiles in Cuba, as this would have given Bolivia some diplomatic leverage vis-à-vis the United States.

76. 15 H.A.R., December 1962, pp. 1154-1155. See also República Oriental del Uruguay, *Mensaje del Poder Ejecutivo a la Asamblea General al inaugurarse el l período de la XXXIX Legislatura* (1963), pp. II/6-7. See also "La posición uruguaya frente a la propuesta de Estados Unidos," *Tribuna* (Montevideo), October 26, 1962.

77. *El Mercurio*, October 31, 1962.

78. Ibid.

79. See Senator S. Allende's speech in the Senate in República de Chile, *Diario de Sesiones del Senado, Legislatura Extraordinaria*, Sesión 9a, October 23, 1962.

80. See E. Frei, *Chile tiene un destino: pasado y presente de una crísis* (Santiago, 1962); and L. Gross, *The Last, Best Hope. Eduardo Frei and Chilean Democracy* (New York, 1967), p. 197.

Chapter IX

THE AFTERMATH OF THE MISSILE CRISIS

After the missile crisis three basic choices were open to Cuba. In the first place, she could seek an immediate accommodation with the United States, which would have been tantamount to acceding to the Khrushchev-Kennedy agreement. Secondly, she could opt for a permanent condition of hostile suspense with the United States, relying on the moral and economic support of the Soviet Union. Thirdly, she could choose a policy of hostility *á outrance* to the United States by launching guerrillas at strategic points in Latin America, with or without the connivance of the Soviet Union. For the moment Cuba chose the second option. Diplomatic identity with the Soviet Union was gradually and cautiously modified in favor of greater autonomy in foreign policy. On February 28, 1963, Khrushchev had stated that "if an attack is made on Cuba . . . the Soviet Union will deliver a crushing blow at the aggressors,"[1] but though the Soviet troops stationed in Cuba included some of the best in the Soviet armed forces, their number was falling steadily.[2] A gulf began to open in the relations between Cuba and the Soviet Union as the two adopted different attitudes on prime issues of world affairs.

In November 1962 Mikoyan had discussed the possibility of a nuclear test-ban agreement with Kennedy in Washington,[3] but Castro insisted on the fulfillment of his five conditions before he would consider taking steps in this direction, and not even the supplications of fellow Latin American states taking fresh initiatives towards a nuclear-free zone in Latin America could move him. When the test-ban agreement was signed in August 1963, Cuba was not a party to it.[4]

However, the Soviet leaders could rest assured that, lacking nuclear power, Cuba was in no position to upset their agreement with the United States. What gave them real cause for alarm was Castro's disposition to listen to overtures from Peking. On January 16, 1963, *Revolución* stated flatly that "Cuba wishes to remain outside the controversies within the Soviet camp," and in March 1963 Castro told Claude Julien, a French journalist, that the Chinese were "right in saying that we must not yield to imperialism. We are well placed to know that imperialism is not a paper tiger."[5] It is therefore likely that, more than anything else, it was Soviet anxiety to keep Castro out of the Chinese orbit that was the chief consideration in inviting him to the Soviet Union.

The Cuban delegation remained in the Soviet Union from April 27 to May 24, 1963, and the Soviet leaders appear to have converted them to the principle of "peaceful coexistence"[6] in "international," meaning in this context "inter-state," relations. That, in spite of verbal hostility, the Cubans were sincere in their adherence to the principle was demonstrated by Cuban state practice during 1963. Typical in this respect was the Cuban reaction to the conciliatory speech made by Kennedy at Harvard University on June 10, 1963, which was seen as a reversal of United States policy. Kennedy's sincerity was stressed, and blame for the trends of United States foreign policy attributed to a conspiracy between Pentagon generals and industrialists.[7]

On the other hand, Castro's position regarding armed revolutionary struggle in Latin America was far from clear. On January 16, 1963, in a speech to the Congress of Women of the Americas in Havana, he had pledged support for armed insurrection, and in his March 1963 interview with Claude Julien he referred in contemptuous language to the inactivity of Latin America's Muscovite Communists, with the exception of those of Venezuela, shown during the missile crisis. The question of what tactics to pursue in order to produce Communist revolutions in Latin America was therefore a prime issue. The joint Soviet-Cuban declaration published at the end of Castro's stay in the Soviet Union laid it down that national liberation struggles were to be waged according to tactics appropriate to local conditions,[8] a compromise formula which settled nothing. Moreover, the Soviet leaders could hardly have been gratified when in August 1963 *Cuba Socialista* published the Chinese policy statement of June 14, 1963, in its entirety.

If Cuba was still the prime catalyst in Latin America, Brazil was beginning to rival her in this respect, as by virtue of her size and strategic importance, her increasingly controversial politics became a cause of major concern. On January 6, 1963, the presidential system of government was restored, and this enabled Goulart to pursue his policies with greater vigor. Subsequent developments can be divided into three phases: (a) the experiment of the "positive Left," from January to June 1963; (b) the period of adjustment, from June 1963 to March 1964; and (c) the final period, from March 1964 to the end of the Goulart régime on April 1, 1964.[9]

The success of the "positive Left" hinged on its ability to solve the problem of the Brazilian balance of payments with the help of the United States and the International Monetary Fund. Dantas, now minister of finance, went to Washington for talks with officials of the United States Administration; but both he and Roberto Campos, Brazil's ambassador there, were so gravely disappointed by the unhelpful attitude encountered that they seriously considered breaking off the talks. Second thoughts were entertained only because both were well aware of the lack of cohesion of the new cabinet, and Campos also feared the ascendancy of the "negative Left" in the event of a rift with the United States.[10] In March 1963, Dantas was more fortunate in reaching agreement with the IMF, which had just adopted a new policy of compensation for a fall in export earnings of underdeveloped countries.[11] However, the experiment of the positive Left failed in spite of some support abroad, as Dantas was unable to prevent a series of salary increases of about 70 percent in May. He was more successful in concluding a trade agreement with the Soviet Union in April 1963 which covered a period of five years and provided for an annual exchange of $100 million, compared with Soviet-Brazilian trade of only $70 million in 1962. This new figure equalled Soviet trade with Cuba in 1960.[12]

As regards Cuba, Goulart intimated to the United States that he would attempt to induce Castro to adopt a "Yugoslav" policy, with emphasis on a new brand of "Latin American socialism" and benevolent neutralism. Under this plan—an extension of a previous attempt by Dantas to achieve the neutralization of Cuba through a statute of negative obligations at the Punta del Este conference in January 1962—Cuba would obtain economic aid in return for a pledge not to export communism and not to allow the use of Cuba as a base for medium-range Soviet missiles or bombers.[13] But his plan was not adopted and, in spite of his rapprochement with Mexico, Goulart still felt relatively isolated.

After the collapse of the experiment of the positive Left in June 1963, the ideological influence of Populists of the further Left became more noticeable both at home and abroad.[14] Muscovite Communism in Latin America at that particular juncture was much preoccupied with the possible growth of Chinese influence, and it was therefore natural that pains should be taken to stress the need for cooperation with the urban sectors.[15] Their emphasis on developmental elements in Brazil's policy show that there were certain features which Muscovite Communist policy had in common with the Brazilian developmentalist school as it had evolved since the days of Kubitschek.[16] But affinity must not be confused with association, let alone subordination.

A turning point came at the end of the year, when a clear connection was established in President Goulart's New Year's message between welfare at home and the direction of policy abroad.[17] In many ways now the foreign policy of Brazil began to resemble that of Cuba during the first half of 1960, before the flow of Soviet arms began. In a way also, the trade agreement with the Soviet Union of April 1963 could be compared with Mikoyan's trade arrangements with the Cuban government of February 1960. On August 22, 1963, J. A. de Araújo Castro, a career diplomat, had taken over the Ministry of Foreign Affairs from Lins e Silva. Whether that was intended to strengthen presidential decision-making power is not certain, but there cannot be much doubt that, after New Year's Eve, foreign policy was made largely by the president. A new edge was given to policies inaugurated long ago but hitherto pursued only half-heartedly. Anti-imperialism, cooperation with the underdeveloped countries, and an increasingly critical attitude towards the Organization of American States were cases in point. When General de Gaulle decided to recognize the Communist government of China, Goulart was said to be in favor of following suit; but de Araújo Castro felt it proper to allow a "decent interval" to elapse after French recognition.[18]

The quasi-neutralist foreign policy adopted by Goulart was not, however, the only facet of his diplomacy, for Brazil tried to compensate for the loss of her erstwhile partner in the Uruguaiana axis, Frondizi's Argentina, by assuming the leadership of the non-interventionist governments of Latin America. After October 1962, Brazil began to switch the main weight of her neutralism from the political to the functional side, taking the initiative toward a denuclearized zone in Latin America, and in the promotion of the closer economic integration of the region. At the UNCTAD in Geneva in 1964 Brazil acted as the militant spokesman of the underdeveloped world.[19]

A return to diplomatic normalcy was gradually taking place in Mexican foreign policy as the traditional middle-of-the-road stance was being reinforced by the clamors emanating from the increasingly important urban economic complex[20] for fresh markets overseas. Thus, from late 1963 onwards, Mexico was doing relatively brisk business with Communist China. Mexican congressmen toured China in February 1964, and there were even rumors of an impending recognition of China's Communist government.[21] In November 1963 Mexico entered into a contract to sell 440,000 tons of her wheat harvest to China.[22] In December China was allowed to open a fair in Mexico City, and in the same month López Mateos and Chang Kuang-tau, head of a Chinese commercial mission, contracted for the purchase by Communist China of 200,000 bales of Mexican cotton in the following year.[23]

Social and political conditions in Bolivia showed a steady decline in this period without, as yet, having a profound effect on Bolivia's foreign policies. During the revolution of 1952 the armed forces had been dissolved and replaced by a politically reliable militia. In response to political disorders in the tin mines by the traditionally unruly miners, President V. Paz Estenssoro recreated an armed counterforce. The majority of tin miners were staunchly left-wing, and in the peculiar circumstances engendered by the Cold War in Latin America, tended to attract the attention of Cuba. In August 1963 a crisis had developed in the relations between the two countries, following political disturbances emanating from the mining areas. It is typical of the nationalist sentiment which pervaded Bolivia that the Senate, which had come out in favor of Cuba during the missile crisis in October 1962, and had on previous occasions voted in favor of establishing diplomatic relations with the Soviet Union and of expelling the French ambassador, now resolved to ask the president to declare Roberto Lasalle, the Cuban ambassador, persona non grata.[24] Paz Estenssoro rejected that advice, preferring merely to call the Cuban ambassador sharply to order.[25] Shortly before his own fall in November 1964, the president saw himself compelled to break off diplomatic relations with Czechoslovakia.[26]

Meanwhile, Bolivia tried to steer an uneasy middle course, and shortly before Tito's visit in September 1963,[27] J. Fellman Velarde, the foreign minister, thought it proper to insist that Bolivia was not a member of any neutral group of states, adding that "we must maintain the respect of our people, and this we cannot do if there is any suspicion that the United States has a hand in our foreign policy."[28]

The policy succeeded. On arrival, Tito obliged by affirming that he had not come to Latin America to enroll recruits for a neutralist bloc,[29] and when Paz Estenssoro visited Kennedy in Washington in October 1963, the latter gave an explicit endorsement of the Bolivian régime.[30]

In Chile the missile crisis caused a debate within the Left, with the main line of division running between the Socialists and Communists, the principal partners in the left-wing *Frente de Acción Popular* (FRAP). Raúl Ampuero emerged as the chief spokesman of the Socialists, whilst Luis Corvalan, secretary-general of the Communist Party, led the Communists. The disagreement between the two parties was one over tactics, with the Communists backing Soviet policy to the hilt and looking at world politics in terms of world power politics, while the Socialists favored the neutralist states and stressed the ideological side of the struggle.[31]

Ampuero set the tone in an article written in May 1963 in which he declared roundly that his independent Marxism made him feel a greater sympathy for Cuba and Algeria than for the Soviet Union or China.[32] He emphatically denied that the "Socialist world system" had a leading role, and maintained that the stimulating influence of Soviet economic success in the underdeveloped world had been exaggerated.[33] The Communists, on the other hand, insisted on the indispensability of the Soviet connection, arguing that "neither the solidarity of the Latin American nations nor the aid . . . of a country such as Yugoslavia, will suffice."[34]

The military takeover in Argentina on March 19, 1962, had led to a sharp reversal of foreign policy. A return to civilian government based on the *Unión Cívica Radical del Pueblo* was effected in 1963 and made possible a subtle change in foreign policy in the direction of a return to the traditional independence of Argentina. While, for instance, E. D. del Carril, the first foreign minister of the military régime, had condemned "so-called neutralism," M. A. Zavala Ortiz, President Illia's foreign minister, foreshadowed a foreign policy based on "neither equanimity nor neutralism" and remarked obliquely, with reference to the problem of Cuba, that "one has to get used to it that there is room for various conceptions in the world" and that "where circumstances made it impossible for Argentina to be friendly, at least Argentina will show respect."[35]

The Illia Administration at once proceeded with surprising energy to annul the contracts concluded between the United States oil companies and YPF in 1960. While this action was hardly designed to please the Western powers, [36] there could as yet be no question of restoring diplomatic relations with Cuba, and the result was a lukewarm conformity with United States policies.

NOTES

1. *Pravda,* March 1, 1963.

2. In January 1963 the number of Soviet troops stationed in Cuba was put by United States estimates at 17,000. See 16 H.A.R., January 1963, p. 31; by March the figure had dropped to 8,000. See ibid., March 1963, p. 248; in October 1963 it was down to 7,000. See ibid., October 1963, p. 963.

3. *New York Times,* November 20, 1962.

4. Nor was Castro willing to tolerate any misgivings on that score from members of his own entourage, as the highly cultured but politically unimaginative former leader of the Cuban Communist Party, Juan Marinello, who had openly canvassed a solution of the missile crisis along lines proposed by the Soviet Union, was to find to his cost. Having publicly approved of the test-ban treaty, he was eventually posted to UNESCO in Paris, a politically innocuous post. See H.A.R., Vols. 15 and 16, pp. 1103 and 31 respectively.

5. *Le Monde,* March 22 and 23, 1963, quoted in Goldenberg, op. cit., p. 283. For a general appraisal of China's attitude, see J. J. Lee, "Communist China's Latin American Policy," 4 *Asian Survey,* November 1964, pp. 1123-1134.

6. The joint declaration (see 3 *Cuba Socialista,* June 1963, pp. 1-19) says on this point that "In conditions in which States with different social and political systems exist, the principles of peaceful coexistence present the only correct and reasonable basis for international relations."

7. See L. Gómez Wangüemert, "Panorama y Perspectiva de la situación internacional," 1 *Política Internacional* (Havana, 1963), pp. 111-120.

8. The operative passage reads as follows: "The question of a peaceful or non-peaceful road to socialism, in one country or another, will be settled in the final analysis by the struggling peoples themselves in accordance with the concrete correlation of class-forces and the extent of the resistance by the exploiting classes to the socialist re-organization of society." *Cuba Socialista,* loc. cit.

9. The terms "positive" and "negative" Left were coined by Dantas to make a distinction between middle-of-the-road Populists, like himself, and the quasi-Marxist variety of Populists and outright fellow-travellers. The former was working loyally for reform and development within the Goulart Administration, while the latter was trying to infiltrate it. See "Brazil: economic problems and political solutions," by an anonymous author in 19 *The World Today* (1963), pp. 476-484.

10. See T. E. Skidmore, *Politics in Brazil, 1930-1964* (New York: Oxford University Press, 1967), pp. 240-241.

11. 16 H.A.R., March 1963, p. 304, and June 1963, p. 623. The reconciliation between Brazil and the IMF was based on a Three Year Plan and included a standby agreement of $200 million. See *Financial Times*, March 26, 1963.

12. See 6 *Revista Brasileira de Política Internacional*, March 1963, pp. 107-108. For a critical view of the agreement, see M. Bueseu, *Ensaio sôbre o intercâmbio Brasil-URSS* (Rio de Janeiro: Leonardo da Vinci, 1964).

13. 16 H.A.R., January 1963, p. 83; and Irenee Guimaraes, "Cuba a sa place dans le systéme panaméricain, estime le Brésil," *Le Monde Diplomatique* (Paris), January 1963, p. 7.

14. I. L. Horowitz, *Revolution in Brazil* (1964), p. 378, seems to imply that a quiet revolution was in progress in Brazil after June 1963. Evandro Lins e Silva, a lawyer belonging to no political party, was appointed foreign minister, and it is perhaps significant that in his speech on taking over he announced that he had received instructions from President Goulart "to project Brazil's international policy as the external facet of our internal effort towards economic and social development and of the country's security." See *Discurso pronunciado pelo Ministro Lins e Silva na solenidade de transmissão da pasta das relações exteriores, em 20 de Junho de 1963.*

15. Horowitz, op. cit., p. 372.

16. See Skidmore, op. cit., pp. 180 and 361.

17. 17 H.A.R., January 1964, pp. 80-81.

18. Ibid., February 1964, pp. 178-179.

19. H. Gall, "Conferencia de las Nacionés Unidas sobre comercio y desarrollo," 5 *Foro Internacional* (1964), pp. 99-129. See also his statement at the fourth Plenary Meeting of the Conference, UN Doc E/CONF. 46/STA/7 pp. 7-8, and his article, "Time is Running Short," *New University Thought*, December 1963–January 1964, pp. 57-69, on the task of the United Nations in overcoming underdevelopment. See also J. Azevedo Rodrígues, "A Unidade do Mundo Subdesenvolvido e o conflicto Norte-Sul: A Conferencia das Nações Unidas sobre Comercio e Desenvolvimento," 1 *Revista Civilização Prasileira*, March 1965, pp. 89-113; and the same author, "O Sistema Interamericano contra a América Latina," 1 *Política Externa Independente*, May 1965, pp. 81-102.

20. The urban interests carried much more weight than those of the agrarian sector. Mexican sugar production, for instance, was reaching record levels and would have required the adoption of a policy hostile to Cuba in order to qualify for a larger slice of the vital quota of the sugar market of the United States. For Mexico's place in the Alliance for Progress, see W. J. Kemnitzer, "México en la Alianza para el Progreso," *Foro Internacional*, July/September 1963, pp. 41-59.

21. *New York Times*, January 30, 1964.

22. 16 H.A.R., November 1963, p. 1042.

23. Ibid., December 1963, p. 1137.

24. *New York Herald Tribune*, August 28, 1963. J. Fellman Velarde, Bolivia's foreign minister, had previously protested to the Cuban government over the latter's intervention in a general trade union strike. See *New York Times*, August 25, 1963.

25. *Neue Zürcher Zeitung*, September 5, 1963.

26. *The Times*, October 31, 1964.

27. See *Le Monde*, September 28, 1963; and *The Times*, September 30, 1963.

28. 16 H.A.R., September 1963, p. 899.
29. *The Times,* September 30, 1963.
30. 16 H.A.R., October 1963, p. 995.
31. See E. Halperin, *Nationalism and Communism in Chile* (Cambridge, Mass., 1965).
32. R. Ampuero, "Los distintos caminos hacia el socialismo," *Arauco,* May 1963, pp. 10-16.
33. Halperin, op. cit., p. 157.
34. Ibid., p. 34.
35. *Neue Zürcher Zeitung,* October 27, 1963.
36. A. Harriman, special ambassador of the United States, flew to Buenos Aires to try to settle the oil dispute. See *New York Times,* November 8, 1963; but in June 1964 drilling was begun by YPF in three areas in which foreign companies were still at work. See *Financial Times,* June 25, 1964.

Chapter X

THE VENEZUELAN CRISIS (1963-1964)

The Khrushchev-Kennedy agreement had been valuable in terminating the missile crisis and in solving a large part of the Cuban problem. By it the United States had undertaken (a) to respect Cuba's territorial integrity; (b) by way of corrollary, to control and curb the activities of Cuban exiles; and (c) to stop all attempts to subvert the Castro régime. In return, the Soviet Union had agreed not to send to Cuba strategic weapons (ground-to-ground missiles and Ilyushin fighter-bombers, and so on) and to reduce Soviet forces in Cuba to a token number. The administration of President Johnson gave no indication of going back on the agreement.

However, the implications of the agreement for the rest of Latin America were as yet far from clear. Since the autumn of 1961 hard line governments in Latin America had attempted to induce the United States to adopt more energetic policies against the Castro régime, and Venezuela provided a further instance of this sort in 1963.[1]

During 1962 Venezuela was moving steadily towards the center of conflict in Latin America. With elections due in December 1963, the internal situation began to verge on civil war. The dominating figure on the government side continued to be President Betancourt. On May 22, 1963, he announced emergency legislation against both left-wing parties, the Communists and the *Movimiento de la Izquierda Revolucionaria* (MIR),[2] and, after an attempt had been made to assassinate him, he gave orders for the arrest of leading Communists and "Miristas."[3] In the same month the Communists came out in favor of both participation through legal channels in the elections and the pursuit of *guerrillero* activity, the beginning of Communist ambiguity in the face of successful government measures against the Left.[4]

Betancourt's drive against the Left at home was matched by attempts to isolate Cuba abroad. Thus, he met President Kennedy in February 1963 to propose a three-fold strategy by the OAS to stop all flights to Cuba; to ban all OAS nationals from visiting Cuba; and to establish air and sea patrols to enforce these measures.

As the date of the presidential elections in Venezuela was approaching and internal tensions were reaching breaking point, an announcement by the Venezuelan government on November 3, 1963, disclosed the discovery of a cache of arms buried in the Paraguana Peninsula which contained three tons of arms of United States, Belgian, and Italian manufacture. Ministerial statements announcing the discovery indicated that the arms might have been stolen from the Venezuelan army, though the first announcement had spoken of their Cuban origin. On November 29, 1963, two days before the presidential elections, the government confirmed the Cuban origin of the arms, and at a special conference of ambassadors, M. Falcón-Briceño, the foreign minister, and Briceño Linares, the minister of defense, displayed the Cuban emblems to lend weight to these assertions.[5] On the same day Venezuela took the matter to the OAS for action under Article 6 of the Rio Treaty, and on December 3, 1963, the Council of the OAS decided by a vote of 16 to 0 to investigate the charges, with Brazil, still under President Goulart, insisting that her assenting vote should not affect the merits of the case,[6] and Mexico abstaining. Brazil suggested that Cuba should be allowed to answer these charges, but this was rejected by the latter on the ground that she was no longer a member of the OAS.[7] An investigating committee was established by the OAS, composed of representatives of the United States, Argentina, Costa Rica, Colombia, and Uruguay, which arrived in Caracas on December 8, 1963, and made its preliminary report behind closed doors on December 20, 1963.[8] Its full report, submitted towards the end of February 1964, concluded unanimously that there was a "policy of aggression" conducted by Cuba against the "territorial sovereignty, the political integrity and the stability of democratic institutions of Venezuela."[9] Venezuela eventually asked for a meeting of consultation of foreign ministers, and the Council of the OAS decided, with Mexico abstaining, to hold the meeting on July 21, 1964.[10] The delay may be explained by a desire not to risk divisions at the meeting, as had happened at Punta del Este in January 1962.[11]

At the meeting, held in Washington between July 21 and July 26, 1964, the question of sanctions against Cuba was the central issue. Venezuela asked for a collective breach of diplomatic and consular relations and the interruption of all trade and communications with Cuba, and was supported by the remaining hard-liners and the United States. After a lengthy period of difficult negotiations two resolutions were passed. Resolution I, adopted by a vote of 15 to 0 with Bolivia, Chile, Mexico, and Uruguay abstaining, called for (a) a break of diplomatic and consular relations; (b) the suspension of all trade, whether direct or indirect (except on humanitarian grounds); and (c) the suspension of all sea communications with Cuba. Resolution II, adopted also by a vote of 16 to 0 with Bolivia, Chile, and Mexico abstaining, presented a "Declaration to the people of Cuba."[12]

The conference revealed a sharp division between sanctionist and non-sanctionist states, with Mexico, Chile, Bolivia, and Uruguay ranged on the side of the latter, and Argentina trying to play the role of a mediator as she had done at Punta del Este in 1962. The non-sanctionist front had, however, been considerably weakened by the defection of Brazil, which had a change of régime on April 1, 1964. Since a two-thirds decision of the meeting was legally binding on all OAS members, Mexico, Chile, Bolivia, and Uruguay were faced with the awkward choice of complying with the OAS decision and risking political repercussions at home, or refusing to comply and thereby weaken the authority of the OAS.

Mexico made it clear from the beginning that she would not impose sanctions, but after a great deal of heart-searching Chile decided to comply on August 11, 1964, Bolivia on August 21, 1964, and Uruguay on September 8, 1964. The non-sanctionist front had collapsed, and Cuba found herself, but for Mexico, completely isolated in the Americas.

Ex-President Betancourt of Venezuela told the Investigating Committee of the OAS that Castro had chosen his country as his primary target because "with our production of three and a half million barrels of oil per day, we are the principal supplier of the primary strategic raw material for the Western world, in time of peace and war."[13] But though R. Leoni, the AD candidate, had won the presidential elections on December 1, 1963, he only obtained 33 percent of the votes cast. Facing relentless militancy on the Left, he had to seek support on the Right in forming a broadly based government able to carry Venezuela through the crisis. The fruits of the policy were reaped when the Ninth Meeting of Foreign Ministers of the OAS adopted mandatory sanctions broadly in line with what Venezuela had demanded.

In order to make the sanctions watertight, the new Venezuelan government had threatened in February to take action against governments trading with Cuba, and Dr. E. Tejera-Paris, Venezuelan ambassador to the OAS, announced that these would soon have to decide whether they wished to trade with Cuba or with Venezuela.[14] In August 1964 Iribarren Borges, the foreign minister, hinted at possible collective action against Mexico if she made good her intention to ignore the OAS decision regarding sanctions.[15] Even President de Gaulle was not left unchallenged on this point during his stay in Caracas in September 1964.[16] However, it was one thing to persuade the OAS but quite another to take on the governments of the rest of the world trading with Cuba, and Venezuela's efforts in this direction were unsuccessful.

It is possible that the diplomatic success of Venezuela in the OAS was a contributory cause of deep division within the Left, where some rebels embraced the Peking line and others, such as A. Rangel, leader of MIR, abandoned the hard - line and were warmly recommended for it by *Pravda*.[17] As early as April 1964—some months before the ninth OAS meeting—the Sixth Plenum of the Venezuelan Communist Party foreshadowed a change in its own tactics by placing less emphasis on the armed struggle as a revolutionary technique.[18]

The extent to which Cuba had been implicated in Venezuela's internal disorders in 1963 remained unclear. On December 6, 1963, Castro said that the cache of arms discovered in Venezuela had been placed there by the CIA in order to compromise Cuba. He referred to the Betancourt Administration as representing "the principal instrument of Yankee imperialism and its plans of aggression" against Cuba.[19] Contradicting himself, he informed Herbert Matthews of the *New York Times* some time later that, "Of course, we engaged in subversion, the training of guerrillas, propaganda! Why not? This is exactly what you are doing to us."[20] This did not prevent Cuba from using legal tactics to gain her political ends when Raúl Roa refused the Investigating Committee of the OAS access and cooperation on the narrow formal grounds that the Cuban government had been illegally excluded from the OAS and, more narrow still, that no member state represented on the investigating committee, with the sole exception of Uruguay, had any diplomatic relations with Cuba.[21]

Castro's kite-flying attempts vis-à-vis the United States were probably designed to frustrate the imposition of a comprehensive embargo on Cuba. That may have been the central strategy behind the interview granted to the *New York Times* on July 5, 1964, in which Castro spelt out his willingness to stop intervening in Latin America in return for the cessation of subversive activities on the part of the United States and its Latin American allies in Cuba.

If Castro's offer was connected with the forthcoming Ninth Meeting of Consultation of Foreign Ministers of the OAS, it was made too late. The State Department rejected it the day after it was made; Venezuela succeeded in producing the OAS vote it wanted; and Dean Rusk dismissed Castro's offer on the ground that what he had proposed was "not a subject for bargaining."[22]

But if Castro's offers had come too late, so had OAS sanctions. Cuba could now rely on the Soviet Union underwriting her economy. Cuba's trade with the Western Hemisphere was nearly all in food and worth no more than $18 million.[23] Nor was Castro impressed by Betancourt's threat to halt trade with Britain, France, and Spain if those countries insisted on trading with Cuba. As Castro rightly observed, Venezuela exported more to those countries than she imported, and therefore her threat was an empty one.[24]

In April 1964 there were signs of a withdrawal of Soviet military experts from Cuba, giving rise to United States fears that certain types of sophisticated ground-to-air missiles capable of shooting down U-2 planes had been handed over to Cuban control. It was ironical that the United States should now be anxious to favor direct Soviet control over Cuban arms in order to ensure the smooth implementation of the Khrushchev-Kennedy agreement of 1962.

Castro's Diplomatic Offensive in the Underdeveloped World

Castro never set any great store by any Latin American government after the Punta del Este conference of 1962 and the crumbling of the quasi-neutralist group of states during the missile crisis. The outcome of the Washington conference of July 1964 seemed to confirm his judgement. Further disappointments were to follow: the fall of Goulart in Brazil, soon followed by that of Paz Estenssoro of Bolivia; and the overwhelming defeat of Allende, presidential candidate of FRAP, at the Chilean elections of September 4, 1964. The Cuban leader's scant respect for even moderate Latin American presidents, such as Arturo Illia in Argentina, to whom he contemptuously referred as "a cheap social doctor,"[25] indicates his growing indifference towards Latin American governments. Simultaneously, Castro developed a contempt of Muscovite Communist Parties in Latin America.

Disillusioned with Latin America and the Soviet Union alike, Castro began to seek fresh diplomatic outlets in the underdeveloped world outside Latin America. So far, there had not been any evidence that the concept of a neutralist "third world" had held much appeal for him. On the contrary, the underdeveloped world, which others saw as *terra optima* of neutralism, was regarded by him as a promising field of revolutionary possibilities.[26]

At the Second Conference of Non-aligned Nations, held in Cairo during October 5-10, 1964, President Dorticós took the opportunity to define Cuba's foreign policy: "Cuba considers it is not allied to any military bloc . . . but we must make clear that non-alignment as far as Cuba or any other country represented here is concerned, should not imply a neutral attitude towards mankind's great problems."[27] Consequently the Cubans began to develop intense political activity in Africa, focussing on African governments with a marked radical slant and indigenous revolutionary movements.

Whitaker maintains that the Goulart régime in Brazil blocked proceedings leading to the Ninth OAS Meeting of Foreign Ministers of July 1964, and that it was only after its fall that "things got moving again."[28] The point is well made, though Brazil was not in this particular instance more militant than the other non-sanctionist states. The foreign minister, de Araújo Castro, after consultation with Goulart, had made it clear as early as January 3, 1964, that Brazil would neither break relations with Cuba nor approve sanctions against her.[29] In this respect Brazil's attitude was similar to that of Bolivia, and like Bolivia, she might have undergone a change of heart if faced with the unpalatable alternatives of either complying with sanctions or flouting the law of the OAS.

The *Revolução* of April 1, 1964, which had unseated the Goulart Administration and brought to power the military under Marshal Castelo Branco, was a turning point.[30] At first there was some ambiguity about the policy adopted by the Castelo Branco régime, but this was due to caution rather than to inclination, and it was some time before its precise policies emerged. Vasco Leitão da Cunha, the new foreign minister, had been ambassador to Havana and Moscow as well as secretary-general of the Itamaratí under Kubitschek and Quadros, but he appears to have been disillusioned by the policies pursued by these two presidents. In his first declaration on foreign policy on April 29, 1964, he maintained that the new régime's foreign policy would amount to a mere rectification, and not an outright reformulation, of previous policy. Yet, his speech already contained the seeds of future developments as he explained how in the modern world there was a tendency for absolute sovereignty to turn itself into interdependence, and how the new régime would pursue bilateral policies in place of "impracticable" multilateral ones.[31]

The president, who took an active interest in foreign policy, made it clear beyond all doubt in a speech to cadets of the Itamaratí on July 31, 1964, that Brazil would be a faithful adherent to "the Western democratic system." He emphasized that the concept of independence could only. operate within certain practical conditions. Within the present bipolar context, the maintenance of independence assumed the recognition of a certain degree of interdependence in military, economic, and political matters. No country in either the Western or the Soviet world would be able to defend itself on its own against either center of power. Similarly, an acknowledgement of economic interdependence was inevitable in trade and investments. Relations with the East which were of a commercial, technical, or financial nature were "therefore possible without prejudice to Brazil's 'basic option.' " Neutralism was criticized by Castelo Branco as encouraging passivity, uncertainty in internal policy and the economic system, and breeding a "hybrid" inefficiency all round. It showed an emotional immaturity springing from a resentment of the resources at the disposal of the two superpowers, and represented a flight from international reality and the risks implicit in it.[32]

The president's speech left no room for any doubt as to Brazil's new role in international affairs. At the same time it clearly revealed the doctrines held by the *Escola Superior de Guerra,* founded at the height of the Cold War in 1949 and preserved unaltered since then, as the source of the president's views.

However, there was no diplomatic break with the Soviet Union, and Brazil's announcement in the Committee of Eighteen composing the Disarmament Conference in Geneva that henceforth her official status of "neutral" in that committee was to be treated as a mere formality, was largely balanced by her attendance as an observer at the Second Conference of Non-aligned Nations in Cairo in October 1964.

Brazil's attitude during the ninth OAS meeting was surprisingly cautious. That she was the key state at the conference was attested by the election of Vasco Leitão da Cunha as chairman.[33] That her attitude was far from impartial may be inferred from statements made before the conference. Thus, the minister of war, A. Costa e Silva, declared in April that a break with Cuba was "an aspiration of the people."[34] On May 11, 1964, Brazil did break diplomatic relations with Cuba, with the reservation that this was done without prejudice to any decisions to be taken at the conference regarding collective sanctions.

Though electorally weak, Dr. Illia's Argentine government enjoyed a certain amount of support in its foreign policy. In Washington, Argentina was at the head of a group of countries willing to go along with those demanding sanctions against Cuba but opposed to their compulsory nature.

Conceding the principle, Argentina tried to prevent its full application by pointing out that, while failing to hurt Cuba, sanctions would have grave internal consequences in some sanctionist countries. Argentina was also opposed to the idea of armed action against Cuba in the event of non-compliance, preferring a solution based on mere condemnation of Castro's infiltration of Venezuela, a warning to Cuba, and the establishment of a vigilance committee.[35] On July 23, 1964, M. A. Zavala Ortiz, Argentina's foreign minister, anxious still to ride a middle course, was beginning to yield in his opposition to sanctions.[36] Argentina had failed in her original purpose and eventually voted with the majority.

Unlike Bolivia, Chile, and Uruguay, all of whom had proclaimed their disagreement with a policy of mandatory collective sanctions, both before and during the conference, Mexico continued to hold firm even after the conference, justifying her non-participation in sanctions on legal grounds. After his Palm Springs (California) meeting of February 22, 1964, with President Johnson, President López Mateos announced publicly that because Cuba was no longer a member state of the OAS, it was for the United Nations to handle the conflict between Venezuela and Cuba, since a non-member could not legally be subjected to sanctions.[37] The force of this statement was explosive, as it ran directly counter to the strenuous attempts of the hard line countries to obtain a mandate for sanctions from the OAS. The effect was in no way mitigated by the president's suggestion that it was the OAS that was the appropriate place for settling the dispute between the United States and Panama, then approaching a climax. It was hardly likely that the United States was eager to be subjected to a decision by the OAS in this dispute. To heighten the effect of the presidential statement, the foreign minister intimated that if the OAS should insist on dealing with the Venezuelan-Cuban dispute, then Mexico would not consider herself bound by any decisions it might take.[38]

Whitaker implies that the timing was deliberate, designed to precede the publication of the report of the investigating committee by a few days—the contents of which must have been known to the Mexican government—and he suggests that the remarks were expressly calculated to soften the impact of that report.[39] This may have been so, but it does not explain why, some time after the Punta del Este conference, at which Cuba had been excluded from the OAS, President López Mateos should have insisted that the dispute between the United States and Cuba should be dealt with by the OAS.[40]

There are two possible explanations for the increasing militancy of Mexico's foreign policy at this particular juncture. First, Mexico may have felt growing alarm at the prospect of the OAS Investigating Committee encroaching on the internal sovereignty of member states of the OAS, a development that no Mexican Administration can afford to contemplate with equanimity. And secondly, though there is no tangible evidence of this, there may have been some strength in the position of the Left in the councils of PRI, at least in the field of foreign policy.

J. Gorostiza, Mexico's foreign minister, did not attend the conference, and his place was taken by V. Sánchez Gavito, a career diplomat known for his vigorous powers of presenting a case. In May, Mexico had intimated that she would prefer a conference on an ambassadorial level. The arguments developed by Sánchez Gavito were of a juridical nature and focussed on the interpretation of the facts and the law appertaining to the situation. He said it had not been shown that the territorial integrity of Venezuela had been affected in ways described in Article 6 of the Rio Treaty and that the objective of that treaty was "primarily the maintenance of a system of collective defense against the possibility of armed attack from the outside." The peace of Venezuela had not been broken and the situation "at no time represented a threat to the peace of the hemisphere," and the proposal that four countries should break off relations with Cuba would be "completely irregular" since it would represent the adoption of measures affecting only a minimal part of the members of the OAS.[41] Whilst the logic of some of the arguments is open to doubt, the strength of the Mexican determination was plain.

At the end of the ninth meeting, Mexico voted against paragraphs 1-3 and 5 of Resolution I, abstained on paragraphs 4 and 6, and voted in favor of paragraph 7, and early in August the foreign minister went so far as to issue a communiqué announcing the president's resolve to continue relations with Cuba. It also announced that Mexico would abide by an advisory opinion of the International Court.[42] This was a course which Cuba had tried to pursue after her exclusion from the OAS at the Punta del Este Conference in 1962, and which Mexico on that occasion had failed to support. Mexico's change of mind on that subject marked a considerable stiffening in her attitude.

Two mutually compatible explanations have been put forward for Mexico's attitude on this occasion. One author suggests that Cárdenas may have extracted a promise from López Mateos and those PRI members who had agreed to support the candidacy of Gustavo Díaz Ordaz at the forthcoming presidential elections not to agree to the imposition of sanctions on Cuba during the ninth meeting of consultation as a condition for giving his support to Díaz Ordaz also.[43] Another author thinks that the economic program worked out by López Mateos in 1962, which envisaged close ties between government and private industry, had succeeded in creating an optimistic atmosphere in which Mexico's rate of economic growth had once more become one of the highest in Latin America. It was because of her economic strength in 1964, as compared with her economic weakness in 1961, that Mexico was able to stand up to the United States at the ninth meeting where she had to give in at the eighth.[44]

Uruguay backed Venezuela's demand for a meeting of OAS foreign ministers, but shortly before the meeting the foreign minister pronounced himself opposed to collective sanctions.[45] When the question of casting Uruguay's vote at the conference on Resolution I arose, the National Executive Council voted unanimously against it. *El Debate*, representing the *ortódoxo* wing of the *blanco* party on August 6, 1964, fiercely attacked the Latin American governments which had voted in favor of sanctions, and Haedo recorded his firm support for continued relations with Cuba, whilst the *colorado* paper *La Mañana*, on August 26, 1964, expressed the view that the choice facing Uruguay after the OAS decision was either to honor or to disavow the Rio Treaty.

Once again Uruguay was in a dilemma over foreign policy. Zorrilla de

San Martín, an ardent noninterventionist, was at the center of the storm since he refused to consider a break until the legal validity of the sanctions envisaged could be tested in the United Nations, and in doing so came close to the radical attitude adopted by the Mexican government.[46] A majority of the National Executive Council seemed to favor him. Only the Herrerista (blanco) leader, M. Echegoyen, and Senator W. Guadalupe favored a break, provided this was followed by similar action with regard to the other Communist countries; a formidable reservation.

On August 30, 1964, a commission of experts set up by the government to make a recommendation in this highly controversial matter reported in favor of compliance with the Washington decision to impose sanctions. [47] Carlos Velazquez, Uruguay's representative at the United Nations, wished the decision to be referred to that body.

Uruguay decided on September 8, 1964, to comply with the OAS ruling, but the official declaration of the break with Cuba was followed by a significant request to the OAS to reconsider the case in plenary session. The voting in the National Executive Council was narrow.[48]

This must have been the hardest, closest, and most controversial decision taken by Uruguay since the war. Whitaker suggests that it was not finally adopted until the unexpectedly decisive victory of Eduardo Frei in the presidential elections in Chile on September 4, 1964—only four days before the critical meeting of the Uruguayan Council—created a new political mood in South America.

In Chile the two main contenders for the presidential election due on September 4, 1964, Eduardo Frei, a Christian Democrat, and Salvador Allende, leader of FRAP, had to clarify their attitudes towards Cuba. The position was complicated by the issue of the future of Chilean copper. FRAP advocated the expropriation of foreign copper companies in Chile, while Frei opposed this on the ground that "Chile only consumes 12,000 tons yearly out of the 500,000 tons she produces," and nationalization would close international markets against her. It would not therefore be reasonable to embark on such a course which might place the country "in the same position as Cuba."[49] Allende countered by asserting that retaliatory measures after expropriation would fail because of the great demand for Chilean copper, and because Chile's reserves are among the best in the world.[50]

Allende furthermore emphatically rejected any suggestions that, in the event of his victory, Chile might become a Soviet base.[51] On this issue there was open conflict between the two party leaders, but both disliked the idea of sanctions against Cuba, Allende going so far as to inform a correspondent of the Italian Communist paper *Paese Sera* that he would take Chile out of the Rio Treaty.[52]

In view of the consensus in this matter, the dying Alessandri Administration had little choice but to act accordingly. Julio Philippi, Chile's foreign minister, therefore denounced the Cuban government forcefully for its intervention in Venezuela, but firmly opposed the idea of sanctions at the ninth OAS meeting. When the ninth meeting decided to impose non-military sanctions on Cuba, Alessandri had to decide whether or not to comply with the majority decision taken at the conference.

Three courses were open to Alessandri. He could (a) adopt a strictly legalistic attitude, which would have implied a recognition of the legality of the processes by which the Ninth Meeting had reached the decision to apply sanctions. In such an event he was equipped with all powers under Chile's constitution to act without any need of consultation at home; or (b) he could cast doubt on the legality of the conference decision, in which case he should have been ready to refer the matter to the United Nations for an advisory opinion; or (c) he could pass on responsibility over this highly controversial issue to a new president, in the conviction that it would not be right for an outgoing administration to take such a grave decision. That Alessandri did not act at once would suggest that he was not certain in his own mind which of the three available solutions he should adopt.[53]

Although it has been suggested that the United States had tacitly agreed that Chile should wait until the presidential elections were over,[54] Alessandri in fact broke with Cuba on August 11, 1964, explaining that his action was "in compliance with Chile's traditional policy of observing international treaties and agreements arrived at democratically by the necessary majorities," and avowing, in flat contradiction to the relevant rule of international law, that this action would not be binding on his successor.[55] And although R. Tomic, an influential left-wing Christian Democrat, was to condemn the decision as "a judicial crime and a political stupidity,"[56] Frei announced during a televised press conference on August 15, 1964, that, though he considered the Washington decision to be an erroneous one, once the Chilean government had decided to comply with it, "it was not within our power to modify it." Frei pleaded with his viewers not to turn this matter into an election issue.[57]

It would be easy to suspect collusion between Alessandri and Frei behind the scenes in order to embarrass Allende in the event of the latter's triumph at the polls, but no such evidence exists, and there are good reasons for assuming that Alessandri had opted for compliance on at least three grounds: (a) because the maxim *pacta sunt servanda* had been one of the principal themes of his administration; [58] (b) because the pending dispute with Bolivia over the River Lauca made a strictly legalistic posture politically more necessary than ever; and (c) because Alessandri's own sense of presidential authority demanded that he should fulfil his duty, irrespective of the consequences for his successor in office.

Bolivia was presented with a similarly difficult decision. The Bolivian representative's attitude at the ninth OAS meeting showed his government's dislike of the idea of sanctions when he joined with Mexico and Uruguay in abstaining from the vote on this issue. Emphasizing the legally binding character of the decision taken at the conference, Gen. L. Rodríguez Bidegaín, Bolivia's acting foreign minister, announced that his government would abide by the decision, but his announcement produced wide political repercussions in the country, especially within the ruling MNR. Only the Liberal Party unanimously favored compliance with the decision.

The president at first refused to impose sanctions, and congressional reaction was sharply divided. In the Senate, in which emotional nationalism is always marked in matters concerning foreign policy, a motion asking the executive to impose non-military sanctions on Cuba was rejected; but the Chamber of Deputies voted overwhelmingly (37 to 5) in favor of sanctions. Though relations with Cuba had been good, all controversy was eventually terminated by the firm decision of the government on August 21, 1964, in favor of carrying out loyally Bolivia's obligations under the OAS charter. [59]

NOTES

1. This is the principal thesis of J. Slater, in op. cit.

2. 15 H.A.R., May 1963, pp. 472-474.

3. *New York Times,* June 14, 1963.

4. See E. Mansera, "Events in Venezuela," *World Marxist Review,* June 1963, pp. 53-56.

5. See *New York Times,* November 4, 7, 9, and 29, 1963.

6. OAS, *Acta del Consejo,* December 3, 1963, pp. 23-25 and 33-34.

7. OAS Council, Report of the *Investigating Committee appointed by the Council of the OAS, acting provisionally as Organ of Consultation, in accordance with the Resolution of December 3, 1963.*

8. *New York Times,* December 22, 1963.

9. *New York Times*, February 25, 1964. This issue of the paper contains the full report.

10. OAS, *Acta del Consejo*, June 26, 1964, p. 15.

11. See A. P. Whitaker, "Cuba's Intervention in Venezuela: A Test of the OAS," 8 *Orbis*, Autumn 1964, pp. 511-536.

12. OAS, *Novena Reunión*, Doc. No. 17, pp. 2 and 4.

13. OAS, *Report of the Investigating Committee* (1964), pp. 44-45.

14. *The Times*, February 26, 1964. See also *Financial Times*, March 3, 1964.

15. 17 H.A.R., August 1964, p. 724.

16. Ibid., September 1964, p. 724.

17. See *The Economist*, September 26, 1964. The URD itself came under pressure from its own radical youth sector under Fabricio Ojeda. See R. Robledo Limón, "El Partido Comunista de Venezuela. Sus tacticas políticas de 1964 a 1969," 4 *Foro Internacional*, April/June 1970, pp. 531-551.

18. Ibid.

19. 16 H.A.R., December 1963, p. 1152.

20. H. Matthews, *Return to Cuba* (Berkeley, 1964), p. 15.

21. See A. Rodríguez, "La Conferencia de la OEA," 5 *Foro Internacional*, April/June 1965, pp. 547-575.

22. Whitaker, op. cit., p. 527.

23. *New York Times*, July 23, 1964.

24. *Financial Times*, March 5, 1965. By way of contrast it was estimated in Britain, France, and Canada, all carrying on trade with Cuba, that the latter had about $100-120 million available for trade with the West outside the Western Hemisphere. See *New York Times*, November 24, 1964. See also G. Zhukov, "Capitalist Trade with Cuba," *New Times* (Moscow), April 15, 1964, pp. 16-17.

25. *New York Times*, October 12, 1964.

26. As Guevara explained to a Uruguayan journalist on September 20, 1964: "The Third World is a world of transition, and it is a world which cannot stay isolated. Even Algeria, to the extent that it becomes more deeply a part of the socialist system, is withdrawing from the Third World." See 17 H.A.R., September 1964, p. 799.

27. Cuba, Ministry of Foreign Affairs, *Cuba at the Second Conference of Non-Aligned Nations* (Havana, 1964), p. 16.

28. Op. cit., p. 512.

29. *New York Times*, January 6, 1964.

30. Opinions about the complicity of the United States in the *Revolução* vary. According to Skidmore, the United States Administration was not involved, though no doubt pleased at the outcome. Ambassador Gordon Lincoln described the event as "one of the major turning points in history." See op. cit., pp. 322-330.

Ex-President Goulart informed the present author during an interview kindly granted in Montevideo on May 29, 1971, that he had received a congratulatory message from the US Administration addressed to the new revolutionary government before he had actually vacated his seat of authority at Brasilia.

31. *O Estado de S. Paulo*, April 30, 1964.

32. Ministério das Relações Exteriores, *Textos e Declarações sobre política externa (de abril de 1964 a abril de 1965)* (Brasilia, 1965), pp. 7-14. On the general

change, see V. Reisky de Dubnic, "Brasiliens neue Aussenpolitik. Von der Block-freiheit zur Solidarität mit dem Westen," 20 *Europa-Archiv,* February 10, 1965, pp. 91-100.

33. 17 H.A.R., July 1964, p. 663.
34. *O Estado de S. Paulo,* April 12, 1964. There was substance in the minister's assertion only insofar as at a meeting of the presidents of the legislative assemblies of fifteen Brazilian states, held in São Paulo, the representatives of Guanabara, Minas Gerais, and São Paulo had issued a manifesto calling for a break with Cuba which commanded the unanimous acceptance of those representatives, as well as the signatures of 29 parliamentarians who were present. See ibid., April 11, 1964.
35. Whitaker, op. cit., p. 524. The pro-Perón *Confederación General de Trabajo* officially and publicly encouraged the government to oppose sanctions. Ibid., p. 522.
36. See Panamerican Union, *Novena Reunión de Consulta de Ministros de Rela-ciones Exteriores, 21-26 de julio de 1964* (Washington, D.C., 1965), pp. 145-153.
37. *New York Times,* February 23, 1964.
38. Whitaker, op. cit., p. 516.
39. Ibid., p. 517.
40. Nor would this have justified the director-general of the Mexican *Banco de Comercio Exterior,* R. Zaveda, to announce with triumphant defiance, during a press conference in Warsaw on June 23, 1964, that Mexico was selling Cuba articles which were enabling the latter to extricate herself from the difficulties created by the United States blockade. See *New York Herald Tribune,* June 24, 1964.
41. OAS, *Novena Reunión,* Doc. No. 47, p. 2.
42. Ibid., pp. 218-219.
43. A. K. Smith, *Mexico and the Cuban Revolution. Foreign Policy Making in Mexico under President López Mateos, 1958-1964* (Ithaca, N.Y.: Cornell University, 1970), pp. 249-250.
44. Olga Pellicer de Brody, *México y la Revolución Cubana* (Mexico City, 1971).
45. Whitaker, op. cit., p. 525.
46. The foreign minister was even reported to have been confident that, if the matter were referred to the United Nations, the latter would reject the decision taken at the ninth meeting. See *Revolución* (Havana), July 30, 1964.
47. The Commission was composed of Dr. Pratt de Maria, director of the Treaty Department at the Foreign Ministry; Dr. A. Aguirre, director of the Diplomatic Department at that ministry; A. Freyre and H. Grey Espiell.
48. See *El País,* September 9, 1964.
49. See *Financial Times,* March 24, 1964.
50. *New York Times,* June 7, 1964.
51. Ibid.
52. See 17 H.A.R., July 1964, p. 647. This point was in any case provided for in the electoral program of FRAP.
53. J. Duran, a right-wing Radical, favored compliance with the OAS decision; but the Radical Party itself, and all parties to the left of it, opposed the imposition of sanctions.
54. Slater, op. cit., p. 170.
55. 17 H.A.R., October 1964, p. 741; Whitaker, op. cit., p. 534.
56. *El Mercurio,* August 19, 1964.

57. Ibid., August 16, 1964.

58. See, for instance, a prominent declaration to this effect by G. Vergara Donoso, Alessandri's first foreign minister, on February 6, 1959, in *El Mercurio,* February 7, 1959.

59. Ex-President Paz Estenssoro informed this writer in 1971 that Bolivia's decision had been greatly influenced by that of Chile, which preceded it by ten days.

It has been suggested that the United States and Bolivia had been "just short of open quarrel" because of the latter's failure to break off diplomatic relations with Cuba following the reelection of Paz Estenssore for another presidential term on May 31, 1964, and that economic pressures had been applied subsequently by the United States through a "highly political aid program." Paz Estenssoro was overthrown in a military coup on November 4, 1964. Juan de Onis, writing in the *New York Times,* August 9, 1964.

Chapter XI

CRISIS IN THE DOMINICAN REPUBLIC (1965-1966)

Nearly all ties between Cuba and the OAS countries, with the exception of Mexico, had now been severed. And while Cuban trade with the rest of the world remained unaffected, the Cuban economy could not have survived without the support of the Soviet Union.

The United States rested content with maintaining a high degree of isolation of Cuba in the hope that this would prevent the latter from fomenting upheaval in Latin America. The validity of the Khrushchev-Kennedy agreement continued to be upheld, but there persisted a nagging suspicion that the Soviet Union was merely biding her time to make a comeback under more favorable conditions somewhere else in the sub-continent. To avoid this, United States policy—especially after the death of Kennedy—sought above all the preservation of the status quo in Latin America. This was a sound enough calculation, but it failed to cover contingencies in which spontaneous revolution implicating neither Havana nor Moscow could bring in its train consequences which these policies were supposed to prevent. A situation of this kind arose unexpectedly in the Dominican Republic in April 1965.

Intervention

In December 1962, 60 percent of all votes went to Juan D. Bosch, a prominent intellectual and middle-of-the-road politician, in a free presidential election. The new president, basically a left-of-center reformer, met numerous difficulties in carrying out his program and, after nine months in office, was overthrown in a military coup in September 1963. The junta which supplanted him failed to make any headway, and before long its unity disintegrated. An open bid for power by reforming elements among the military and their civilian allies was made on April 4, 1965, but the attempt was only partially successful and dissolved amid general confusion within four days.

Acting on the advice of his ambassador in Santo Domingo, J. B. Martin, President Johnson ordered United States marines into the Dominican Republic on April 28, 1965, ostensibly to evacuate United States nationals who were alleged to be in mortal danger, but actually in order to prevent the establishment of "another Communist State in the Western Hemisphere," as President Johnson had to admit on May 2, 1965.[1] The action by the United States was taken without consulting the OAS.[2]

Eventually, the Tenth Meeting of Consultation of OAS Foreign Ministers assembled in Washington and resolved to dispatch an Inter-American Force to the Dominican Republic, in which the United States troops already there were to be integrated. After a great deal of indecision and confusion, elections were held on June 1, 1966, under the supervision of the OAS, and the Inter-American Force was eventually withdrawn.

The Revolutionaries

The policy which would have been adopted by the party of Bosch—the *Partido Revolucionario Dominicano*—is known, as it had been revealed during the nine months while he was in office. Three features stand out in its record. One was enthusiastic espousal of the Alliance for Progress, especially its reforming aspects, some of them enshrined in the Bosch Constitution of 1963.[3] The second was uncompromising hostility to the Communists at home. When he appealed to the United States on April 29, 1965, to refrain from intervention, it was done in the name of anti-Communism.[4] Thirdly, in his foreign policy Bosch proved to be a moderate with isolationist tendencies. On the one hand he refused to establish relations with Cuba, but on the other he performed no positively hostile act against Cuba nor showed any hostile intent against the Castro régime, which may have aroused suspicion in Washington. Col. F. Caamaño, the commander of the pro-Bosch revolutionaries in Santo Domingo, pursued policies identical with those practiced by Bosch in office.

Unlike the Communists of Guatemala and Cuba, the Communists of the Dominican Republic were neither well-organized nor able to throw up men possessing high qualities of leadership. Above all, they were split into three factions:[5] the *Partido Socialista Popular Dominicano* (Moscow-oriented); the *Movimiento Popular Dominicano* (Peking-oriented); and the *Agrupación Política Catorze de Junio* (Havana-oriented). Of these three, the last probably contained some well-trained *guerrilleros* who were able to hold General Wessin's tanks at bay at a time when even Caamaño had taken to the shelter of an embassy. It would not, therefore, on the surface, seem that the Communists constituted a basic element of the revolutionary pattern.

Forewarned by their experience during the Cuban missile crisis of 1962, the Soviet leadership remained extremely careful during the crisis not to do or say anything that might encourage suspicions of Soviet military aid to the rebels. And though Cuba was well-placed for providing military assistance,[6] she remained content with sounding a clarion call to Latin America to raise to the occasion by giving military aid to the rebels, while burying the diplomatic hatchet temporarily with those Latin American governments critical of the United States in this matter.[7]

The remainder of Latin America was divided in its reaction. Uruguay, Chile, and Mexico provided the hard core of resistance to the action taken by the United States, with Argentina, Ecuador, Peru, and Venezuela disapproving in less intransigent terminology. At the other end of the scale Brazil, flanked by the traditional client states of the United States, supported the United States, while Bolivia and Colombia tended to stand aloof.

In Chile, President Frei sought support in Western Europe to cope with the oppressive hegemony of the United States in Latin America.[8] And while proposing the creation of a Latin American common market which would include Cuba,[9] he was determined not to do anything to endanger the prospects of continued United States aid, and allowed Gabriel Valdés, his foreign minister, to praise the Alliance for Progress on January 6, 1965, as "the most impressive" effort of its kind in America.[10]

Frei took much of the wind out of the sails of the Left by speedily restoring diplomatic relations with the Soviet Union on November 24, 1963, in accordance with an election promise and after an interval of interruption of 17 years, as well as with other Communist countries with which Chile had had diplomatic relations in the past. In the autumn of 1964 a trade mission from Communist China was established in Santiago, and in November 1965 Chile abstained in the United Nations in the vote on the admission of the government of that country.

Over Cuba, however, Frei displayed considerable caution. In November 1964 he maintained that, in spite of ideological differences that separated him from Cuba, he was hopeful of seeing a Latin American effort to readmit Cuba to membership of the American community, and Enrique Bernstein, Chile's chief delegate at the United Nations, was allowed to approach Guevara on his own initiative in New York with a view to exploring possibilities in that direction.[11]

Valdés, Frei's foreign minister, who differed considerably from the president in both temperament and style, wished to see the reestablishment of commercial relations with Cuba as a prelude to full diplomatic relations, and the Chilean embassy in Paris, where Bernstein had been transferred meanwhile, was subsequently the scene of unsuccessful private soundings for a suitable formula for Cuba's return to the OAS.[12] In public, Valdés hedged his offer to Cuba during a comprehensive review of Chile's foreign policy in the Senate on January 6, 1965, with a number of unacceptable conditions. "The Cuban adventure," he said, "has been invalidated not by its Marxist character, but by its lack of autonomy," and if Cuba was to qualify for Chilean support, the Havana government would have to "revert to its original direction, whatever the socio-economic régime in force."[13]

Frei's objective in cultivating Western Europe, promoting Latin American economic integration, and normalizing relations with the Communist countries seems to have been to build on the conception of a West resting on three pillars of an Anglo-Saxon North America, Western Europe, and Latin America on a footing of strict equality.[14] That in order to achieve this he was prepared to go to some lengths in curbing United States hegemony in the Western Hemisphere was proved during the crisis in the Dominican Republic. On April 29, 1965, the Chilean government instructed its representative in the OAS to demand "immediate collective action of the OAS instead of unilateral measures," and to agree to a proposal received from President Leoni of Venezuela on the same day to take common action. When there was no abatement of the intensity and scale of the intervention, Chilean attitudes began to stiffen noticeably, and a Mexican resolution in the OAS on May 1, 1965, to appoint a five-man committee composed of representatives of Argentina, Brazil, Colombia, Guatemala, and Panama was opposed by the Chilean representative on the ground that acceptance would be tantamount to approving the action of the United States.[15]

The tone of these statements and the openly defiant attitude adopted by Chile at this stage could not, however, conceal the fact that by having proposed collective OAS action earlier on, Chile had limited her own subsequent freedom of action in offering outright opposition to the United States. She had therefore to modify her position somewhat, yielding the role of leader of the Latin American opposition to Uruguay and Mexico. Thus, when on June 2, 1965, the Tenth Meeting adopted the decision to put responsibility for mediation in the hands of a Commission of Three, Chile, in common with Venezuela, merely abstained, whilst Uruguay and Mexico voted against the proposal.[16] The Chilean attitude remained distinctly critical, however, as regards the basic nature of the intervention, and her representatives denied that it could in any way be justified on ideological grounds.[17] Chile subsequently resisted any attempt to reform the OAS in such a way as to invest its Council with powers of decision in political matters in advance of those already enjoyed by the Meeting of Foreign Ministers under the Rio Treaty.

The harshest opposition offered to the United States came from Uruguay. This caused surprise, since the country had been in the throes of a general crisis for some years.[18] During the crisis in the Dominican Republic, Uruguay happened, with Bolivia, to be one of Latin America's non-permanent members on the Security Council, and it was this body, rather than the ninth meeting, in which Uruguay's voice was heard loudest through its representative, Carlos M. Velazquez, a politician in the Herrerista tradition of independent action in foreign affairs.

On April 29, 1965, the Chamber of Deputies in Montevideo adopted by a majority of 65 to 74 a resolution protesting against the landing of United States marines in the Dominican Republic,[19] and on May 3, 1965, the National Executive Council instructed the Uruguayan representative in the OAS to demand the withdrawal of the United States from the Dominican Republic. When the French representative on the Security Council voiced an identical demand that day, the two Latin American representatives expressed opposing views: while the Bolivian representative sided with the United States by arguing that the resolution of the conflict should be left to the OAS, the Uruguayan representative considered the United States action illegal and as having gone "beyond all the norms known in the inter-American system." He proposed that the Security Council deal with the problem and call for an immediate cessation of unilateral action in the Dominican Republic, referring throughout his address disparagingly to the action of the United States as based on what he called the "Johnson doctrine."[20]

In the OAS, meanwhile, Uruguay was one of five states (the others were Chile, Ecuador, Mexico, and Venezuela) to vote against participation in an Inter-American Force for despatch to the Dominican Republic. It came as a most unpleasant surprise to the United States to be confronted so resolutely in the Security Council by a fellow American government, as the paramountcy of the OAS in the resolution of inter-American conflicts had been taken for granted since the Guatemalan crisis.[21]

Following instructions formulated by the National Executive Council, Velazquez took the initiative on May 14, 1965, in proposing a resolution authorizing the secretary-general of the United Nations "to follow closely the events in the Dominican Republic and take such measures as he may deem appropriate for the purpose of reporting to the Security Council."[22] This the representative of the United States opposed, revealing to the world at large the breach that existed between it and some Latin American states. Matters were made worse by the fact that the Uruguayan initiative in the Security Council was taken in response to an urgent request to it by Dr. Jolti Cury, Colonel Caamaño's foreign minister. In the end the United States had to acquiesce in the dispatch of a United Nations mission headed by A. J. Mayobre, executive-secretary of ECLA, in his capacity as U Thant's special representative.

There were signs that at this point elements in the Uruguayan Administration were taking fright at the intransigent attitude to which its representative on the Security Council had committed himself, and a second line of policy was developed to ensure speedy retreat. The stage chosen was the OAS rather than the United Nations. On May 22, 1965, the same day on which Velazquez was so eloquently asserting the priority of the Security Council, Uruguay's representative in the OAS, E. Oribe, voted in favor of a proposal to create an Inter-American Force in the Dominican Republic, a complete reversal of attitudes, after the Uruguayan delegate in the OAS had on no less than eleven previous occasions voted against the establishment of such a force.[23] On June 3, 1965, Uruguay associated herself with Chile, Ecuador, Mexico, and Venezuela in refusing to sign a letter of permanent Latin American representatives to the United Nations urging the coordination of efforts between the OAS and the United Nations in the Dominican Republic.[24] Finally, Velazquez announced categorically in the Security Council on June 7, 1965, that "no collective action . . . can flow legitimately from the Tenth Consultative Meeting (of the OAS) and this includes the creation of that Inter-American Force to be used in an American State."[25]

An anti-climax followed almost immediately. On June 11, 1965, a correspondent of the *New York Times* in Montevideo reported that according to "government sources," Uruguay's foreign minister, L. Vidal Zaglio, had informed the National Executive Council that Velazquez had "distorted and exceeded" his instructions in attacking the United States; he had given a false slant, and allowed his own feelings to influence his presentation of the case in demanding that the problem of the Dominican Republic be removed from the jurisdiction of the OAS. According to the same source, Uruguay's new diplomatic position was that a neutral provisional government should be formed, and that early elections should be held under the supervision of the United Nations.[26] At the same time it was announced that Velazquez would shortly become ambassador in London. The Uruguayan ambassador in Washington denied expressly that Velazquez' action in the Security Council had anything to do with this appointment.[27]

That at this juncture there had been a sharp reversal in Uruguay's foreign policy can scarcely be doubted. In mid-June the Uruguayan foreign minister travelled to Chile and Peru in an effort to canvas support for the idea that the neutrals in Latin America—Chile, Mexico, Peru, and Uruguay—should form a group capable of taking over from the OAS in the event of the latter failing in its task of pacification and conciliation in the Dominican Republic, and on June 13, 1965, he announced officially that Velazquez had not departed from his instructions in addressing the Security Council.[28]

Mexico's performance in regard to the crisis in the Dominican Republic fell below expectations, considering her robust refusal to agree to the decisions of the Ninth Meeting of OAS Foreign Ministers taken in July 1964. The election of President G. Díaz Ordaz in 1964 with the support of ex-President Cárdenas had been interpreted to mean that changes in foreign policy would be a matter of emphasis only. During the first six years of the Castro régime, the Left in Mexico had blamed business for trying, by all means including the withdrawal of capital, to compel the government to condemn Cuba. The Right had blamed the flight of capital that had taken place on the climate created by the Left and the weak governmental reactions to it.[29]

Under Díaz Ordaz the Right seems to have taken some heart. The United States was criticized for not doing enough for Mexico under the Alliance for Progress,[30] and businessmen would inveigh against the gringo invasion of capital from the North. Under the impact of the shock occasioned by the invasion of the Dominican Republic, the fairly wide differences between Left and Right disappeared, with both sides rallying behind the policy of the government.[31]

The first responses of the Mexican Administration to reports coming in from the Dominican Republic showed a caution so marked as to seem to confirm the supposed conservative character of the Díaz Ordaz régime. On April 30, 1965, A. Carrillo Flores, the foreign minister, said he hoped the marine landings would be "as brief as possible" and that he recognized the humanitarian reasons for the intervention. It was only at the end of May that Mexico refused to sign an address to the Security Council canvassed by twelve Latin American countries to reaffirm their adherence to the OAS.[32] On June 1, 1965, the Ministry of Foreign Affairs reminded the world that the furthest that the founders of the OAS had gone in 1948 in the way of collective intervention was to create an Inter-American Defense Committee.[33]

When the fighting had stopped, however, Mexico abandoned its root-and-branch opposition to the United States by assuming the role of conciliator at the Extraordinary OAS Rio conference in November 1965.[34] When the Colombian representative there wished to introduce a resolution in which a clear and adverse allusion was made to the invasion, R. de la Colina, the Mexican representative, persuaded him to withdraw it.[35]

With Uruguay, Chile, and Mexico in the vanguard of opposition to the United States, Argentina tried to play the role of mediator, but in doing so was brought to the point of internal political disruption, as differences of opinion were revealed between M. A. Zavala Ortiz, the foreign minister, and Arturo Illia, the president. Argentina's attitude in the crisis also provoked a contest between the executive and legislative branches of the government.

At first the government, with Zavala Ortiz as its spokesman, tried to seek refuge in a formula whereby any state was entitled to use measures of self-defense, individually or collectively, against Communist subversion from Cuba; but as United States action in the Dominican Republic escalated, the government was forced to modify its attitude. Uneasily, Argentina approved of the creation of an Inter-American Force, while Zavala Ortiz added the rider that nobody would be compelled to contribute any forces.[36]

In Congress, meanwhile, even the Conservatives expressed severe misgivings about the United States actions, while the Peronists clamored for a withdrawal of United States forces and the left-wing Socialists, led by R. Muñiz, wanted Argentina to leave the OAS by way of protest.[37] The foreign minister tried to beat a retreat by denying the right of intervention to the United States,[38] advising Congress to agree to the participation of Argentine troops in the Inter-American Force,[39] and informing the United States ambassador that no political interference in the operations of this force could be tolerated. This ingenious scheme was, however, frustrated by an adverse vote in Congress on May 19, 1965.[40]

This left Argentina virtually without a policy. In despair, Zaval Ortiz called a conference of foreign ministers of Argentina, Brazil, Chile, Paraguay, Uruguay, Peru, and Bolivia from which he hoped to obtain some guidance. The refusal of Brazil, Peru, and Chile to attend the conference frustrated his initiative, while the Bolivian government added to Argentina's embarrassment by inquiring whether Argentina would be prepared to send troops to Bolivia in the event of a Communist coup there.[41]

Early in June 1965, J. R. Vázquez, under-secretary of foreign affairs, resigned in protest against what he described as Argentina's neutrality, reflected in the many votes of abstention cast at OAS meetings during the crisis. Zavala Ortiz offered his resignation several times, but on each occasion his policy was approved by the cabinet, which remained united at the crucial moments of the crisis even though President Illia would have preferred a consistently hard line against the action taken by the United States.[42] Discontent with Argentina's policy among the hard liners in the armed forces reached a peak when Gen. J. Onganía, the commander-in-chief, advocated an ideological alliance with Brazil against Communism, thereby challenging the reserved attitude of the government towards the military régime in Brazil. The general was made to resign in December 1965, but succeeded in seizing the presidency in a coup on June 26, 1966.

Venezuela's reaction caused some surprise. A determined opponent of the Castro régime—it was on her insistence that OAS sanctions had been imposed on Cuba in 1964—her policy may to some extent have been dictated by the fear that an inconsistent attitude on this occasion might lose her the continued support of the Latin American countries maintaining these sanctions.

Public opinion was outraged by the action taken by the United States, especially as there had been close personal ties between Betancourt and Bosch when they were both exiles.[43] On April 29, 1965, Venezuela was among the Latin American states calling for the immediate convocation of an OAS meeting of consultation. A congressional resolution urged that a strong protest be sent also to the United States government calling for the withdrawal of forces from the Dominican Republic.[44]

When the Tenth Meeting called for a vote in support of a resolution to set up an Inter-American Force, the Venezuelan delegate was among the five abstainers, trying unsuccessfully to amend the resolution by calling for the replacement of all United States forces by an OAS force drawn exclusively from Latin American countries.[45]

Brazil backed the action taken by the United States to the hilt. In March 1965 Vasco Leitão da Cunha, the foreign minister, had disclosed in Miami his government's intention to "do everything possible" short of establishing a Cuban government in exile on Brazilian soil to enable the Cuban people to "liberate themselves from the régime of Fidel Castro." [46] Brazil consequently made the only substantial Latin American contribution to the Inter-American Force and, in the person of Gen. H. Panasco Alvim, supplied the nominal commander of that force.[47] Throughout 1965 Brazilian statesmen tried, without notable success, to canvas the notion of "ideological frontiers" which had supposedly supplanted the outworn concept of territorial sovereignty in its strictly formal sense. [48] The new concept was to fit in neatly with the arguments in favor of a permanent inter-American force.

That Brazil was never to break off relations with the Soviet Union and its satellites in Eastern Europe was perhaps due to the influence of Roberto de Oliveira Campos, minister of planning and economic coordination, who was eager to secure new markets for Brazil;[49] to the resilience of the diplomatic service which had been taken over by the new régime almost intact and had succeeded in preserving its esprit de corps;[50] and also to the personal influence of Vasco Leitão da Cunha, basically an Anglophile Liberal who knew the Soviet Union from personal experience as ambassador in Moscow.

United States intervention in the Dominican Republic had solved nothing. New life was imparted to the moribund idea that the United

States was determined to prevent socio-economic change in Latin America, and a fresh impetus was provided for the far Left in Latin America to engage in all-out action to reduce United States political influence on the sub-continent.

The action taken by the United States may have demonstrated the ability of her forces to quell any Latin American rising, but if the Soviet Union was impressed by this United States resolve, Latin American revolutionary movements associated with Havana certainly were not. On the contrary, they would draw fresh hope from the general indignation displayed in Latin America at the intervention and set out to perfect the techniques of the guerrilla thought appropriate to the new conditions.

NOTES

1. See Connell-Smith, op. cit., p. 336 et seq.
2. *New York Times*, May 9, 1965.
3. Under Bosch the republic received loans and grants worth nearly $50 million from Alliance for Progress funds. See *The Economist*, September 28, 1963. During his visit to Washington in January 1963 Bosch welcomed the Alliance for Progress policy of the United States. See *Neue Zürcher Zeitung*, January 8, 1963. But in his memoirs, written after 1965, he showed some reserve about the way the Alliance operated in practice. See *The Unfinished Experiment* (London: Pall Mall, 1965), pp. 146-166.
4. *The Times*, April 30, 1965.
5. For a brief historical sketch, see *L'Est et Ouest*, May 1-15, 1966.
6. Cuba had no excuse for lacking the military means for helping the constitutionalist side in the Dominican Republic. In addition to ample tank forces, Cuba in 1965 possessed heavy artillery and possibly more than 100 Soviet jet fighters. Cuba also retained short-range missiles of various kinds. See *New York Times*, March 22, 1965. See also E. Ameijeiros, Cuba's deputy-minister of defense, "Gracias a la URSS, contamos hoy con el mejor ejército de la América Latina," *Revolución*, February 22, 1964.
7. See *Revolución*, May 5, 1965. See also the special edition of 10 *Política Internacional* (Havana), April/June 1965. On April 30, 1965, Roa merely called on U Thant to take action. See *New York Times*, May 1, 1965.
8. As Frei explained, it was "preferable to have a strong (Western) Europe rather than two blocs only." See *Le Monde*, October 4-5, 1964.
9. See A. Craig, "Chile's Revolution in Freedom," *The British Survey*, December 1965, p. 9.
10. See G. W. Grayson, "The Significance of the Frei Administration for Latin America," 9 *Orbis*, Autumn 1965, pp. 760-779.
11. It was typical of Frei's reserve that he made the significant amendment in

Bernstein's draft of a speech to the General Assembly that the guarantee of human rights in Cuba would be an essential prerequisite of any restoration of Cuba's rights in the OAS.

According to an account of Bernstein's talks with Guevara, provided by the Chilean Ministry of Foreign Affairs for the benefit of other Latin American governments, Chile had offered a guarantee, couched in abstract terms, of non-intervention and self-determination in return for a Cuban undertaking to break her military ties with the Soviet Union. Guevara rejected this as useless. See *New York Times*, December 29, 1964.

12. *New York Times*, December 28, 1964.

13. See G. Valdés, *Resumen de las proposiciones que formulara Chile en la próxima Conferencia Interamericana Extraordinaria de la OEA* (Santiago, 1965).

14. On this point, see Frei's general statement on election day, as reported in *Le Monde*, September 4-5, 1964.

15. *New York Times*, April 30, 1965, and May 1 and 2, 1965.

16. *The Times*, June 7, 1965.

17. According to an opinion poll taken by Professor E. Hamuy, only 6.8 percent of Chileans supported United States intervention in the Dominican Republic, whilst 48.8 percent were against it. See L. Gross, *The Last, Best Hope. Eduardo Frei and Chilean Democracy* (New York, 1967), p. 198.

18. Though the blanco party had won the elections of 1962 and held a majority of seats in the National Executive Council, it was outnumbered in Congress. The Nardone faction within the party had disintegrated following the death of its founder in 1964, and the colorados were split into ten identifiable factions.

19. *Cámara de Representantes, Diario de Sesiones*, April 29, 1965, p. 537.

20. See *Washington Post*, May 5, 1965.

21. For a legal appraisal of the conflict of jurisdiction, see G. I. A. D. Draper, "Regional Arrangements and Enforcement Action," 20 *Revue Egyptienne de droit international* (1964), pp. 1-44. See also I. L. Claude, "The OAS, the United Nations and the United States," *International Conciliation*, No. 547, March 1964; and D. Baron, "The Dominican Republic Crisis of 1965, A Case-Study of the Regional v. the Global Approach to International Peace and Security," in A. W. Cordier's (ed.), *Columbia Essays on International Affairs*, Vol. III (1967), pp. 1-37.

22. *New York Times*, May 15, 1965. For details of the instructions, see *Carta de Montevideo*, May 10, 1965.

23. *New York Times*, May 23, 1965. Those voting against on this occasion were Chile, Exuador, Mexico, and Peru; Argentina and Venezuela abstained; the remainder voted in favor.

24. UN Doc. S/PV. 1220, June 3, 1965.

25. UN Doc. S/PV. 1221, June 7, 1965.

26. *New York Times*, June 11, 1965.

27. Ibid.

28. *New York Times*, June 14, 1965.

29. M. Ojeda Gómez, "México en el ámbito internacional," 6 *Foro Internacional*, October/December 1965, pp. 247-270.

30. See an article printed in *Comercio Exterior*, March 1965, a government organ often reflecting the views of businessmen close to the government, by T. Moscoso,

former Puerto Rican-born coordinator of the Alliance for Progress under President Kennedy. "Es adecuado la actitud de EE UU hacia la Alianza para el Progreso?" (March 1965). President Díaz Ordaz went out of his way in his State of the Union message of September 1, 1965, to praise the Alliance. See *Latin America Times,* September 3, 1965.

31. Congratulations poured in from the Central Committee of the Trade Union of Electricians; from students; from the National Confederation of Peasants, as well as from entrepreneurs. See *Novedades,* May 7, 1965; *El Nacional,* May 11, 1965; *El Universal,* May 8, 1965; and ibid. respectively.

32. *Le Monde,* May 30-31, 1965.

33. *Latin American Times,* July 20, 1965. J. Torres Bodet, Mexico's minister of foreign affairs at the Bogotá Conference of 1948, had expressly rejected the idea of an inter-American force. See A. de Rosenzweig Díaz, "Siete aspectos cruciales de la política exterior de Mexico," *Polémica,* May/June 1969, pp. 82-83. The protest was double-barrelled, for the ruling *Partido Revolucionario Institucional* entered a strong protest against intervention in the affairs of the Dominican Republic. Like the document issued by the Foreign Ministry, the Party document attacked the concept of an Inter-American Force ("the so-called Inter-American Force") and supported Mexico's resolve, expressed by Díaz Ordaz, not to have any part in it. Partido Revolucionario Institucional, *Democracia y justicia social* (June, 1965).

34. For details, see Olga Pellicer de Brody, "México en la OEA," 6 *Foro Internacional,* October/December 1965, and January/March 1966, pp. 228-302, in footnote 9 at p. 302.

35. For details, see ibid., p. 295.

36. Zavala Ortiz was convinced of the uselessness of opposing the United States as a matter of principle, and preferred a course which was both pragmatic and less difficult. (Information kindly supplied to this writer by the former foreign minister in an interview granted in Buenos Aires on June 17, 1971.)

37. *La Prensa,* May 8, 1965.

38. B. Goldenberg, "Die dominikanische Tragödie," 14 *Europa-Archiv* (1965), p. 527.

39. *Le Monde,* May 9-10, 1965.

40. Goldenberg, op. cit.

41. *Neue Zürcher Zeitung,* May 21, 1965. Ex-President Frondizi chose this moment to predict that if a policy of mutual insurance of régimes were to be adopted in Latin America, it would lead to the wholesale intervention of Latin American governments in each other's affairs. See A. Frondizi, *La cuestion dominicana y la soberanía argentina* (Buenos Aires, 1965), especially pp. 11-12. According to one source, Zavala Ortiz expressed himself outside Congress as being cautiously in favor of the action by the United States, which he saw as being directed against the possibility of a Communist subversion of the Caamaño forces. See *Neue Zürcher Zeitung,* May 22, 1965.

42. Information kindly supplied to the present writer by M. A. Zavala Ortiz in an interview granted in Buenos Aires on June 17, 1971.

43. Betancourt condemned the United States intervention on May 3, 1965, in New York. See *New York Times,* May 4, 1965. He tried to influence the Johnson Administration to soften the "hard-line." See *Le Monde,* May 7, 1965.

44. *New York Times,* May 1, 1965.

45. *New York Times,* May 7, 1965.

46. *O Estado de S. Paulo,* March 11, 1965.

47. On July 3, 1965, that force was composed as follows: United States, 10,900 troops; Brazil, 1,115; Costa Rica, 20 policemen; El Salvador, 3 general staff officers; Honduras, 250 men; Nicoragua, 164; Paraguay, 183. See *OAS Chronicle,* August 1965, p. 5.

48. For a critical voice, see *Correio da Manhã,* May 23, 1965.

49. See R. de Oliveira Campos' plea for new markets in *O Estado de S. Paulo,* September 16, 1965. For details of his trip to Moscow in search of trade, see ibid., September 5-17, 1965.

50. Only five members of the diplomatic corps lost their posts as a result of the *Revolução;* one of them at the express behest of a European government.

Chapter XII

THE RISE OF THE GUERRILLA (1965-1967)

Nothing illustrated more forcefully the demise of the Cold War in Latin America in its classical form than the desperate efforts made by the Cubans to stir its embers. Stripped of missile power, only half-willing to accept the terms of the Khruschchev-Kennedy agreement and feeling betrayed by the Soviet Union, Cuba felt isolated. Until October 1962 the Cuban leadership may have been convinced of the willingness of the Soviet Union to support Cuban-type revolutions in Latin America. That conviction was severely shaken but not altogether destroyed by the outcome of the missile crisis, for a purely strategic accommodation between the two world powers over Cuba need not necessarily have affected the principle of Soviet support for revolution elsewhere in Latin America.[1]

Since the missile crisis, and possibly even before, it had been established Soviet policy to sanction the use of violence in Latin America only where it held out real prospects of success.[2] In all other cases the Soviets contented themselves with fostering a transitory process from coalition government with Communist participation to full-fledged Socialism, Moscow-style—or at least sanctioned by Moscow—through an extended period of "national democracy."[3]

The Soviet leaders were sufficiently alarmed to call a secret meeting of pro-Moscow Communist parties of Latin America in Havana in December 1964. To accommodate Cuba, they were prepared to shift their strategy somewhat and, in two articles in the Party periodical *Kommunist* in August 1964, had veered from an unspecified position in the matter of the use of violence to one of positive approval of this form of struggle in certain circumstances.[4]

That Cuba's policy was undergoing substantial change could be inferred not only from statements made in Havana, but also from the publication in 1965 of *La Révolution dans la révolution,* a study of revolutionary strategy by Régis Debray, a young French philosopher, who had at one time been lecturing at Havana University.[5] According to Leninist revolutionary theory, the presence of objectively revolutionary conditions must be the central factor determining the moment of revolutionary action. The maturing process may be hastened by political agitation and organization, but the existence of revolutionary mass conscience was at all times to be an essential preliminary for revolutionary action. Without ostensibly calling this doctrine into question, Debray neatly reversed the operational priorities. A revolutionary situation, according to Debray, could be created by taking revolutionary action first, and promoting a revolutionary conscience among the masses in the wake of action subsequently. The most revolutionary action was military struggle, because it carried the most powerful effect of demonstration. Operational demonstration was more important than political education. In the field, Debray argued consistently, military leadership must be accorded primacy over political leadership whenever necessary. Disclaiming that his strategic theories derived from the historical model of the Cuban Revolution and criticizing the Algerian model as too narrowly confined within the national frame to be useful as a universal precept, Debray recommended the application of the Vietnamese type of guerrilla on a continental scale.[6]

In November 1964 at the latest, the decision must have been taken in Havana to launch a guerrilla movement in Latin America expressly designed to open a second front against the United States, now that she had become deeply involved in Vietnam, and by doing so not only create a military diversion on a world scale, but also promote the revolutionary consciousness of the discontented masses of Latin America. It was hoped the United States would be goaded into intervening in Latin America on a massive scale, and that various guerrilla groups already operating in various places would coalesce. The moderate measure of Soviet encouragement of existing *guerrillas* in Latin America was considered as quite inadequate.[7] In December 1964 Guevara, who appears to have been in charge of the entire guerrilla operation from the start, embarked on a tour of several African countries, including Algeria, Mali, the Congo (Brazzaville), Guinea, and Tanzania, and proclaimed hopefully that Africa presented "one of the most important, if not the most important battlefield against all the forms of exploitation in the world, against imperialism, colonialism and neo-colonialism."[8] As always a revolutionist rather than a statesman, and inclined to seek macro-solutions on a continental scale rather than micro-solutions within the narrow confines of the nation-state, Guevara was convinced at the end of his African tour of "the possibility of creating a common front against colonialism, imperialism and neo-colonialism,"[9] thereby establishing the concept of a universally coordinated struggle on a "tricontinental" canvas.

Cuba's interest in militant Afro-Asian politics was again emphasized when President Dorticós and foreign minister Roa attended the Cairo Conference of Non-Aligned States in October 1964, and there was evidence of growing contacts between Cuba and the rebels in the Congo (Léopoldville).[10] Before long further evidence of the tricontinental nature of Cuba's guerrilla diplomacy emerged. The Congress of Peoples of Asia, a Soviet-sponsored organization of nongovernmental character, had been formed in New Delhi in March 1955, and subsequently expanded into the Organization of Solidarity of the Peoples of Asia and Africa (OSPAA) in Cairo in December 1957. Following the advent of the Castro régime in Cuba, the inclusion of suitably qualified representatives from Latin America was suggested in April 1961. At the Moshi (Tanzania) conference of OSPAA in 1963 Latin American observers were admitted, and the Cuban spokesman offered Havana as the site of the next meeting of the organization. Keen Sino-Soviet competition followed for the promotion of Cuba's representation in OSPAA,[11] and the first regular representation of Latin America was made at the Winneba (Ghana) conference in 1965.

Bolivia had been chosen as a suitable focus for Guevara's projected guerrilla. Centrally placed in the South American continent and relatively inaccessible to the military might of the United States, Bolivia was to provide a base from which a guerrilla, once established, could spread into Argentina, Paraguay, Brazil, Chile, and Peru, setting alight the entire *cono sur* and rendering the intervention of the United States inevitable.

Bolivia was within easy reach of Uruguay, a liberal country through which arms could be channelled without attracting undue attention, and of Chile, from where active support in terms of military aid could be provided by enthusiastic members of the Socialist Party. Politically, it was true, Bolivia was not very promising after the major agrarian reforms carried out there by the Paz Estenssoro Administration since the Revolution of 1952. But Paz Estenssoro was now in exile, and some Bolivian landowners had hopefully returned to the country in order to reclaim their land, thus creating a sense of apprehension among the emancipated peasantry.

The Tricontinental Conference (January 1966)

There was now a distinct possibility of the Soviet Union and China being outflanked on the Left by an OSPAA charismatically refurbished by the adherence of revolutionary Cuba and a number of nongovernmental, pro-Cuban delegations from Latin America.[12] To be disparaging about Castro in these circumstances was hardly practical politics. The only alternative course was to promote him. The Soviet leaders were willing to fall in with the idea of forming a new worldwide, tricontinental organization—an expanded version of OSPAA—and to have it centered in Havana. But once the Cubans were in charge of the conference, they introduced the maximum number of pro-Castro delegations from Latin America, thereby enabling Castro to stave off Soviet and Chinese pressures alike by clever stage management and by the ingenious political device of following the Soviet line in respect of interstate relations while retaining an individual position with regard to world revolutionary strategy.[13]

The Soviet Union, grown wary of Cuba, wanted Cairo to be retained as headquarters; but the Chinese, sensing an advantage, suggested Havana. The Cubans needed little persuasion and the point was carried by the conference. The seat and effective control of the new body, called Organization of the Peoples of Asia, Africa and Latin America (OSPAAL), passed into Cuban hands, and Osmani Cienfuegos, chairman of the Cuban government's Commission on International Relations, was elected its secretary-general.

The Chinese were not allowed to triumph for long, because—whether with cynical deliberation in an attempt to balance Chinese gains against Soviet losses, or just by an extraordinary coincidence—Castro seized on a Chinese refusal to barter rice for sugar [14] to pick a quarrel, thereby restoring Cuban neutrality in the Sino-Soviet dispute.[15]

The OLAS Conference (August 1967)

Castro also succeeded in carving out an exclusive political domain for himself. On January 16, 1966, an announcement was made about the creation of a separate Organization of Latin American Solidarity (OLAS), with its seat in Havana. Ideologically and organizationally, the OLAS conference was weighted against the old guard Communists.[16] And whilst the resolution of the Tricontinental (OSPAAL) to hold its first conference in Cairo was never allowed to be implemented, OLAS was to hold its first conference in Havana during the summer of 1967. The rivalry between Muscovite Communism and revolutionary Castroism had supplanted that between Muscovite and pro-Chinese Communism as the main subject of contention among Marxist-Leninist movements in Latin America.[17] In nearly every Communist Party of the region there were now strong currents favoring Castro against Moscow. Some Communist Parties were split three ways between the Muscovites, the Castroites, and the pro-Chinese, but the latter were no longer of any consequence. The real battle was between Castro and Moscow, and—as the totally inconclusive meeting in Havana between Kosygin, the Soviet prime minister, and Castro had shown in July 1967—neither side was willing to make concessions.[18]

At the OLAS conference assembled in Havana in August 1967 the Cuban leadership, and above all Castro himself, launched open attacks on the Soviet Union and the Muscovite Communist Parties of Latin America, blaming the Soviet government for making diplomatic overtures towards anti-Castro governments in the region,[19] and accusing both the Soviet Union and Latin America's Muscovite Communist Parties of failing to support the armed struggle in the continent.[20]

Invoking the historical memories of Bolívar and Sucre, the conference declared the revolutionary struggle in Latin America to be of an international, all-continental, and Pan-Latin American character,[21] and it was hinted mysteriously that the struggle was already in progress. At long last there seemed a good chance that Latin America would be converted into a guerrilla under the inspiration and detailed direction of Havana. Soviet warnings were brushed aside contemptuously.[22]

A cruel anticlimax was to follow the euphoria of the OLAS conference. Guevara's expedition to Bolivia ended in miserable failure when on October 8, 1967, Che himself was captured and shot by forces of the Bolivian army, exposing the latest and boldest strategy adopted by the Castro régime towards Latin America as ill-conceived. Not only did Bolivia's peasantry fail to be recruited, but–far more decisive–the United States, alerted by the unfavorable effects of its invasion of the Dominican Republic in April 1965, refused to be drawn in, and far from intervening in strength, rested content with the training of a relatively efficient anti-guerrilla force within the Bolivian army which succeeded in stamping out Guevara's guerrilla.

Historical developments had overtaken Guevara. During the early planning stages of the operation, between October 1964 and mid-1965, the prospects of a United States intervention on the one hand, and the coalescence of isolated guerrillas in Latin America under Guevara's central direction on the other, had been fair if not brilliant. By the time Guevara's guerrilla could be operationalized, the United States had learned the lesson of the futility of military intervention in Latin America; Luis de la Puente's guerrilla in Peru had been stamped out by the military in 1965; and the Venezuelan guerrilla was dwindling.

Latin America's Reaction

Latin American governments also reacted in a distinctly low key, as few of them saw themselves directly threatened by guerrillas. Diplomatic action was confined to an extraordinary meeting of the Council of the OAS held in Washington on February 2, 1966, which condemned the intention of the Tricontinental Conference to launch wars of national liberation. Chile and Mexico abstained from the final vote on legal grounds but associated themselves with the sentiments expressed in it. Ten days later all OAS governments except that of Mexico addressed a letter to the president of the Security Council of the United Nations, alleging a breach of the Charter of that organization.[23]

In Brazil, Juracy Magalhães, Castelo Branco's new foreign minister, still pursued what was now the will-of-the-wisp of an inter-American force during his travels to Bolivia, Chile, Argentina, and Uruguay in 1966,[24] and also tried to keep alive the companion doctrine of "limited sovereignty."[25] In Argentina, the Illia Administration contented itself with a protest to the Soviet embassy, but both tone and direction of policy began to change under General J. C. Onganía, made president in a coup in June 1966. The general defended publicly the thesis of "ideological frontiers" to contain "international Communist subversion" and began to lean on the Brazilian military government in what looked like an informal resurrection of the Uruguaiana axis with a strong anti-Communist bias.[26]

Mexico, taken aback by the vigor and thrust of the guerrillero offensive, as proclaimed at the Tricontinental, reacted strongly at first, and R. de la Colina, Mexico's representative at the OAS, maintained that not only armed attack but also other forms of intervention "or offensive menaces" fell under the technical heading of aggression.[27] Mexico never approved of the idea of "ideological frontiers," and refrained from either supporting a complaint regarding the Tricontinental to the OAS[28] or from signing a letter of complaint to the Security Council. Nonetheless, Carrillo Flores, Mexico's foreign minister, felt obliged to warn Castro in September 1967 to abandon his policy of continental violence "before it is too late."[29]

Chile's position, now that President Frei was the subject of attack from Havana,[30] was complicated by the attitude taken by many Socialists, whose imagination had been captured by the new spirit of continental revolutionism. Because the Communists never approved wholeheartedly of this unbridled revolutionism, their relations with the Socialists reached an all-time low during and after the OLAS conference, especially since the Chilean Congress of the Socialist Party in 1967 had accepted the "vía armada" as a suitable method of attaining power for Latin American Socialists.[31] Allende, who had attended the OLAS conference in Havana and given support to its general resolutions, began to attack Frei's foreign policy at the end of July 1967, but was careful to exempt him from any fault for his conduct during the crisis in the Dominican Republic.[32]

The new spirit of continental revolutionism was also affecting Frei's own party, the Christian Democrats. In April 1967 the president felt it incumbent upon himself to warn that if Latin America failed to revolutionize itself voluntarily within a decade, a total revolution would follow,[33] and in mid-July 1967 the national council of the Party announced that OLAS could operate freely in Chile provided it did not create or suggest insurgency there.[34] To make matters worse, Frei explained almost at the same time that though he was morally against its policies, he had no legal means of preventing OLAS from working in Chile, thus clearing the way for Allende, who had agreed to set up an OLAS office in Santiago.

Strong protests poured into Christian Democrat headquarters from the governments of Colombia, Venezuela, and Guatemala, invested by guerrillero activity.[35] At this point the Chilean under-secretary of state at the foreign ministry saw fit to announce that Chile will join no inter-American guerrilla organization.[36] And while Frei was severely critical of those Chileans who had taken part in the OLAS conference, Rafael Gumucio, generally considered to be on the left of the Christian Democrat Party, conspicuously failed to attack the political principles underlying OLAS, questioning merely the wisdom of its tactics on the ground that these would provide a pretext for the creation of an inter-American force.[37] The whole political system of Chile was thrown out of gear by the prospect of an all-Latin American guerrilla.

In Venezuela, President Leoni favored the imposition of effective sanctions on Cuba as the Venezuelan Left was further split by Castro's new policies. On the one hand, Douglas Bravo, a former member of the politburo of the Venezuelan Communist Party, founded in December 1966 the pro-Castro *Partido de la Revolución Venezolana*, with himself as secretary-general; but on the other hand the Communists opposed the idea of a continued guerrilla in Venezuela and tried to work their way back into political legality.[38]

While Castro's energetic initiatives in Latin America seemed to produce some initial successes, all they achieved in the end was the alienation of most governments in the area and deep divisions within the Left. Castro's attempt to break out of Cuba's isolation had failed.

NOTES

1. On Cuba's position between the Soviet Union and China, see *Hoy*, March 16, 1963, as cited by Clissold, op. cit., pp. 282-283, 289, and 290-291. Castro had remarked explicitly that "Cuba wished to remain outside the controversies within the Socialist camp." See *Revolución*, January 16, 1963.

2. The countries in which violence was considered a worthwhile risk were Colombia, Guatemala, Peru, and Venezuela.

3. On this point, see H. S. Dinerstein, "Soviet Policy in Latin America," 61 *American Political Science Review* (1967) pp. 88-90. The author quotes the Uruguayan Communist leader Rodney Arismendi, writing in the Moscow *Kommunist* in March 1961, as follows: "The unity of the Latin American revolution does not exclude, but on the contrary, presupposes various national processes, a wealth of tactics, dissimilar tempos of development, various levels of the sharpness of the class struggle, and an endless gamut of political struggle in each country, region or group of countries."

4. See R. Gott, *Guerrilla Movements in Latin America* (London: Nelson, 1970), p. 21.

5. Note, for instance, Guevara's unusually aggressive criticism of Soviet and Soviet-satellite aid policy at the Algiers Afro-Asian Economic Seminar held between February 22 and March 1, 1965. On this point, see P. Schenkel, "Kuba und die kommunistische Welt," 19 *Osteuropa* (1969), pp. 267-285; also Clissold, op. cit., pp. 289-290.

The original article by Debray, "América Latina: algunos problemas de estrategia revolucionaria," appeared in *Bohemia,* Nos. 57 and 58, on November 19 and 26, 1965, on the eve of the Tricontinental Conference in Havana to be held in January 1966. See also Gott, op. cit., pp. 24-25.

6. It is worth recalling that Juan Bosch, former president of the Dominican Republic, expressed the view in 1963 that Latin America was on the brink of a revolution that would probably be "bloody, destructive and prolonged," thus presenting impartial evidence of the existence of an objective revolutionary situation. See *New York Times,* October 13, 1963.

7. See Guevara's remarks in Algiers, cited in footnote 5 above.

8. *Hoy,* December 23, 1964.

9. *Revolución,* February 19, 1965.

10. *New York Times,* January 14, 1965. For a comprehensive treatment, see "Les Cubains en Afrique noire," *Est et L'Ouest,* June 1-15, 1967.

11. See A. Entralgo, "De Bundung a Moshi," 2 *Política Internacional* (Havana, 1963), pp. 39-52.

12. On this point, see E. Halperin, "Die Ausstrahlung des Castrismus in Lateinamerika," 21 *Europa-Archiv* (1965), pp. 759-768.

13. See Clissold, op. cit., pp. 28-29. The documents of the Tricontinental Conference may be found in the special issue of *Cuba Socialista* of February 1966; and in 21 *Europa-Archiv* (1966), D 507. See also A. P. Lentin, *La lutte tricontinentale* (Paris, 1966).

14. On this point, see Schenkel, op. cit., p. 274. See also "Arroz chino, azucar cubano," *Marcha* (Montevideo), March 21, 1966.

15. In May 1966 a new trade agreement was signed between Cuba and China.

16. See K. Devlin, "The Castroist Challenge to Communism," pp. 159-173, in J. G. Oswald and A. J. Strover (eds.) *The Soviet Union and Latin America* (London, 1970).

17. Castroite tendencies had made considerable inroads in such Marxist-oriented Socialist parties as those of Chile, Argentina, and Ecuador. Trotskyist currents were never strong anywhere in Latin America except, in a spurious manner, in Bolivia and among some of the guerrilleros in Guatemala. Castro attacked the latter, the MR-13 *(Movimiento Revolucionario 13 de noviembre)* of Yon Sosa after the Tricontinental Conference. See L. Mercier Vega, *Etat et Contre-Etat* (Paris, 1968), p. 63.

18. *International Herald Tribune,* July 28, 1967. No communique was issued at the end of these talks.

19. A prominent Soviet writer was driven to remark in 1967 that "The countries of Asia, Africa and Latin America cannot, naturally, count on the Socialist States being in a position to provide all their requirements for capital, equipment and technical assistance. A significant portion of their requirements has to be satisfied through the agency of the imperialist States." See V. Tiagunenko, "Aktualniye voprosy nekapitalisticheskovo puti razvitiya," *Mirovaya ekonomika i mezhdunarodnye otnosheniya,* November 1967, p. 17.

20. For a Muscovite Communist counterblast, see Luis Corvalan's article in *Pravda,* July 30, 1967, alluding to the petit-bourgeois nature of Castro's policies. In April 1967 Douglas Bravo, pro-Castro guerrillero and member of the Central Com-

mittee of the Venezuelan Communist Party, was expelled from that Party. In May 1967 a mixed Cuban-Venezuelan group of Castroite guerrilleros landed in Venezuela. In June 1967 the Bravo group was reorganized in accordance with Debray's precepts.

21. See J. B. More Benitez, "La solidaridad revolucionaria en América Latina," 19 *Política Internacional* (Havana, 1967), pp. 1-7.

22. Having originally discountenanced Havana's ultra-revolutionary strategy on practical grounds, the Soviet government began to frown on the guerrilleros on grounds of explicit principle, describing them as "Bakuninists." See *Pravda*, September 26, 1967. For further details, see R. F. Lamberg, "La formación de la línea castrista desde la Conferencia Tricontinental," 8 *Foro Internacional*, January/March 1968, pp. 278-301; and W. W. Berner, "Castro's und Moskau's lateinamerikanische Strategie," 18 *Aussenpolitik*, June 1968, pp. 357-367.

23. *Le Monde*, February 4 and 11, 1966.

24. *Jornal da Tarde*, February 4, 1966, had reported some hesitation in the Itamaratí as to the precise attitude to adopt vis-à-vis the Soviet Union after the Tricontinental.

25. See his speech to the Rotary Club in Rio in August 1966. *Jornal do Brasil*, August 16, 1966.

26. See "Hay acuerdo argentino-brasileño sobre los problemas hemisféricos," *La Mañana* (Montevideo), October 20, 1966. On the geopolitics of the military régime in Brazil, see a number of articles in 2 *Revista Brasileira de Estudos Politicos*, July 1966.

27. For the full text of de la Colina's speech, see *El Excelsior*, February 4, 1966.

28. *El Excelsior*, February 8, 1966.

29. *El Universal*, September 26, 1967.

30. For Castro's attacks on President Frei, see W. R. Duncan, "Chilean Christian Democracy," 53 *Current History*, November 1967, pp. 263-308. Also Clissold, op. cit., pp. 292-293.

31. See E. Labarca Goddard, *Chile al rojo* (Santiago: Universidad Técnica del Estado, 1971), pp. 193-194.

32. *El Mercurio*, July 29, 1967. During a conference organized by the Institute of International Studies at Santiago, Allende insisted that "revolutionary violence must be pitted against reactionary violence." See *El Mercurio*, August 8, 1967. These views were echoed by the prominent Socialist Clodomiro Almeyda, "La OLAS y la crísis en América latina," 1 *Estudios Internacionales* (Santiago), October 1967–March 1968, pp. 427-442.

33. *New York Times*, April 11, 1967.

34. Ibid., July 16, 1967.

35. Ibid., July 27, 1967.

36. *Frankfurter Allgemeine Zeitung*, August 11, 1967.

37. *El Mercurio*, August 17, 1967.

38. See R. Robledo Limón, "El Partido Comunista de Venezuela. Sus tácticas políticas de 1964 a 1969," 44 *Foro Internacional*, April/June 1970, pp. 531-551.

Chapter XIII

THE DECLINE OF THE GUERRILLA (1967-1968)

Having staked all on a successful guerrilla to break out of isolation and to shuffle off Soviet patronage, Castro now found himself more dependent on Soviet favors than ever before. This showed itself plainly in the economic sphere. Trade picked up in 1968, as a Soviet credit of $327.8 million was extended to Cuba, but the crux of Cuba's economic relationship with the Soviet Union concerned the terms on which the Soviets were prepared to supply crude oil for Cuba's growing needs of fuel.[1] Cuba's demands on the Soviet Union for raw materials at subsidized prices had been growing steadily for some time. The turning point came in April 1968, when Moscow insisted that henceforth annual increases of Soviet supplies of crude oil to Cuba had to be kept within a limit of 2 percent until further notice, and as a result of this restriction Cuba had to resort to the unpopular device of rationing petrol.[2]

By taking this measure the Soviet Union had shown—whether deliberately or not—that it was within her power to decide at what pace the Cuban economy was to develop, and Cuban acknowledgment of this reality was made when, on January 1, 1969, Castro admitted that Cuba would not be economically self-sufficient in the near future.[3]

The scepticism of the Soviet Union regarding Cuba's guerrilla diplomacy had been fully vindicated, while her own policy of fostering closer diplomatic and economic ties with existing Latin American governments was acquiring a new plausibility.[4]

On August 24, 1968—three days after the Soviet invasion of Czechoslovakia—Castro gave his qualified approval to the action taken by the Soviet Union. Frankly admitting that the invasion represented a flagrant breach of international law, Castro maintained that it was justifiable nevertheless on political grounds since revisionist tendencies within the Dubcek regime had got out of control. Concentrating his analysis on the causes of steady revolutionary decay in Czechoslovakia, Castro concluded that it was due to a general slackening of revolutionary discipline. By according a roundabout approval to the newly fashioned Brezhnev Doctrine of "limited sovereignty," Castro turned the argument neatly against the Soviet government by asking it to give up supporting "leading forces which are Right-inclined, reformist and ready to compromise in Latin America."[5] This must have been interpreted in Moscow as a positive gesture, for it was followed by the appointment of Aleksandr A. Soldatov, a most experienced diplomat, as Soviet ambassador to Havana in September 1968.

The shock of Guevara's defeat in rural guerrilla was such that the Cuban leadership found it hard to take to the idea of encouraging urban ones. The standard manual on urban guerrilla methods by the Brazilian Carlos Marighella was printed eventually in the organ of OSPAAL in such a way as to suggest that it was more in the nature of a tribute to a brave fighter than a serious recommendation to Castroite practitioners in the field.[6] Support of urban guerrilleros where appropriate—as in the case of Uruguay—did, however, eventually form part of Cuban strategy.

Changes towards moderate foreign policies also began to be made in countries whose governments had hitherto taken a hard line against Cuba. Thus, the presidency of Marshal Arthur Costa e Silva in Brazil (March 1967-September 1969)[7] saw a swing-back in foreign policy from the rigid conceptions held by Castelo Branco to something like the lines of diplomacy which could have been pursued under Quadros and Goulart if internal crises had not frustrated their purpose. Though he had played the key part in the overthrow of the old régime in 1964, José Magalhães Pinto, the president-marshal's foreign minister, had at one time been an admirer of Quadros' foreign policy; and it seemed inconceivable that he would not abandon the diplomacy of Juracy Magalhães, his predecessor at the Itamaratí. While continuing to recognize subversion as a possible threat and not ruling out collective military action in concrete cases of subversion,[8] Magalhães Pinto placed his main emphasis on the concept of state sovereignty, which was to be achieved by means of energetic economic development through the agency of both Brazilian and foreign capitalism.[9] There were even signs that Brazil intended to trace out an independent policy on a world canvas. Thus, Magalhães Pinto sought to prevent a world nuclear "oligopoly" which could deprive the underdeveloped countries, and Brazil in particular, of achieving a rapid economic transformation through the peaceful application of nuclear power.[10] He also insisted on the principle of international economic equality, as expressed by him at the second United Nations Conference on Trade and Development (UNCTAD) at New Delhi in February 1968, and was instrumental in bringing about the Consensus of Viña del Mar in May 1969, by which Latin America agreed to the joint presentation of her economic demands to the United States.[11] It would appear that the developmentalist conception was once more coming to the fore.[12]

The overall effect of Magalhães Pinto's new style of foreign policy was to break the informal axis that had been forged between Brazil and Argentina under the presidencies of Castelo Branco and General Onganía respectively.[13]

After the foundering of Argentina's last bid for the creation of an inter-American force during the Buenos Aires conference of February 1967, Onganía concentrated his endeavors on the economic development of the country. In March 1968[14] he made a plea for all Latin American integration in the military as well as in the economic field, but this "Bolivarian" version of an inter-American force fell on deaf ears. The *cordobazo* of 1969, in which students and workers united for the first time to oppose his policies, proved a serious blow to him, and in January 1970 he was willing to associate himself with President Frei of Chile in stressing the importance of all-Latin American solidarity as evidenced in the Consensus of Viña del Mar.[15] In June 1970 he was replaced by Gen. R. Levingston.

In Mexico, according to at least one report,[16] officials of the Ministry of Foreign Affairs had expressed themselves in private that the country's continued link with Cuba provided its "first line of defense" against pressures from the United States. But in 1968 the link with Cuba hardly served such purpose any longer. Mexican trade with Cuba had not increased after 1964, and in a period of détente on a world scale, the continued link with Cuba was fast losing its terror—if terror it ever was—to the United States. Moreover, Mexico proved unwilling to trade away lightly in politically risky enterprises the high reputation of commercial respectability which she had acquired.[17]

In Venezuela the end of the rural guerrilla began to be in sight. As early as 1966, Douglas Bravo, the hard-pressed Castroite guerrillero chief in Venezuela, began to throw out hints in his *Manifesto de Iracara* to COPEI, the Christian Democrat movement then still in opposition, that help from almost any quarter would be welcome.[18] In December 1968, Rafael Caldera, the COPEI candidate in the presidential election, won a dead-heat victory over González Barrios, candidate of *Acción Democrática*, which had supplied the incumbents of the presidency since 1958.[19] The Communist Party, now disapproving of the guerrilla in Venezuela, was almost immediately legalized, and the threat of the guerrilleros was played down by Caldera.[20] A new and calmer political climate was beginning to pervade Venezuela.

NOTES

1. See P. Schenkel, "Kuba und die kommunistische Welt," 19 *Osteuropa* (1969), pp. 267-285. For previous developments in Soviet-Cuban trade, see R. S. Walters, "Soviet Economic Aid to Cuba, 1959-1964," 42 *International Affairs* (London), January 1966, pp. 74-86; and J. D. Cochrane, "América Latina y Europa oriental: algunas notas y estadísticas sobre comercio," 8 *Foro Internacional*, January/March 1968, pp. 317-327, which contains useful statistical tables.

2. See R. F. Lamberg, "The Cuban Economy and the Soviet Bloc, 1963-1968: a commentary," in J. G. Oswald and A. J. Strover (eds.). *The Soviet Union and Latin America* (London, 1970), pp. 116-126.

3. *Granma* (weekly review), January 2, 1969. In view of the low yield of the sugar harvest for 1968, a mere 5 million tons, Castro could hardly conceal the seriousness of Cuba's economic situation from the world.

4. Professor V. Volsky, director of the Institute of Latin American Affairs in the Soviet Academy of Sciences, had told a meeting of the United Nations Economic Commission for Latin America (ECLA), held in Caracas in May 1967, that the Soviet Union was "interested in securing bilateral agreements with countries all over Latin America in order to show the people that there is an alternative to exploitation by the capitalist world." See *Latin America*, May 19, 1967. See also "L'URSS applique en Amérique latine une politique de coexistence surtout orientée vers le développement des relations économiques," *Le Monde Diplomatique*, January 1968.

5. Speech of August 24, 1968, reported in *Granma*, August 25, 1968. For an interesting commentary, see "Fidel Castro y los tanques de Praga," *Marcha* (Montevideo), September 20, 1968, pp. 16-17.

6. Carlos Marighella, "Minimanual del guerrillero urbano," *Tricontinental,* January/February 1970. See also R. F. Lamberg, "La Guerrilla Urbana: condiciones y perspectivas de la 'segunda ola' guerrillera," 4 *Foro Internacional,* January/March 1971, pp. 431-443.

7. The best analytical treatment of the administration of Marshal Costa e Silva is to be found in C. Chagas, *Cento días da Presidencia Costa e Silva* (Rio de Janeiro, 1970). In an address to the diplomats of the Itamaratí in Brasilia on April 5, 1967, the president referred significantly to the "inherent dynamism of the international situation which has evolved from the rigidity of positions characteristic of the Cold War towards a relaxation of tensions." See Ministério das Relações Exteriores, *Documentos de Política Externa, (de 15 de março a 15 de outubro de 1967)* (Brasilia, 1967), p. 12.

8. In May 1968 it was decided by the OAS to finance a special committee composed of five military men and two civilians to watch the subversive activities of "Castro-Communism" in the Western Hemisphere. Only the bare two-thirds majority necessary for a motion of this kind was obtained, with Brazil abstaining. *Daily Telegraph,* May 7, 1968.

9. Already at the first meeting of the cabinet of the new administration, held on March 16, 1967, the president had announced that "Brazil's foreign policy cannot continue to represent simple reflexes of our condition of underdevelopment, but will have to express the aspirations of a country determined to push forward its development energetically." See Ministério das Relações Exteriores, *Documentos de Política Externa (de 15 de março a 15 de outubro de 1967)* (Brasilia, 1967), p. 5.

10. Consequently, instructions were given to Brazil's representative at the disarmament talks proceeding at Geneva—Sérgio Corrêa da Costa—to prevent such a conclusion. This was a point to which Magalhães Pinto would return time and again during his tenure at the Itamarati. See, for instance, his speech to the General Assembly of the United Nations on September 21, 1967, in which he upheld the Treaty of Tlatelolco—which the Costa e Silva Administration had ratified—with its careful distinctions between the military and peaceful uses of nuclear energy, as being perfectly adequate for adoption of a world scale; see ibid., pp. 109-110. See also his attack on the world powers at the Second Meeting of UNCTAD, New Delhi, on February 5, 1968, in Ministério das Relações Exteriores, *Documentos de Política Externa II (28 de outubro de 1967 a 3 de maio de 1968)* (Brasilia, 1968), pp. 55-60.

11. See his address to the *Escola Superior de Guerra* of July 3, 1969.

12. The year 1969 saw the publication of another comprehensive work by Hélio Jaguaribe, who had been one of the main intellectual pillars of I.S.E.B. See Jaguaribe, *Desenvolvimento econômico e desenvolvimento político* (Rio de Janeiro: Paz e Terra, 1969).

13. The urban guerrilla in Brazil seems not to have caused the administration of Marshal Arthur Costa e Silva undue concern. In May 1968 a Communist splinter group, the Workers Communist Party, came into being to act as urban guerrilla, but the movement, heavily dependent on the strong personality of Carlos Marighella, collapsed when their leader fell in battle in November 1969. See R. F. Lamberg, "La Guerrilla Urbana: condiciones y perspectivas de la 'segunda ola' guerrillera," 11 *Foro Internacional,* January/March 1971, pp. 421-443.

14. *El Mercurio* (Santiago), March 7, 1968.

15. *Latin America,* January 16, 1970.

16. Ibid., September 22, 1967. The present writer had numerous occasions to have this story retailed to him by unauthorized but generally well-informed persons in September 1971.

17. In March 1968 Antonio Carillo Flores, Mexico's foreign minister, made it perfectly clear that his government would in no way associate itself at the forthcoming UNCTAD in New Delhi with any demands for the amortization of debts. Mexico's reputation as a commercially sound proposition must be maintained, he said. See *Financial Times,* March 6, 1968.

18. See Mercier Vega, op. cit.

19. The official figures were: Caldera, 29.06 percent of all votes cast, against González Barrios' 28.31 percent.

20. See K. Lindenberg, "Der Regierungswechsel in Venezuela in lateinamerikanischer Perspektive," *Vierteljahrshefte,* June 1969, published by the Research Institute of the Friedrich Ebert-Stiftung (Berlin).

Chapter XIV

TOWARDS A NEW DIPLOMACY

With the Cold War largely out of the way, a new diplomatic climate was beginning to pervade Latin America. Except in Cuba, Soviet military influence existed nowhere in the region, and the United States, chastened by the two traumatic experiences of the Dominican Republic and, far more deeply, of Vietnam, was willing to project a "low profile" towards Latin America.[1] Thus, the expropriation in Peru and Bolivia in 1968 and 1969, respectively, of the two United States-owned corporations IPC and Gulf Oil[2] failed to produce an energetic response from the Nixon Administration.

For their part, the governments of Latin America began to close their ranks in matters of world trade and to diversify their foreign policies in general. Quasi-neutralist foreign policies were adopted by the military régimes of General Velasco Alvarado in Peru and General Ovando Candia in Bolivia, and the latter began to accept Soviet aid.[3] Salvador Allende's unexpected victory at the polls in September 1970, which led to the expropriation of the United States-owned copper mines and a shift in Chile's foreign policy, pointed in the same direction, and was followed within a month by the accession to power in Bolivia by General J. J.

Torres, under whose presidency the Marxist Left gained a marked political ascendancy and Soviet economic influence increased in leaps and bounds. Within the Peruvian military, who provided the fountainhead of the revolution and who would brook no civilian interference in their policies, several tendencies contended for supremacy.[4] The left wing, which had produced the internal "revolution from above" in the first place, had at least three origins: (a) social: 55 percent of all generals promoted between 1940 and 1965 had come from the *sierra;*[5] (b) ideological: the *Centro de Altos Estudios Militares* (CAEM), founded in Lima in 1958, had been a source at which younger and middle-range officers were able to imbibe left-wing doctrines of a Populist and, less so, Marxist variety, implicit in the lectures given there regularly by university dons—both Peruvian and foreign—on political science, economics, and sociology; (c) psychological: during the suppression of the Castroite *guerrilla,* organized in the *sierra* by Luis de la Puente in 1965, the officers involved came into close contact with the *indio* peasant population of the areas concerned, and concluded that many—perhaps most—of their grievances were substantially justified.

Other tendencies which proved to be important in the making of foreign policy could be traced to periods of professional residence abroad, whether for the purpose of training or on active service as military attachés. This group could be divided between those officers who were influenced by what they had seen and heard in the United States, and those who had served in Europe. Among the latter, General Juan Velasco Alvarado—the head of the junta—whilst acting as military attaché in Paris, had been enthralled by the example of the foreign policies of General de Gaulle, and, above a thicket of left-wing verbiage, the "Gaullist" tendency asserted itself time and again, showing the immense influence of the president and those military of a similar cast of mind. The dislike of disproportionate power of United States corporations, the resentment of the exercise of United States military hegemony in Peru through the supplies of arms under the mantle of anti-Sovietism, and an open posture towards the underdeveloped world; all these were distinctly Gaullist elements. Moreover, "Gaullism," thus defined, provided the ideal formula for bringing politically diverse sections of the military under one cover, and had the additional advantage of satisfying the Communists.

Relations between the United States and Peru had begun to worsen under President Belaúnde since the beginning of 1966, when the question of the International Petroleum Company's deposits at La Brea y Pariñas became acute.[6] At the suggestion of T. C. Mann—who had masterminded the invasion of the Dominican Republic in 1965 on behalf of the State Department—the decision was taken to suspend aid to Peru until a settlement was reached with the IPC. Walt Rostow, prominent adviser on foreign policy at the White House, saw Belaúnde in March 1966 to advise against nationalization in return for the resumption of United States aid, and his advice was accepted.[7]

Gen. Velasco Alvarado reversed his predecessor's decision, and IPC was nationalized in October 1968.[8] In February 1969, Foreign Minister E. Mercado Jarrín made it clear that if reprisals were taken by the United States, Peru would appeal to the world. Forestalling any boycott regarding aid, Mercado Jarrín explained that Peru was not interested in "conditional" aid.[9] At the same time the Peruvian foreign minister was careful to make it clear that the IPC was a "special case" and not part of a general policy of expropriation.[10] In April 1969 the United States announced in face of growing Latin American solidarity with Peru that no sanctions would be imposed. Peru had scored an impressive victory.[11]

In March 1970 Mercado Jarrín had an important meeting with Charles Meyer, trouble-shooter for Latin America of the Nixon Administration, in which he was assured that the imposition of restrictive measures by the United States against any country in Latin America would be preceded by previous consultation within the OAS,[12] and in 1971 the situation had eased sufficiently to allow Mercado Jarrín to visit Brazil.[13]

President Belaúnde had prepared the ground for an eventual reestablishment of diplomatic relations with the Soviet Union, and the military régime completed the process on February 1, 1969.[14] A trade agreement between the two countries was signed on February 17, 1969.[15] This, alongside trade agreements with other Communist countries in Eastern Europe, helped Peru to withstand the investment freeze which followed the expropriation of the IPC.[16] In August 1970 a Soviet credit of $30 million was extended to Peru.[17] However, in October 1970 the president warned that there could be no question of a transition of Peru's revolution to that "of another type," considered by some as "genuine" (*verdadera*),[18] and eventually it was stated emphatically that Peru did not consider herself a Socialist country.[19]

Peru's cautious rapprochement with Communist China betrayed a desire neither to offend the United States nor to find herself isolated in this respect within Latin America. A first hint was given by the foreign minister in the United Nations in 1970, when he said he shared the "restlessness" of others about the absence of Mao Tse-tung's government in that body.[20]

In June 1971 a commercial mission under the minister of fisheries, General J. Tantaleán Vanini, visited China to explore new possibilities of marketing Peru's two leading export commodities, fishmeal and copper.[21] As a result, the two countries established commercial missions in each other's capitals and concluded a trade agreement.[22] This development was capped on November 2, 1971, by the extension of full recognition and the exchange of ambassadors with Communist China.

Peru's attitudes towards Cuba changed also under the military régime. In mid-January 1970, the foreign minister had denied emphatically any rumors of an "axis" with Bolivia and Cuba, expressing the government's wish to see Cuba return to a dialogue and link with the inter-American system,[23] and Peru's new representative in the United Nations announced in February 1971 that his government would favor a change of policy towards Cuba "within the OAS."[24] Diplomatic relations with Cuba were finally renewed on July 8, 1972.

As to the rest of the underdeveloped world, General Mercado Jarrín's "Decalogue of Torre Tagle," a ten-point statement of positions which he considered to be desirable of application by at least the underdeveloped countries of Latin America, provided the basis for the 1969 Consensus of Viña del Mar.[25] Peru sent an observer to the Lusaka Conference of Non-aligned Countries in September 1970, and Mercado Jarrín explained in this connection that Peru regarded herself as "a leading country of some seventy nations whose 'alignment' does not necessarily imply the possibility of an ineffective neutralism, but an offensive one of a powerful anti-imperialist element."[26]

In Ecuador the winds of change were felt also. The hitherto explosive issue of the Marañon territory, disputed with Peru since 1942, was resolved eventually in 1971 after the election to the presidency of J. M. Velasco Ibarra in 1968.[27]

On February 3, 1969, Velasco Ibarra announced the establishment of diplomatic relations with the Soviet Union, and was supported by the Socialist Party and opposed by both Conservatives and the *Partido de Acción Revolucionaria Nacionalista*.[28] The Socialists also wanted the starting of negotiations with Cuba. Gonzalo Oleas, their secretary-general, addressing the 28th conference of his party, remarked that it was "absurd that our international relations should be conditioned by the points of view of the State Department."[29] At the end of January 1971 the military mission of the United States in Quito was compelled to leave,[30] and on November 17, 1971, the government announced that it was ceasing to recognize Nationalist China. This has not, however, been followed by the establishment of diplomatic relations with Peking. Velasco Ibarra was overthrown in a coup in February 1972, and no further diplomatic developments have taken place.

In Bolivia, President René Barrientos had pursued a friendly policy towards the United States and mercilessly hunted down the guerrilla of Che Guevara, but in January 1968, a few months after the collapse of Guevara's guerrila, he invited the Soviet Union to open trade relations with Bolivia. In February 1969—following the military coup in Peru—he implied that the establishment of diplomatic relations with the Soviet Union—no longer a novelty in Latin America—would depend on Soviet aid to Bolivia's budding oil industry. A delegation of Bolivian miners was allowed to visit the Soviet Union, and the compliment was allowed to be returned a year later.

Barrientos himself lost his life in an air accident on April 27, 1969. [31] Barely a few days later, the OAS rejected a proposal by the Bolivian ambassador accredited to that body that could have created the ground-work for eventual participation of Cuba in the inter-American system, [32] an act that must still have formed part of Barrientos' diplomacy.

The weak government succeeding Barrientos failed to withstand the growing strains to which it was subjected, and Gen. Ovando Candia seized power on September 26, 1969. Partly responsible for the suppression of the guerrilla in 1967, he followed in the footsteps of Peru in nationalizing the United States-owned Gulf Oil Company in November 1969.[33] In his New Year's message of 1969-1970 he announced, moreover, that henceforth Bolivia would pursue an independent diplomacy, and at the end of January 1970 the new Bolivian ambassador in Moscow described the establishment of diplomatic relations as a "victory of the independent foreign policy of President Ovando Candia" while praising the Soviet Union for "its role as counter-weight to imperialism." [34] Ovando also praised the important contribution Guevara had made to the Bolivian Revolution and expressed his willingness to trade with Cuba.[35] The United States military mission was closed down, and Ovando offered to cooperate with Peru and Chile in eliminating the hegemony of the United States in Latin America. He was even prepared to leave the OAS.[36]

These were strong actions for which Ovando had not prepared the ground politically. His cabinet included some civilians, among them some Marxists. The position of the latter was explained by Gen. J. J. Torres, who maintained that even Marxists believed nowadays that in countries in which the proletariat was not strong enough, the army must be made the avant-garde of the struggle for liberation.[37] These measures came too late to save Ovando. The Right had recovered its wits. Alarmed by the demands of the Fourth Workers Congress in May 1970 for the establishment of relations with Cuba and Communist China, and the expulsion of the military mission of the United States and of the Peace Corps, pressures began to be applied on Ovando. And though at the end of August he was still able to receive Zhukov, head of the Latin American desk of the Soviet Foreign Ministry, and to despatch Gen. J. J. Torres to attend the Lusaka Conference of Non-aligned Countries as an observer,[38] he had to retreat from September onwards. On September 11, 1970, he agreed to pay compensation of $78 million to the Gulf Oil Company,[39] and also announced that he would not brook the expulsion of Formosa from the United Nations.[40]

In a swift coup and countercoup, power passed eventually to Gen. J. J. Torres on October 8, 1970, who promised to form a government with the participation of workers, students, peasants, and the military.[41]

Yet, unlike the Peruvian junta, Torres had failed to unite the military behind him. The Left, encouraged by the victory of Allende in Chile, now began to make demands for the adoption of drastic left-wing measures. On March 18, 1971, Torres reshuffled his cabinet to satisfy his left-wing critics.[42] At this point the Bolivian Revolution had left that of Peru far behind. A political command of the Left began to function in the form of a Popular Assembly in June 1971 and demanded the reestablishment of diplomatic relations with both Cuba and Chile.[43] Early in May, Bolivia's delegate at the ECLA conference at Santiago had, on explicit instructions from Huascar Taboaga, the foreign minister, supported Chile's demand that socialism, as a strategy of economic development, should be included in the agenda of the next session.[44] Much more ominous in the long run was the politically reckless act of installing a "secretariat of militia" in the Popular Assembly,[45] a Marxist-inspired attempt to gather the popular forces of the Left, whose task would be "to arm the people on a national scale and place it under a single command."[46]

Soviet influence in Bolivia began to grow fast. In January 1971 the miners union petitioned Torres to import Soviet technology into the Bolivian mines.[47] In April 1971 the Soviet Union granted a credit of $275 million for the purchase by Bolivia of machinery and industrial equipment.[48] In June it was announced that the Soviet Union would grant Bolivia technical aid in exploring oil deposits in the *altiplano*,[49] and a few days later it was made public knowledge that, as from 1972, the Soviet Union would purchase more than half the output of the state-owned Bolivian tin mine "Matilda."[50] In August the news broke that a Soviet mission was shortly to visit Bolivia to study the possibility of granting a huge loan of $3,750 million for the extraction of iron ore.[51]

Arrangements were completed for a direct telephone conversation between Presidents Torres and Allende, to take place at night on August 20, 1971, to clinch the final details for the resumption of diplomatic relations between the two countries.[52] But Torres still wavered between establishing the unity of the armed forces as an essential preliminary for further momentous political decisions, and throwing his weight fully behind the revolutionary Left, risking a civil war in the process. In the meantime the right wing of the armed forces—reinforced by military commanders who until recently had been considered loyal to Torres—struck and won the day on August 21, 1971, thus thwarting a development that could have led to the creation of an international front of left and left-inclined governments stretching from Chile via Bolivia to Peru and Ecuador.

The new régime of Col. Hugo Banzer, based on the right wing of the armed forces, especially the Rangers, and on a political coalition of the two former enemies, the *Falange* and the *Movimiento Nacional Revolucionario,* reversed nearly all of the policies introduced since the death of Barrientos. The new foreign minister, Mario Gutiérrez, leader of the Falange, ruled out any relations with Chile so long as the latter would not grant Bolivia her long-desired corridor to the sea. Relations with Brazil were greatly improved,[53] and the new government had every intention to improve its relations with the United States.[54] To complete the reversal of diplomatic relations, 119 Soviet diplomats were expelled from La Paz on March 29, 1972.[55] Bolivia had moved full circle from Barrientos to Banzer.

While the Peruvian junta was consolidating its position and successive Bolivian military leaders staggering under the impact of new political forces, the administration of President Frei in Chile sought continually to reinvigorate its foreign policy. But neither the president nor his foreign minister were entirely their own masters any longer, since a three-fold rift had opened within the Christian Democratic Party in 1967 over the attitude to be adopted in the face of revolutionary developments in Latin

America. As the date of the forthcoming presidential elections approached, the Frei Administration began to move to the Left, both abroad and at home.

An opportunity[56] of taking the lead in Latin America was to offer itself presently. In March 1969 Valdés predicted a considerable stiffening of Latin American attitudes vis-à-vis the United States at the forthcoming conference of CECLA[57] at Viña del Mar (Chile) in May 1969,[58] where, in the event, a memorandum—the Consensus of Viña del Mar—was composed containing the collective demands of Latin America for a substantial revision of United States policies towards that continent.[59] It was typical of Valdés that in delivering the letter to President Nixon he exceeded by far the compromise mandate he had obtained at Viña del Mar in pressing the claims of Latin America.[60]

During its last two years in office the Frei Administration had moved substantially to the Left. Abroad, its most spectacular innovation had been to foster the rehabilitation of Cuba within the Americas, whilst at home there began an ominous move away from "Chileanization" towards the principle of the outright nationalization of copper.[61] The road seemed to be clear for a new, much more radical Christian Democrat president—or so it was believed in Christian Democrat circles[62]—well-equipped politically to steal the thunder of the Left.

Chile's reputation in foreign affairs was further enhanced by her gradually changing attitude towards Cuba. That Frei, let alone Valdés, was unhappy about Cuba's ostracism in Latin America was well-known. Chile never ceased to make soundings in Latin America with a view to end Cuba's isolation.[63] Following an intimation by the Cuban government to an unofficial Chilean trade mission in Havana that no further military or financial aid would be granted to guerrilleros still active in Latin America,[64] Valdés called unequivocally for the reintegration of Cuba into the inter-American system in February 1970.

However, on September 4, 1970, Dr. Salvador Allende, head of the left-wing coalition *Unidad Popular* comprising Socialists, Communists, Radicals, and a few left-of-center splinter parties, was elected president of Chile, taking office on November 4, 1970. His victory was in no way influenced by events in either Peru or Bolivia,[65] as, on the same showing, he could have won in 1964 if he could have split the forces on his Right as he did in 1970.[66]

If Allende had been elected in 1958, as he nearly was, his foreign policy may not have differed much from that pursued by Fidel Castro. Thus, the section of the program of *Unidad Popular* dealing with foreign affairs had been largely taken over from the program of FRAP used in 1958, and was out of date in 1970. It called for the relinquishment of Chile's ties with the World Bank and the IMF, the denunciation of both Rio Treaty and the Mutual Assistance Agreement with the United States, as well as for the substantial reform of the OAS, and presupposed the existence of an unbridgeable gulf between Latin America and the United States in conditions of Cold War.[67] Such policies were no longer practical in a climate of world détente in 1970, and even Castro seemed to appreciate the dangers of diplomatic intransigence when he sent warning four days after Allende's election not to jeopardize the dollar markets of copper or to allow an exodus of copper technicians.[68]

It soon became evident that Allende needed no prompting in appreciating the realities of the situation, and he consequently made a careful distinction in the treatment he meted out to United States private enterprise on the one hand, which was harsh, and of the United States government, which was markedly circumspect. The president also charted a safe course between the Charybdis of clamors for more polemical attitudes emanating from left-wing intellectuals in the Socialist Party and the pragmatism urged on him by the Ministry of Foreign Affairs, and to avoid antagonizing the armed forces. The latter were assured of a level of military supplies to which they had become accustomed under Frei, and since Allende showed no intention of switching his sources of procurement from the United States, this alone made the denunciation of the Rio Treaty and the Mutual Assistance Agreement with the United States impossible.

On the other hand, Allende showed no hesitation in recognizing the governments of Communist China and Eastern Germany, and, defying an OAS decision of 1964, in reestablishing relations with Cuba. It was only over the recognition of the governments of North Korea and North Vietnam that considerable delays occurred, grounded in fears that such steps might enable Congress in the United States to cut off aid to Chile. [69] Similar reasoning may have deterred the Allende Administration from leaving the World Bank and the IMF, and from expelling the United States military mission in Santiago.

In a number of ways Allende's foreign policies differed in emphasis and style only from those pursued by his predecessor in office. Where Frei sought to counteract the hegemony of the United States in Latin America by drawing closer to Western Europe and by promoting the economic integration of Latin America,[70] Allende tried to achieve similar ends by leaning on Eastern Europe and by fostering the political, rather than the economic, unity of Latin America, at any rate outside Brazil. But the foundations of the latter policy had been laid by Frei, who was the initiator of the Andean Pact.

Abjuring any pronounced ideological intentions in the field of foreign policy, Allende's primary objective has been the accommodation of both world powers with the purpose of carrying out his program of basic reforms at home without let or hindrance by diplomatic complications. Consequently, Allende made trips to Chile's partners in the Andean Pact—Peru, Ecuador, and Colombia—in September 1971, and sealed his friendship with the Communist world by visits to Cuba and Eastern Europe in November 1972. He also seized the opportunity of normalizing relations with Argentina during two meetings with President Lanusse in Salta in July 1971 and in Antofagasta in October of the same year, and used Orlando Letelier, his ambassador in Washington, to maintain relations with the United States on an even keel. Those who had expected Allende to allow his ideological convictions to overrule his diplomatic prudence by reviving the Cold War in Latin America must have been severely disappointed. When Allende fell in September 1973, this was due entirely to domestic reasons.[71]

That events in Peru, Bolivia, Ecuador, and Chile had not left the policies of Cuba unaffected was borne out by a British newspaper correspondent who was informed in mid-November 1971 by officials in the Cuban Ministry of Foreign Affairs that Cuba was responding to "new conditions" in Latin America, such as the upsurge of economic nationalism and regional cooperation, with "new policies."[72]

Cuban foreign policy began to evolve accordingly. In April 1969 Carlos Rafael Rodríguez could still maintain—somewhat arrogantly—that to have relations with other Latin American governments or form common fronts with other movements was not important to Cuba;[73] but on July 14, 1969, Castro pledged his support to "any true revolution" in Latin America and to the military government of Peru.[74] In October 1969 a Cuban periodical did not rule out relations between Cuba and Bolivia, now under General Ovando Candia,[75] and in March 1970 it was reported that the Soviet Union was trying to lend a helping hand to those Latin American governments which were willing to smile on Havana.[76] In August 1970—after an important meeting with the Chilean Communist

Sen. Volodia Teitelboim at the end of June 1970—Castro declared his willingness to have relations with Chile, but not with Peru "because imperialism would take it as a pretext for launching aggressions against the present government" there. Chile was different because her internal developments would not be affected by diplomatic relations with Havana; Socialism in Chile could be obtained through the ballot box; she was "one of the few Latin American countries in which the political struggle was waged constitutionally . . . in this concrete case, in Chile in 1970, Socialism can gain an electoral victory."[77] On July 26, 1971, he conceded that the same might happen in Uruguay in November 1971.[78]

Castro's former enthusiasm for Latin American guerrilleros was on the wane also. In March 1970 it was reported that Cuban aid to guerrilleros in Colombia had dropped from $24,000 in 1968 to $4000 in 1969,[79] and in May 1970 Castro announced that Cuban support for revolutionary movements was not confined to guerrilleros "but any government that sincerely adopts a policy of social and economic development, and liberation of its country from the Yankee imperialist yoke."[80] In July 1970 the Cuban leader delivered himself of a heavy broadside of sarcasm against "super-revolutionaries."[81] Régis Debray swiftly made use of the fall of General Torres' left-wing government in Bolivia on August 21, 1971, by reaffirming his belief in the need of revolutionary violence,[82] and was echoed by Castro.[83]

As regards the OAS, Castro denied expressly on July 14, 1969, any intention of rejoining that body, stating his conditions for a resumption of relations with Latin American governments thus: "Any Latin American country wishing to establish relations with Cuba has to declare that OAS accords are arbitrary and unjust, and that as compensation for crimes committed against our country in complicity with Yankee imperialism, it is ready to disregard these accords";[84] but—presumably following the advent of the Allende Administration in Chile in November 1970 and its relatively moderate attitude towards the OAS—this position was revised in August 1971: "We only accept relations with governments giving authentic proof of their sovereignty and national independence in relation to imperialism."[85]

These developments could not leave relations with the Soviet Union unaffected. From mid-1968 onwards, Cuban newspapers were taking the Soviet side in the Sino-Soviet dispute. After all, when it came to hard facts, Cuba had received a total of $1,500 million in Soviet military aid over eleven years.[86] In November 1969, Marshal Grechko of the Soviet Union spent a week in Cuba,[87] and in May 1970 Castro envisaged "more military links with the Soviet Union."[88] In September 1970, eight years exactly after the onset of the momentous missile crisis, Soviet naval operations were reported in the Cuban port of Cienfuegos, looking suspiciously like the building of a submarine base or the installation of a submarine tender. After a warning from the White House, these operations ceased in October 1970. The warning had contained the ominous statement, "In the event that nuclear submarines were serviced either in Cuba or from Cuba, that would be a violation of the understanding."[89] The United States could not have been more explicit on this point. "The crucial factor for submarine-based missiles is not absolute totals per se, but the number on station within firing range of enemy targets at any particular time."[90] Cienfuegos may, therefore, have been regarded as strategically suitable to neutralize the advantage—enjoyed in this sense at the moment by United States nuclear-armed submarines—in the use of the Holy Loch base in Scotland[91] or Rota in Spain. The Soviet naval presence in the Caribbean is believed to be considerably larger than the one in the Indian Ocean.[92]

An extension of the scale of Soviet economic aid to Cuba could not be far off in these circumstances. On July 26, 1970, Castro admitted failure in his economic policies,[93] and on the following day *Izvestia,* organ of the Soviet government, dwelled on the importance of Soviet economic aid to Cuba.[94] In May 1970 Castro admitted that he had set the annual sugar target at ten millions mainly in order to pay off some of Cuba's debts to the Soviet Union.[95] In April 1971 Mr. Baibakov, head of the Soviet Planning Commission, made a prolonged visit to Cuba, allegedly asking them to make better use of Soviet equipment.[96] Castro obliged by acknowledging this need publicly at Alamar (Cuba) in the presence of A. Kosygin, the Soviet prime minister, who was visiting the island after an absence of four years.[97] In July 1972 Cuba was finally admitted as a full member of COMECON, and this was followed by the announcement in January 1973 of a Soviet moratorium on the repayment of Cuba's debts, as well as further Soviet long-term aid on favorable terms.

Allende's advent to power caused some concern in Buenos Aires. Gen. López Aufranc—a right-wing general, not a member of the top decision-making echelons within the Argentine military junta, but commanding wide respect nonetheless—probably reflected the general mood when he proclaimed, somewhat hastily, that "united, Brazil and Argentina will oppose the invasion of Latin America by harmful ideologies."[98] But L. M. de Pablo Pardo, President R. Levingston's foreign minister, informed the world that the resumption of diplomatic relations between Chile and Cuba was not affecting Argentina in any way.[99]

After the coup in which Gen. Alejandro Lanusse unseated the ruling president, Gen. R. Levingston, Argentina began to draw noticeably closer to Chile, mainly in order to offset the growing stature of Brazil,[100] which began to encroach on Argentina's traditional zone of influence, comprised of Paraguay, Uruguay, and Bolivia. It seemed as if Brazil, rather than Chile, presented the prime problem of Argentina's foreign policy.[101]

The new pragmatism in Argentina's foreign policy was reflected in the preferences shown by de Pablo Pardo—taken over as foreign minister by Lanusse—who, "according to sources in the Foreign Ministry," favored a rapprochement with both left-wing Bolivia and Chile under Allende,[102] and signalled the final demise of the concept of "ideological frontiers." Henceforth, the new pragmatic principle of "ideological pluralism" was to govern the diplomatic relations between the two countries, and it found its first affirmation during the meeting between Lanusse and Allende at Salta (Argentina) on July 23, 1971.[103] By entering into an entente with Chile, Argentina made it clear that she was unwilling to subordinate her Latin American policies to those of Brazil, or to act as the ideological stalking horse of either Brazil or the United States against Chile, Bolivia, or Peru. The principle of ideological pluralism was subsequently extended during official visits by Lanusse and Allende to Peru, Ecuador, Colombia, Venezuela, and Mexico, thus applying to the whole of Spanish-speaking Latin America outside the Central American-Caribbean area, excepting only a narrow belt of small states composed of Uruguay, Paraguay, and Bolivia. To complete the process of the pragmatization of her foreign policy, Argentina accorded full recognition to Communist China on February 19, 1972.[104] The pro-Perón President Héctor Cámpora, who succeeded Lanusse in May 1973, took these policies to their logical conclusion by recognizing North Vietnam and by resuming relations with Cuba on May 28, 1973. Perón himself clearly favored close relations with Peru and Cuba, but it remains to be seen whether he will want to push the encirclement of Brazil much further, thus repeating his own diplomatic patterns of 1952 and 1953, or whether on the contrary he might, given the chance, promote a rapprochement with Brazil along the lines of that achieved by Frondizi and Quadros in their Uruguaiana axis of April 1961.

Mexico, traditionally eager to pursue a cautious policy towards the United States while remaining sympathetic toward general Latin American desires to achieve wider margins of independence,[105] began to fall in gradually with the new mood under her new president, Luis Echeverría. Through the 1960s the real gross national product had risen annually by about 3 percent faster than the Mexican population, and United States investment in the country, at $1,500 million, was among the highest in Latin America.[106] Nonetheless, according to ECLA, half the population received a very small proportion of the total income.[107] Consequently, Echeverría tried to curb the economic influence of the giant of the North [108] and eventually aligned himself with the policies of the Andean countries and Argentina.

It was expected that under Echeverría relations with the Communist world would undergo some improvement. However, complications arose unexpectedly when in March 1971 five Soviet diplomats were suddenly expelled on the allegation that a number of Mexicans trying to subvert public order had received guerrillero training in North Korea and that the Soviet embassy in Mexico City, by granting those men scholarships, had enabled them to proceed to Pyönyang, the North Korean capital.[109] It is not, however, by any means certain that there was Soviet-North Korean collusion in the matter,[110] though it is possible that, with Cuba losing interest in the further promotion of guerrillas in Latin America, Mexican would-be guerrilleros had to use this circuitous route to reach North Korean training camps.[111]

Cuba, too, with which Mexico had never broken off relations, was to pose an awkward problem. On May 25, 1970, a Mexican Boeing-727 aircraft was highjacked to Cuba,[112] and Carrillo Flores, Mexico's foreign minister, asked for the extradition of the four highjackers. Cuba replied that there were Cuban laws for the punishment of hijackers, but that she reserved the sovereign right of extradition.[113] In retaliation, Mexico announced in July 1970 that she wished to put an end to the existing agreement regulating air travel between the two countries. One would therefore have expected Mexico to adopt a hard line at the OAS conference held in Washington in February 1971, but this was not to be the case.[114]

In May 1971—under the Echeverría Administration, and facing the prospect of the early reestablishment of aerial communications between Allende's Chile and Castro's Cuba—Mexico began to beat a retreat when Rabasa, the foreign minister, announced that the question of a renewal of the aerial agreement with Cuba was merely a matter of economics.[115] A new agreement—held up as a model—was signed on July 30, 1971,[116] and the question of principle was conveniently forgotten.

The speedy recognition of the Communist government in China should have been a matter of routine, if Mexico's past practice in the field of recognition is any guide.[117] However, almost certainly inhibited by the strong stand taken by the United States over this question, Mexico failed to do so until the forthcoming trip by Nixon to Peking was announced in July 1971, and in spite of a growing chorus of voices outside Latin America demanding the seating of the Chinese Communists in the United Nations. As late as October 1970, A. Carrillo Flores, foreign minister in the outgoing Ordaz Díaz Administration, issued a tortuously phrased statement justifying Mexico's vote against the seating of the representatives of Communist China in the United Nations on the curious ground of his government's unwillingness to break with Formosa.[118] In October 1971, however, Echeverría, considering himself snubbed by the United States over its high-handed attitude towards a Mexican delegation sent to protest over the economic measures taken in August 1971, travelled to New York to make a militant speech in the United Nations in justification of Mexico's vote in favor of Formosa's expulsion,[119] and this was followed on February 2, 1972, by the assumption of full diplomatic relations with Communist China. Later in the year, Echeverría travelled to Chile to meet Allende, and in turn played host to the Chilean president in Mexico City in November 1972. His diplomacy was capped in 1973 by a world tour, which included Moscow and Peking but studiously evaded Washington.

The new pragmatism in Latin America's international relations also affected Venezuela, which resumed diplomatic relations with Moscow in April 1970 under her Christian Democratic President Caldera. This was probably done on economic rather than on political grounds, having been determined by the fact that the Soviet Union was a major producer of oil.[120] As to Cuba, President Caldera expressed the wish at the Caracas meeting of the Inter-American Economic and Social Council in February 1970 that she might be allowed "to rejoin the Latin American family," and that her boycott was an inefficient means of coercion.

Internally, the pro-Soviet Communist party had been allowed a legal existence again in March 1969 after it had withdrawn its support from the *mirista*-type of guerrilleros in 1967, and after it had been split by the Soviet action in Czechoslovakia in 1968,[121] an action greatly facilitated by Castro's withdrawal of support from the guerrilleros in 1969, for which he was to be denounced by Douglas Bravo, the guerrillero leader, in January 1970.[122]

While the Andean countries and Mexico represented the new spirit of independence in Latin America, and Bolivia, originally part of that informal diplomatic alignment, reversed the course of her foreign policy under President Banzer, Brazil was riding on a wave of economic prosperity to a status of unparalleled political importance in Latin America, which carried with it some dangers of isolation.

The Garrastazú Médici régime, which had taken over from the Costa e Silva Administration in the autumn of 1969, carried on the lines of foreign policy laid down by J. Magalhães Pinto under the previous government, but expanded its scope in two directions. First, it raised the concept of development on a par with that of security; and second, closely connected, it placed greater emphasis on geopolitics, as evidenced by the grandiose scheme of opening the territories of Trans-Amazonia and insisting on a 200 mile limit of her territorial waters. From mid-1970 onwards the high rate of economic growth encouraged many Brazilians, both inside and outside the government, to visualize Brazil as a world power by the year 2000, [123] and, in the short run, to regard her as a possible leader of at least the South American states in world affairs.[124]

Brazil continued to identify with the underdeveloped world in such bodies as CECLA and UNCTAD, and was prepared, if necessary, to oppose the United States on the economic plane.[125] However, O. Bilac Pinto, Brazilian observer to a Belgrade meeting of non-aligned countries in November 1969, made it perfectly clear that Brazilian cooperation must be confined strictly to the economic plane, as Brazil continued to regard herself as a politically committed country under the terms of the Rio Treaty.[126]

Relations with the Soviet Union remained unchanged, with trade between the two countries expanding in an impressive way,[127] and in view of lessening world tensions, political relations with the United States were losing much of their former appeal. There could be no doubt, however, that general United States influence in Brazil was still considerable,[128] as witness to the massive influx of United States capital, a process deliberately encouraged by A. Delfim Neto, minister of finance under the Costa e Silva and Médici Administrations. In 1969 foreign investment in Brazil reached the astonishing level of $1,185 million,[129] rising to $3,400 million in 1973.

The first reaction of Brazil to the advent of Allende was to draw closer to Argentina[130] and to take certain restrictive measures. When Argentina moved closer to Chile, the building of strategic roads was pushed forward with great vigor, as Brazil sensed a possibility of being isolated in South America.

Because of her rapidly growing power and status and the suspicion aroused in the remainder of South America that she is aiming at a form of *liderança,* Brazil is now regarded as the most important diplomatic factor in that part of Latin America, especially since her rise happens to coincide with a steady decline of interest shown by the United States. Her ascendancy is also one of the causes of the new spirit of pragmatism that marks the present phase of diplomatic relations in Latin America.

There are, moreover, signs of a growing Brazilian awareness of the danger of isolation. With the term of office of the Médici Administration drawing to a close, there are now some indications of a more emphatically Latin American outlook on the part of the government and an understanding of Brazil's need to balance her continuing economic expansion on the continent—as witnessed by her agreement with Paraguay regarding Itaipú in 1973—by a studied political rapprochement with the Andean group and, depending on favorable circumstances, with Argentina.

In Uruguay the *tupamaros*—an urban guerrilla active since 1968—stepped up the pace of their operations from March 1969 onwards. Allende's peaceful victory in Chile in 1970 seemed to have given them some pause and led to the formation of the *frente amplio,* a left-wing cartel closely modelled on *Unidad Popular* in Chile, composed of Communists, Socialists, and Christian Democrats, as well as some disaffected groups drawn from both traditional parties.[131] The frente amplio began to function in February 1971 under General Liber Seregni, of no party affiliation.

The government seems to have taken fright at the prospect of a left-wing victory at the polls, and in May 1971 President J. Pacheco Areco saw fit to call for N. Demidov, the Soviet ambassador, an act widely interpreted as an official warning not to show undue interest in trade union, student, social, and other activities connected with the tupamaros.[132] It was indeed remarkable that the Soviet embassy in Brasilia should have gone out of its way in March 1971 to dissociate itself publicly from urban guerrilleros in Brazil, while its counterpart in Montevideo preserved a silence on the subject of the tupamaros.[133] In June 1971 the Uruguayan government strengthened its censorship of the press and closed the Cuban news agency, *Prensa Latina,* in Montevideo.[134]

In the event, the candidate of the frente amplio polled 16 percent of the vote on November 28, 1971, and J. M. Bordaberry, a *colorado*, was elected as new president. The previous administration had been under some pressure to resume trade relations with Cuba,[135] but Bordaberry made it clear that he shared the political outlook of the military regimes of Brazil and Argentina, to which he would also look for closer economic ties. It was to become evident before long that—like the Banzer régime in Bolivia—he would draw closer to Brazil, if not to Argentina. When the tupamaros resumed their activities, the government took drastic measures to suppress them. In the course of 1973 Bordaberry assumed extraordinary powers reminiscent of the Terra dictatorship of 1933. While it is clear that, for the moment at least, Uruguay under Bordaberry prefers a Brazilian orientation to an Argentine one, it remains to be seen to what extent the country can isolate itself from the effects of the *Peronista* revival across the River Plate.

During the period under review in this chapter, Latin America made some progress towards normalizing her relationship with the former principals in the Cold War. The new policy of the "low profile" of the United States was facilitating this, but the Soviet government, by its circumspect policy, also made a contribution. Its breaking of diplomatic relations with Chile following the military coup there in September 1973 must be regarded as falling outside the norms of Soviet behavior of recent years.

Soviet policy towards Latin America appeared to be guided by three principles: (a) no arms to Latin America except to Cuba; (b) peaceful economic relations with all governments in the area; and (c) advice to Moscow-oriented Communist Parties to limit their methods to either the infiltration of existing Populist governments or the electoral support of left-wing cartels which include Muscovite Communist representation.

In intra-Latin American relations the severely rigid forms of anticommunism associated with the doctrine of "ideological frontiers" began to crumble and to give way to the idea of "ideological pluralism."[136] Consequently, the movement for the diplomatic reassociation of Cuba within Latin America and towards the normalization of relations with the Communist world outside the area have gathered strength.[137] The break in diplomatic relations with Chile, following upon the military coup there on September 11, 1973, represented a setback but is unlikely to act as a final barrier to eventual integration. With the direct influence of the world powers declining in the underdeveloped world in general, intra-Latin American issues are likely to acquire a new importance,[138] with greater attention being paid consequently to the notion of the balance of power.[139] It is not impossible that, under these conditions, the future of Latin America's international system will begin to resemble that of the nineteenth century rather more than that of the twentieth.[140]

NOTES

1. D. Fascell, chairman of the Committee on Foreign Relations of the House of Representatives in Washington, thought it possible that the United States would coexist with a predominantly Socialist Latin America. He thought that Latin America must evolve its own patterns of development, profiting from both Marxist and capitalist experience. See *Jornal do Brasil*, December 17, 1970 and April 17, 1971.

2. The assets of Standard Oil were first taken over by Bolivia in 1937, but Esso was allowed back in 1956.

3. At first, events in Bolivia tended to follow the trend set by the new military government of Peru.

4. See also M. R. Millar, "Algunos aspectos de la política exterior del nuevo régimen peruano," 10 *Foro Internacional*, April/June 1970, pp. 407-424.

5. See L. Einaudi, in an interview with *Caretas* (Lima), June 11-24, 1971, pp. 14-15 and 41-42. For other articles on the Peruvian military, see S. L. Rozman, "The Evolution of the Political Role of the Peruvian Military," 12 *Journal of Inter-American Studies and World Affiars*, October 1970, pp. 539-564; R. I. Clinton, "The Modernizing Military. The Case of Peru," 24 *Inter-American Economic Affairs*, Spring 1971, pp. 43-66; and E. Alonso, "Fuerzas armadas y revolución nacional en Bolivia y Peru," 9 *Estrategia* (Buenos Aires), September 1970-February 1971, pp. 15-26.

6. President Belaúnde consulted the two principal opposition leaders, former President Manuel Odría and A.P.R.A. leader R. Haya de la Torre. See *La Prensa* (Lima), January 1, 1966.

7. These revelations were made in *La Prensa* (Lima), on June 3, 1969, by the former assistance secretary of state of the United States, R. N. Goodwin.

8. "Observers forecast that Washington would apply devastating economic sanctions under the terms of the Hickenlooper Amendment, which decrees that the United States should cut off aid to a country that nationalizes United States property without paying fair compensation. They also forecast that other foreign investors would pull out overnight. They were wrong on both counts." See *The Economist*, February 21, 1970.

9. *El Comercio* (Lima), February 1, 1969.

10. *La Prensa* (Lima), February 2, 1969.

11. See "Tres de octubre. Balance y perspectivas," *Oiga*, October 3, 1969, pp. 11-13 and 41-42.

12. *Expreso*, March 17, 1970.

13. Ministerio de Relaciones Exteriores del Perú, *Visita del canciller del Perú al Brasil* (Lima, 1971).

14. This followed the renewal of relations with Czechoslovakia, Rumania, and Yugoslavia. See *Christian Science Monitor*, February 8, 1969.

15. *International Herald Tribune*, February 18, 1969.
16. *The Economist*, February 21, 1970.
17. *Le Monde*, August 28, 1970. On the level of Communist parties, it was decided in June 1971 that they must give support to Peru's Revolution. Both *Pravda* of Moscow and Jorge del Prado, secretary-general of the Peruvian Communist Party, made simultaneous statements to this effect. See *La Prensa* (Lima), June 26, 1971. *Pravda* of July 2, 1971, carried an additional message of del Prado listing the reasons for this decision.
18. *La Prensa*, October 4, 1970.
19. An official denial was published in response to a rumor that the government was supporting a request by Cuba and Chile, at the Santiago Conference of the United Nations Economic Commission for Latin America (ECLA), to place on the agenda of the next meeting of that body an item calling for the express consideration of the "Socialist road to development." See *El Comercio* (Lima), May 7, 1971.
20. *Expreso*, September 21, 1970.
21. *Oiga*, July 30, 1971. It was rumored at the time, however, that the government's unilateral increase of the price of fishmeal had resulted in considerable contractions in the export market of that commodity, and that the approach towards Communist China was a measure of despair.
22. *La Opinión* (Buenos Aires), August 15, 1971, and *El Excelsior* (Mexico City), August 15, 1971.
23. *La Prensa*, January 16, 1970.
24. *La Prensa* (Lima), February 23, 1971.
25. See Ministerio de Relaciones Exteriores del Perú, *El Perú en la CECLA, en 1970* (Lima, 1970).
26. Ministerio de Relaciones Exteriores del Perú, *Discurso pronunciado por el Minister de Relaciones Exteriores, el 18 de septiembre de 1970 en la Asamblea General de Naciones Unidas* (Lima, 1970), p. 11.
27. See "Integración peruano-ecuatoriana," *El Mercurio*, July 20, 1971.
28. *Latin America*, February 14, 1969. In 1971 Ecuador relied on Eastern Europe for marketing its bananas. The personnel of the Soviet embassy is larger than that of the United States embassy.
29. Ibid., February 21, 1969.
30. *El Mercurio*, February 3, 1971.
31. For an analysis of developments within Bolivia before April 1970, see L. Whitehead, "Bolivia's Conflict with the United States," 26 *The World Today*, April 1970, pp. 167-178.
32. *New York Times*, May 8, 1969.
33. Whitehead, op. cit., pp. 172-173.
34. *Jornal do Brasil*, January 31, 1970.
35. Whitehead, op. cit., p. 167. In August 1970 a Soviet loan of $27.5 million, repayable over twenty years, was extended to Bolivia. See *Financial Times*, August 18, 1970.
36. Whitehead, op. cit., p. 175.
37. The lecture was delivered to an audience of university students. See *Süddeutsche Zeitung*, April 17, 1970.
38. *Latin America*, September 11, 1970.

39. *Financial Times,* October 10, 1970.

40. *Latin America,* September 11; 1970.

41. Already in his dialogue with the Left in January 1970, Torres had defined the duty of the armed forces as "allying themselves with the oppressed classes . . . to the exclusion of the Right and the internationalized Left." And on November 14, 1969, he had told the Inter-American Defense Board assembled in La Paz that the armed forces must not regard themselves as performing exclusively "the repression of international communism, but as cooperators and agents in the battle against . . . economic underdevelopment." See E. Alonso, "Fuerzas armadas y revolución nacional en Bolivia y Perú," 9 *Estrategia* (Buenos Aires), September 1970-February 1971, p. 19.

42. *Financial Times,* March 19, 1971.

43. *La Segunda* (Santiago), June 25, 1971.

44. *O Estado de S. Paulo,* May 8, 1971.

45. *Correio da Manhã,* May 3, 1971.

46. Ibid.

47. *Jornal do Brasil,* January 16, 1971.

48. Ibid., April 15, 1971.

49. *O Estado de S. Paulo,* June 3, 1971; and *Argentinisches Tageblatt,* June 21, 1971.

50. *El Siglo* (Santiago), June 26, 1971.

51. *El Excelsior* (Mexico City), August 10, 1971.

52. *El Día* (Mexico City), August 24, 1971.

53. *Latin America,* September 10, 1971.

54. Ibid. Ernest Siracuse, United States ambassador in La Paz, reported jubilantly that he was "in the fortunate position . . . to be able to give an assurance that international confidence in Bolivia has been restored." See *Der Spiegel,* November 1, 1971.

55. *Evening Standard,* March 30, 1972.

56. See "Política de acercamiento con países del Pacífico," *El Mercurio,* September 15, 1969.

57. *Comisión Especial para la Coordinación Latinoamericana.*

58. *El Mercurio,* March 29, 1969. Frei himself asked the conference to concert its actions. Argentina, Brazil, and Mexico wanted these to be taken through existing inter-American organs, notably the Inter-American Economic and Social Council; but Chile wanted to see new machinery created for energetic negotiations with the United States.

59. For the text, see *Estudios Internacionales* (Santiago), October/December 1969, pp. 403-418.

60. See "Aspiraciones de Latinoamérica expuso el canciller chileno a Richard Nixon," *El Mercurio,* June 12, 1969.

61. See *Mensaje del Presidente Eduardo Frei al Congreso Nacional. Seis años del gobierno (21 de mayo de 1970)* (Santiago, 1970), pp. 55-59.

62. See R. Tomic, *Revolución chilena y UP* (Santiago, 1969).

63. See *Latin America,* January 10, 1969; and "Chile: El PDC apoya el reintegro de Cuba," *El País* (Montevideo), January 7, 1969.
  In April 1969 Chile decided to sell Cuba $11 million worth of agricultural

produce in defiance of the OAS ban. Baltasar Castro, a Socialist politician, was used by the Chilean government as the unofficial emissary to Fidel Castro.

64. *Financial Times*, September 10, 1969.

65. See E. Labarca Goddard, *Chile al rojo* (Santiago, 1971).

66. The figures were as follows: Alessandri, 1,036,278 votes; Allende, 1,075,616 votes; Tomic, 824,849 votes. A comparative analysis of the percentage of votes cast in 1964 and 1970 respectively for the three candidates gives the following picture:

1964			1970		
Allende	*Frei*	*Duran*	*Allende*	*Alessandri*	*Tomic*
38.9	56.1	5.0	36.3	34.9	27.8

67. On this point, see E. Labarca Goddard, *Chile al rojo* (Santiago, 1971), p. 220.

Allende had opposed the Rio Treaty and voted against the Mutual Assistance Agreement with the United States. See *El Mercurio*, June 16, 1952.

68. See *New York Times*, November 1, 1970.

69. See United States, *US States Code, 1970 Edition, containing the general and permanent laws of the United States in force on January 20, 1970* (Washington, D.C., 1970), Vol. V, Title 221, "Foreign Relations and Intercourse," p. 5903, par. 2370, section (f), sub-section (b), sub-paragraph (i), "Denial of assistance to countries preparing for aggressive military efforts."

70. Radomiro Tomic, Christian Democrat candidate at the presidential elections of 1970, wished to pursue a neutralist foreign policy modelled on that of Algeria and Yugoslavia and wanted the outright nationalization of the copper industry. See *El Programa de Tomic* (Santiago, 1970).

On Chile's need of aid from the United States, see Gabriel Valdés, *Conciencia latinoamericana y Realidad internacional* (Santiago, 1970), p. 138.

71. See L. Whitehead, "Why Allende Fell," *The World Today*, November 1973, pp. 461-474.

72. D. Doder, writing in *The Guardian*, November 23, 1971.

73. *New York Times*, April 27, 1969.

74. *The Economist* (Latin American edition), July 23, 1969.

75. *Bohemia*, October 17, 1969.

76. *Neue Zürcher Zeitung*, March 8, 1970.

77. *El Excelsior*, August 5, 1970.

78. *La Prensa* (Lima), July 30, 1971.

79. *Frankfurter Allgemeine Zeitung*, March 5, 1970.

80. *Latin America*, May 8, 1970.

81. *El Mercurio*, July 29, 1970.

82. *El Excelsior*, August 25, 1971.

83. *Granma*, August 29, 1971.

84. Ibid., July 15, 1969.

85. *El Día*, August 29, 1971.

86. *Granma*, April 24, 1970.

87. *Neue Zürcher Zeitung*, November 21, 1969.

88. *Latin America,* May 8, 1970.

89. See G. H. Quester, "Missiles in Cuba, 1970," 49 *Foreign Affairs,* April 1971, pp. 493-506.

90. Quester, op. cit., p. 496.

91. Ibid.

92. For a general background, see M. McGwire, "The Background to Soviet Naval Developments," 27 *The World Today,* March 1971, pp. 93-103; and P. Hanson, "The Rise of the Soviet Merchant Marine," ibid., Vol. 26, March 1970, pp. 130-136.

93. *Granma,* July 27, 1970.

94. *Izvestia,* July 27, 1970.

95. H. Marchant, former British ambassador to Cuba, writing in *New Society,* October 8, 1970, p. 627.

96. *The Economist,* November 6, 1971.

97. *Observer,* October 31, 1971.

98. *Der Spiegel,* August 16, 1971.

99. *El Excelsior* (Mexico City), November 13, 1970.

100. See two articles by the editors of 5 *Estrategia,* January/February 1970, on "Relaciones argentino-brasileños," pp. 48-57; and "Argentina y Brasil. Estudio comparative de algunos de sus aspectos fundamentales," pp. 72-96.

101. Mariano Grondona, leading commentator and distinguished political scientist, remarked in July 1971 that if Argentina and Brazil were allowed to combine in a "capitalist" axis against the predominantly radical Andean Group, the latter will be driven to call on the Soviet Union for aid. See *Visión,* July 3-17, 1971.

102. *El Mercurio,* June 26, 1971.

103. On April 6, 1972, a treaty of arbitration was signed between Argentina and Chile.

104. The talks between Presidents Lanusse and Médici in Brasilia in March 1972, while kept on a friendly level, proved inconclusive.

105. R. de La Colina, Mexico's ambassador at the OAS, said that his country's voting record in that body was mixed, with Mexico voting with other underdeveloped countries at times. See *El Excelsior,* November 1, 1970.

106. See J. Womack, "The Spoils of the Mexican Revolution," *Foreign Affairs,* July 1970, pp. 677-687.

107. As quoted in the *Financial Times,* December 2, 1970.

108. In July 1971 President Echeverría told journalists that a fresh impulse was needed for *capitalismo nacionalista,* but that foreign capital must be made "complementary to national capital." See *El Excelsior,* July 5, 1971.

109. See *El Excelsior,* March 19, 1971. *El Día* published both Soviet and Mexican communiqués in its issue of March 20, 1971.

110. Witness C. Foley's informative article on this point in *The Observer,* March 26, 1971.

111. It was in November 1966 that the secretariat of the Tricontinental in Havana announced that, in accordance with a hitherto secret resolution passed at the Tricontinental Conference in January 1966, Cuba and North Korea were setting up "schools for the training of political cadres for the revolutionary movements of their respective continents." At the time the North Koreans would neither deny nor

confirm this. See also K. Devlin, "The Castroist Challenge to Communism," pp. 159-173, in J. G. Oswald and A. J. Strover (eds.) *The Soviet Union and Latin America* (London, 1970).

112. *El Excelsior,* June 2, 1970.

113. Ibid.

114. Ibid., February 7, 1971.

115. *El Excelsior,* May 27, 1971.

116. Ibid., July 31, 1971. See also text of the agreement in Universidad Nacional Autónoma de México, *Boletín del Centro de Relaciones Internacionales,* September 1971, pp. 60-63.

117. On the subject of Mexico's policy or recognition, see M. Seara Vázquez, "México y la República Popular," in Universidad Nacional Autónoma de México, *Boletín del Centro de Relaciones Internacionales,* September 1971, pp. 75-79.

118. *El Excelsior,* October 16, 1970. Ex-President Emílio Gil, on the other hand, pronounced himself in favor of Communist China's entry.

119. In his speech of October 5, 1971, the president referred to China as "juridically indivisible."

120. Viktor Likhatchev, the new Soviet ambassador in Caracas, is an oil expert. See *L'Express* (Paris), November 23-29, 1970.

Venezuela's foreign minister, Calvani, stated at Tegucigalpa on November 29, 1969, that he was fully alive to the dangers of ideological and economic penetration inherent in the act of creating diplomatic relations.

121. T. Petkov, prominent Communist and at one time active *guerrillero,* wrote a book, *Checoeslovaquia—el socialismo como problema* (Caracas: Domingo Fuentes, 1970), in which he denied the right of intervention to the Soviet Union.

122. *The Interpreter,* August 1970, p. 16.

123. This was expressly stated by the president in a speech on October 30, 1969. See E. Garrastazú Médici, *O Jôgo da Verdade* (Brasilia, 1970), p. 35.

124. See the leading article in *Correio da Manhã,* May 2-3, 1971.

125. See an article by Brazil's foreign minister, M. Gibson Barbosa, "Política Brasileira de Comercio Exterior," 13 *Revista Brasileira de Política Internacional,* March/June 1970, pp. 63-70.

126. *Jornal do Brasil,* November 7, 1969.

127. *Financial Times,* May 7, 1970. See also "Ofensiva de vender da URSS no Brasil é consequencia do nôvo acôrdo de comércio," *Jornal do Brasil,* March 16, 1969.

128. *Jornal do Brasil,* May 20, 1971, gives precise figures of the large numbers of United States civilian and military officials stationed in Brazil.

129. *Latin America,* May 21, 1971. For various criticisms, see P. R. Schilling, *Una historia sucia: el capital extranjero en el Brasil* (Montevideo: L.Y.S., 1968); F. Gasparian, "Debate Rages on the Role of Foreign Capital," *Financial Times,* November 18, 1970; and R. Medina, *Desnacionalização. Crime contra Brasil?* (Rio de Janeiro: Editora Saga, 1970).

130. See "Cumbre militar sobre Chile se cumple en Brasil," *Ya* (Montevideo), October 22, 1970.

131. See *Bases programáticas del Frente Amplio* (Montevideo, 1971).

132. *O Estado de S. Paulo,* May 19, 1971.

133. *Le Monde*, March 24, 1971. The Communist Party placed heavy emphasis on the importance of the *frente amplio*, while playing down the side of the tupamaros.

134. *Argentinisches Tageblatt*, June 18, 1971.

135. Zorrilla de San Martín, foreign minister when Uruguay severed relations with Cuba in 1964, called for the resumption of trade with Havana. See *Latin America*, June 26, 1970.

136. The predominant internal ideology in Latin America is economic development ("desarrollo" in Spanish; "desenvolvimento" in Portuguese). The principle is clear but fierce dispute persists as to the exact strategy by which the principle is to be realized. See, for instance, O. Sunkel, "Capitalismo transnacional y desintegración nacional en América Latina," 4 *Estudios Internacionales*, January/March 1971, pp. 3-61; Roberto de Oliveira Campos, *Do outro lado da cêrca* (Rio de Janeiro: APEC, 1967); and Instituto Latinoamericano de Planificación Económica y Social, *Dos polémicas sobre el desarrollo de América Latina* (Buenos Aires: Editorial Universitaria, 1970).

137. Galo Plaza, secretary-general of the OAS, said in Paris that Chile was not defying that body in resuming relations with Cuba. Each member country had the right of raising the question of lifting existing sanctions on Cuba. See *El Excelsior*, November 13, 1970.

138. See, for instance, P. Seaborn Smith, "Bolivian Oil and Brazilian Nationalism," 12 *Journal of Inter-American Studies and World Affairs*, April 1971, pp. 163-181.

139. The new distribution of power within the area was reflected in the vote on the expulsion of Formosa from the United Nations in October 1971, when Chile, Cuba, Ecuador, Mexico, Peru, and Trinidad and Tobago voted for expulsion, while Bolivia, Brazil, Costa Rica, El Salvador, Guatemala, Haiti, Honduras, Nicaragua, Uruguay, and Venezuela voted against, and Argentina, Colombia, Jamaica, and Panama abstained.

140. Though still functioning as an annual forum, the OAS was seen to be in decline, a fact clearly to be witnessed by the fiasco of its Washington conference on terrorism, diplomatic status, and asylum in January 1971.

BIBLIOGRAPHY

A NOTE ON SOURCES

Textbooks
No basic textbook on the foreign policies of Latin American countries covering the present period exists in any language, although a limited number of texts deals with the relations between the United States and Latin America, focusing on the United States end of the relationship. Numerous works purporting to be comprehensive analyses of the subject turn out to be, on closer inspection, no more than commentaries, but some of these have been of moderate value. Information on the present subject therefore had to be sought from an unusually large number of secondary works.

Memoirs
Some memoirs have been written by leading Latin American statesmen, but the overwhelming majority of these take the form of personal commentary rather than a critical examination of the events covered. There is a wealth of commentaries by writers either not involved or involved only peripherally in the making of Latin American foreign policies, but these have been of limited usefulness.

Documents
There are few collections of government sources of Latin American origin. Many government papers and annuals contain a mass of information on a wide range of subjects, but very little that is relevant to this subject. On the other hand, nearly all records of OAS conferences have been at hand.

Periodicals
Investigators are better served by the existence of a reasonably wide range of periodicals in English, Spanish, and Portuguese. Only a few of these specialize in Latin American affairs. Thus, the *Journal of Inter-American Studies and World Affairs* and *Inter-American Economic Affairs* (both published in the United States), whose contributions vary considerably in quality, contain some useful material. Occasional articles in *The Economist* (London) and *Marcha* (Montevideo) have been informative, as have been some papers in *The World Today* and *International Affairs*

(London). Among the Latin American periodicals devoted wholly or partially to foreign affairs, mention should be made of *Foro Internacional* (Mexico City), *El Boletín del Centro de Estudios Internacionales* of the Universidad Nacional Autónoma of Mexico, *Estudios Internacionales* (Santiago), *Política Internacional* (Havana), and the *Revista Brasileira de Política Internacional* (Rio de Janeiro).

Newspapers

Pride of place among sources in this category must belong to the *Hispanic-American Report*, published monthly by Stanford University (Stanford, Calif.) between 1947 and 1964. While it was appreciated that this Report based its information on a wide range of newspaper sources of varying quality, the information produced has invariably proved accurate. Its commentaries of events have been made the subject of critical scrutiny, like other sources, as a matter of principle.

To fill the gap, there has in recent years been published on a monthly basis *Latin America* (London), which is steadily improving in quality.

Among Latin American newspapers, *O Jornal do Brasil, O Estado de São Paulo* and *Correio da Manhã* (Brazil), *Carta de Montevideo* (a weekly digest of *La Mañana*, Uruguay), *La Prensa* and *La Nación* (Argentina), *El Mercurio* (Chile), *La Prensa* (Peru), *El Excelsior* and *El Día* (Mexico), and *Granma* (formerly *Hoy* and *Revolución*, Cuba) have proved useful sources.

Information culled from the high-quality press of the United States (*New York Times, New York Herald Tribune, Christian Science Monitor*, etc.), of France (*Le Monde, Le Figaro*, etc.), of Switzerland (*Neue Zürcher Zeitung, Tribune de Geneve*, etc.), of Western Germany (*Frankfurter Allgemeine Zeitung, Süddeutsche Zeitung*) and of England (*The Times, The Guardian, Daily Telegraph*, etc.) has been invaluable.

I. GENERAL

Latin America and the World

BOOKS

BLAKEMORE, H. and SMITH, C. T. (eds.) *Latin America. Geographical Perspectives* (London: Methuen, 1971).

BRIANO, J. T. *Geopolítica y geostrategia americana* (Buenos Aires: Pleamar, 1966).

CALDERA RODRÍGUEZ, R. *El bloque latinoamericano* (Santiago: Pacífico, 1961).

CLISSOLD, S. *Latin America* (London: Oxford University Press, 1970).

COROMINAS, E. V. *En las áreas políticas del Caribe* (Buenos Aires: El Ateneo, 1952).

CÚNEO, D. *La batalla de América latina* (Buenos Aires: Siglo Veinte, 1964).

DILLON, M. (ed.) *Latin America in World Affairs. The Politics of Inequality* (New York: Barrons, 1973).

DUGGAN, L. *The Americas. The Search for Hemisphere Security* (New York: Holt, Rineholt & Winston, 1949).

EISENHOWER, M. S. *The Wine is Bitter* (New York: Doubleday, 1963).

GÓMEZ ROBLEDO, A. *Idea y experiencia de América* (Mexico City: Fondo de Cultura Económica, 1958).

HIRSCHMAN, A. O. *Latin American Issues* (New York: Twentieth Century Fund, 1961).

JAGUARIBE, H. et al. *La Dominación de América Latina* (Lima: Moncloa, 1968).

KRIEGER VASENA, A. and J. PAZOS. *Latin America* (London: Benn, 1973).

Organisation of American States, Pan American Union. *Bilateral Treaty Developments in Latin America, 1942-1952* (Washington, D.C., 1953).

PÉREZ TRIANA, S. *The Neutrality of Latin America* (Santiago: Hispania, 1916).

RIPPY, J. F. *Globe and Hemisphere. Latin America's Place in the Postwar Foreign Relations of the United States* (Chicago: Reghery, 1958).

ROWE, L. S. et al. *Latin America in World Affairs, 1914-1940* (Philadelphia: University of Pennsylvania Press, 1941).

TRIAS, V. *Imperialismo y geopolítica en América Latina* (Montevideo: Ediciones Sol, 1967).

United Kingdom. *Treaty for the Prohibition of Nuclear Weapons in Latin America* (London: HMSO Cmnd. 3615, 1968).

United States, Arms Control and Disarmament Agency. *International Negotiations on the Non-Proliferation of Nuclear Weapons* (Washington, D.C., 1969).

URQUIDI, V. L. and R. THORP (eds.) *Latin America in the International Economy* (London: Macmillan, 1973).

WHITAKER, A. P. *The Western Hemisphere Idea* (Ithaca, N.Y.: Cornell University Press, 1954).

WIONCZEK, M. S. *Latin American Economic Integration* (New York: Praeger, 1966).

YRARRÁZAVAL CONCHA, E. *América Latina en la guerra fría* (Santiago: Nascimiento, 1959).

ARTICLES

GERMANI, G. "Pertenece América Latina al Tercer Mundo?" *Aportes* (October 1968), pp. 7-32.

IVOVICH, E. "Latin America's Position in Relation to World Changes in Trade Policy." *Economic Bulletin for Latin America* (February 1962), pp. 53-72.

PREISWERK, R. "The Relevance of Latin America to the Foreign Policy of Commonwealth Caribbean States." *Journal of Inter-American Studies* (April 1969), pp. 245-271.

RIPPY, J. F. "The Unsatisfactory State of Inter-American Relations." *Current History* (March 1959), pp. 165-170.

RODRÍGUEZ DE MAGIS, M. E. "Una interpretación de la guerra fría en Latinoamérica." *Foro Internacional* (1964), pp. 517-531.

STUBENRAUCH, W. "Osthandelsprobleme der lateinamerikanischen Länder." *Wirtschaftsdienst* (May 1961), pp. 232-236.

The World Powers and Latin America

BOOKS

AGUILAR MONTEVERDE, A. *El Panamericanismo: de la Doctrina Monroe a la Doctrina Johnson* (Mexico City: Cuadernos Americanos, 1965).

ALLEN, R. L. *Soviet Influence in Latin America. The Role of Economic Relations* (Washington, D.C.: Public Affairs Press, 1959).

BARBER, W. F. and C. N. NEALE RONNING. *Internal Security and Military Power: Counterinsurgency and Civil Action in Latin America* (Columbus: Ohio State University Press, 1966).

BEMIS, S. F. *The Latin American Policy of the United States* (New York: Norton, 1967).

BURR, R. N. *Our Troubled Hemisphere* (Washington, D.C.: The Brookings Institute, 1967).

CLISSOLD, S. *Soviet Relations with Latin America, 1918-1968* (London: Oxford University Press, 1970).

DOZER, D. M. *Are We Good Neighbors?* (Gainesville: University of Florida Press, 1959).

FRANCO, P. *La influencia de los Estados Unidos en América Latina* (Montevideo: Tauro, 1967).

GONYONSKY, S. A. *Latinskaya Amerika i S.Sh.A., 1939-1959* (Moscow: Izdatelstvo Instituta Mezhdunarodnykh Otnoshenya, 1960).

JOHNSON, L. L. *U.S. Private Investment in Latin America: some questions of national policy* (Santa Monica, Calif.: Rand Corporation, 1964).

MAY, S. and G. PLAZA LASSO. *The United Fruit Company in Latin America* (Washington, D.C.: National Planning Association, 1958).

MECHAM, J. L. *The United States and Inter-American Security, 1889-1960* (Austin: Texas University Press, 1961).

MORRISON, L. S. *Latin American Mission* (New York: Simon & Schuster, 1965).

MÜLLER, K. (ed.) *The Soviet Bloc and the Developing Countries* (Hanover: Verlag für Literatur und Zeitgeschichte, 1964).

OSWALD, J. G. (comp.) *Soviet Images of Contemporary Latin America. A Documentary History, 1960-1968* (Austin: University of Texas Press, 1971).

RIEMENS, H. *L'Europe devant l'Amérique Latine* (The Hague: Nijhoff, 1962).

SCHLESINGER, A. *A Thousand Days* (London: Deutsch, 1965).

SLATER, J. *The OAS and United States Foreign Policy* (Columbus: Ohio State University Press, 1967).

ARTICLES

DINERSTEIN, H. S. "Soviet Policy in Latin America." *American Political Science Review* (1967), pp. 80-90.

MANIGAT, L. F. "Les Etats-Unis et le secteur caraïbe de l'Amérique latine." *Revue Française de Science Politique* (1969), pp. 645-683.

NAUMANN, J. "Lateinamerika und die beiden deutschen Staaten." *Deutsche Aussenpolitik* (August 1964), pp. 760-767.

OWEN, C. F. "United States and Soviet Relations with Underdeveloped Countries. Latin America–a Case Study." *Inter-American Economic Affairs* (1960), pp. 85-116.

RICHARDS, E. B. "Marxism and Marxist Movements in Latin America in Recent Soviet Historical Writing." *Hispanic-American Historical Review* (November 1965), pp. 577-590.

SMITH, R. F. "The United States and Latin American Revolution." *Journal of Inter-American Studies* (1962), pp. 89-104.

International Organizations Involving Latin America
BOOKS
CANYES, S. M. *The OAS and the United Nations* (Washington, D.C.: Pan American Union, 1955).
CONNELL-SMITH, G. *The Inter-American System* (London: Oxford University Press, 1966).
GREGG, R. W. (ed.) *International Organization in the Western Hemisphere* (Syracuse, N.Y.: Syracuse University Press, 1968).
HOUSTON, J. A. *Latin America in the United Nations* (New York: Carnegie Endowment for International Peace, 1956).
Organisation of American States. *The Inter-American Treaty of Reciprocal Assistance. Applications.* Volume I, 1948-1959. Volume II, 1960-1964 (Washington, D.C., 1964).
———. Inter-American Peace Committee. *Report to the Eighth Meeting of Consultation* (Washington, D.C., 1962).
———. Pan American Union. *Strengthening of Internal Security, 1951* (Washington, D.C., 1953).
PRAT GAY, G. de. *Política internacional del grupo latinoamericano* (Buenos Aires: Abeledo Perrot, 1967).

ARTICLES
CLARET DE VOEGD, L. "La coordinación entre las Naciones Unídas y la OEA en el arreglo de las controversias: el caso Cuba." *Revista de derecho internacional y ciencias diplomáticas* (1968), pp. 32-41.
CLAUDE, I. L. "The OAS, the United Nations and the United States." *International Conciliation,* special number (March 1964).
CORNELIUS, W. G. "The Latin American 'bloc' in the United Nations." *Journal of Inter-American Studies* (1961), pp. 419-435.
DRAPER, G. I. A. D. "Regional Arrangements and Enforcement Action." *Revue Egyptienne de droit international* (1964), pp. 1-44.
LAREDO, I. M. "Latinoamérica en las Naciones Unídas." *Foro Internacional* (1964), pp. 571-611.
MAURTUA, F. M. "El grupo latinoamericano en las Naciones Unídas y algunos problemas jurídicos." *Revista peruana de derecho internacional* (1956), pp. 10-43.
MORALES, M. and B. WOOD. "Latin America and the United Nations." *International Organization* (1965), pp. 714-727.
ROBINSON, D. R. "The Treaty of Tlatelolco and the United States: a Latin American nuclear free zone." *American Journal of International Law* (April 1970), pp. 282-309.
RUDA, J. M. "Relaciones de la OEA y las Naciones Unídas en cuanto al mantenamiento de la paz y la seguridad internacionales." *Revista Jurídica de Buenos Aires* (January/June 1961), pp. 21-30.
SAENZ, P. "A Latin American-African Partnership." *Journal of Inter-American Studies* (April 1969), pp. 317-327.

Latin American Politics
BOOKS
AGUILAR, L. E. (ed.) *Marxism in Latin America* (New York: Knopf, 1968).
ALEXANDER, R. J. *Latin American Political Parties* (New York: Praeger, 1973).
–––. *Communism in Latin America* (New Brunswick, N.J.: Rutgers University Press, 1957).
BURNETT, B. G. and K. F. JOHNSON. *Political Forces in Latin America. Dimensions of the Quest for Stability* (Belmont, Mass.: Wadsworth Publishing, 1970).
CALVERT, P. *Latin America: Internal Conflict and International Peace* (London: Macmillan, 1969).
DILLON, D. *International Communism and Latin America* (Gainesville: University of Florida Press, 1962).
FITZGIBBON, R. H. *Latin America. A Panorama of Contemporary Politics* (New York: Appleton, 1971).
GOTT, R. *Guerrilla Movements in Latin America* (London: Nelson, 1970).
MAIER, J. B. and R. W. WEATHERHEAD. *Political Change in Latin America* (New York: Praeger, 1964).
MARTZ, J. D. (ed.) *The Dynamics of Change in Latin American Politics* (Englewood Cliffs, N.J.: Prentice-Hall, 1971).
MERCIER VEGA, L. *Etat et Contre-Etat* (Paris: Belfond, 1968).
POPPINO, R. E. *International Communism in Latin America. A History of the Movement, 1917-1963* (New York: Free Press, 1966).

ARTICLES
ALEXANDER, R. J. "Outside Control of Latin American Communists." *Thought Patterns* (1964), pp. 35-49.
JOHNSON, K. F. "Causal Factors in Latin American Political Instability." *Western Political Quarterly* (1964), pp. 432-446.
SIMON, S. F. "Anarchism and Anarcho-Syndicalism in South America." *Hispanic-American Historical Review* (1949), pp. 281-286.

Social Change in Latin America
BOOKS
ADAMS, R. N. (ed.) *Social Change in Latin America Today* (New York: Harper & Row, 1960).
BLASIER, S. C. (ed.) *Constructive Change in Latin America* (Pittsburgh: Pittsburgh University Press, 1968).
FALS BORDA, O. *Las revoluciones inconclusas en América Latina, 1809-1968* (Mexico City: Siglo Veintiuno, 1968).
HALPER, S. A. and J. R. STERLING (eds.) *Latin America. The Dynamics of Social Change* (New York: St. Martin, 1973).
KEPNER, C. D. *Social Aspects of the Banana Industry* (New York: Columbia University Press, 1956).
LAMBERT, J. *Amérique latine: structures sociales et institutions politiques* (Paris: Presses Universitaires de France, 1963).
PETRAS, J. and M. ZEITLIN (eds.) *Latin America: Reform or Revolution?* (New York: Fawcett World, 1968).

II. INDIVIDUAL COUNTRIES

Argentina

BOOKS

ALEXANDER, R. J. *The Perón Era* (London: Gollancz, 1952).

Argentina, Ministerio de Relaciones Exteriores y Culto. *La República Argentina en la IX Conferencia Inter-Americana* (Buenos Aires, 1948).

Argentina, Secretaría de la Presidencia. *Speeches by Perón* (Buenos Aires, 1947).

BAGÚ, S. *Argentina en el mundo* (Mexico City: Fondo de Cultura Económica, 1961).

BLANKSTEN, G. I. *Perón's Argentina* (Chicago: University of Chicago Press, 1953).

CAILLET-BOIS, R. R. *Cuestiones internacionales, 1852-1966* (Buenos Aires: Eudeba, 1970).

CÁRDENAS, G. et al. *El Peronismo* (Buenos Aires: Carlos Pérez, 1969).

CONIL PAZ, A. A. and G. E. FERRARI. *Argentina's Foreign Policy, 1930-1962* (South Bend, Ind.: University of Notre Dame Press, 1966).

CRISTÍA, P. C. et al. *Argentina en la postguerra* (Buenos Aires: Emece, 1946).

CÚNEO, D. *Las nuevas fronteras* (Buenos Aires: Transición, 1964).

FERNS, H. S. *Argentina* (London: Benn, 1969).

FLORIT, C. A. *Las Fuerzas Armadas y la guerra psicológica* (Buenos Aires: Arayú, 1963).

———. *Política Exterior nacional* (Buenos Aires: Arayú, 1961).

FRIGERIO, R. *El desarrollo argentino y la comunidad americana* (Buenos Aires: Gure, 1959).

FRONDIZI, A. *La política económica nacional* (Buenos Aires: Arayú, 1963).

———. *Petróleo y nación* (Buenos Aires: Transición, 1963).

———. *La política exterior argentina* (Buenos Aires: Transición, 1962).

———. *La Argentina ante los problemas mundiales* (Buenos Aires: Prensa de la Nación, 1961).

———. *El gobierno y el comunismo* (Buenos Aires: Prensa de la nación, 1960).

———. *La lucha antiimperialista* (Buenos Aires: Debate, 1955).

———. *El Tratado de Río de Janeiro de 1947. Recopilación de antecedentes. Posición internacional de la Unión Cívica Radical* (Buenos Aires: Union Civica Radical, 1950).

GARCÍA, E. A. *La política internacional de la República* (Buenos Aires: Emecé, 1964).

GOLDWERT, M. *Democracy, Militarism and Nationalism in Argentina, 1930-1966* (Austin: University of Texas Press, 1972).

GRONDONA, M. *La Argentina en el tiempo y en el mundo* (Buenos Aires: Primera Plana, 1967).

IMAZ, J. L. de. *Los que mandan* (Buenos Aires: Eudeba, 1964).

LUETOLF, F. *Die argentinische Wirtschaftspolitik seit dem zweiten Weltkrieg* (Zürich: Polygraphischer Verlag, 1957).

LUNA, F. *Diálogos con Frondizi* (Buenos Aires: Editoria Desarrollo, 1963).

LUX-WURM, P. *Le Péronisme* (Paris: Librairie générale de droit et de jurisprudence, 1965).

McGANN, T. F. *Argentina, the United States and the Inter-American System, 1880-1914* (Cambridge, Mass.: Harvard University Press, 1957).

MAGNET, A. *Nuestros vecinos justicialistas* (Santiago: Pacífico, 1955).

PALACIOS, A. L. *Nuestra América y el imperialismo* (Buenos Aires: Palestra, 1961).

PERÓN, J. D. *Mensaje del Presidente de la Nación Argentina General Juan Perón, 84ta Sesión del Honorable Congreso. Primer Mayo, 1950* (Buenos Aires: Prensa de la Nación, 1950).

———. *Perón habla* (Buenos Aires: Subsecretaría de Informaciones, 1952).

———. *Policy and Strategy. Without attacking anyone I offer criticism* (Buenos Aires: Presidencia, 1951).

PETERSON, H. F. *Argentina and the United States, 1810-1960* (New York: University of New York, 1963).

RAMOS, J. A. *Historia del stalinismo en la Argentina* (Buenos Aires: Mar Dulce, 1969).

REMORINO, J. *Política internacional argentina. Compilación de documentos, 1951-1955.* Volume I (Buenos Aires: Establicimiento Gráfico, 1968).

RUMBO, E. I. *Petróleo y vasallaje: carne de vaca y carnero contra carbón mas petróleo* (Buenos Aires: Hechos e ideas, 1957).

SCOBIE, J. R. *Argentina. A City and a Nation* (New York: Oxford University Press, 1971).

SELSER, G. *Punta del Este contra Sierra Maestra* (Buenos Aires: Hernández, 1968).

SILVA, C. A. *La politica internacional de la Nación Argentina* (Buenos Aires: Imprenta de la Cámara de Diputados, 1946).

SMITH, O. E. *Yankee Diplomacy. United States Intervention in Argentina* (Dallas: Southern Methodist University Press, 1953).

SILENZI DE STAGNI, A. *El petróleo argentino* (Buenos Aires: Problemas Nacionales, 1955).

USINGER, O. G. *Fundamentos de la política internacional argentina* (Rosario: Universidad del Litoral, 1952).

WHITAKER, A. P. *Argentina* (Englewood Cliffs, N.J.: Prentice-Hall, 1964).

———. *Argentine Upheaval* (London: Atlantic Press, 1955).

ARTICLES

HOLMES, O. "Argentina and the Dream of Southern Union," in *Political, Economic and Social Problems of the Latin-American Nations of Southern South America* (Austin: Texas University Press, 1949), pp. 43-57.

HECHEN, S. "La política exterior argentina y el desarrollo." *Foro Internacional* (1965), pp. 489-510.

LA ROSA, P. "La conferencia de Bogotá." *Boletín del Ministerio de Relaciones Exteriores y Culto,* 32 (August 1948), pp. 65-83.

MORENO QUINTANA, L. M. and C. M. BOLLINI SHAW. "La política internacional." *Revista de la facultad de derecho y ciencias sociales* (September/October 1948), pp. 1107-1147; (November/December 1948), pp. 1475-1506.

MURKLAND, H. B. "Latin America at Havana." *Current History* (June 1948), pp. 332-335.

PABLO PARDO, L. M. de. "La posición de la Argentina como factor de su política exterior." *Revista de la facultad de derecho y ciencias sociales* (January/April 1949), pp. 205-215.

SANTA PINTER, J. J. "The Foreign Policy of Argentina," in J. E. Black and K. W. Thompson (eds.) *Foreign Policies in a World of Change* (New York: Harper & Row, 1963), pp. 591-616.

SNOW, P. G. "Argentine Radicalism, 1957-1963." *Journal of Inter-American Studies* (October 1963), pp. 507-531.

The World Today. "Stalin and Bravo" (March 1953), pp. 97-98.

Bolivia

BOOKS

ALEXANDER, R. J. *The Bolivian National Revolution* (New Brunswick, N.J.: Rutgers University Press, 1959).

BEDREGAL, C. and A. CRESPEDES. *Economía nacional y defensa de Latinoamérica. Imperialismo y desarrollo* (La Paz: Tupa Amaru, 1963).

FELLMAN VELARDE, J. *Memorandum sobre la política exterior boliviana* (La Paz: Juventud, 1967).

———. *Víctor Paz Estenssoro. El hombre y la revolución* (La Paz: Tejerina, 1955).

MALLOY, J. M. *The Uncompleted Revolution* (Pittsburgh: University of Pittsburgh Press, 1970).

MARTIN, L. D. *Bolivia in 1956* (Stanford, Calif.: Hispanic American Report, 1958).

Partido Comunista de Bolivia. *Réponse de Oscar Zamora, 1er secrétaire du Parti communiste bolivien Marxiste-Leniniste, à Fidel Castro, juillet-août 1968* (Paris: Gat-leCoeur, 1969).

PAZ ESTENSSORO, V. *Bolivia se suma a la Alianza para el Progreso* (La Paz: Dirección Nacional de Informaciones, 1962).

SELSER, G. *La CIA en Bolivia* (Buenos Aires: Hernández, 1970).

WHITEHEAD, L. *The United States and Bolivia* (Beckenham, Kent: Haslemere Publication, 1969).

ZONDAG, C. H. *The Bolivian Economy, 1952-1965. The Revolution and its Aftermath* (New York: Praeger, 1966).

ARTICLES

ALONSO, E. "Fuerzas armadas y revolución nacional en Bolivia y Perú." *Estrategia* (September/December 1970), pp. 10-14; (January/February 1971), pp. 35-40.

WHITEHEAD, L. "Bolivia's Conflict with the United States." *The World Today* (April 1970), pp. 167-178.

Brazil

BOOKS

ALENCASTRE, A. *O Brasil e as Relações con o Leste e a URSS* (Rio de Janeiro: Nap, 1959).

———. *Oswaldo Aranha, o mundo áfro-asiático e a paz* (Rio de Janeiro: Nap, 1961).

AMADO, J. *O cavaleiro da esperança* (Rio de Janeiro: Vitória, 1956).

ARCHER, M. *Brasil, Fronteira da Africa* (São Paulo: Felman/Rêgo, 1963).

ARINOS DE MELO FRANCO, A. *Evolução do crise brasileira* (São Paulo: Editora Nacional, 1965).

AZEVEDO, T. de. *Social Change in Brazil* (Gainesville: University of Florida Press, 1965).

BARROS, J. de. *A Política Exterior do Brasil, 1930-1942* (Rio de Janeiro: Zelio Valverde, 1943).

BASBAUM, L. *História sincera de república de 1930 a 1960: em apendice, as razões e as consequências de vitoria e da renúncia do Sr. Jânio Quadros* (São Paulo: Editôra Edaglit, 1962).

Brazil, Ministério das Relações Exteriores. *Viagem do Presidente João Goulart aos Estados Unidos da América e ao México* (Rio de Janeiro, 1962).

————. *Gestão do Ministro Láfer na pasta das Relações Exteriores* (Rio de Janeiro, 1961).

Brazil, Presidência da República. *Resenha de Govêrno do Brasil, Juscelino Kubitschek, 1956-1961.* Volume 5, 1950 (Rio de Janeiro, 1961).

BOURNE, R. *Getúlio Vargas of Brazil, 1883-1954* (London: Knight, 1974).

CABRAL, C. C. *Tempos de Jânio e outros tempos* (Rio de Janeiro: Civilização Brasileira, 1962).

CARDOSO, F. E. and J. E. FALLETTO. *Dependencia y desarrollo en América Latina* (Mexico City: Siglo Veintiuno, 1969).

CARVALHO, C. M. D. de. *Atlas de Relacões Internacionais* (Rio de Janeiro: Conselho Nacional de Geografía, 1960).

CHAGAS, C. *Cento e treze días de angústia: impedimento e morte de um presidente* (Rio de Janeiro: Agência Journalística Image, 1970).

DANTAS, F. C. SANTIAGO. *Política Externa Independente* (Rio de Janeiro: Civilização Brasileira, 1962).

DULLES, J. W. F. *Unrest in Brazil* (Austin: University of Texas Press, 1970).

————. *Vargas of Brazil* (Austin: University of Texas Press, 1967).

DUTRA, E. G. *Discursos e alocuções preferidos em 1947 pelo Presidente* (Rio de Janeiro: Imprensa Nacional, 1948).

FONTES, L. and G. CARNEIRO. *A Face Final de Vargas. Os bilhetes de Getúlio* (Rio de Janeiro: O Cruzeiro, 1966).

FREE, L. A. *Some International Implications of the Political Psychology of Brazilians* (Princeton, N.J.: Institute for International Social Research, 1961).

FREYRE, G. *Uma política transnacional de cultura para o Brasil de hoje* (Belo Horizonte, Minas Gerais: Facultade de Direita da Universidade de Minas Gerais, 1960).

————. *New World in the Tropics: the Culture of Modern Brazil* (New York: Knopf, 1959).

GOLBERY DO COUTO, S. *Geopolítica do Brasil* (Rio de Janeiro: Olympio, 1967).

GOMES, R. P. *O Brasil entre as cinco maiores potências* (Rio de Janeiro: Leitura, 1969).

GOULART, J. *Mensagem ao Congresso Nacional* (Brasilia: Imprensa Nacional, 1963).

GUILHERME, O. *O Brasil e a Era Atômica* (Rio de Janeiro: Vitória, 1957).

HECHEN, S. *Proyección internacional de Brasil* (Santa Fé, Argentina: Castellví, 1964).

HOROWITZ, I. L. *Revolution in Brazil* (New York: Dutton, 1964).

IANNI, O. *Raças e classes sociais no Brasil* (Rio de Janeiro: Civilizaçao Brasileira, 1966).

JAGUARIBE, H. *O nacionalismo na atualidade brasileira* (Rio de Janeiro: Instituto Superior de Estudos Brasileiros, 1958).

Jornal do Commercio. *A política exterior do Brasil na gestão do chanceler Raul Fernandes* (Rio de Janeiro, 1951).

KUBITSCHEK, J. *A Marcha do amanhecer* (São Paulo: 'Bestseller,' 1962).

———. *Discursos preferidos no quinto ano do mandato presidencial, 1960* (Rio de Janeiro: Imprensa Nacional, 1961).

———. *Mensagem ao Congresso Nacional remetida pelo Presidente da República na apertura da sessão legislativa de 1959* (Rio de Janeiro: Congresso Nacional, 1959).

———. *Uma campanha democrática* (Rio de Janeiro: Olympio, 1959).

LOEWENSTEIN, K. *Brazil under Vargas* (New York: Macmillan, 1942).

MARIGHELA, C. *For the Liberation of Brazil* (Harmondsworth, Middlesex: Penguin, 1971).

MEIRA PENNA, J. O. de. *Política externa: segurança e desenvolvimento* (Rio de Janeiro: Agir, 1967).

MENDES DE ALMEIDA, C. A. *Nacionalismo e Desenvolvimento* (Rio de Janeiro: Instituto Brasileiro de Estudos Áfro-Asiáticos, 1963).

MENEZES, A. J. B. de. *O Brasil e o mundo ásio-africano* (Rio de Janeiro: Pongetti, 1955).

NERY DA FONSECA, L. *Geopolítica* (Rio de Janeiro: Bedeschi, 1940).

NEVES DA FONTOURA, J. *Depoimentos de um ex-ministro* (Rio de Janeiro: Simões, 1957).

OLIVEIRA, J. T. de. *O Govêrno Dutra, 1946-1950* (Rio de Janeiro: Civilizaçâo Brasileira, 1956).

OLIVEIRA CAMPOS, R. *Reflections on Latin American Development* (Austin: University of Texas Press, 1967).

PEDROSA, M. *A opção brasileira* (Rio de Janeiro: Civilizaçâo Brasileira, 1966).

———. *A opção imperialista* (Rio de Janeiro: Civilizaçâo Brasileira, 1966).

PICCIOLI, I. A. C. *As pressões na renúncia de Jânio* (Rio de Janeiro, 1962).

PRESTES, L. C. *Por que os comunistas apóian Lott e Jango* (Rio de Janeiro: Vitória, 1960).

REISKY DE DUBNIC, V. *Political Trends in Brazil* (Washington, D.C.: Public Affairs Press, 1968).

RODRÍGUES, J. H. *Brazil and Africa* (Berkeley: University of California Press, 1965).

SCHNEIDER, R. M. *The Political System of Brazil, 1964-1970* (New York: Columbia University Press, 1971).

SELCHER, W. A. *The Afro-Asian Dimension of Brazilian Foreign Policy* (Gainesville: University of Florida Press, 1970).

SKIDMORE, T. E. *Politics in Brazil, 1930-1964* (New York: Oxford University Press, 1967).

SOUZA, A. de. *O Brasil e a terceira guerra mundial* (São Paulo: Biblioteca do Exército, 1959).

STORRS, K. L. *Brazil's Independent Foreign Policy, 1961-1964* (Ithaca, N.Y.: Cornell University Press, 1973).

TAVORA, J. *Átomos para o Brasil* (Rio de Janeiro: Olympio, 1958).

VARGAS, G. *Mensagem ao Congresso Nacional apresentada pelo Presidente da República por ocasão de abertura da sessão legislativa de 1953.* 2 volumes (Rio de Janeiro: Congresso Nacional, 1954).

————. *A campanha presidencial* (Rio de Janeiro: Olympio, 1951).
VILELA LUZ, N. *A luta pela industrialização do Brasil* (São Paulo: Difusão Européia do livro, 1961).
WERNECK SODRÉ, N. *História Militar do Brasil* (Rio de Janeiro: Civilização Brasileira, 1965).

ARTICLES

ARANHA, O. "Regional Systems and the Future of the United Nations." *Foreign Affairs* (1948), pp. 415-420.
BARRETTO, N. "O Brasil e o terceiro mundo." *Cadernos Brasileiros* (January/February 1968), pp. 15-21.
FERREIRA, O. S. "La geopolítica y el ejército brasileño." *Aportes* (April 1969), pp. 112-131.
FISCHLOWITZ, E. "Subsidios para a 'doutrina africana' do Brasil." *Revista Brasileira de Política Internacional* (1960), pp. 82-95.
GORDON, L. "Brazil's Future World Role." *Orbis* (Autumn 1972), pp. 621-631.
HICKEY, J. "The day Mr. Berle talked with Mr. Quadros." *Inter-American Economic Affairs* (1961), pp. 58-71.
JAGUARIBE, H. "A renúncia do Presidente Quadros e a cris política brasileira." *Revista Brasileira de Ciências Sociais* (1961), pp. 272-311.
LEITE LINHARES, M. Y. "Brazilian Foreign Policy and Africa." *The World Today* (1962), pp. 532-540.
LIMA, A. A. "A polição do Brasil em Punta del Este." *Revista Brasileira de Política Internacional* (1962), pp. 5-16.
MARINI, R. M. and O. PELLICER Y BRODY. "Militarismo y desnuclearización en América Latina: el caso de Brasil." *Foro Internacional* (July/September 1967), pp. 1-22.
OLIVEIRA CAMPOS, R. "The Foreign Policy of Brazil." *Brazilian Business* (November 1962), pp. 43-46.
————. "Sôbre o conceito de neutralismo." *Revista Brasileira de Política Internacional* (1961), pp. 5-12.
Orbis. "Brazil's International Role in the Seventies: A Conference Report" (Summer 1972), pp. 545-560.
QUADROS, J. "Brazil's New Foreign Policy." *Foreign Affairs* (1961), pp. 19-27.
REISKY DE DUBNIC, V. "Brasiliens neue Aussenpolitik. Von der Blockfreiheit zur Solidarität mit dem Westen." *Europa-Archiv* (1965), pp. 91-100.
RODRÍGUES, J. H. "Nueva actitud exterior de Brasil." *Foro Internacional* (1962), pp. 408-422.
————. "O presente e o futuro das relações africano-brasileiros." *Revista Brasileira de Política Internacional* (1962), pp. 501-516.
————. "The Foundations of Brazil's Foreign Policy." *International Affairs* (1962), pp. 324-338.
————. "Aspirações e interesses de Brasil." *Journal of Inter-American Studies* (1961), pp. 147-185.
SOUSA SAMPAIO, N. de. "The Foreign Policy of Brazil," in J. E. Black and K. W. Thompson (eds.) *Foreign Policies in a World of Change* (New York: Harper & Row, 1963), pp. 617-642.

SOUZA GOMES, H. de. "A ação do Brasil, em dez anos, nas Nações Unidas." *Boletim da Sociedade Brasileira do Direito Internacional* (1955), pp. 35-48.
WALLIS, V. "La experiencia de Brasil con una política exterior independiente." *Estudios Internacionales* (1967), pp. 189-211.

Chile

BOOKS

ALLENDE GOSSENS, S. *Chile's Road to Socialism* (Harmondsworth, Middlesex: Penguin, 1973).
———. *Cuba, un camino* (Santiago: Prensa Latinoamericana, 1960).
ALMEYDA MEDINA, C. *Reflexiones políticas* (Santiago: Prensa Lationoamericana, 1958).
———. *Hacia una teoría marxista del estado* (Santiago: Prensa Latinoamericana, 1948).
ANGELL, A. *Politics and the Labour Movement in Chile* (London: Oxford University Press, 1972).
BOWERS, C. G. *Chile through Embassy Windows, 1939-1953* (New York: Simon & Schuster, 1958).
——— (in Spanish translation) *Misión en Chile, 1939-1953* (1957).
Chile, Ministerio de Relaciones Exteriores. *Address by H. E. Gabriel Valdés, Minister of Foreign Affairs of Chile, delivered on November 22, 1965, at the Second Special Inter-American Conference of Rio de Janeiro* (Santiago, 1965).
———. *Chile y la conferencia de San Francisco* (Santiago, 1945).
CORVALAN, L. *Chile hoy: la lucha de los comunistas chilenos en las condiciones del gobierno de Frei* (Buenos Aires: Anteo, 1965).
CRUZ CAMPO, L. D. *The Totalitarian Neo-Czarism of the Soviet Union* (Santiago: Imprenta Chile, 1949).
DEBRAY, R. *Conversations with Allende* (London: New Left Books; 1971).
DURÁN BERNALES, F. *El Partido Radical* (Santiago: Nascimiento, 1958).
EDWARDS, E. (ed.) *Pensamiento político de don Jorge Alessandri* (Santiago, 1970).
FREI MONTALVA, E. *Chile tiene un destino: pasado y presente de una crísis* (Santiago: Raposo, 1962).
———. *Pensamiento y acción* (Santiago: Pacifico, 1956).
Frente de Acción Popular. *Un camino nuevo para Chile: programa del gobierno popular* (Santiago, 1958).
GROSS, L. *The Last, Best Hope. Eduardo Frei and Chilean Democracy* (New York: Random House, 1967).
GUZMÁN HERNÁNDEZ, J. *Gabriel González Videla. Biografia y análisis crítica de su programa* (Santiago: Universo, 1946).
HALPERIN, E. *Nationalism and Communism in Chile* (Cambridge, Mass.: MIT Press, 1965).
JOHNSON, D. L. (ed.) *The Chilean Road to Socialism* (New York: Doubleday, 1973).
LABARCA GODDARD, E. *Chile al rojo* (Santiago: Universidad Técnica del Estado, 1971).
MELLO MOURÃO, G. *Frei y la revolución en América Latina* (Santiago: Pacífico, 1966).

ORREGO VICUÑO, C. *Solidaridad y violencia. El dilema de Chile* (Santiago, 1969).
PIKE, F. B. *Chile and the United States, 1880-1962* (South Bend, Ind.: University of Notre Dame Press, 1963).
SILVERT, K. H. *Chile Yesterday and Today* (New York: Holt, Rhinehart & Winston, 1965).
STEVENSON, J. R. *The Chilean Popular Front* (Philadelphia: University of Pennsylvania Press, 1942).
TOMIC, R. *Sobre el sistema interamericano* (Santiago, 1963).
———. *El Tratado Interamericano de Ayuda Mutua: Oportunidad perdida para la unidad de América!* (Santiago, 1949).
VALDÉS, G. *Conciencia latinoamericana y realidad internacional* (Santiago: Pacífico, 1970).
WÜRTH-ROJAS, E. *Ibáñez. Caudillo enigmático* (Santiago: Pacífico, 1958).

ARTICLES
BERNSTEIN CARABANTES, E. "Punta del Este y las erróneas interpretaciones de un tratado." *Foro Internacional* (1962), pp. 518-534.
BLASIER, S. C. "Chile: A Communist Battleground." *Political Science Quarterly* (1950), pp. 353-375.
DUNCAN, W. R. "Chilean Christian Democracy." *Current History* (November 1967), pp. 263-267.
FREI MONTALVA, E. "Tendencias e perspectivas interamericanas." *Revista Brasileira de Política Internacional* (1959), pp. 5-19.
HAMBURG, R. P. "Soviet Foreign Policy, the Church, the Christian Democrats and Chile." *Journal of Inter-American Studies* (October 1969), pp. 605-615.
RODRÍGUEZ, A. "La conferencia de la OEA." *Foro Internacional* (1965), pp. 547-575.
VÉLIZ, C. "The Chilean Experiment." *Foreign Affairs* (April 1971), pp. 442-453.

Colombia

BOOKS
ANDRADE, R. *Cuba: el vecino socialista: con una nota de Alfonso López Michelsen* (Bogotá: D.E., 1961).
FLUHARTY, V. L. *Dance of the Millions. Military Rule and the Social Revolution in Colombia, 1930-1956* (Pittsburgh: University of Pittsburgh Press, 1957).
MARTZ, J. D. *Colombia* (Chapel Hill: University of North Carolina Press, 1962).
TURBAY AYALA, J. C. *Polítca internacional de Colombia* (Bogotá: Imprenta Nacional, 1961).

ARTICLES
CAICEDO CASTILLA, J. J. "La conferencia de Petrópolis y el Tratado Interamericano de Asistencia Recíproca." *Universidad Nacional de Colombia* (February/April 1948), pp. 123-231.
HOBSBAWM, E. J. "The Revolutionary Situation in Colombia." *The World Today* (1963), pp. 248-258.
LLERAS CAMARGO, A. "Posição da Colombia no Sistema Jurídico Interamericano." *Revista Brasileira de Política Internacional* (1961), pp. 5-17.

SANTOS, E. "Mis conferencias con el Presidente Roosevelt y los planes de organización militar interamericanos." *Revista América* (April 1947), pp. 3-14.

Cuba

BOOKS

ABEL, E. *The Missiles of October* (London: MacGibbon, 1966).

ACUÑA, J. A. *Cuba: revolución traicionada. Documentos irrefutables de la alianza del comunismo con el tirano Batista* (Montevideo: Editorial 'Goes', 1962).

ALLEN, J. S. (ed.) *Fidel Castro in Chile* (New York: International Publishing, 1972).

BATISTA, F. *Cuba Betrayed* (New York: Vantage, 1962).

———. *Paradojismo: Cuba, víctima de las contradicciones internacionales* (Mexico City: Bota, 1964).

BEKAREVITCH, A. D. *Kuba: vneshne-ekonomicheskiye otnoshenya* (Moscow: Nauka, 1970).

BERNER, W. *Der Evangelist des Castroismus-Guevarismus: Régis Debray und seine Guerrilla-Doktrin* (Velbert: Blick und Bild, 1969).

BLANCO, E. J. *De Playa Girón a Punta del Este* (Buenos Aires, 1962).

BONSAL, P. W. *Cuba, Castro and the United States* (Pittsburgh: University of Pittsburgh Press, 1971).

CASUSO, T. *Cuba and Castro* (New York: Random House, 1961).

CEPERO BONILLA, R. *El convenio cubano-soviético* (Havana: Echeverría, 1960).

———. *Política azucarera, 1952-1958* (Mexico City: Futuro, 1958).

CHAYES, A. *The Cuban Missile Crisis* (London: Oxford University Press, 1974).

China, Information Services. *Cuba sí, Yanquis no! En apoyo de la lucha del pueblo cubano y de los otros pueblos latinoamericanos contra el imperialismo de los Estados Unidos* (Peking, 1962).

COROMINAS, E. V. *Cuba en Punta del Este* (Buenos Aires: Política, Economía y Finanzas, 1963).

———. *México, Cuba y la OEA* (Buenos Aires: Política, Economia y Finanzas, 1965).

Cuba, Comisión de Orientación Revolucionaria de la Dirección Nacional de PURSC. *Fidel en la URSS* (Havana, 1963).

Cuba, Ministerio de las Relaciones Exteriores. *Cuba en la OEA* (Havana, 1960).

———. *The Appeal of Cuba to the Security Council of the United Nations* (Havana, 1960).

Cuba. *Playa Girón. Derrota del imperialismo.* 4 volumes (Havana: Ediciones R, 1961 and 1962).

DEBRAY, R. *La Révolution dans la Révolution* (Paris: Maspero, 1967).

DORTICOS TORRADO, O. *Cuba is a Sovereign Nation* (Havana: Ministry of Foreign Relations, 1960).

DRAPER, T. *Castroism. Theory and Practice* (London: Pall Mall, 1965).

———. *Castro's Revolution: Myths and Realities* (London: Thames & Hudson, 1962).

FURTAK, R. K. *Kuba und der Weltkommunismus* (Opladen: Westdeutscher Verlag, 1967).

GARELLI FARIAS, M. J. *La crisis internacional de 1962 y el bloqueo de Cuba* (Mexico City: UNAM, 1967).

GOLDENBERG, B. *The Cuban Revolution and Latin America* (London: Allen & Unwin, 1965).

GONZÁLEZ PEDRERO, E. *La revolución cubana* (Mexico City: UNAM, 1959).
GUEVARA, E. *Bolivian Diary* (London: Cape/Lorimer, 1968).
———. *La Guerrilla de guerrillas* (Havana, 1960).
HORELICK, A. *The Cuban Missile Crisis. An Analysis of Soviet Calculations and Behavior* (Santa Monica, Calif.: RAND, 1963).
JENKS, L. H. *Our Cuban Colony. A Study in Sugar* (New York: Arno, 1970).
JOHNSON, H. B. *The Bay of Pigs* (London: Hutchinson, 1965).
JOHNSON, L. L. *The Course of United States Private Investment since the Rise of Castro* (Santa Monica, Calif.: RAND, 1964).
KENNER, M. and J. PETRAS (eds.) *Fidel Castro Speaks* (Harmondsworth, Middlesex: Penguin, 1970).
KRAKAU, K. *Die kubanische Revolution und die Monroe-Doktrin* (Frankfurt: Metzner, 1968).
LAMBERG, R. F. *Die castristische Guerrilla in Lateinamerika. Theorie und Praxis eines revolutionaren Modells* (Hanover: Neue Gesellschaft, 1971).
LARSON, D. L. (ed.) *The Cuban Crisis of 1962: selected documents and chronology* (Boston: Houghton-Mifflin, 1963).
LENTIN, A. P. *La lutte tricontinentale; impérialisme et revolution après la conférence de la Havana* (Paris: Maspéro, 1966).
MORA, J. M. de *Punta del Este: historia íntima de una conferencia* (Mexico City: Galvala, 1962).
PACHTER, H. M. *Collision Course. The Cuban Missile Crisis and Coexistence* (London: Pall Mall, 1963).
PERAZA, F. *Revolutionary Cuba. A bibliographical guide* (Gainesville: University of Miami Press, 1969).
PHILLIPS, R. H. *The Cuban Dilemma* (New York: Astor/Honor, 1962).
PIRIZ, H. et al. *La "culpa" tiene Cuba: seis periodistas latinoamericanos desnudan la farsa de la OEA y sus cancilleres en Punta del Este* (Montevideo: Estrella, 1962).
ROCA, B. *29 artículos sobre la revolución cubana* (Havana: Partido Socialista Popular, 1960).
ROIG DE LEUCHSENRING, E. *Cuba no debe su independencia a los Estados Unidos* (Havana: Tertulia, 1960).
SANTOVENIA, E. S. *Armonías y conflictos en torno a Cuba* (Mexico City, 1956).
SCHEER, R. and M. ZEITLIN. *Cuba: An American Tragedy* (New York: Grove, 1964).
SCHLESINGER, A. *A Thousand Days* (Boston: Houghton-Mifflin, 1965).
SEERS, D. (ed.) *Cuba. The Economic and Social Revolution* (Chapel Hill: University of North Carolina, 1964).
SELSER, G. *Punta del Este contra Sierra Maestra* (Buenos Aires, 1968).
SEMIDEI, M. *Les États-Unis et la Révolution Cubaine, 1959-1964* (Paris: Armand Colin, 1968).
SMITH, E. E. T. *The Fourth Floor: An Account of the Castro Communist Revolution* (New York: Random House, 1962).
SMITH, R. F. *Background to Revolution. The Development of Modern Cuba* (New York: Knopf, 1966).
———. *What Happened in Cuba: A Documentary History* (New York: Twayne, 1963).

———. *The United States and Cuba: Business and Diplomacy, 1917-1960* (New York: Bookman Associates, 1961).

SUÁREZ, A. *Cuba: Castroism and Communism, 1959-1966* (Cambridge, Mass.: MIT Press, 1967).

SUCHLICKI, J. (ed.) *Cuba, Castro and Revolution* (Coral Gables: University of Miami Press, 1972).

TORRES RAMÍREZ, B. R. *Las relaciones cubano-soviéticas, 1959-1968* (Mexico City, 1969).

TRAPPEN, F. *Die kubanische Volksrevolution* (Berlin: Staatsverlag der DDR, 1965).

TRETIAK, D. *Cuba and the Soviet Union: the growing accommodation* (Santa Monica, Calif.: RAND, 1966).

United States, Department of State. *Events in United States-Cuban Relations. A Chronology, 1957-1963* (Washington, D.C., 1963).

———. *The Soviet Military Build-Up in Cuba* (Washington, D.C., 1962).

URRUTIA, M. *Fidel Castro & Co., Inc.* (New York: Praeger, 1964).

WILKERSON, L. *Fidel Castro's Political Programs from Reformism to Marxism-Leninism* (Gainesville: University of Florida Press, 1965).

WILLIAMS, W. A. *The United States, Cuba and Castro: an Essay on the Dynamics of Revolution and the Dissolution of Empire* (New York: Monthly Review Press, 1962).

WOLPIN, C. *Cuban Foreign Policy and Chilean Politics* (Lexington, Mass.: Lexington Books, 1971).

ZEITLIN, M. *Revolutionary Politics and the Cuban Working Class* (Princeton, N.J.: Princeton University Press, 1967).

ARTICLES

ALLISON, R. C. "Cuba's Seizure of American Business." *American Bar Association Journal* (1961), pp. 187-195.

ALVAREZ TABÍO, F. "La base naval de Guantánamo y el derecho internacional." *Cuba Socialista* (1962), pp. 91-108.

ANGELL, A. "Castro and the Cuban Communist Party." *Government and Opposition* (1967), pp. 241-252.

BERLE, A. A. "The Cuban Crisis, Failure of American Foreign Policy." *Foreign Affairs* (1960), pp. 40-55.

BERNER, W. W. "Castro's und Moskau's lateinamerikanische Strategie." *Aussenpolitik* (1968), pp. 357-367.

BRIEUX, J. J. "La Tricontinentale." *Politique Etrangère* (1966), pp. 19-43.

CRANE, R. D. "The Cuban Crisis: a Strategic Analysis of American and Soviet Policy." *Orbis* (1963), pp. 528-563.

———. "The Sino-Soviet Dispute on War and the Cuban Crisis." *Orbis* (1964), pp. 537-549.

CRONON, E. D. "Interpreting the New Good Neighbor Policy. The Cuban Crisis of 1933." *Hispanic-American Historical Review* (1959), pp. 538-567.

Cuba. "Declaración conjunta soviético-cubana." *Cuba Socialista* (1963), pp. 1-19.

D'ESTÉFANO PISANI, M. A. "Presencia y precisión de no alineación." *Política Internacional* (1965), pp. 73-105.

FENWICK, C. C. "The Issue at Punta del Este: Non-Intervention versus Collective Security." *American Journal of International Law* (1962), pp. 466-474.

GIL, F. G. "La Revolución cubana y el mundo socialista." *Foro Internacional* (1968), pp. 384-393.

GLICK, E. B. "Cuba and the 15th United Nations General Assembly: A Case Study of Regional Dissociation." *Journal of Inter-American Studies* (1964), pp. 235-248.

———. "Isolating the Guerrilla. Some Latin American Examples." *Orbis* (Autumn 1968), pp. 873-886.

GÓMEZ WANGÜEMERT, L. "Panorama y Perspectiva de la situación internacional." *Política Internacional* (1963), pp. 111-120.

GONZALEZ, E. "Castro's Revolution, Cuban Communist Appeal, and the Soviet Response." *World Politics* (1968), pp. 39-68.

HAGAN, R. and B. BERNSTEIN. "Military Value of Missiles in Cuba." *Brazilian-American Survey* (February 1963), pp. 8-13.

HALPERIN, E. "Die Ausstrahlung des Castrismus in Lateinamerika." *Europa-Archiv* (1965), pp. 759-768.

HENNESSY, C. A. M. "The Roots of Cuban Nationalism." *International Affairs* (1963), pp. 345-359.

LAMBERG, R. F. "La formación de la línea castrista desde la Conferencia Tricontinental." *Foro Internacional* (January/March 1968), pp. 278-301.

LUCINDA GARZA, C. "Causas y desarrollo del conflicto cubano-norteamericano de enero de 1958 a julio de 1960." *Foro Internacional* (April/May 1969), pp. 354-386.

McWHINNEY, E. " 'Coexistence' and Cold War in International Law." *International Journal* (Winter 1962-1963), pp. 67-74.

MORENO, I. "Las Reuniones de San José." *Foro Internacional* (1961), pp. 341-359.

ROA, R. "Perspectivas de la Revolución Cubana." *Revista de Ciencias políticas y sociales* (1960), pp. 243-252.

ROCA, B. "El desarrollo histórico de la revolución cubana." *Cuba Socialista* (1964), pp. 8-27.

———. "Los planteamientos de Fidel Castro sobre las relaciones Cuba-Estados Unidos." *Cuba Socialista* (1964), pp. 1-14.

SMITH, R. F. "Castro's Revolution. Domestic Source and Consequence," in J. Plank (ed.) *Cuba and the United States. Long-range Perspectives* (Washington, D.C.: The Brookings Institute, 1967), pp. 45-68.

STOKES, W. S. "The Cuban Parliamentary System in Action." *Journal of Politics* (1949), pp. 335-364.

TORRAS, J. "Dos años de relaciones fraternales entre Cuba y la Unión Soviética." *Cuba Socialista* (1962), pp. 1-7.

TORRAS, P. "Cuba, Estados Unidos y la desnuclearización de América Latina." *Cuba Socialista* (October 1965), pp. 12-20.

———. "La política imperialista de Estados Unidos hacia Cuba." *Comercio Exterior* (April/June 1964), pp. 14-23.

United States, Department of State. "Sino-Soviet Military Aid to Cuba Summarized." *Department of State Bulletin* (April 16, 1962), pp. 644-646.

VALDÉS, N. P. "La diplomacia del azucar. Cuba y Estados Unidos." *Foro Internacional* (July/September 1971), pp. 46-65.

WALTERS, R. S. "Soviet Economic Aid to Cuba." *International Affairs* (1966), pp. 74-86.

WILSON, D. P. "Strategic Projections and Policy Options in the Soviet-Cuban Relationship." *Orbis* (1968), pp. 504-517.

Dominican Republic

BOOKS

BOSCH, J. *The Unfinished Experiment* (London: Pall Mall, 1966).

DÍAZ ORDOÑEZ, V. *La política exterior de Trujillo* (Santo Domingo: Impresora Dominicana, 1955).

GALÍNDEZ, J. de. *La era de Trujillo* (Buenos Aires: Americana, 1966).

MARTIN, J. B. *Overtaken by Events* (New York: Doubleday, 1966).

MONCLÚS, M. A. *El caudillismo en la República Dominicana* (Santo Domingo: Editora del Caribe, 1962).

NIEDERGANG, M. *La Revolution de Saint-Domingue* (Paris: Plon, 1966).

RODMAN, S. *Quisquaya: a History of the Dominican Republic* (Seattle: University of Washington Press, 1964).

WIARDA, M. J. *The Dominican Republic. Nation in Transition* (London: Pall Mall, 1969).

ARTICLES

BARON, D. "The Dominican Republic Crisis of 1965. A Case-Study of the Regional versus the Global Approach to International Peace and Security." A. W. Cordier (ed.) in *Columbia Essays in International Affairs.* Volume III (New York: Columbia University Press, 1967), pp. 1-37.

PARKINSON, F. "Santo Domingo and After," in *Year Book of World Affairs* (London: London Institute of World Afairs, 1966), pp. 143-168.

Ecuador

BOOKS

Organisation of American States, Inter-American Peace Committee. *Report on the Case Presented by the Government of Ecuador* (Washington, D.C., 1960).

TAMAYO MANCHENO, G. *El Velazquismo. Una interpretación* (Guayaquil: Royal Print, 1960).

VELASCO IBARRA, J. M. *Servidumbre y Liberación: del imperialismo atómico a la claridad del espiritu* (Buenos Aires: Americales, 1968).

WILSON, V. H. *Política Internacional del Ecuador, 1960-1961* (Quito: Minerva, 1961).

ARTICLES

URBANSKI, E. S. "Ecuador's Socioeconomic Mosaic." *Current History* (January 1964), pp. 19-25.

Guatemala

BOOKS

ARÉVALO, J. J. *The Shark and the Sardines* (New York: Lyle Stuart, 1961).

———. *Guatemala, la Democracia y el Imperio* (Santiago: Renacimiento, 1954).

CARDOZA Y ARAGON, L. *La revolución guatemalteca* (Mexico City: Cuadernos Americanos, 1955).

CASTRO, J. R. *Política Internacional de Guatemala, 1944-1951* (Havana: Imprenta 'H.C.', 1951).

DEAMBROSIS MARTINS, C. *La Conferencia de Bogotá y la posición de Guatemala* (Guatemala City: Tipografía Nacional, 1948).

EDEN, SIR A. *Full Circle* (London: Cassell, 1960).

GALICH, M. *Por qué lucha Guatemala? Arévalo y Arbenz: dos hombres contra un imperio* (Buenos Aires: Elmer, 1956).

Guatemala, Ministerio de Relaciones Exteriores. *Guatemala ante América. La verdad sobre la Cuarta Union de Consulta de Cancilleres americanos* (Guatemala City, 1951).

MARTZ, J. D. *Communist Infiltration of Guatemala* (New York: Vantage, 1956).

MONTEFORTE TOLEDO, M. *Guatemala: Monografía sociológica* (Mexico City: UNAM, 1959).

MUÑOZ MEANY, E. *El hombre y la encrucijada. Textos políticos en defensa de la democracia* (Guatemala City: Tipografia Nacional, 1950).

OSEGUEDA, R. *Operación Guatemala* (Santiago: Prensa Latinoamericana, 1958).

SCHNEIDER, R. M. *Communism in Guatemala, 1944-1954* (New York: Praeger, 1959).

TORIELLO, G. *La batalla de Guatemala* (Buenos Aires: Pueblos de América, 1956).

United Kingdom, Her Majesty's Stationery Office. *Report on Events leading to and arising out of the change of régime in Guatemala* (London: HMSO. Cmd. 9277, 1954).

United States, Department of State. *Intervention of International Communism in Guatemala* (Washington, D.C., 1954).

YDÍGORAS FUENTES, M. *My War with Communism* (Englewood Cliffs, N.J.: Prentice-Hall, 1963).

ARTICLES

BRITWELL, G. E. "Underdeveloped Countries: The Theory and Practice of Technical Assistance. Factors in the Economic Development of Guatemala." *American Economic Review* (1953), pp. 104-135.

PIKE, F. B. "Guatemala, the United States and Communism in the Americas." *Review of Politics* (1955), pp. 232-261.

TAYLOR, P. B. "The Guatemalan Affair: A Critique of United States Foreign Policy." *American Political Science Review* (1956), pp. 787-806.

United States, State Department. "Expropriation of United Fruit Company Property by the Government of Guatemala." *Department of State Bulletin* (September 14, 1953), pp. 357-360.

Haiti

MANIGAT, L. F. *Haiti in the Sixties, Object of International Concern* (Washington, D.C.: Center of Foreign Policy Research, 1964).

Mexico

BOOKS

ÁVILA CAMACHO, M. *La ruta de México* (Mexico City: Secretaría de Educación Pública, 1946).

BASSOLS, N. *La Revolución Mexicana cuesta abajo* (Mexico City: Guión de Acontecimientos Nacionales y Internacionales, 1960).

BETETA, R. *Entrevistas y pláticas* (Mexico City: Renovación, 1961).

BORTSCH, A. and W. KÖNIG. *La política mexicana sobre inversiones extranjeras* (Mexico City: Colegio de Mexico, 1968).

BOSCH, C. G. *Problemas diplomáticos de México independiente* (Mexico City: Colegio de Mexico, 1947).

BRANDENBURG, F. *The Making of Modern Mexico* (Englewood Cliffs, N.J.: Prentice-Hall, 1964).

CABRERA, L. *El pensamiento de L. Cabrera: selección y prólogo de E. Luquin* (Mexico City: Biblioteca del Instituto Nacional de Estudios Históricos de la Revolución Mexicana, 1960).

– – –. (Pseudonym, B. Urrea) *Una opinión sobre el conflicto mundial* (Mexico City, 1951).

CASTAÑEDA, J. *Mexico and the United Nations* (New York: Manhattan Publishing, 1958).

CLARK, M. J. *A Biography of Miguel Alemán, President of Mexico* (Austin, 1951).

CLENDENEN, C. C. *The United States and Pancho Villa: A Study in Conventional Diplomacy* (Ithaca, N.Y.: Cornell University Press, 1961).

CLINE, H. F. *The United States and Mexico* (Cambridge, Mass.: Harvard University Press, 1967).

COROMINAS, E. V. *México, Cuba y la OEA* (Buenos Aires: Política, Economía y Finanzas, 1965).

COSÍO VILLEGAS, D. *Cuestiones internacionales de Mexico: una bibliografia* (Mexico City: Secretaria de Relaciones Exteriores, 1966).

– – –. *American Extremes* (Austin: University of Texas Press, 1964).

– – –. *Change in Latin America. The Mexican and Cuban Revolutions* (Lincoln: University of Nebraska Press, 1961).

DÍAZ ORDAZ, G. *La doctrina internacional de México* (Mexico City: Centro de Estudios Nacionales, 1965).

FABELA, I. *Intervención* (Mexico City: Escuela Nacional de Ciencias Políticas y Sociales, 1959).

– – –. *Buena y mala vecindad* (Mexico City: America Nueva, 1958).

– – –. *La conferencia de Caracas y la actitud anti-comunista de México* (Mexico City: Cuadernos Americanos, 1954).

– – –. *Los precursores de la diplomacia mexicana* (Mexico City: Secretaría de Relaciones Exteriores, 1926).

FREITHALER, W. O. *Mexico's Foreign Trade and Economic Development* (New York: Praeger, 1968).

GARCÍA ROBLES, A. *México en las Naciones Unidas* 2 Volumes. (Mexico City: UNAM, 1970).

GARCÍA TREVIÑO, R. *La ingerencia rusa en México y Sudamérica* (Mexico City: América, 1959).

GONZÁLEZ, N. et al. *México en el mundo de hoy* (Mexico City: Guarania, 1952).

GONZÁLEZ CASANOVA, P. *Democracy in Mexico* (London: Oxford University Press, 1972).

HECHEN, S. *Programación y elaboración de la política exterior de México* (Rosario: Universidad del Litoral, 1968).

JIMÉNEZ MORENO, W. et al. *Historia de México* (Mexico City: ECLALSA, 1963).

LOMBARDO TOLEDANO, V. *¿Moscú o Pekín? La vía mexicana hacia el socialismo* (Mexico City: Partido Popular Socialista, 1963).

LÓPEZ MATEOS, A. *Presencia internacional de Adolfo López Mateos* (Mexico City: La Justicia, 1963).

———. *Nueva dimensión internacional de México: las relaciones de México y Yugoslavia* (Mexico City: La Justicia, 1963).

———. *Informe que rinde al II Congreso de la Nación, de 1 de septiembre 1961 al 31 de agosto 1962* (Mexico City: La Justicia, 1962).

———. *Pensamiento y programa* (Mexico City: La Justicia, 1961).

———. *Presencia de México en Sudamérica. Discursos* (Mexico City: Pri, 1960).

México, Secretaría de las Relaciones Exteriores. *La política internacional de México, 1952-1956* (Mexico City, 1957).

———. *México en la IX conferencia internacional 1948* (Mexico City, 1949).

———. *The Continental Doctrine of the Mexican Senate* (Mexico City, 1941).

MILLON, R. P. *Mexican Marxist. Vicente Lombardo Toledano* (Chapel Hill: University of North Carolina Press, 1966).

MORA, J. M. de. *Punta del Este: historia íntima de una conferencia* (Mexico City: Galvala, 1962).

MORA ORTIZ, G. *L'évolution du commerce extérieur du Mexique* (Paris, 1957).

PADILLA NERVO, L. *Discursos y declaraciones, 1948-1958* (Mexico City: Secretaría de Relaciones Exteriores, 1958).

Partido Revolucionario Institucional. *The Voice of Mexico in the United States and Canada. Speeches by Adolfo López Mateos* (Mexico City, 1959).

RONDERO, J. *Nacionalismo mexicano y política mundial* (Mexico City, 1969).

SCHMITT, K. M. *Communism in Mexico* (Austin: University of Texas Press, 1965).

SEARA VÁZQUEZ, M. *La política exterior de México. La práctica de México en el derecho internacional* (Mexico City: Esfinge, 1969).

SHEREMETIEV, I. *El Capitalismo de Estado en México* (Mexico City, 1969).

SILVA HERZOG, J. *Meditaciones sobre México* (Mexico City: Cuadernos Americanos, 1948).

SMITH, A. K. *Mexico and the Cuban Revolution: foreign policy-making in Mexico under President Adolfo López Mateos, 1958-1964* (Ithaca, N.Y.: Cornell University Press, 1970).

TORRES BODET, J. *Memorias*, 4 volumes (Mexico City: Porrúa, 1969).

TOWNSEND, W. C. *Lázaro Cárdenas. Mexican Democrat* (Ann Arbor, Mich.: WAHR, 1952).

UNZUETA, G. *Lombardo Toledano y el Marxismo leninismo* (Mexico City: Fondo de Cultura Popular, 1966).

WEBSTER, A. *Woodrow Wilso y México* (Mexico City: De Andrea, 1964).

WIONCZEK, M. S. *El nacionalismo mexicano y la inversión extranjera* (Mexico City: Siglo Veintiuno, 1967).

YAÑEZ, A. (ed.) *Proyección universal de México. Crónica del viaje realizado por el Presidente de México Lic. Adolfo López Mateos a India, Japón, Indonesia y Filipinas en año 1962* (Mexico City: Torres, 1963).

ARTICLES

BASSOLS, N. "Veinte ratones y un gato, o la conferencia de Washington." *Revista guatemalteca* (July/September 1951), pp. 5-18.

BLANKSTEN, G. I. "Foreign Policy of Mexico," in R. C. Macridis (ed.) *Foreign Policy in World Politics* (Englewood Cliffs, N.J.: Prentice-Hall, 1962), pp. 311-334.

BROWN, P. M. "Mexico and the Monroe Doctrine." *American Journal of International Law* (1932), pp. 117-120.

CARDONA, S. "La política de México y el Derecho internacional." *Revista de Ciencias políticas y sociales* (1962), pp. 27-48.

CARILLO FLORES, A. "Mexico and Latin America." *Proceedings of the Academy of Political Science* (May 1964), pp. 356-371.

CASTAÑEDA, J. "Revolution and Foreign Policy: Mexico's Experience." *Political Science Quarterly* (1963), pp. 391-417.

CUEVAS CANCINO, F. "The Bogotá Conference and Recent Developments in Pan American Relations: a Mexican View." *International Affairs* (1948), pp. 523-533.

———. "The Foreign Policy of Mexico," in J. E. Black and K. W. Thompson (eds.) *Foreign Policies in a World of Change* (New York: Harper & Row, 1963), pp. 643-672.

ENGEL, J. E. "The Revolution and Mexican Foreign Policy." *Journal of Inter-American Studies* (October 1969), pp. 518-532.

FABELA, I. "La conferencia de Caracas y la actitud anti-comunista de México." *Cuadernoas Americanos* (1954), pp. 7-17.

GARCÍA REYNOSO, G. "México en la segunda UNCTAD." *Comercio Exterior* (February 1968), pp. 5-7.

GONZÁLEZ NAVARRO, M. "La ideología de la Revolución Mexicana." *Historia Mexicana* (April/June 1961), pp. 628-636.

KAHLE, G. "Ursprünge und Entwicklung der mexikanischen Guerrillatradition." *Jahrbuch für Geschichte von Staat, Wirtschaft und Gesellschaft Lateinamerikas* (1967), pp. 35-42.

PADILLA, E. "The Meaning of Pan-Americanism." *Foreign Affairs* (1954), pp. 270-281.

PELLICER DE BRODY, O. "Los grupos patronales y la política exterior méxicana: las relaciones con la Revolución Cubana." *Foro Internacional* (1969), pp. 1-27.

———. "La Revolución Cubana en México." *Foro Internacional* (1967), pp. 360-383.

———. "México en la OEA." *Foro Internacional.* Volume 6 (October 1965-March 1966), pp. 288-302.
RONDERO, J. "México en Punta del Este." *Revista de Ciencias políticas y sociales* (1962), pp. 49-72.
ROSS, S. R. "Mexico: Cool Revolution and Cold War." *Current History* (February 1963), pp. 89-94, and 117.

Panama

CASTILLERO PIMENTEL, E. *Panamà y los Estados Unidos* (Panama City: Editora Panama, 1964).
EALY, L. O. *The Republic of Panama in World Affairs, 1903-1950* (Philadelphia: University of Pennsylvania Press, 1951).

Peru

BOOKS
COTLER, J. *Crísis política y populismo militar* (Lima: Instituto de Estudios Peruanos, 1969).
———. *El populismo militar como modelo de desarrollo nacional: el caso peruano* (Lima: Instituto de Estudios Peruanos, 1969).
HAYA DE LA TORRE, R. *La Defensa continental* (Buenos Aires: Americano, 1946).
OWENS, R. J. *Peru* (London: Oxford University Press, 1963).
Peru, Ministerio de Guerra. *Las guerrillas en el Perú y su represión* (Lima, 1966).
QUIJANO, A. *Nationalism and Capitalism in Peru: A Study in Neo-Imperialism* (New York: Monthly Review Press, 1971).
SHARP, D. (ed.) *United States Foreign Policy and Peru* (Austin: University of Texas Press, 1972).
TUDELA, F. *La posición jurídica internacional del Perú en el proceso de la determinación de su frontera con Ecuador* (Lima: Torres Aguirre, 1952).

ARTICLES
HERRING, H. "Peru in serious trouble." *Current History* (February 1963), pp. 95-99, and 117.
MEJÍA VALERA, J. "La estratificación social en el Perú." *Cuadernos Americanos* (1964), pp. 107-117.

Uruguay

BOOKS
CIASULLO, A. L. *El Uruguay y la solidaridad interamericana. El Tratado de Asistencia Militar con Estados Unidos* (Montevideo: Revista de derecho público y privado, 1952).
FRUGONI, E. *La esfinge roja. Memorial de un aprendiz de diplomático en la Unión Soviética* (Buenos Aires: Claridad, 1948).
GILIO, M. E. *La guerrilla tupamara* (Havana: Casa de las Américas, 1970).
HAEDO, E. V. *En defensa de la soberanía: discursos pronunciados en la Cámara de Senadores de la República Oriental del Uruguay durante el período 1942-1946* (Montevideo: Congreso, 1946).

LABROUSSE, A. *The Tupamaros* (Harmondsworth, Middlesex: Penguin, 1970).
LACARTE MURO, J. A. *Política Economica exterior del Uruguay* (Montevideo: Consejo Interamericano de Comercio y Produccion, 1955).
PENDLE, G. *Uruguay* (London: Oxford University Press, 1963).
QUÍJANO, C. *El Tratado con los Estados Unidos* (Montevideo: Marcha, 1950).
TAYLOR, P. B. *Government and Politics of Uruguay* (New Orleans, La.: University of Tulane Press, 1962).
United States, Department of Commerce. *The Foreign Trade of Uruguay, 1956-1957* (Washington, D.C., 1958).
Uruguay. *Constitution of October 26, 1951* (Montevido: Presidencia, 1952).
———. Institute of International Law. *Uruguay and the United Nations* (New York, 1958).
VELÁZQUEZ, C. M. *La política internacional en el pensamiento de Luis Alberto de Herrera* (London, 1968).

ARTICLES
CRAIG, A. "Uruguay: Back to One-Man Rule." *The World Today* (1967), pp. 43-46.
FRUGONI, E. "Meditación política sobre Latinoamérica." *Combate* (June 1959), pp. 15-23.
SHAPIRO, S. "Uruguay: A Bankrupt Welfare State." *Current History* (January 1969), pp. 36-41.
TAYLOR, P. B. "Interests and Institutional Dysfunction in Uruguay." *American Political Science Review* (1963), pp. 62-74.

Venezuela

BOOKS
BETANCOURT, R. *Hacia una América Latina democrática e integrada* (Caracas: Sendero, 1967).
———. *Tres años de gobierno democrático, 1959-1962.* 3 volumes (Caracas: Imprenta Nacional, 1962).
———. *Venezuela rinde cuenta* (Caracas: Imprenta Nacional, 1962).
CABIESE DONOSO, M. *Venezuela Okey* (Santiago: Ediciones del Litoral, 1963).
FALCÓN BRICEÑO, M. *Venezuela en las Naciones Unídas* (Caracas: Ministerio de Relaciones Exteriores, 1963).
HERRERA OROPEZA, J. *Hacia una Venezuela nacionalista* (Caracas: Pensamiento Vivo, 1968).
MAGALLANES, M. V. *Pertidos políticos venezolanos* (Caracas, 1959).
MARTZ, J. D. *Acción Democrática* (Princeton, N.J.: Princeton University Press, 1966).
OJEDA, F. *La guerra del pueblo* (Caracas: Fuentes, 1970).
Venezuela, Presidencia de la República. *Gobierno y nación defienden en Venezuela el régimen democrático. Actos contra el terrorismo comunista* (Caracas, 1963).

ARTICLES
AHUMADA, J. "Hypotheses for the Diagnosis of a Situation of Social Change. The Case of Venezuela." *International Social Science Journal* (1964), pp. 192-201.

INDEX